THE
WHITE
BONUS

ALSO BY TRACIE McMILLAN

The American Way of Eating: Undercover at Walmart, Applebee's,

Farm Fields and the Dinner Table

THE
WHITE
BONUS

FIVE FAMILIES AND THE CASH VALUE
OF RACISM IN AMERICA

Tracie McMillan

HENRY HOLT AND COMPANY
NEW YORK

Henry Holt and Company

Publishers since 1866

120 Broadway

New York, New York 10271

www.henryholt.com

Henry Holt® and Ⓗ® are registered trademarks of Macmillan Publishing Group, LLC.

Distributed in Canada by Raincoast Book Distribution Limited

Library of Congress Cataloging-in-Publication Data is available.

ISBN 9781250619426

Our books may be purchased in bulk for promotional, educational, or business use. Please contact your local bookseller or the Macmillan Corporate and Premium Sales Department at (800) 221-7945, extension 5442, or by e-mail at MacmillanSpecialMarkets@macmillan.com.

First Edition 2024

Designed by Omar Chapa

Printed in the United States of America

1 3 5 7 9 10 8 6 4 2

For Harper, Isaac, and Lucy

I am so tired of waiting,
Aren't you,
For the world to become good
And beautiful and kind?
Let us take a knife
And cut the world in two—
And see what worms are eating
At the rind.

—LANGSTON HUGHES, "TIRED," 1930

CONTENTS

A U T H O R ' S   N O T E

On Method and Language

Method

This is a work of journalism, based on documented facts. This is true of the stories of my subjects, of myself and my family, and of the larger historic, political, and social story I tell about this country. Still, because this is also the story of five families and communities over time, I often had to rely on personal recollections as well.

When drawing on interviews and recollections, I've tried to indicate the degree of verification of each with the following formatting:

- "Quotes in regular text" have been quoted from a reliable transcript or contemporaneous account in a journal or diary, or quoted from a reliable document;
- *"Quotes in italics"* are quotes drawn from memory;
- *Italicized quotes without quote marks* represent internal monologue or interior thoughts.

Still, I depended heavily on documentation rather than personal recall to reconstruct and tell these stories. You can see some of the breadth and depth of this in the notes and bibliography, which include census reports, property deeds, city directories, congressional reports, medical bills, diary entries, photographs, letters, newspaper articles, and far more. I have conducted hundreds of hours of interviews, cumulatively, with my subjects and their friends and family and colleagues, and interviewed my own family. In some instances, placing my subjects' stories in context required the development of original histories, datasets, and calculations, all of which were done in consultation with scholars trained in the relevant disciplines. Many of these can be found on whitebonus.com.

Language

This is a book about race in America. It should not be surprising, then, that the most powerful racial epithet in our language—the one that begins with N, and ends in R—came up intermittently. As a journalist, I resist changing language as it is spoken or in using general euphemisms ("a racial slur") when a specific term is being referenced. That said, I've no interest in subjecting readers to the visceral reaction that can arise from reading violent language. In an attempt to strike a middle ground, where referencing that word was required as part of accurate documentation, I have substituted "the N-word" for the epithet. If it was part of a quote, I use "n—".

I have chosen to capitalize "Black," but not "white." I think there are good arguments to be made for capitalizing both. For now, my instinct is to follow the guidance of the Associated Press, which does not capitalize "white." When editors explained that decision in 2020, they noted that "capitalizing the term white, as is done by white supremacists, risks subtly conveying legitimacy to such beliefs." As a white writer, my goal is to undermine rather than legitimate the same.

PROLOGUE

In 2014, I watched footage of tanks facing off against unarmed protesters in Ferguson, Missouri. I thought: *I knew this was what my country is like, but I pretended I did not.*

In 2016, I watched my professional peers scoff at Donald Trump's campaign, and my friends go along with them. I thought the sinking feeling in my stomach, the deep suspicion that he'd win, was a fluke, one more example of how I was too broke and too cynical to understand the new day dawning. When he won, I thought: *I knew this was what my country is like, and I pretended I did not.*

In 2018, I watched Brett Kavanaugh's confirmation hearing for the Supreme Court. I watched a grown man sputter and spew and sneer as he was asked to face consequences for his treatment of others. It was the same way my father spoke to me after that time he abused me. I thought: *I knew this was what my country is like, and I pretended I did not.*

By 2020, when I watched the news about the deaths of Ahmaud Arbery, Breonna Taylor, and George Floyd, I had exhausted my capacity to pretend. For the first time in my life, I could make out the long, heartbroken thread that began with being raised to endure, excuse, and ignore abuse directed at me; that ran on through my learning to endure, excuse, and ignore abuse directed at other people; and ended with me abusing people, too. I quivered with rage at myself and my country and thought: *I knew this was what we were like, and I cannot pretend any more.*

THE
WHITE
BONUS

INTRODUCTION

If American life is a river, relief from poverty and strife sits atop one of its slippery banks, and the American Dream sits safely back from its edge. Few of us manage to plant our feet firmly enough in that soil to have no fear of it falling away; fewer still are born there in the first place. Most of us, instead, start out somewhere in the water and do what we can to make it across. Family wealth determines our starting point. Economic class is the distance we must cover.

In the river, our various privileges help us to stay afloat and ease our crossings. The biggest privileges are whiteness and maleness, but other aids may come along—physical attractiveness, heterosexuality, physical strength, cunning social intuition, innate abilities. Nobody is guaranteed safe crossing, but each buoyant scrap can be the difference between making it across the river and foundering in the current, each privilege of varying use if we make it ashore. It is dishonest to say that we all start to swim in the same place and with the same advantages—or that, once we've arrived, we each enjoy the same security and comfort. It is an unsettling rejection of American meritocracy to admit that we do not.

White Americans rarely talk about the differences in our crossings.

Those who've reached the far bank often stay silent, content in having arrived. Many of those still in the river remain silent, too, certain that speaking up will only make their crossing more difficult. Few of us consider how we might make getting across the river safer for everyone, or how to make that slippery bank a bit easier to climb. I have often stayed silent, and it has had its benefits. But I am no longer convinced it is for the best.

That is a long way of saying that for a very long time I thought race and racism "happened" only to people who were not white. As a journalist, I reported on poverty and hardship, and could see plainly how racism kept nonwhite people down. I did not yet see how it pulled white people up. That limited approach mirrored the way that I'd been taught to understand race and racism: It wasn't about me. As a journalist who has long documented America's multiracial poor and working classes, and as a white woman raised here, I use this book to explore the flip side of that understanding: how race benefits people who are white. I start with my family and myself.

For most of my adult life, I understood my place in the world through the lens of economic class. I grew up in a white, middle-class family.* My mother fell ill when I was five years old. The adults in my family discussed

---

* Class identity is vastly more complicated than income, also comprising, at minimum, wealth, culture, and the private safety net that each can provide. I engage with this broader experience of class throughout the book, but in the interest of storytelling I use "class" as a shorthand for income. To that end, unless otherwise noted, reference to specific individuals' class status indicates where their estimated household income falls along the class-income definitions developed by researchers at the Pew Research Center, and initially shared as part of the methodology of their December 2015 report, *The American Middle Class Is Losing Ground*. As explained to me by Pew senior researcher Rakesh Kochhar, those brackets—as a percentage of median income across the United States, adjusted for household size—are: lowest-income/poor, 0–50 percent of median income; lower-middle class, 50–67 percent; middle class, 67–200 percent; upper-middle class, 200–300 percent; upper-class/rich, 300 percent of median income and above. Unless otherwise noted, estimates referenced are based on the median income for all Americans, of all races, combined.

medical debt constantly. When I was twelve, my mother moved to a nursing home. My father began to belittle me. Sometimes, his temper boiled over and he flew into rages. To escape, I worked: My first paycheck came at fourteen, from an orchard. I have supported myself since college, when I juggled up to five jobs to make rent and tuition and pay for food. In those early years of independence, which I stubbornly insisted on to avoid my father's abuse, I was so malnourished I developed vertigo. Later, when I chose to pursue a career as a journalist covering the poor despite its low pay, I often found myself without much more income than the people about whom I wrote. Unwittingly and always somewhat unnecessarily, I have periodically experienced something of what it is like to live in America without a net. It has terrified me each time. It terrifies me still.

Few of the people I interacted with at the private university I attended or in the journalism circles in which I worked seemed to have had similar experiences—whatever their race. Most of my peers came from families with enough wealth that they were baffled, if sometimes sympathetic, when I mentioned my financial stresses. In these circles, being white and without family support made me strange, which carried its own ironic benefits. More than anything, my struggles seemed to make me a curiosity—someone with an entertaining backstory for cocktail parties, or a target for sympathy and, importantly, help.

In college, when people heard that I worked to cover my living expenses, they assumed *my* lack of money in the present meant that my *family* was poor. Later, professional colleagues made similar assumptions when I said I'd worked service jobs in college and had avoided graduate school because I could not fathom its expense. I knew, dimly, that my grandfather had some wealth, but my access to it was limited by both family custom and my objection to my father's abuse. I avoided discussing those fraught topics with colleagues. Instead, I let my peers use the phrases they felt best described me. Eventually, "working class" stuck, and, for self-interested reasons I discuss later, I made it my own.

Until recently, it has been unusual in America to have a broad, mainstream discussion about how race works for white people, or how white advantage, much of it facilitated by government, intersects with the other factors that shape life in this country. For a very long time, I understood my race only dimly: as a vague, immutable power about which I had limited knowledge, and even less control. Given the power my whiteness holds, it now feels strange—bizarre, even dangerous—that I entered adulthood with so little conscious understanding about how whiteness works and what whiteness means. This fact frustrates and embarrasses me, but it is nothing new for a white American.

As a reporter, I know how to be specific about how race works for people who are not white, especially when they are Black. I know that Black children born poor in America are one-quarter as likely to become rich as poor children who are white, and I know that Black boys born rich are half as likely to stay rich as their white peers. I know that Black people are no more likely than whites to use or sell drugs, but they are three to four times more likely to be arrested on drug charges. And I know that when they are convicted of any crime, Black people are more likely to be sent to prison than white people. I know Black families have 13 percent of the wealth of white ones. In this country I am rarely expected to acknowledge the obvious inverse: That white people born rich are twice as likely as Black people to stay that way. That we are two-thirds to three-quarters less likely to be arrested on drug charges. That we have eight times as much wealth.

Indeed, for all the difficulties of my crossing, whiteness has buoyed me up in my hardest moments. Some of the benefits of my race are hard to measure: my ability to blend in among white people with more power, to safely express anger in public, or to prompt sympathy with my tears. Others are easier to quantify: Racist policies in housing let my grandparents build middle-class wealth that was denied to Americans who were not white; racist administration of the G.I. Bill gave them access to college that was largely denied to Americans who were not white; and racism ingrained in the publishing industry gave me advantages that led to the contract for my first book—and the contract for this one, too. There are many others, and they are documented in these pages. I tally their approximate—and bare minimum—value in the White Bonus Index at the end of this book.

I know that this book puts white people at its center, myopically focused on our experience as if it is the only one worth understanding. I know that mainstream journalists, in particular, have practiced this myopia almost as if it were a religion. And, as I document later, I know that I have not only observed these damaging practices; I have participated in them, too. But if there is any story about white Americans that this country has left untold, it is the story of how we—how *I*—directly benefit from racism. I've spent my career documenting how racism harms people who are not white, especially in the form of poverty, in hopes of making the lives of our poorest better. Not much has changed. Maybe I can do more good by documenting this untold story of exactly how racism helps me, just as it helps nearly all white Americans. That is the story at the center of this book.

★ ★ ★ ★ ★

This is a sprawling story. To tell it, I must break it into smaller, more manageable stories, and then weave them together into that larger whole. I begin with my family's story and end with my own, tallying what I have come to call a "white bonus" along the way. This concept is a clear inverse of what scholars and journalists have long referred to as the "Black tax"— the higher costs faced by Black Americans who have been denied so much of the aid extended freely to whites.*

To begin tallying that bonus, I've chosen a crude but telling measure: the total money my family has spent on me since I left home at seventeen years old. The reasoning is simple: It is money I did nothing to earn, that my family had no legal obligation to spend on me, and that my family was able to give. Then I look at my family's history and use my skills as a journalist

---

* Although it has many roots, the concept of the Black tax received a thorough journalistic treatment by *Chicago Tribune* journalist Clarence Page in 1980. Today, its greatest chronicler is Georgetown law scholar Dorothy Brown, whose work—summarized in her 2021 book, *The Whiteness of Wealth*—has rigorously documented the racist effects of American tax policy.

to investigate: Would my family have had that money to give if they were not white? When the answer is no, the money comes from racial advantage. This initial "family bonus" is almost exclusively a measure of how American public policy, which built the twentieth-century's middle class, has trickled down to the current day. This is the first piece of my white bonus.

The next element of white advantage I consider derives from what the pioneering nineteenth-century Black sociologist W. E. B. Du Bois called whiteness's "psychological wage": the comforts and benefits that come from being a member of a dominant group. These are the small, interpersonal ways that doorways to power are opened: the offering of benefit of the doubt and encouragement, rather than suspicion and dismissal, which in turn encourages white people to tacitly believe they are entitled to things that others are not. Although these advantages begin as intangible privileges, they facilitate access to material advantages. This indirect relationship makes it difficult to measure this element of white advantage, what I call a "social bonus" of whiteness. Still, when any event arose in my subjects' lives where it appeared that implicit white advantage yielded material benefits, I have tallied those, too.

Any honest consideration of a white bonus, though, must also address a related element: racism's cost to all of us. This is different from the amorphous concepts of "privilege" and "fragility" that have dominated America's discussion of whiteness in recent years. Its most recent champion is writer and policy expert Heather McGhee, who speaks compellingly about how racism hits "the target first and worst." Racism, then, hurts nonwhite, and especially Black, people the most—but it hurts many whites as well. This broader understanding of racism is an important complement to, not a replacement for, the extraordinary body of work chronicling racism's harms to its direct targets.* It also begs a question that drives this book: If

---

* While the list of cited works in the bibliography provides deeper guidance to this work, I am thinking here of the journalism of Ta-Nehisi Coates, Nikole Hannah-Jones, Clint Smith, and Isabel Wilkerson; the memoirs of Sarah Broom, Jesmyn Ward, and Kiese Laymon; and the scholarship of Dorothy Brown, Tressie McMillan Cottom, Nell Irvin Painter, and William A. Darity Jr.

racism in American policy has given so much to whites, is there a point at which its costs outweigh its benefits, even to white people?

This book is, by its nature, limited. There are many caveats: I work as a journalist, not a scholar, and certainly not an economist. I cannot take a full measure of the material benefits of racism—and, as many economists have told me, it is likely that no one can. Racism is too complex, too slippery, too multifaceted to pin down its value in a definitive way. The same is true of racism's costs, which land on the bodies and psyches of its targets in ways that defy monetary calculation. Indeed, public health scholar Arline Geronimus coined the term "weathering" to describe the way that the stresses of oppression of all kinds directly create poor health. But while this stress effect shows up across many hardships, it is most pronounced and most widespread among Black Americans—whose health, researchers have found, does not improve with income and education the way it does for whites. For Black people in the middle and upper classes, research suggests a lifetime of managing a constant flow of white assumptions, ranging from banal to lethal, can spur disease at an early age and even shorten their lives, regardless of how much money they make. There is, as of yet, no firm dollar value for *that*.* In this way, any estimate I offer will be woefully, dramatically, impossibly insufficient.

And yet there is value in posing a powerful question and following the answers where they lead, even if the math is rough. There is no algorithm here, no econometric model. There is only a question that needed to be asked, and the stories I learned when I tried to answer it.

I begin with my family because I know our story best. This is different from how I have approached most of my work as a journalist. For many

---

* In a forthcoming 2024 article, William A. Darity Jr., the Duke economist, explores the idea of paying reparations to Black Americans based on their shorter life spans—as opposed to the bulk of his work on reparations, which focuses on the racial wealth gap. In *RSF: The Russell Sage Foundation Journal of the Social Sciences*, Darity estimates that the cost of a reparations program based on longevity would be "about $29 trillion, more than twice the estimate generated by focusing on the wealth gap."

years, my job has been to approach other people and ask them to explain a foreign experience to me, so that I might explain it to others. But it didn't feel right to ask other white people to explain whiteness to me—as if I had no experience with it myself, as if I had any claim to objectivity at all. Following journalistic convention, I aim to accurately reflect the thoughts and experiences of my subjects, while leaving most of the work of judgment to readers. Following the conventions of memoir, I am more direct about how I see myself and my family.

As this work evolved, it became clear that any honest consideration of my own relationship to racism—which, as a white woman, means my relationship to unearned power—also meant being honest about the hardships that have shaped me. For a long time, I shrugged off my difficult childhood. I told myself that it was in the past, and that at least it had made me stronger and more empathetic. I suppose those things are true insofar as they go. I see now that they made me more resentful, too: more willing to endure abuse, more willing to expect others to endure it; angry when others got sympathy where I expected derision. Because white Americans' resentment is so central to modern racism here, my hardships are a part of my relationship to racism, too.

Still, the story of white advantage in America is a bigger story than any single family can tell. So, in between the six chapters that tell my family's story, I have written four profiles of other white people. They are from different parts of the country, different generations, different gradations of economic class. Each subject has spent most, if not all, of their life in America's shrinking middle class. Several are poised near the downward slide from middle-class to poor, reflecting, I think, an uncertainty about whether their economic stability will last. But the most important criterion was that they each agreed to speak with me openly about their lives, and to consider the role that their race has played in shaping them. With each person, I estimate their white bonus in the same manner I measure my own—and I tally it for each of us in the index at the end of this book. My hope is that this cross section of stories will help me understand how racism has shaped histories and policies to which my own family has few ties. I also suspect it will let me see how racism echoes across time and place; how it morphs, and whether parts of it disappear.

As big as this story is, I have limited its scope in three important ways. First, I cover only the twentieth and twenty-first centuries. This excludes the 246 years during which enslavement based on race was a legally codified part of America's economic and political structure, as well as the 35 years, including Reconstruction, that followed the Civil War.* I had to draw a line somewhere—and I believe the last 124 years provide plenty of insight into how racism has given advantage to white Americans.†

Second, this book is primarily concerned with the divide between the experiences of Black Americans and white Americans. I have chosen this approach because the divide between Black and white is so enduring here that to call it "caste," as the journalist Isabel Wilkerson does, is accurate. I hope that future work, by me or other writers, will clearly contrast white advantage against the complex histories between white and other nonwhite Americans, including those of Hispanic, Indigenous, and Asian descent.

Third, all of my primary subjects are white, and I do not systematically compare them to subjects who are not white. I have made this decision in hopes of forcing myself to study white advantage, and white advantage alone. I do not like to admit it, but there is a relief I feel when I listen to stories of how racism hurts people who don't look like me. There is the relief of absolution in exchange for having borne witness, and the relief of maintaining my innocence. Most of all there is the relief of having kept the

---

* Here, I am using the year 1619 as the introduction of enslavement as part of the American economy, continuing through late 1865, when passage of the Thirteenth Amendment to the Constitution outlawed enslavement in all states.

† Readers interested in learning more about whiteness in the nineteenth century and earlier should seek out the work of W. E. B. Du Bois, particularly *Black Reconstruction in America*, and Nell Irvin Painter's *The History of White People*. I've also learned from David R. Roediger's *The Wages of Whiteness*; Noel Ignatiev's *How the Irish Became White*; and Keri Leigh Merritt's *Masterless Men*.

focus off of me. I do not trust this relief, which keeps me so comfortable and does so little to change anything. I am curious about what I might learn about racism by leaving that relief behind, and practicing honesty instead.

This book does not highlight the extraordinary, and it does not study an average, either. None of my subjects have faced hardships that will sound foreign to most Americans. None of us have gone through life guaranteed the comforts of great wealth. Indeed, there is nothing about my family or the people I profile that is remarkable. Nor is any one of us an "everyman" who could represent an average of anything. Instead, my hope is that, by studying the ways that racism has shaped this handful of white American families, including my own, I can better understand why racism continues to fester in my country, why so many white Americans treat racial hierarchy as a fact they cannot change rather than a problem they will confront, and whether there's any chance that the benefits it gives are not worth what they cost. I hope that writing this book can help me find a better way to cross the river—for myself, of course, and for all Americans.

I believe we all deserve safe passage. The story that follows is what I learned by trying to find it.

MY GRANDPARENTS

SOUTHEAST MICHIGAN, CANADA, AND MICHIGAN'S UPPER PENINSULA

1907–1943

For most of my adulthood, I've understood myself to be on the border of the working and middle class. Even so, I have longed to feel myself on solid financial ground—far enough into the middle class that I have no immediate worry of falling back into the river. So when my father moved out of my childhood home in 2016 and handed me the family albums he no longer wanted to keep, the old pictures I found of his parents surprised me.

The images are black and white, some with stark contrast and others a rainbow of grays. My favorite set contains four images of his parents, my Grandmar and Grandpa Mac, with their mothers. It must have been March or April. There is no snow, but everyone is in overcoats. The women wear hats. Grandpa Mac wears a three-piece suit, the vest buttoned. They stand in the driveway of my grandparents' new house, solidly built with brick and white clapboards. One shows Grandmar, slender and birdlike, a cloud of dark curls around her shoulders. The mothers stand with her in front of a black Hudson Terraplane, all curving wheel wells and chrome grille. Another photo shows Grandmar in front of the house with her mother. A third shows Grandpa Mac with his. There's no date written on the photos, but they would have been taken in the late 1930s. Maybe the early 1940s.

My favorite photo shows my grandfather with both mothers, in front of the car. My grandfather is on the left, overcoat open, one hand casually in his pocket, holding back the coat. He is lean, olive-skinned, and handsome, a broad prominent nose above a pencil mustache, dark curly hair cropped close to his scalp, hazel eyes fixed just beyond the camera. His mother stands in the middle, thin, awkward, and stiff, a tall hat draped in black netting atop her head, her mouth a flat line. Grandmar's mother is on the right, shorter and rounder, leaning comfortably on the Hudson's front wheel. She is giving my grandfather an amused look. I like to think she said, *Can you get a load of all this?*

When I look at these photos, I want to say things like "Look at how happy they were." Or, "Grandpa's mom must've been a piece of work, huh?" Or, "I would have liked to have known Grandmar's mom." Sometimes, I admire the coats and the car and Grandpa Mac's style. Today, a good eighty years after those photos were taken, the details I notice do not surprise me. Instead, I am surprised by an obvious fact that I, and my family, had long left unsaid.

My dad's parents had money. Later, my mom's parents would have some, too. As a child, I could not see this because I did not understand how to spot money or its lack. As a young adult, I could not see it because a lack of money defined my options, separated me from my peers at college, limited the jobs I could take or the trips I might make. And, until very recently, I'd failed to see the most important reason they had that money in the first place: They were white.

I have avoided observing their race on instinct—my quiet subterranean compulsion to be mindful of power: to do what I can to acquire it, and to do what I can to avoid it being used against me. This instinct is why, when I look at old photos, I do the same thing my peers and my family and my country do with anything that suggests unearned advantage: I do not talk about it.

★ ★ ★ ★ ★

My grandparents were all from Michigan. It is where my parents are from, and it is where they raised me. Today, my home state gets mentioned in the news mostly because of Detroit's troubles and glories, the state's storied college football programs, or its swing state status in national elections. But when my grandparents were growing up, Michigan was a larger and more glittering force. For my family, Michigan and its cities must have seemed full of possibilities.

Detroit drew Grandpa Mac from his childhood home in Sault Sainte Marie, which sits at the eastern edge of Michigan's Upper Peninsula, across the St. Marys River from Sault Sainte Marie, Canada. Long before the first French explorers arrived in 1618, native bands of Ojibwa lived off the rich flora and fauna: fish, deer, maple sugar, wild rice. Meanwhile, down south, slavery was laying the foundation for a plantation economy that would fuel industrial manufacturing in the Northeast. Commerce in the northern wilderness operated somewhat separately and relied on what the forests and waters produced unaided: fur, fish, and timber. France claimed the land, then ceded it to Britain after losing the French and Indian War in 1760. When Britain lost the Revolutionary War, the area fell within the bounds of the United States. In 1836, Ojibwa leaders signed a treaty with the United States, exchanging more than 13.8 million acres of land for $300,000 and promises of smaller annual payments. That is a price, in-hand, of roughly two cents an acre.

My grandfather was born in 1907, most likely at home, in Steelton, an industrial town on the Canadian side of the river. Ship traffic crowded the locks connecting Lake Huron, at the river's southern end, to Lake Superior, twenty feet higher and to the north, since the 1850s. Freighters carried lumber, copper, and iron from the Upper Peninsula, Minnesota, and Wisconsin to the Great Lakes' industrial centers: Chicago and Detroit,

Toronto and Buffalo. Ships could transport freight far more cheaply than railroads, and this lowered the prices for anything made from what they carried: steel and cars and telephone wire. "These narrow walls made Pittsburgh and Gary [Indiana] possible," observes a boosterish account of the period. The freighters also connected the granaries of the Great Plains with ports along the Great Lakes, easing the work of feeding city dwellers. By the late 1910s, the Sault's four locks passed more freight annually than all of America's saltwater ports combined. Even so, the American Sault was a small town. When its population more than quintupled from 1880 to 1900, it only reached 10,588.

My grandfather rarely spoke about his childhood, but it sounded difficult in the way that life at the start of the twentieth century always sounds difficult. His father died in 1913, asphyxiated overnight by a gas lamp in a Cleveland boardinghouse; he had been working at a steel plant there. According to news reports, my grandfather's mother, Ella, then the mother of three boys, was "prostrated with grief." She worked, and in 1919 she remarried, this time to an American innkeeper. That husband passed away a couple years later, and she remarried another American, this time a painter. In 1925, my grandfather graduated from Sault Sainte Marie High School, on the American side. Soon he was working as a messenger and clerk at the local branch of a national bank.

There's no record of why my grandfather left the Sault. I don't know if it felt small to him or if he felt crowded out by the layers of stepfamily being added. I don't know if he yearned for adventure, if he could not find work he liked, or if family pressured him to leave. But for whatever reason, in 1929, he took a job as a bank teller in Detroit. It was a boomtown then, and the fourth-largest city in the country.

My grandfather traded a town of fourteen thousand for a city of roughly 1.5 million, but he was not leaping into the unknown. His uncle Norman, Ella's brother, had emigrated from Canada to Detroit in 1920. Around the time my grandfather joined him, Norman, a pharmacist, owned a house in a new subdivision on the city's northwest side, built as part of a national home-building boom. It was fairly unusual back then for anyone to buy a home without paying the full price outright. In 1920, less than half of Americans owned their homes—largely because mortgages were short and expensive. Most ran for three to seven years, required down payments of 50 percent, and only credited payments toward interest—leaving borrowers as deep in debt at the end as at the beginning.

Despite those barriers, Norman had managed to buy a home built by B. E. Taylor, a Detroit developer. Taylor had bought up huge tracts of farmland and woods at the city's edge, then turned it into housing with modern amenities like sewers and pavement. A block away, a new streetcar ran along Grand River Avenue, linking the neighborhood with downtown, nine miles to the southeast. Some of Taylor's subdivisions were spacious, with houses built on multiple lots set back far from the street. Norman's block was more modest, with shallow yards and houses on every lot.

This is where my grandfather arrived when he first left home. He lived there for a year. His part of Detroit must have looked so different from the Sault: new homes crowded with new families, a streetcar roaring its way downtown. Yet in at least one way it was very much the same: Every resident on Norman's block, like everyone in our family and nearly everyone in the Sault, was white.

* * * * *

At the time my grandfather moved to Detroit, mainstream white America largely considered race to be a biological fact, something "essential" and inborn that determined your abilities. This was never true, and in the early 2000s advances in genetic mapping allowed scientists to prove that skin color does no more to shape a person's talents or flaws than hair and eye color. But in the early part of the twentieth century, white American society broadly accepted that skin color dictated personality and intelligence, conveyed value or its lack.* This prejudice not only

---

* Although the assumption that skin color correlates with other inborn traits has receded from mainstream American discourse, the concept has persisted well into the twenty-first century. In 2005, sociologists found that 22 percent of nonwhite Americans attributed the income gap between Black and white

shaped individual interactions. It also shaped how the American government used its power to influence the lives of its citizens—including their housing.

Sometimes racial prejudice showed up in housing as case-by-case discrimination by individual landlords, which preserved white neighborhoods and helped give rise to enclaves like San Francisco's Chinatown and Harlem in New York City. Sometimes homeowners and developers added racial covenants to property or housing deeds to prohibit people who were not white from living in them. But at the very start of the twentieth century, the most common practice was to standardize discrimination through law. Across the country—though mostly in the South—cities began to pass zoning ordinances restricting neighborhoods by race.

Racial zoning was introduced in Baltimore in 1910, after George McMechen, a Black Yale-trained attorney, rented a vacant rowhouse on a previously all-white block. On his first night in the home, on McCulloh Street near Druid Hill, rocks were thrown through his windows, and a brick was thrown through the third-floor skylight. There was more white violence when more Black families moved into other vacant buildings on the block.

Officials took this as a sign that violence was an unavoidable consequence of integration and argued—without providing evidence—that integration would cut the value of white-owned property in half. Baltimore passed a new zoning rule that prohibited Black or white people from buying homes in neighborhoods where they were not part of the racial majority. Breaking it risked a fine of up to nearly one hundred dollars and up to a year in jail. The author of the ordinance, a white attorney named Milton Dashiell, said that the city "has a right—indeed, not only

---

Americans to "unspecified genetic differences between the two groups." More recently, a 2016 study found that half of white medical students believed there were significant biological differences between Black people and white people. The link between skin color and other genetic traits has been so thoroughly disproven that in 2023 the National Academy of Sciences advised researchers that they "should not use race as a proxy for human genetic variation."

has the right, but should hold it as its bounden duty—to step in and, by the prohibition of further influx of negro population into the white districts, prevent further destruction in value." This right, reasoned Dashiell, could be enforced by the city.

The ordinance was controversial, gaining national attention—as well as critics and mimics. Over the next seven years, twenty-seven cities enacted racial zoning. With the exception of Colwyn, Pennsylvania, all of those cities were in the South, where they were part of the ever-shifting segregation laws known as Jim Crow, or in states that bordered the region. Zoning based on race stayed legal until 1917, when the Supreme Court struck it down in *Buchanan v. Warley*. Government, held the court, could not violate "the civil right of a white man to dispose of his property if he saw fit to do so to a person of color and of a colored person to make such disposition to a white person." The issue at hand was not equal protection under the law for people who were not white, but the state's ability to intervene in a private contract.

★ ★ ★ ★ ★

When Grandpa Mac landed in Detroit, my mother's parents, Donald Weddle and Katheryn Nichols, were children in Pontiac, a General Motors town thirty miles northwest. Pontiac is smaller than both Detroit and Flint, but it's no less a part of the automobile's heartland; its factories were turning out hand-built Model Ts by 1909—four years before Detroit would introduce the assembly line. Pontiac is also a kind of heartland for my mother's family, so far removed from immigration that no stories of the old country remain. It is where my mother's parents were born, where my mother was born, and where my sisters and I were born.

My mother's father, Grandpa Don to me, was born to southern migrants with German roots, both of them from the Ozarks. The families of Bert and Mary Weddle, my great-great-grandparents, farmed the land and worked in lead mines. Neither living offered much comfort or security. I imagine, but cannot prove, that Bert and Mary, newlyweds, came north seeking opportunity. Unlike Black people leaving the South in those days, they did not need to flee racial violence, which was persistent in Missouri. From 1877 to 1950, sixty black men were lynched in that state, more than half of whom were killed after 1900.

By 1917, Bert and Mary had arrived in Pontiac, having watched the Ozarks' mountains give way to Illinois fields before, most likely, changing trains in Chicago. From there, they would've skirted the shores of Lake Michigan before heading east, finally disembarking at Detroit's extravagant Michigan Central Station, an icon modeled after ancient Roman bathhouses. The Grand Trunk Railroad would have carried them northwest, through swamp and farmland, to Pontiac. Bert signed a draft card for the First World War and indicated he was a welder at a local foundry. Soon, he was welding at an auto factory, and by 1930 he was at a private welding company. They rented homes from General Motors, a block or two from the plant. They changed neighborhoods but always lived among mechanics and factory workers, always in communities without any Black residents. Their last house in the city was in a section without sewers.

City life did not erase their rural upbringing. This was particularly true for Mary, the daughter of a farmer—and great-granddaughter of a Methodist circuit preacher who pastored at several churches. To hear my grandfather tell it years later, chicken dinners in Pontiac began on Sunday mornings, with Mary in the backyard, her hand grasped tightly around the head of a live chicken. She'd raise her arm and snap her elbow, spinning the chicken until its neck broke, then chopped off the head. Their city yard was small enough for neighbors to see the scene unfold: A headless chicken puttering around under the clothesline, bleeding, as my grandfather, a dark-haired boy of six or seven, chased it, wrestled it into scalding water, then plucked its feathers. I remember my grandfather telling this story with good humor. He liked to share it with me whenever I complained about modern meat.

This was the kind of story my family told me about themselves: Country people in the city. Factory workers and bankers. Well-intentioned, not bothering anybody, keeping to themselves. I assumed, like children do, that my family's story represented the way things were. In this way, I assumed that my family was telling me the whole story about the place I was from.

Like most children, I was wrong.

* * * * *

My mother's maternal grandparents, the Nicholses, had come from rural families, laborers and farmers in small Michigan towns up north. Her father, Harley, made it through seventh grade before he went to work; her mother, Evelyn, got through eighth. They married in 1912, ages twenty-two and twenty, and by 1930 the couple had moved to Pontiac. I imagine the same promises that drew the Weddles had beckoned to the Nicholses, too. Harley found work at a carriage company that had retooled itself to make car bodies for Henry Ford. The work would have likely offered steadier and higher pay than farming—an admittedly low bar. Unions had yet to be recognized by the government then, and factory work could be unsafe and income unpredictable. Even so, by 1930 they had four children—including my grandmother, then a toddler—and owned their home. Three more children followed.

The Great Depression began in 1929, halting the boom in home building. Construction all but stopped. People lost work and stopped paying their mortgages. By 1940, the Nicholses were renting again, sharing a small home with the two parents, Harley's brother, and six children from toddlers to twentysomethings. Only one child, the oldest daughter, Eleanor, had gotten married and moved out.

These stories are new to me. Before I began working on this book, I knew little of the mining and settling and train riding, the farming or the steady march toward the promises of cities. My family speaks so little of its past that, when people have asked me what I "am," I've shrugged and changed the subject, as my parents have before me. Our ignorance of our past feels odd to me, given how neatly it fits into America's story of itself: European immigrants escaped manual labor, watched their children work in factories, their grandchildren in offices. Instead, we shrug and say

we are American and do not take it further. We know, instinctively, that
we could not be American without being at least partly white, but that is
another thing we do not talk about.

* * * * *

The threat of white violence has long been active and intense in the
North—though I never learned about that growing up. From the early
1800s through the 1930s, white racial violence was endemic in the North.
It spiked in the 1910s and 1920s, as African Americans fleeing the South,
as well as immigrants, began arriving in northern cities. In the 1920s, the
Ku Klux Klan reported seventy thousand members in Michigan. In the
spring and summer of 1923, the organization held several mass gatherings outside the city limits—some of which included cross burnings that
drew between two thousand and eight thousand people each. There was
a Klavern in Pontiac, too. My mother's cousin remembers that Harley and
Evelyn Nichols, Grandma Kate's parents, talked admiringly of the Klan.
She tells me they had joined its ranks.

The KKK was not the only white supremacist group active in my
birthplace. From the early 1920s to the late 1930s, a covert white supremacist terrorist organization called the Black Legion was active in Michigan, including Pontiac. Founded in the mid-1920s, the group operated
primarily in Detroit but had members across the Midwest. Scholars con-
servatively estimate its peak membership, in the mid-1930s, at between
sixty thousand and a hundred thousand. Its members worked in auto-plant
management, police departments, city governments, and, it is believed,
auto-plant security forces.

The Black Legion became national news in 1936, after the media blew
up the story of its murder of Charles Poole, a white, Catholic employee
of the Works Progress Administration. There had been little news coverage of the group's earlier violence: Not of the 1933 murder of George
Marchuk, a white union leader, or the attempted murder of Edward
Armour, a Black steelworker, undertaken because a Legion member
wanted to kill a Black person. Not of the 1934 murder of white union

organizer John Bielak, or the burning, that year, of the farmhouse and barn of William Mollenhauer, a suspected Communist in rural Oakland County. And not even of the 1935 murder of Silas Coleman, a Black man that members had kidnapped, taken to a swamp, wounded with gunshots, and then chased for sport before killing him. Those activities had earned only passing interest from the FBI's J. Edgar Hoover, who opened an investigation in late 1935—then closed it the month before the Poole murder. He did not reopen the case.

In Oakland County, where Pontiac is located, a one-man grand-jury investigation by Circuit Judge George Hartrick yielded an estimate of between 2,200 and 4,500 Black Legion members in the county, 86 of them public officials and public employees. Public outcry over the Poole murder led to the group's dissolution, but the Black Legion became a media sensation. National news coverage led to a magazine serial, a novel, a radio drama featuring Orson Welles, and two films—one of which starred Humphrey Bogart and earned an Oscar nomination. Even so, the Black Legion and the commonness of racial violence it represented is one more thing my family, and my community, do not talk about.*

★ ★ ★ ★ ★

Across the country, racism was beginning to morph into less blatant—but no less powerful—forms, particularly in housing. Once the Supreme Court declared segregation by zoning unconstitutional, many white leaders turned to racially restrictive covenants—the kind of deed provision that prohibited my grandfather's home from being sold to Black buyers. Historians have found racial covenants on property deeds as early as 1843, in both the North and the South, but they became much more common

---

* White supremacist hate groups remain a notable presence across the United States. As of 2021, the Southern Poverty Law Center had documented ninety-eight white nationalist hate groups active in forty-five of the fifty states, as well as fifty-four neo-Nazi groups, eighteen chapters of the Ku Klux Klan, seventeen racist skinhead groups, sixteen neo-Confederate organizations, and nine Christian-identity hate groups.

after the zoning ruling. And while zoning had been almost exclusive to the South and its border states, racial covenants spanned the whole country: Charlottesville, Chicago, Detroit, Los Angeles, Minneapolis, Oakland, Oklahoma City, Philadelphia, Phoenix, Queens, San Antonio, Seattle, and Washington, D.C. For the next three decades, courts nationwide upheld racial covenants as legal and enforceable by law.

Every racial covenant used broadly white-supremacist language, but the specifics could differ. Some were florid: One 1932 covenant for a California subdivision promised that "[the] premises and each and every structure erected thereon shall not be sold, leased or conveyed to or occupied or inherited by any person whose blood is not that entirely of the Caucasian race." Others were plain and specific. I have read about covenants in Canada prohibiting the sale of homes to Jewish people; covenants in Saint Louis that prohibited Asian Americans, referred to as "Mongolian," from living in homes; and deed restrictions in Texas that prohibited Mexicans, among others, from doing the same. But whomever else was excluded, covenants almost always placed a ban on Black people, usually referred to as "Negro." Indeed, while the list of prohibited or included groups may expand or contract, the language across racist covenants is startlingly similar, as if cut and pasted from one master template.

There is a reason for that.

In 1924, the National Association of Real Estate Boards, a private confederation of real estate brokers from across the country, instructed its members that an ethical Realtor "should never be instrumental in introducing into a neighborhood a character of property or occupancy, members of any race or nationality, or any individuals whose presence will clearly be detrimental to property values in that neighborhood." NAREB training materials and appraisal guides stated as fact that when minorities came into a white neighborhood, property values went down. In 1927, the group wrote a template racial covenant and circulated it to its members. Developers and homeowner associations across the country began to adopt the language. By 1930, a model licensing act with the same language had been adopted by thirty-two states. In order to be licensed as a real estate broker, you had to promise to discriminate by race.* If you did not, you risked being expelled from the profession.

But if covenants had become central to the American home industry, fighting them had become central to the fight for racial justice—even, argued civil rights attorneys, to American democracy itself. Covenants were "absurd and un-American," James Weldon Johnson, the NAACP's executive secretary, wrote to colleagues working on a covenants case. "If you begin by segregating members of one race, you may easily come to the point where segregation is made into a matter of creed as well as race. . . . It would undermine the very foundation of American citizenship."

Outside of lawsuits aiming for the Supreme Court, though, opponents of covenants more often made their case by highlighting the pedigree and class status of Black homeowners. There was no lofty language about the foundation of citizenship. There was no discussion of how few Americans—and how exceedingly few Black Americans—were financially able, at least through the mid-1930s, to buy a home. Instead, says the historian Kevin Boyle, "respectability politics plays out a lot of the time because . . . Black people who could afford to test the covenant were well-to-do people. It didn't tend to be poor people who could afford to move into white neighborhoods."

* * * * *

Housing was a central concern for the Roosevelt administration when it took power in 1933. The home ownership industry that government had encouraged in the 1920s was stalling out. In that first year, officials directed agencies to expand low-cost housing—and to help keep existing homeowners in their homes. When officials launched the Home Owners' Loan Corporation that year, they tasked it with helping homeowners who were struggling to pay their mortgages through no fault of their own.

---

* In 2020, the president of NAR (National Association of Realtors), Charlie Oppler, issued a public apology for the organization's past discrimination.

HOLC began buying distressed mortgages from banks, then refinanc-
ing people's mortgages on forgiving terms. Instead of short, interest-only
loans, HOLC offered the first mortgages that were affordable to middle-
class people—similar to the terms offered today. Payment was spread out
over fifteen to twenty-five years, interest rates were below 5 percent, and
the loans were amortized, allowing homeowners to gain equity as they
paid. Since the agency was intended to help *existing* homeowners, it maintained the status quo, neither advancing nor challenging segregation. The
demographics of HOLC's mortgage clients in this period closely matched
the demographics of home ownership: mostly white, but with a notable
minority of Black homeowners. In cities across the country, most of the
agency's mortgages were in neighborhoods it eventually coded as "declining" or "hazardous," shaded yellow and red.

The Federal Housing Administration was different. HOLC had been
intended to rescue people who already owned homes. The FHA was
charged with creating more homeowners by offering affordable mortgages. In the process, went the thinking, the agency could solve two
problems. First, it would help the economy by rescuing the construction industry—which had seen a 90 percent drop in business during the
Depression. Second, it would address the housing crisis by making homeownership affordable to the middle class.

In financial terms, the FHA accomplished this by expanding the insurance of affordable, amortized, long-term mortgages like the ones HOLC
had introduced. This meant that private banks would loan to less-affluent
homebuyers since, if the homebuyers failed to pay, the government would
cover their losses. The FHA finalized its first loans in 1935. Soon, it was
underwriting whole suburban developments. By 1950, FHA financing
underwrote more than a quarter of all new homes—485,933 that year
alone. Recent scholarship suggests that the FHA also shaped private banks'
lending practices, and therefore fueled redlining in a way that, in practice,
HOLC did not. All of this made the FHA instrumental in the postwar push
that drew white residents out of cities and into suburbs.

As the FHA created the template for modern homeownership, it consistently treated Black residents as less valuable than white ones. Its founding documents required the agency to use "economically sound" investment criteria—and the agency, much like Baltimore officials in 1910 and NAREB officials, considered Black residents a danger to property values. The agency's 1935 underwriting manual instructed staff that "a change in social or racial occupancy generally leads to instability and a reduction in values." It said that "important among adverse influences . . . are infiltration of inharmonious racial or nationality groups," and warned that "all mortgages on properties protected against [such] unfavorable influences, to the extent such protecting is possible, will obtain a 'high rating.'" Its 1936 manual recommended racist covenants to promote the "prohibition of the occupancy of properties except by the race for which they are intended." A decade later, the FHA removed direct references to race from the manual. The agency nonetheless continued to equate "compatibility among the neighborhood occupants" with higher value for much of the 1950s.

Both HOLC and the FHA used maps to manage their portfolios. In the 1930s, as HOLC refinanced more than one million mortgages, the agency used local Realtors to assess the real estate markets in 239 cities where it held mortgages. Each city was divided into districts based on how local Realtors—licensed by NAREB—understood neighborhood boundaries. Each district was color-coded for risk. Green for districts where values were high or Realtors believed they would increase, blue for districts that would hold value, yellow for districts that were less valuable or likely to decline, and red for districts where values were low or dropping. Most Americans did not know about these maps until the historian Kenneth T. Jackson began writing about them in the 1980s. Visually striking and infinitely shareable, the maps are often pointed to as the root of modern racial disparities in homeownership.

Scholars, however, will point to an important detail: Neither HOLC nor its maps *changed* much about homeownership in America. They were not used to determine who would get new mortgages, but to manage the resale of properties the agency already possessed through foreclosure. The more interesting maps would be those of the FHA—an agency that

openly practiced racist discrimination for decades, and cast the mold for
homeownership in twentieth-century America. Federal officials, though,
destroyed most of them in 1969 in response to a lawsuit.

A map is not required, of course, to judge discrimination by the FHA.
For that, its track record will suffice. One study using 1940 data found
that out of the roughly 1,300 Black homeowners in Greensboro, North Carolina, only one got an FHA loan. Another, in Peoria, Illinois, found that
the FHA did not insure any of the town's two hundred Black residents.
In Baltimore, the FHA helped finance loans for an estimated 8 percent of
white homeowners—but only an estimated 2 percent of Black ones, nearly
half of whom lived in a relatively affluent Black community near Morgan
College. The FHA did not limit its borrowers' use of racial covenants until
1950, when the agency began to refuse to insure mortgages for properties
with new racial covenants. It made no ban on insuring homes that contained old ones.

It's easy to find echoes of the FHA's logic throughout home financing
institutions. The Federal Home Loan Bank Board, which oversaw savings and loan associations, did not oppose denying mortgages on the basis
of race until 1961. Erle Cocke Sr., then the chair of the Federal Deposit
Insurance Corporation, told the U.S. Commission on Civil Rights that
his agency was morally and legally obligated to allow its member banks
to consider race when making mortgages, given that "financing of a real
estate purchase for a member of a minority group might have a serious
effect upon values in a neighborhood."

This was the world in which my grandparents built their families and
their financial lives. But they would need to meet each other first.

* * * * *

My father's mother, born Margaret Masten, would have been twenty-seven
or twenty-eight years old when she met Grandpa Mac. She was part of a
working-class, German Catholic family, three generations deep in Ann
Arbor. Her dad was a painter for the university, and her mother cleaned
houses. They rented their homes and moved often. Little wonder that

Margaret studied stenography in high school, graduating in 1928. By 1929, she was working at a bank. That fall, Black Thursday sent the country into the Great Depression.

In 1936, the banks they each worked at merged. I imagine them eyeing each other in marble-floored hallways, flirting, and falling in love. They would have made an appealing couple: he was just shy of tall, dapper, and attentive, she had a dry wit, a taste for liquor, and a devout Catholic faith. They courted long enough that, despite the distance between Ann Arbor and Sault Ste. Marie, both families had met, and liked, the love their child had chosen.

In August of 1936, just as HOLC and the FHA were hitting their stride, my grandparents eloped to Angola, Indiana, a hundred miles away. They chose a more glamorous honeymoon, spending a night or two at the Statler Hotel in Detroit, an eight-hundred-room Renaissance Revival overlooking a park. When Ella, my grandfather's mother, learned of the marriage, she wrote a letter urging the couple to visit and promising a wedding present. "Hope you will be the happiest couple ever lived," she wrote. "I think you both were meant for one another." When my grandparents returned to Ann Arbor, they lived in an apartment, occupying the second floor of a house on the city's west side. This was the start of their life together.

Shortly after they were married, my grandparents took out a land contract to pay for a lot in a new subdivision nearby. Land contracts are risky: If the borrower misses a single payment, the owner can take back the house, and the borrower loses everything they've spent on the house up to then. There are no documents to tell me why my grandparents chose this setup to build their home. Experts tell me it is strange that my grandfather, who would have had access to information about the new world of FHA loans, chose this path. Within a few years, my grandparents built a handsome brick bungalow with a full basement, full attic, and two bedrooms. They looked forward to parenthood, but had no luck in bearing children of their own.

Other things went more smoothly for my father's parents, particularly when it came to finances. They met and married toward the end of the

Great Depression. While unemployment in the Depression had peaked around 25 percent nationwide—and at 34 percent in Michigan—things had begun to improve. In 1938, the national unemployment rate had dropped to 19 percent; in Michigan, where wartime manufacturing boomed, less than 9 percent of white men were unemployed. By comparison, more than 18 percent of Black men were unemployed.* There is no record of either of my grandparents losing their jobs, and by 1940 they reported earning $3,300 a year as a couple. That income put them at the boundary between the middle and upper-middle class. There's no documentation of the amount of the land contract for the house, but I remember my father's cousin telling me it cost about $8,000.†

When my grandparents bought the land, it had already been subdivided for development. Each deed in the subdivision was subject to restrictions intended to set a standard for the neighborhood and the house itself. If a buyer breached any of the provisions, they could be sued by the seller or by their new neighbors; in extreme cases, police could be called to force compliance. One provision set a minimum sales price, to prevent the development of slums. Another outlined owner obligations in terms of building a sidewalk. A third required the developer to connect the house to city sewers. You would find similar provisions in deeds written last year. But you would not find the sixth on any deed written today, though you might find it readily in the archives of the National Association of Real Estate Boards—known today as the National Association of Realtors. This provision, the final one on the list, prohibited the sale,

---

* The late economist William E. Spriggs spent much of his career documenting that the African American unemployment rate has historically, and quite consistently, been double that of white Americans. While Spriggs published extensively over his career on the topic, a 2018 article in Law and Inequality, "A Look at Inequality, Workers' Rights, and Race," provides a useful overview to the topic and his work.

† According to the Bureau of Labor Statistics, their combined $3,300 income in January 1940 was equivalent to $71,026 in January 2023. The $8,000 land contract in January 1937 was equivalent to $169,742 in January 2023.

rental, or occupation of the property by "any Negro or persons of African descent."

That covenant gave my grandfather a house, which gave him stability and, eventually, wealth. Like so many things in my family, we do not talk about that. I don't know any white families that do.

★ ★ ★ ★ ★

Grandpa Mac did not get to enjoy his new house for long. In 1941, the United States joined World War II and expanded the draft to include men as young as eighteen and as old as forty-five; the latter clause snagged Grandpa Mac. Still, he was a bit old for combat, and his class status, a function of his profession—and therefore his age and race—made it easy for men with power to see themselves in him. He stayed stateside for the duration of the war, as did about a quarter of soldiers.

The military was segregated then, from its draft to its bunks to its blood banks, with the 1.2 million Black soldiers who served in World War II working in separate units from white soldiers. I think it was his first time living under segregation codified in law. His assignments—North Carolina first, then Florida—took him to states that operated under Jim Crow rules. This must have shaped his time in the service, but that is one more thing my family does not talk about. Family photos show him and my grandmother when she visited him in Tampa, enjoying the beaches, which were segregated, and a Tampa teahouse that hosted segregated events.

It was different for my mother's father. Tall, with dark eyes and a strong hooked nose, my grandpa Don was a nineteen-year-old civil engineering student at a local college when the army lowered the age of service to eighteen and included college students in the draft. When he was drafted, he ended up going to war.

Even so, Grandpa Don had advantages over many others caught by the draft—and particularly over Black recruits. Most notably, he was better educated than most Americans, of any race. In 1940, just 11 percent of white American men received any education after high school, and nearly two-thirds didn't make it past eighth grade. For Black boys, most of whom still lived in the Deep South and faced underfunded or nonexistent schools, the average was to get a fifth-grade education. Just over 3 percent of Black boys received any post–high school education at all.

Education mattered in the military, because it helped determine your assignment. When my grandfather took the Army General Classification Test, he did well—just as most educated recruits, Black or white, did. Because my grandfather did well, the army gave him six months of engineering classes in 1943. This bought him time safely stateside. More than 99 percent of the recruits who received this same reprieve were white.

In this way, being white bought my grandfather time. It couldn't protect him forever. As the war intensified, bodies became more important than skills. Three months after D-Day, Grandpa Don landed in Normandy. For the next eight months, he helped man a cannon on the front lines of the war. He came home after the Nazis surrendered, returning on July 20, 1945, the day before my grandmother turned eighteen. On August 6, the United States dropped an atomic bomb on Hiroshima, Japan. On August 9, it dropped a plutonium bomb on Nagasaki. Within days, Japan surrendered and the war was over, and this meant that Grandpa Don was safe.

When I was in my twenties, I talked with my grandma Kate, Don's wife, about the atomic bombs. I had become friends with a woman whose grandmother had survived the Nagasaki bombing. I imagine I told Grandma Kate I felt, as I do now, that the bombings were horrible and that my country had been inhumane to use them, that my country would never have treated the bombs as necessary if the tables had been turned. My grandmother shrugged: Maybe so, but they had made her marriage possible, and therefore my life. Enjoying the spoils, I was to understand, was my right. I was not to question it at all.

★ ★ ★ ★ ★

After the war ended, both my grandfathers began to build their families using what resources they had. Anxious to fill their second bedroom, Grandmar and Grandpa Mac began to look into adoption. Grandpa Mac returned to the bank, stepping back in as if he had never left. In October 1946, they brought home a round-cheeked newborn baby boy with a shadow of ebony hair and pale blue eyes. They named him John, after my grandfather, and called him Johnny.

My mother's parents, younger and with less money, were drifting toward each other in Pontiac. The army discharged Donald just before Thanksgiving, and he moved back in with his parents. By then his parents had bought a handsome two-story brick Colonial on a wide expanse of lawn in Waterford Township, just outside the city limits. Waterford's population nearly tripled from 1930 to 1950; all but a couple dozen of its residents were white. In Pontiac, meanwhile, the second wave of the Great Migration had begun to introduce more Black workers into factories, and more Black families were settling in its neighborhoods.

If the inaugural deed for Donald's parents' home is any indication, the segregated divide between Pontiac and its neighboring townships was intentional, fueled by developers. The deed shows that my family's handsome Colonial was subject to the restrictions of the Oakwood Subdivision, which included racial covenants: "No person of any race other than the Caucasian race shall use or occupy any building or any lot, except that this covenant shall not prevent occupancy by domestic servants of a different race domiciled with an owner or tenant," they read. The same deed names the subdivision's three trustees: Edward Howlett, Fred Harger, and William Ransom. All of them were known around town, but only Ransom, who served as Pontiac's tax assessor in the 1930s, had been named publicly as a member of the Black Legion.

Grandpa Don resumed classes at Lawrence Technological University. He would have been eligible for the G.I. Bill, which covered tuition and living expenses for veterans approved for study. The policy launched many poor and working-class white men into the professional middle class that defined mid-century affluence, and doubled the number of college graduates nationwide. Yet, at the insistence of southern politicians—and the quiet acceptance of many northern politicians—the educational benefit required the approval of local officials, which meant that any Black veteran seeking to use their benefit would need the approval of local, white officials. This gatekeeping meant that white veterans were dramatically more likely to see their military service open the door to a college education. Indeed, while the G.I. Bill was in theory available to any veteran, use of its benefits was deeply segregated. Today, many scholars regard the postwar G.I. Bill as a source not only of social mobility (for whites), but of racial disparity, too.

Still, there are no formal records documenting how Grandpa Don paid for this round of classes, and no relatives can recall anything about it. However he paid for classes, Grandpa Don also worked at his dad's welding shop and began settling back into civilian life. For a while, he was dating a woman named Mary.

Back in Pontiac, Katheryn—my grandma Kate—several years his junior, had just turned eighteen. She was medium height and full-bottomed, with dark hair and pale blue eyes. Toward strangers, she was cool, but with people she knew, she could be warm and loving. A few months shy of her nineteenth birthday, her mother died. This meant she was the only girl at home in a family with three young boys; it fell to her to care for them. By the standards of the time, she was grown, so she was expected to weather the passing of her mother and her new responsibilities without complaint. As a high school graduate without a job, she had few other options.

Her father remarried within the year, and his new wife, a cousin told me, brought with her a grown son who made passes at Kate. No longer needed as a caregiver for her father and harassed in her home, Kate went to live with her sister, Eleanor, across town. Ten years older than Katheryn and with a husband and two daughters of her own, Eleanor needed the help.

Kate was good at caring for the children, but she was embarrassed by her family's poverty. Sometimes, when she walked downtown for a soda with her nieces and siblings, she'd stride ahead of the pack, head held high, ignoring them; she didn't want anyone to think she was poor. They loved her anyway, shrugging off her snubs as a quirk. Eleanor, maybe out of motherliness, maybe out of wanting fewer mouths to feed, began pushing her younger sister to settle down.

By 1947, Kate and Donald had met, and Eleanor approved of the match. Grandpa Don had a lot to recommend him: He could be charming when he wanted to be, he had a stable job at his father's business, and his family lived in a fine brick home outside the city limits. When Kate asked for permission to drive to New York City with Donald that summer, Eleanor agreed, thinking the couple would elope. They did not.

I wonder about the conversation the sisters had when Kate returned. I picture Eleanor asking leading, expectant questions as my grandmother unpacks a tiny handheld suitcase, puts away her hat, smooths her hair. My grandmother would have feigned confusion and obliviousness at her sister's inquiries, while daydreaming, on the side, of my grandfather. She had a reputation for being a good liar then, and maybe she was proud of her deception. Maybe the trip had been her idea, and she'd done it because she wanted to see the world. Maybe it was my grandfather's idea, and she went to stay in his good graces. Maybe she was just young and reckless. For my part, I see my grandmother's lie of omission as a strategy to get around the fact that, being young and female and without much education, she had little power. She would have learned at home and in public that a direct request rarely got her what she wanted. She would have begun, even then, to wonder whether she could get further by letting the powerful believe what they wanted—and taking what she could get—than by giving them a chance to say no.

Sometime that fall, Kate discovered she was pregnant. Things moved quickly from there. She and my grandfather had a short engagement, and Donald's parents paid for a proper wedding the first week of November. There was a tiered cake cut with a silver server. There was a veil and white gown fitted over my grandmother's still-narrow waist. There was a bow tie beneath my grandfather's clean-shaven chin and already receding hairline. There was a professional photographer who produced a series of stoic pictures of the couple. Within a year, they had rented a house on Pontiac's east side.

When Realtors working for the federal Home Owners' Loan Corporation had categorized the residents of Don and Kate's new neighborhood as
"skilled laborers" in 1937, they put the average income at more than double that of the poorer neighborhoods it abutted. The Realtors noted that
my grandparents' future block was close to the incinerator and a public
dump, but, promisingly, the city had just built a new elementary school
nearby. This, along with its nearly monoracial population—almost all
white—earned it the ranking of "second grade," referenced as "B." I imagine this pleased my grandmother, so keen to avoid looking poor, when they
moved in ten years later. It would have disappointed her, too; she would
have understood there was room for improvement. On June 4, 1948, seven
months after Kate and Don married, my mother was born full-term and
healthy. They named her Charyl.

2

KATRINA RECTENWALD: WORK
B. 1984
PITTSBURGH, PENNSYLVANIA

Maybe Katrina had the mild hot sauce on her wings (one-third butter to two-thirds Frank's hot sauce), or maybe she had the hot ranch (equal parts Frank's and ranch dressing). When I asked her, four years after the fact, which one of the nineteen flavors of wings at Smokin' Joe's Saloon she had that night, she understandably could not remember. The friend she was with, Jasmine, doesn't remember what she got, either—though she might've gone in for the tang of wing dust. Either way, both women agree they'd headed to Pittsburgh's South Side Flats, an early gentrification target where bars and cafés had replaced steel mills, to catch up over wings and cocktails.

Maybe they blended in, maybe they didn't; it's hard to say. Katrina is medium height, built thick. Her light brown hair is streaked with white blond, and her Serbian heritage is obvious in her blue eyes, pink cheeks, and pale skin. Jasmine has a figure like Katrina's and favors lace-front wigs that fall past her shoulders, straight and dark, setting off the smooth brown skin she inherited from her parents. Raised in a mostly white suburb, Jasmine was used to being the lone Black girl in a room full of white people.

Neither the wings nor the drinks from that night in 2017 were memorable. What they both remember, instead, is the question Katrina asked.

She'd turned it over in her head for a few weeks as she'd watched her friends and her union respond to news of a white supremacist rally in Charlottesville, Virginia. The question had come up again in the union office that day. She couldn't stop thinking about it. *All right*, she told her herself as the bartender set down the first round of drinks. *I'm just gonna go for it.*

"Jasmine, I need to ask you a serious question. My organizer told me that, like, there's still racism today."

Jasmine looked at her friend and waited, uncertain. They joked about race between themselves, sometimes: teasing each other about dating men outside their own race, or trading good-natured barbs about the difference between Black and white drinking habits, à la Katt Williams. But this was the first time Katrina had ever brought up *racism*.

The bar would have been loud and boisterous when Katrina glanced over at the Big Buck Hunter console in the corner and spit out her final question—more or less. When she told me the story, I imagined the music in the bar stopping with a record scratch.

"My organizer told me that there's still racism today, and I've been looking and I haven't seen it," Katrina said, rambling. "So, can you tell me, like, does this happen? What's happening here?"

Recalling the conversation later, Jasmine remembered thinking, incredulously, *How didn't you know? Did you think people were arguing and protesting for no reason?* But she did not say this to Katrina. The women had been friends for almost a decade by then, from nursing school to board exams to first jobs to bachelor's degrees. They had vacationed together, and Jasmine had been one of Katrina's bridesmaids. The women were not just friends; there was love between them. Jasmine considered her options.

"Race is such an iffy conversation," Jasmine told me. In her experience, a conversation about racism with white people wasn't worth the trouble. Jasmine could tell her Black friends how a patient assumed she was a nursing aide, not a full nurse, and they'd know, immediately, the sting of being reminded that skin was often the first thing people used to judge her. With her white friends, Jasmine knew from experience, there'd probably be a series of comments: *"Maybe the patient had a bad day,"* or *"Maybe you misunderstood."* Sometimes it'd end with her fending off questions about why she always made things about race. "I just don't even want to go there," says Jasmine. "I don't think a white person would understand."

The talk at the bar was not a long one. They were working women with busy lives, and jobs that required a lot of them. Both understood that this was not a single chat at a bar, but the opening of a new, extended conversation; they didn't need to work it all out tonight. But before they pushed aside the rocks glasses and the plates smeared with hot sauce, Jasmine told Katrina, *"The best way I can describe it to you is that because it doesn't impact you, you don't see it."*

This was a powerful explanation for Katrina, who repeated it verbatim to me each time the story came up. But it wasn't exactly what Jasmine meant.

Jasmine knew, better than Katrina did, that racism *did* impact Katrina. If Jasmine paused to think about it, what she really meant was that racism didn't *hurt* Katrina; it helped her. It was only the difference of one word—saying "impact" instead of "hurt" or "help." But it had nudged the discussion toward safer emotional ground, as if racism "impacted" each of them the same. That kind of subtle redirection was almost subconscious—a reflex Jasmine had developed over a lifetime of keeping friendships as racially mixed as the city itself.

Jasmine would not have welcomed the question—which, out of context, was outrageous—from a white person she did not know well. And she would not have welcomed it from a white person who asked her to explain racism in front of other people, opening the possibility of a group discussion. But Jasmine could sense that Katrina was asking it from a place of love and concern, curiosity and respect; of honestly wanting to *know.* So Jasmine tried to respond with care to one of her best friends telling her—as unbelievable as it seemed—that she wasn't sure racism existed.

★ ★ ★ ★ ★

There were many reasons Katrina hadn't asked Jasmine about racism before. The biggest reason was that she had kind of blindly assumed racism wasn't a problem. In school, she'd learned that Martin Luther King Jr. and Rosa Parks fought for—and won—civil rights. She left her classes thinking that racism was a thing of the past. At home, she'd learned to ignore race. "We were raised in a household where they didn't point out race, and we were taught to treat everybody equal," Katrina told me. "I wasn't told, like, this is a Black person, and this is a white person, and here's differences between [them]." If she thought about race—hers, or that of her coworkers—naming that difference felt the same as being racist. But, mostly, she didn't think about it at all.

Katrina didn't know it, but members of her union's parent organization, the Service Employees International Union, had been puzzling over how to talk about race, too. In May 2016, a couple of days before Donald Trump secured the Republican presidential nomination, union members had voted to require the union to fight "anti-Black and structural racism" in all its work. But SEIU, like most of the country's biggest unions, had little experience with putting that into practice, says Tinselyn Simms, the SEIU staffer charged with figuring out a plan to do so. When it came to workers' rights, most of the big, national unions—including SEIU—tended to focus on wages and paychecks. If there was mention of racial justice, it was treated as a separate concern.* In the wake of the SEIU's resolution, says Simms, "we found that we don't know how to talk about race in the economy in a good way." Part of Simms's job was to find one.

---

* Thoroughly recasting mainstream discussion of labor movements is outside the scope of my work in this book, but it's crucial to note the complex racial history of labor organizing in this country. Racism in various industrial and trade unions is well-documented, but there is also a dynamic history of cross-racial solidarity in labor struggles. "There was/is not a single way the U.S. labor movement approached cross-racial solidarity," says Robin D. G. Kelley, whose 2021 article in *Against the Current* provides an excellent overview to this history. At book length, I've found Nell Irvin Painter's *The Narrative of Hosea Hudson,* Kelley's *Hammer and Hoe,* and the 2023 book *Black Folk,* by Blair LM Kelley (no relation to Robin), to be excellent introductions to this history.

Eventually, Simms connected with a trio that was already working on a similar project. The legal scholar Ian Haney López had published a book, *Dog Whistle Politics*, in 2014. It argued that racism was the biggest threat to the working class. "Unions [are] used to the statement that racism is a weapon in the class war; the rich are winning. They say that all the time," says Haney López. "And then they say, 'And therefore, let's just focus on class.'" But that, he says, is a strategic mistake: "Racism is the weapon. How do you defeat a weapon by not addressing it?"

One of his former students, Heather McGhee, was a leading progressive advocate and had seen that weapon used repeatedly as she advocated for bankruptcy reform and a response to the foreclosure crisis. Yet so much of the broad political left, she says, underappreciated "the extent of racial opposition." Around the time Haney López published his book, McGhee took the helm of a think tank, Demos. She brought on her former professor as a senior fellow to strategize about how, and whether, they could persuade other advocates to talk about race and class at the same time. It was slow going until the 2016 election arrived and racist rhetoric became a central part of American politics.

After Donald Trump won the election, Haney López attended a workshop hosted by Anat Shenker-Osorio, a progressive communications strategist. Her work centered on writing slogans and scripts that politicians could use to win support for campaigns and policies—what political insiders refer to as "messaging." Unions weren't the only institutions that had shied away from discussing race, says Shenker-Osorio. Democratic and progressive campaigns also often assumed that naming racism would lower voters' ability to see common ground with each other.

The trio's working hypothesis in the wake of Trump's election was different: "There is no such thing as race-neutral," says Shenker-Osorio. "Our voters are being bombarded with messaging about race implicitly all the time." And, says Shenker-Osorio, the media attention to voters who'd switched from Obama in 2012 to Trump in 2016 tended to obscure another crucial group: voters who'd supported Obama in 2012 and then stayed home in 2016. It was not *only* that Trump had drawn white voters by using racist language; a lot of Democratic voters, and especially Black Democratic voters, had not voted at all. With the presidency determined by a handful of states where the margin of victory was miniscule, Shenker-Osorio found turnout more promising: There were so many more people who didn't vote than had changed parties.*

As the three of them talked—the professor, the advocate, and the strategist—they came up with a goal: a messaging approach that could "explain how the right had used race as a weapon in the class war, inoculate white voters against race-baiting, and create a narrative that black and brown and other people of color could see themselves in," says McGhee. It was ambitious, and well outside the conventional wisdom of politics. Then again, the Trump election had been, too.

To develop messaging and test it is expensive: focus groups and sensitive dials, endless revisions of door-knocking scripts so short they are practically poems. When the trio learned that SEIU was puzzling over much the same problem, they suggested a collaboration. Demos had staff and infrastructure. SEIU had funding. Shenker-Osorio could lead the research. Haney López offered intellectual framing. The goal was to come up with a messaging approach that would work for SEIU members and candidates. (McGhee, meanwhile, began to think about writing a book for lay readers, which became *The Sum of Us*.)

Research for what became the Race-Class Narrative began in 2017, so it was still in the planning phases when Katrina and Jasmine went out for wings. That night Katrina's take on race was still the one she'd grown up with: Racism wasn't really a problem anymore. Even if it was, her work

---

* Whether to focus campaigns on persuading swing voters or on turning out new and existing ones is a persistent debate in American politics—and particularly among Democrats since 2016. A May 2017 study from the data firm Catalist suggests that turnout was key in 2016. Analysis by Mike Podhorzer, a former political director at the AFL-CIO, in his newsletter "Weekend Reading," suggests turnout has become more important since then. Meanwhile, a 2021 study in the journal *Science Advances* by Hill, Hopkins, and Huber suggests that swing voters were crucial to the 2016 election.

as a union member was only to defend and improve the contract with her name on it; no more, no less. This was how she'd been raised.

It was also how her union mentor saw the world.

* * * * *

By the time Katrina and Jasmine became friends, it had become commonplace for white Americans to believe that not being a racist meant simply not seeing race. When I met Katrina's mother, Becky, she put it to me in terms I'd heard from my own family for years: "I don't look at the color of their skin." (More colorfully, she added: "I don't give a shit. You can be gray with purple polka dots.") It turns out, like a lot of things having to do with race, that this language didn't just happen. It was created on purpose.

America did not start out colorblind.* Even after enslavement had been outlawed, mainstream white American thought held that race was biological. This was not fringe thinking, but the scientific mainstream. Whites' assumption of Black inferiority was used, in turn, to suggest that Black people's poverty and hardships were the result of biological difference—not unfair policy and social custom. One of the most noted social Darwinists of the late nineteenth century, Frederick L. Hoffman, even argued that to offer charity to Black people would only artificially extend the lives of the unfit. White opinion had barely budged by 1939, when nearly three-quarters of white Americans believed Black Americans were less intelligent than us.

It took centuries of pressure, most notably by abolitionists from the 1600s on, then by civil rights activists after emancipation, before whites began to

---

* While assessing constitutional scholarship is beyond the scope of this book, it is worth observing that legal scholars have clearly documented that the U.S. Constitution and its amendments took race into account. During the Supreme Court hearing for *Allen v. Milligan*, an Alabama case testing the Voting Rights Act, Justice Ketanji Brown Jackson observed, "The Framers themselves adopted the equal protection clause, the Fourteenth Amendment, the Fifteenth Amendment, in a race-conscious way." In June 2023, the court issued a decision reaffirming the Voting Rights Act.

consider race differently. By the mid-twentieth century, whites began to see race less as something inborn and more as an ethnic identity—a culture that could be acquired or shed, a history that could be celebrated or ignored. The sociologists Michael Omi and Howard Winant call this approach the "ethnicity paradigm" of race, but the most common term when I was growing up was "the melting pot." Much as immigrants from Europe had assimilated into "American" culture, went the thinking, nonwhite people could match white Americans' economic and social status by assimilating into mainstream, white culture. And behind that idea was the assumption that any difference between white and nonwhite experience—lower wages, less wealth, shorter lives—came from the failure of individual nonwhite Americans to assimilate. The source of the differences in experience by race, then, was personal conduct and cultural norms.

Americans have thought about race in other ways, of course. Some have argued that race is a stand-in for economic class—though this approach falters when trying to explain why some people who are not white attain wealth and why some whites are poor. Others have posited that race could be used to identify a discrete, oppressed group, not unlike a colony under an empire, giving rise to the concept of racial nationhood. But while those two analyses have long circulated in academic and activist circles, they've never attained the mainstream dominance that race-as-biology and race-as-culture held.

The "colorblind" approach I heard from Katrina's mom edged toward the mainstream in the 1960s. Northern opponents of school integration in New York City, Los Angeles, and Chicago all deployed the concept first, says historian Matthew Lassiter. "The idea that racially discriminatory arrangements, like where people live, [are] a race neutral outcome of the free market was really a liberal defense [against] civil rights challenges outside the South," he says. "The southern segregationists weren't claiming their states were colorblind, so they didn't have to use that defense yet." Indeed, when a prominent anti-integration activist in my mother's hometown of Pontiac, Irene McCabe, testified against "forced busing" in front of a Senate committee in 1971, she told the panel, "I like to be colorblind."

This logic migrated to southern school districts in the 1970s, when administrators were gradually abandoning the hope of preserving segregation outright—but saw promise in the northern approach. In 1981, President Reagan's appointee to head the Civil Rights Division of the Department of Justice, William Bradford Reynolds, made colorblindness a touchstone of federal policy. Reynolds declared that the Civil Rights Act of 1964 "mandates color blindness," warned of the dangers of "reverse discrimination," and described affirmative action as a plan to "cure discrimination with discrimination." By the twenty-first century, colorblindness had become so mainstream it was the accepted logic of a majority on the Supreme Court. In 2007, Chief Justice John Roberts wrote an opinion striking down an integration plan in Seattle. The reasoning could have been written by Reynolds: "The way to stop discrimination on the basis of race is to stop discriminating on the basis of race," wrote Roberts.

This is why scholars have come up with the term "colorblind racism." This racism does not show up in the harmful, personal prejudices of white people, as it did in my grandparents' generation. It does not show up in clearly worded restrictions on opportunities by race, as it did in racial zoning and covenants. Colorblindness is the willful refusal to acknowledge that racism has shaped our world, and an unwillingness to repair the harm it has done. It is, as Eduardo Bonilla-Silva, the sociologist who popularized the term "colorblind racism," describes it: "racism without racists."

* * * * *

Katrina started to get involved with her union in 2015, a couple of years after she began working at the hospital, which operates on the union shop model.* At Katrina's hospital, every union member pays 1.8 percent of their

---

* A "union shop" describes a workplace where workers are represented by a union, which they are welcome to join if they like. Workers who choose not to join are still required to pay their fair share toward the union, which advocates on their behalf. By contrast, "open shops" are created by "right to work" laws, which prohibit any requirement to pay dues, regardless of whether a worker

pretax income, up to one hundred dollars per month, toward union dues; nonunion members pay nearly the same in a fair-share fee. In exchange, an organizer experienced in labor issues visits the workplace to talk with workers and helps them advocate for themselves.

When Katrina came into the union, the president of the chapter was a woman named Cathy Stoddart, who'd helped found the chapter in 2000. Cathy took to Katrina immediately. Some people would never really care about the union one way or the other, Cathy knew, but Katrina was different. In her, Cathy saw some of the same traits she valued in herself: a willingness to dig in and get things done, as well as a passion for ensuring that patients were treated well. Maybe, Cathy thought, Katrina might get the same kind of boost from organizing that she did: empowerment. Before long, Cathy was inviting Katrina to union events and encouraging her to participate. One union staffer told me that, the first time they met Katrina, she was "literally under the wing of Cathy Stoddart."

Although Cathy and Katrina were twenty-five years apart in age, the two women had plenty in common. Both came from union families—the men in Cathy's family worked in mines and factories in Appalachian Ohio; the men in Katrina's worked in Pittsburgh's construction trades. Both had attended integrated public high schools. Cathy started high school the year the schools consolidated and desegregated in the 1970s; she remembers her school going from all white to 70 percent Black. Katrina's high school, in Pittsburgh's West End, was half Black and half white by the time she attended. Both women could cite plenty of hardship. Cathy had heard her grandfather's stories of union busting in the mines, watched her hometown crumble as steel withered, and still talks of a battle with medical debt. Katrina's parents, Joe and Becky, were financially stable by the time she was grown, but they'd been so broke when she was small that her mom still talked about feeding a family of five on fifty dollars a month.

---

benefits from a union's advocacy or not. Both the open and union shop models differ from "closed shops," which required any union employer to hire only union members, and were outlawed by the Taft-Hartley Act in 1947.

And while Katrina was moving steadily through adulthood, her siblings struggled. All of her siblings ended up in occasional trouble with drugs. her brother most of all. In the early 2000s, he got convicted on several felony counts for selling cocaine, generating tens of thousands of dollars in fees and fines.*

Partly because of the economic instability of their families, neither woman had taken a straight path to nursing. Cathy says her teachers had discouraged her from trying to be a nurse, so after high school she worked first as a keypunch operator, then selling tractors at Sears. Her parents helped put her through nursing school, she says, and she studied full time while also working full time. Katrina had hoped to become a teacher after high school, but when she headed off to college, she found herself overwhelmed by homesickness. Her parents welcomed her when she came home within a week. Katrina started working at a pizza shop owned by a guy her uncle knew, making five dollars an hour under the table. Eventually, she heard she could earn twice that making beds in a nursing home on the night shift. Becoming a certified nursing assistant, which she remembers took three or four weeks of training, was Katrina's entryway to a career in health care. She just didn't know it yet.

Katrina liked working in the nursing home, chatting with patients, and taking care of her rounds. She took it as a compliment when, she says, an HR manager at the nursing home encouraged her to apply for a nursing scholarship from the corporate chain to which the home belonged. The company would cover the cost of Katrina's books and tuition for an associate's degree in nursing, as long as she promised to work for them for two years after getting the degree. She started classes at the community college in 2008, and finished her associate's degree in 2010. She went on to a bachelor's degree, this time paying for it with her nursing wages, a feat she could pull off because she lived cheaply with her parents. But with more training, she began to see the shortcomings of the care she provided

---

* For a discussion of the sentencing disparities between crack and powder cocaine, as well as the racial implications of them, see chapter 6, page 155.

at the nursing home—"I felt like I was literally going in and throwing pills at people and running out," she told me. She began looking for a better job. By 2015, she was working in a hospital with a union contract, where she met Cathy.

★ ★ ★ ★ ★

Katrina had been flattered when the human resources director at the nursing home suggested she apply for the company's nursing scholarship. As she understood it, there were two slots for each nursing home. The aides were a mix of Black and white, Katrina remembers, but most of the nurses were white. So were the aides getting the scholarship.*

Programs like Katrina's nursing scholarship, which policymakers call "career ladders," became popular in the early 2000s as service-sector jobs expanded—as did the divide between low- and high-paid jobs. In the health care field, the bottom rung of the ladder is the widest, holding 69 percent of the industry's jobs. This is where health care support positions, from nursing aides in group facilities—like Katrina at the start of her career—to hospital janitors, land. On average, these jobs pay about thirteen dollars an hour, and nearly half of the workers are Black or Hispanic. Nurses are the next rung up, making up about a quarter of health care workers. They earn an average of thirty-five dollars an hour, and 19 percent of them are Black or Hispanic. The top rung holds just 5 percent of health care workers—doctors and surgeons. They earn, on average, more than one hundred dollars an hour, and just 16 percent of them are Black or Hispanic.

Jasmine, the friend Katrina had those wings with in 2017, had a different path. During her senior year of high school, Jasmine remembers being one of two Black students in her class. Jasmine persuaded the guidance counselor to let her miss two weeks of school to get trained as a certified nursing assistant. She'd gotten the idea, she says, from an aunt who

---

* The nursing home chain for which Katrina worked went bankrupt in 2018. Its successor, ProMedica, declined to provide details on past skilled-nursing programs.

worked at the same chain of homes where Katrina ended up working. There, an older coworker, a Black woman working as a licensed practical nurse—the lowest rung among nurses—suggested Jasmine become a registered nurse. Jasmine realized she'd never even met a Black RN before and decided to become one. In the spring, as Jasmine listened to the guidance counselor encourage her white friends to aim for four-year degrees, she shared her plan to get a BA. The counselor, remembers Jasmine, wondered why Jasmine would bother; didn't she already have a CNA license? Jasmine ignored this slight and persisted.

Psychological researchers will tell you that, today, much of racial prejudice has taken the form of implicit bias—assumptions people make about others without much conscious thought. A 2009 meta-analysis of implicit association tests, which included thirty-two studies of implicit racial association, found a moderate correlation between holding bias and acting on it. Whether acted on or not, implicit racial bias in the United States is widespread. A recent analysis of 4.7 million implicit association tests suggested that 64 percent of people who took the test "automatically associated the attribute 'good' more with white Americans, and the attribute 'bad' more with Black Americans." These are the kind of associations that might lead an HR staffer to encourage a promising white aide to seek a scholarship—or lead a guidance counselor to discourage an ambitious Black student from applying to college.

By the 2010s, though, both women were working as nurses. Although there is generally a gap in the pay between Black and white nurses, Katrina and Jasmine didn't see one between themselves. Across nursing as a whole, white nurses routinely earn more than Black or Hispanic ones—even when taking differences in training, responsibilities, and experience into account. But when the two friends compared their checks over time, they found they earned about the same. This is likely a reflection of the fact that both women work in union shops. Among the 16 percent of nurses in unions, research suggests that the racial pay gap among unionized nurses is "negligible."

At first, that equity made it a little harder for Katrina to see how persistent racism could be. Nurse pay was set on a union scale in Katrina's hospital, strictly connected to training and career length, and Katrina and Jasmine earned about the same. Where was the racism there? Katrina wondered. But as her work with the union deepened, Katrina began to understand that her workplace was the exception—not the rule.

"I was taking for granted this stuff that we fought for, and won, as a union," she says. "If they look at Jasmine and they're like, 'Hmm, I can pay her less because she's Black,' then whenever I want to bargain my wages, they can say, 'We should only pay this much.' And really, the only reason why people want to pay people less is because of the color of your skin," says Katrina. "At the end of the day, if they're able to get away with paying one person less, then basically we're all impacted."

★ ★ ★ ★ ★

Katrina was an easy mark for union leadership. Cheerful and curious, she's also an inveterate busybody; on neighborhood walks, she's prone to peering into the windows of vacant houses to get a sense of their condition. And, as the daughter of a union construction worker, she already understood there were benefits to paying union dues. When Cathy began showing off her protégée at union events, staff took note. They started inviting Katrina to events, too.

Katrina hadn't heard of the Fight for $15, a national movement pushing to raise the minimum wage to fifteen dollars an hour, before someone in the union mentioned it to her. The campaign debuted in late 2012 in New York City, according to longtime labor reporter Steven Greenhouse. Initially, the campaign was all fast-food workers demanding better pay and was backed by SEIU and New York Communities for Change, an advocacy group. Even though SEIU didn't have members in fast food, the union poured money into the campaign: If workers could get a union at McDonald's, went the thinking, workers everywhere would have an easier time organizing unions at *their* jobs. When corporate employers refused to raise wages, the workers did not give up; they broadened their scope. They began asking government to raise everybody's wages, not just those of fast-food workers, to at least fifteen dollars an hour.

In 2015, Katrina remembers, her union chapter's organizer, Kristy Myers, invited her to testify at a public hearing about low wages. The union was working to organize the hospital's lower-paid workers back then—aides responding to patient call buttons, life-support technicians keeping people alive. So, more than most nurses, Katrina understood the link between what her coworkers made and the quality of care her patients got. Could Katrina talk about what those low wages, and the constant turnover they created, did to the quality of care at the hospital?

The hearing was at a church near the hospital. Rows of folding chairs faced a long panel of community leaders. Katrina had written out testimony in advance with help from union staff, and took a sheet of paper to the podium when they called her name. She talked about what she'd seen at work: How one aide started on the floor, then took a job waiting tables to earn more money. How another had asked nurses for money to help with bills. How only three of the aides that had been in her unit when she started, two years earlier, remained. How the starting wage was ten, maybe eleven dollars an hour. "I'm not an economic expert, but I know that's not a living wage," Katrina testified.

A few days later, Katrina ran into Kristy at the hospital. Kristy asked what Katrina had thought of the event, and Katrina was honest: She'd found it frustrating. "I was like, 'Dude, what the hell? You told me I was going to an action,'" Katrina told me. "'You didn't tell me I was going to show up for a bunch of fast-food workers that say that they should make fifteen dollars an hour!'" What did that have to do with nurses?

This kind of skepticism was a common response to the Fight for $15 from nurses, another union staffer, Zach Zobrist, told me. "It was always like, 'Well, wait a minute. If these folks are going to make fifteen and I only make twenty, that's not really fair because I have a four-year degree' and so on." With some members, he would sense an undercurrent of racism in their objections—even if people didn't say it outright. "The image in their head is people of color working at McDonald's, and if they're going to make that, then I better be doing a lot better," he says. "I think it's inherent when people talk about it."

In Katrina's early involvement with the union, Zach heard that echo of racism in the questions she asked him. He had long heard it in Cathy's objections to the union's involvement in campaigns outside of nursing, too. It ran through the questions many members, especially white ones, asked about the union: Why should nurses help recruit the lower-paid hospital workers into their union, instead of strengthening their own contract? Why should nurses, who made middle-class incomes, show up at rallies for the Fight for $15, where protests were full of McDonald's workers? In the late 2010s, they were asking, too, why organizers were telling nurses about Black Lives Matter protests, instead of being laser-focused on the nurses' wages and working conditions?

Katrina and Cathy had opposite reactions to these developments. Cathy thought the point of the union was to help nurses: to defend and strengthen their contract, and ensure good standards of care. Katrina started out with the same concerns as Cathy, then kept asking more questions. "I'm one of those people that I very, very much want to know the why," she says.

The organizers noticed Katrina's curiosity. When a free labor history class for Pittsburgh's union leaders opened up, Zach invited Katrina to join. She was flattered to be asked. She was curious. The union would pay for it. She had time. So she went.

★ ★ ★ ★ ★

All the while—from her intermittent classes at community college to the shifts at the nursing home, the pizza deliveries giving way to union meetings—Katrina had been living the life of a young, unmarried woman in a city. When she dropped out of college, she'd stayed with her parents, who still lived in the triplex they'd bought in 1981. The house was in Elliott, the lower-income white neighborhood Katrina's parents had both grown up in, on Pittsburgh's South Side. Elliott was thick with family: one set of grandparents in the house behind them, another up the block, uncles and aunts dotting the roller-coaster-hill streets and avenues. For a while she lived in one of the apartments upstairs with a boyfriend, paying family rate—about $400 a month, she thinks, which she split with the boyfriend. When the boyfriend began threatening her, she moved back into her parents' apartment. They didn't charge her rent, then, which left her with money for tuition and even, sometimes, going out. By the time she'd gotten her associate's degree, Katrina had a lively social life, known among her friends for hanging out in the South Side Flats, and for her interpretation of the Wobble.

One night, she started talking to a friend of the bartender, a white guy named Ryan Allard. He worked in a union warehouse for Giant Eagle, a supermarket chain. Ryan was easy to talk to, the son of a union sanitation worker in Beechview—a stable, white working-class neighborhood near Elliott. Katrina bought a round of shots and they began leaving notes for each other, passing them through the bartender. Soon they were dating.

Ryan was born and raised in Beechview, same as his dad. By the time he was dating Katrina, his grandparents had passed on, and the family house had passed to Ryan's dad. At first, the Allards tried renting it out, but mostly they maintained it and paid on the existing debt. Usually it sat empty. When Katrina and Ryan began more or less living with Ryan's parents, around 2013, the Allards made a suggestion: *Why don't you take over the family house?*

Katrina and Ryan moved into a habitable but outdated house, rent-free. The young couple began renovating the house with enthusiasm. They figured it would cost less than $10,000—five if they were lucky—to get it in shape. They hired Katrina's brother, who works construction, to expand and renovate the kitchen. They ended up gutting the entire house. By the end of the first round of work, the bills totaled more than $30,000; Katrina borrowed more than half that from her parents to pay her brother. Katrina estimates they've spent nearly $50,000 on all the renovations, which have included replacing the roof and siding. The Allards still hold title, but have promised to sell the house to the couple for a token amount once the mortgage is paid off.

In 2016, Katrina and Ryan held their wedding on a Saturday at the

Serbian Orthodox Church on Pittsburgh's southern edge, in a ceremony that included nineteen bridesmaids and groomsmen. The wedding party stopped at Allegheny Commons Park on the city's north side for photos, posing on a bridge. Then they headed to the sanitation workers' union hall for the reception in Lawrenceville, a white working-class neighborhood across town that had gentrified at the turn of the century.

The party had been a splurge, and the couple returned to regular life the next day. They argued over the best use of the reception's leftover liquor: tailgating at the house or tailgating outside the Steelers game. But once the game was over and tempers had cooled, they reconciled easily. They headed out for crab and steak at an upscale restaurant by the IKEA—a wedding present from a friend—and talked about their future.

★ ★ ★ ★ ★

Katrina's first labor history class met at the United Steelworkers building downtown, a glass office tower wrapped in a honeycombed steel grid. There were twenty students, five Black and fifteen white, most of them from different unions: the International Brotherhood of Electrical Workers and the Pittsburgh Federation of Teachers had students there, too. For the first class, the teacher, Zach Zobrist, set up a few dozen posters depicting labor history over time so that students could gravitate to whatever captured their interest.

To the surprise of most students, the class began with the story of enslavement. In Katrina's high school history classes, slavery had sounded like a long-past fact with no relevance to her life today. In the class, they talked about how, at the founding of the nation, half the labor force was forced to work without pay—and how that made it harder for free workers, including white ones, to get paid fairly for their own labor. In one class, they watched a scene from the 1987 film *Matewan*, a fictionalized tale based on a bloody 1920 mining strike in West Virginia. When white union members greet a Black miner with racial slurs, it prompts a speech from the white union organizer: "Any union keeps this man out ain't a union, it's a goddamn club. And they've got you fighting white against colored, native against foreign, holler against holler, when you know there ain't but two sides to this world: them that work and them that don't." Recounting the scene to me four years later, Katrina told me it still gave her chills.

The point of the class, Zobrist told me, was to both inspire rising union leaders and to be honest about the movement's weaknesses and mistakes, in hopes of overcoming them. It was the weaknesses, Zobrist knew, that unions tended to overlook when discussing their past. And racism had always been chief among them.

* * * * *

Although Pittsburgh was 95 percent white at the start of the twentieth century, Black workers began arriving en masse during the first Great Migration. From 1910 to 1940, the share of Black residents in the city nearly doubled. The city was hungry for workers then, same as the coal fields outside of it. The story Katrina saw in *Matewan* was real: Companies broke strikes by recruiting impoverished Black and immigrant workers to take striking workers' places. White union members often blamed these replacements for the union's trouble, instead of directing their ire at the companies that had leveraged Black and immigrant workers' poverty and desperation against them. In 1919, there was a national strike of steelworkers—including in Pittsburgh. Nearly all the steelworkers were American-born white men—and the strike failed after companies brought in immigrant and Black men as strikebreakers. Many of the Black workers had been trained in the steel mills of the South; Birmingham, in fact, was sometimes compared to Pittsburgh.

In that era, there were two giant categories of unions: trade and industrial. In general terms, trade unions (also called craft unions) organized highly trained, difficult-to-replace workers who had a single trade—think carpenters and plumbers. There had been trade unions all over the country, each fighting their own battle, until 1886, when about a hundred of them organized into the American Federation of Labor. Industrial unions, by comparison, organized all the workers in a single factory, regardless of what job they held; think workers in the plants that make steel, or textiles, or—like my great-grandfathers in Pontiac—cars. Unions based in factories joined together as the Congress of Industrial Organizations in 1938.

In 1955, the two federations merged into the AFL-CIO—but each branch used distinct methods to get raises and better conditions. The AFL unions demanded high wages primarily by restricting membership, which limited the supply of labor and pushed up wages. In the early trade unions, explains the labor historian Nelson Lichtenstein, "You're exclusive, you keep people out, and you hog the work for yourself and your buddies." The CIO unions, whose workers could be replaced much more easily, didn't have that option. Instead, they relied on the threat of shutting down the factory with a strike across multiple departments.

The AFL and CIO branches addressed racial divides in different ways, too. The trades, most of them started by immigrants who'd initially learned their craft in Europe, kept membership small—and white. In many cases, membership was passed down through families as if it were private property. Leaders "made little effort to conceal their desire to remain a 'lily white' field," writes the historian Joe Trotter.

In 1969, a landmark series of protests in Pittsburgh—big enough to earn several days of national news coverage—won promises of 1,250 jobs for Black workers in construction unions. A study of Pittsburgh craft unions that year, published in 1973, found that of twenty-six unions, twenty-four were at least 92 percent white; four of them were 100 percent white. (The city, by comparison, was 79 percent white and 20 percent Black.) The future didn't look much brighter: only seven of those unions reported any Black apprentices at all. Katrina's dad joined the construction trades a few years later.*

Industrial unions in big factories, like steel plants, couldn't restrict membership like that if they wanted power. They needed as many members across a factory as possible—the more departments that went on strike, the more leverage they had with the company. "Even racists could

---

* There has been no comprehensive assessment of Pittsburgh since 1973 to indicate whether, or how much, racial discrimination by the unions has receded.

understand that if you want to have a strong union, we've got to have a way to incorporate 'these people,'" says Lichtenstein. Although industrial unions could see the strategic benefit of integration, Black workers were rarely treated fairly. A powerful system of occupational segregation offered more jobs, and better ones, to white workers than to Black ones—even in the same factory. At Bethlehem Steel, for example, Black workers made up 60 percent of steelworkers at its plants outside Baltimore—but the safest departments, like timekeeping, machining, and pipe fitting, were 100 percent white. Meanwhile, Black workers made up 75 to 100 percent of the workers in the hottest, dirtiest, most "man-killing" jobs: construction labor, the blast furnace, the coke oven. Black workers' wages, on average, were just 59 percent of those earned by white workers—and, because discrimination had delayed their entry into the jobs in the first place, they were the first to be fired when layoffs arrived. The same divisions were built into the whole economy. "Discrimination is the wrong word," says Lichtenstein. "'Discrimination' makes it sound like some choice is being made by some employer, when actually it's structured."

Katrina's family is scattered with union members, most of whom got their foot in the door through family who'd joined before the unions integrated. Her grandfather on Joe's side was in the Operating Engineers union, while her great-grandfather—on Becky's side—had been a journeyman pile driver, with all the benefits of union membership. He'd gotten his son, Katrina's grandfather Bill, full membership in the union. During those landmark protests in 1969, Bill had been out in the streets protesting *against* integration—at the request, Becky remembers, of his union. A few years later, Bill had pulled Katrina's father, Joe, onto the union's "extras" list. For a while, Joe made ends meet trading off between shifts at a coal plant, driving semis, and picking work with the pile drivers. Those were the days when Katrina's family ate off fifty dollars a month.

Things didn't turn around until Joe got his journeyman's book in 1986, says Becky—a benefit he'd never have been able to get without her family's ties to the union, which in turn they would not have had without being white. At the time, heavy construction workers like Joe earned around

$17,640 a year nationwide. Even with money Becky picked up cutting hair and working for a catering business, they likely were still below half the median income for their family size—functionally poor. The Rectenwalds supplemented that with any profit from the cheap rentals they owned and Becky's occasional work.

When Becky and I talked about this, it was hard for her to see the point in talking about race. "I never gave it a thought," she said. "My whiteness didn't get me anywhere, let's put it that way." Her father had gotten into the union because he was family, not because he was white. And, anyway, if being white had helped her grandfather or her father or Joe get the job, then so be it; they needed the work. "I'm grateful that my husband had a job," she told me. "I get what you're saying, but I don't feel bad in any way."

★ ★ ★ ★ ★

Racism was built into more than just jobs at factories. One of the center-pieces of the New Deal, the 1938 Fair Labor Standards Act, established a minimum wage and the forty-hour work week, but it didn't apply to all workers. Agricultural workers, the majority of whom, at the time, were Black workers in the South, didn't get protected. Neither did service work-ers, including workers doing housework in private homes, in laundries, in hotels and restaurants, even in hospitals. Legislators excluded the same workers from Social Security benefits, and excluded agricultural and domestic workers from the right to organize unions, too.

Racism drove these exclusions. In the South, two-thirds of Black work-ers were employed in domestic labor, agriculture, or service jobs. The comfort of white legislators' families depended, in part, on keeping that work cheap. Accordingly, white supremacist legislators from the South, who controlled important congressional committees, promised to kill any New Deal legislation that extended protections to Black Americans. "You cannot put the Negro and the white man on the same basis and get away with it," said Representative J. Mark Wilcox, a congressman from Florida, during debate on the bill. Indeed, President Roosevelt reassured the press corps that "no law suggested ever intended a minimum wages and hours bill to apply to domestic help." With southern congressmen blocking any effort to make protections universal, politicians were stuck.

What's more, the NAACP had succeeded in getting an antilynching bill introduced in Congress—and southern congressmen used that as leverage, too. As legal scholar Juan Perea has documented, southern legislators promised to kill worker protections, even for whites, if the antilynching bill passed. Walter White, an NAACP leader, recalled that the president, Franklin Delano Roosevelt, told him, "I've got to get legislation passed by Congress to save America. The southerners by reason of the seniority rule in Congress are chairmen or occupy strategic places on most of the Senate and House committees. If I come out for the antilynching bill now, they will block every bill I ask Congress to pass to keep America from collapsing. I just can't take that risk."

Every piece of New Deal legislation related to labor excluded certain jobs from coverage. The jobs that gained labor protections were, in the 1930s, mostly held by white, male workers; the excluded ones, by workers who were Black, female, or both. As a result, Social Security only applied to 13 percent of Black women who worked, and 46 percent of Black workers overall. Meanwhile, more than half of American-born white workers, and two-thirds of white immigrant workers, had jobs that were covered, and gained access to old-age protection.

It took decades for most of the excluded jobs to come under the protection of law—including hospital workers like nurses. In 1966, amid the adoption of federal civil rights legislation, hospital workers and farmworkers gained the right to minimum wages, along with restaurant workers, whose minimum wage was set lower, to a "tipped" wage. In 1974, hospital workers gained the right to organize, the same year that domestic workers gained the right to minimum wage. Tipped wages persist today. These gaping holes in worker protections hurt Black workers the most, but the fact that some workers could be paid less than minimum wage made it harder for all American workers, even white ones, to demand better wages and conditions.

Katrina didn't know about any of this before she took the labor history class: the segregation in the factories, the way that construction unions had worked to stay all-white for generations, the way so many white workers—but only a fraction of Black ones—had been given the safety of a minimum wage, Social Security, and overtime. She just remembered what she'd grown up with: her dad telling the story of calling a Black boy the N-word during a grade-school fight, but inviting Black neighbors to the house for dinner. Her mom telling Katrina that color didn't matter, and debating the definition of the N-word with her best friend, who is Black.*

What Katrina mostly remembered from her childhood was that times had been tough, whether you were in a union or not. Her parents would have known that Black and female workers made inroads in the construction trades and factories in the early 1970s. They would have heard about construction unions' promises to hire Black workers starting in 1970. They would have known about the 1974 consent decree that opened the steel mills to Black and female workers by ending discriminatory seniority systems and mandating diverse hiring. But the region's economy was teetering on a precipice that workers did not know was there. All that change arrived "just in time to for the entire industry to begin its downward spiral," writes historian Gabriel Winant. From 1979 to 1987, Pittsburgh lost 133,000 jobs.

The nadir, wrote local journalists, came in 1983, the year before Katrina was born. By the time Katrina was leaving high school, union members, whatever their color, could no longer promise their children that a lifetime of stable work was possible. A new world of work, christened "the service economy" by economists, had taken the place of industry.

★ ★ ★ ★ ★

In Pittsburgh, health care became the biggest segment of the service economy that replaced the industrial one. This was a direct result of three related facts, writes Winant. As a source of jobs, the supply of health care had expanded steadily from mid-century, paid for largely by the generous health care benefits that unions provided even in retirement. At the same time, manufacturing's decline had pushed women, whose laid-off steel-

---

* For a discussion of my thinking on use of the N-word, see page xii.

worker husbands could no longer support them, into the workforce. This shift expanded the pool of health care workers—as well as the need for childcare and eldercare to replace the caregiving the women had provided at home.

Last, as the economic free fall of the early 1980s hit, and unemployment ballooned to 17.1 percent for all workers—and 25.6 for Black workers—the health effects of so much stress came to the fore. Heart attacks, drug use, and mental illness all spiked. Hospitals and clinics were the only institutions ready to help.

All this combined to make health care the most visible part of the emerging service economy Pittsburgh had adopted. In 1950, roughly 30,000 of the Pittsburgh region's workers had jobs in health care and social assistance, and 170,000 worked in metals industries—steel. By 2010, as Katrina finished her associate's degree in nursing, the numbers had flipped: 30,000 jobs in metals, 185,000 jobs in health care.

A lot of jobs were available, but many had lower pay and fewer benefits than unionized steelwork. Katrina's first health care job, as a nursing assistant, put her near the bottom of the income ladder in health care. She remembers making $10 an hour at her first CNA job, in 2002—the equivalent of $20,000 a year working fifty forty-hour weeks. Even adjusting for inflation, that put her slightly above the average income for both white and Black nursing aides in 2018, when a comprehensive study found they earned $24,809 and $24,755, respectively.*

That low pay for health care workers was built into the industry. During the postwar period, hospitals swelled with new investments in medical care. Yet, as the hospital industry laid its foundation, hardly any of its workers had a legal right to minimum wages, Social Security, or unions. The result was a business model expecting profit margins—referred to as "net earned revenue minus expenditures" in nonprofit institutions—that

---

* According to the Bureau of Labor Statistics, $20,000 in January 2002 was equivalent to $33,785 in January 2023, and $25,000 in 2018 was equivalent to $30,174 in January 2023.

assumed low wages. Similarly, since hospital workers didn't have the right to organize for most of the first decade of Medicare and Medicaid, the economic structure of those programs was built on the assumption that most health care staff had no power to demand higher wages.

Once the pattern was set, aides like Katrina had three choices: endure, fight, or leave. When the HR rep at Katrina's nursing home offered her an affordable path to a nursing degree, around 2008, Katrina no longer needed to endure. She didn't need to fight to improve the job she had, either. Instead, she was gifted the opportunity to leave—the gift, really, of social mobility—and make a better living.

★ ★ ★ ★ ★

When Katrina talked about her career when we first met, she framed it as her fate. "Whenever I was trying to go for teaching, I kept running into all these barriers," she told me the first time we met. By the time she considered nursing, she'd spent four years trying to become a teacher by taking the class or two she could afford each year. "When I moved into going for nursing, I'm not saying that studying wasn't challenging, but it seemed to flow easier, right? It's kind of like there was a path that I was supposed to follow."

But it was also true that the HR director at her nursing home had opened that path for Katrina, giving her the one thing she'd been unable to pull together for teaching: reliable funding for tuition, fees, and books. "Which is yuge," Katrina told me, lapsing into local dialect. "You can't really do anything without funding, right?" Katrina told me that she wasn't sure she'd have become a nurse without it. So much for Katrina hinged on that one act of inclusion—an HR director getting her to apply for the scholarship—that we couldn't avoid discussing, eventually, if Katrina thought she'd have gotten the scholarship if she wasn't white.

It came up after Katrina took me to meet her parents, Joe and Becky, at the modest brick ranch they'd moved to several years earlier, an hour into the hills outside Pittsburgh. Katrina's mom had openly bragged about Katrina's scholarship to me. "They offer her 'You'd make a great nurse' because she's singing and dancing to the patients. I went to go play the lottery that night, and I said, 'It doesn't matter if I win or not. I hit the lottery,'" Becky told me. "My daughter just got a scholarship to nursing school."

Back home in the city, talking it over with me and Jasmine, Katrina wondered if her mother saw the whole picture. "My mom said the other day: 'My daughter got a scholarship to school because she worked hard,'" Katrina said. "I was like, 'But did I work hard? Did I really fucking deserve this?' Like, I don't really know."

Sure, she worked hard, and she had an unusual talent for chatting with ailing patients. So did some of the Black aides she had worked alongside, who didn't get headhunted into the scholarship—plenty of whom were good with patients, the same way she was. *Was that really racism?*

It was hard for Katrina to agree, unequivocally, with what I eventually told her I thought: Yes, that *was* racism, benefiting her—the same as it's often benefited me.

At first, Katrina told me, she felt compelled to figure out if she really deserved the scholarship or not: Was it because she was white? Good with patients? Good at science? Right place, right time? With tuition so expensive, and scholarships so rare, it felt important to make sure she *really* deserved it. But the more she thought about it, the more pointless that distraction seemed. "I was like, 'You know what? Fuck that. School should be free,'" said Katrina.

Katrina did not feel like she had had it easy, of course: long nights studying, enduring and then leaving an abusive boyfriend, years of living with her parents to save on rent. But the work she did with her union, her occasional discussions with Jasmine about race, and her conversations with me, seemed to shift things. It all prompted Katrina to wonder about what, exactly, made her seem "deserving" to others. It felt like such a small

thing, to have a door opened for her—a kindness shown. It was also the
the origin of a long chain reaction that had landed her here: at a dining
table, in a house she expected to soon own, her two little ones napping
upstairs.

★ ★ ★ ★ ★

There is nothing extravagant about Katrina's house. It is small, built for
blue-collar homeowners a century ago. A living-dining room abuts the
ground-floor kitchen, and the bathroom and two bedrooms are stacked
directly on top of them. An addition off the back expanded the kitchen
and added a third bedroom. In 2023, as the housing market cooled off
from its pandemic-fueled bubble, the real estate site Redfin estimated the
house's value around $110,000. Still, provided values hold and the prop-
erty transfer happens as promised, Katrina and Ryan will gain equity
in the house as they enter middle age—which is to say, they will build
wealth.* And unlike my own family, Katrina's has no history of profiting
from racial covenants. When I looked for covenants on the homes of
Katrina's and Ryan's families, I didn't find a single one; both Elliott and
Beechview had been graded "C-declining" by the Home Owners' Loan
Corporation in 1937, marking it as a pointless investment for developers
targeting the upwardly mobile middle class. Given the reality of housing
discrimination, it seems likely that being white was a precondition for
buying homes in these neighborhoods. Elliott remained more than 90
percent white from 1940 through 1990; Beechview didn't drop below
that threshhold util 2010. That said, there's no formal legal structure
that mandated it.

---

* Financially, $110,000 is fairly average wealth for white Americans in their late
  thirties. The median wealth for white American families headed by someone
  under age thirty-five is $25,400, climbing to a median of $185,000 for families
  headed by someone age thirty-six to fifty-four. The median wealth of Black
  Americans in the same age groups, meanwhile, is a fraction of those numbers:
  $600 for young Black families, and $40,100 for middle-aged ones.

Both neighborhoods have been humble since they began, and appear to remain so today. Beechview's main thoroughfare, Broadway, hosts a trolley line that rumbles past vacant storefronts and takeout restaurants. The neighborhood streets branching off it are lined with modest, occupied homes. Elliott is a bit rougher and more isolated, its eastern boundary a bluff overlooking the city's famous point. Homes there, most of them built in the early twentieth century, crowd the steep downslope to Chartiers Avenue. When I visited in 2021, I saw well-kept homes alongside vacant ones posted with condemnation notices.

Today, Beechview offers a little more stability and safety than does Elliott. In the 2010s, city researchers assessed Beechview as "low disadvantage/high advantage." Elliott, where Katrina grew up, is the inverse: high disadvantage/low advantage. Beechview has a third less poverty, a quarter of the unemployment, and half as much gun violence as Elliott. The markers of safety and mobility in Beechview are much more modest than the ones that mark the city's middle- and upper-class strongholds like Squirrel Hill and Point Breeze. But research suggests that even these modest improvements matter deeply in modern American life. Sociologists have found that growing up outside of a poor neighborhood, particularly one that is also violent, is often a powerful predictor of later success—even for young people who grow up in poor families.

That is the power of place. Even before social science had proven it, many families have understood it. That includes, I think, Jasmine's grandparents and great-grandparents, who came to Pittsburgh during the Great Migrations and bought into Bethel Park, a stable suburb just outside the city. It's why Jasmine's own parents had gone a little farther afield, to Castle Shannon, ensuring their daughter would go to a reputable public school. And today it includes Katrina, too, who feels a relief at raising her kids in Beechview. She hadn't disliked Elliot, but as an adult she could more clearly see the instability she'd been immersed in as a child. She remembered a murder at a neighborhood playground. She'd been molested as a little girl by a neighborhood boy, who faced no consequences after she complained. One of her friends had fallen into heroin addiction. Another friend went to a house party and ended up with a brain injury after he tried to go past "security"—three neighborhood guys at the door. All that stuff felt like it was part of life in Elliot. She didn't want that for her own kids.

Both Jasmine and Katrina have built what look like solid paths into the middle class, insofar as I can tell. But I am struck by how different the paths that led each there have been, and how radically different the obstacles visible ahead of them look.

For Katrina, her twenties were marked by a haphazard entry to nursing. Now that she's older, her parents are stable enough to help her invest in her home—thanks in part to decades of union work. Meanwhile, her father's union retirement—along with a lifelong history of property ownership that began before he turned eighteen with help from his father—means they're unlikely to look to Katrina for help as they age. This leaves her and Ryan free to spend whatever they earn on themselves. Depending on how many hours they each put in, Katrina estimates, they can earn anywhere from $80,000 combined to $130,000. In 2022, with two little ones at home and Katrina recovering from a work injury, she says, they made about $82,000. That puts them just below a middle-class income.

It is different for Jasmine, who had to overcome a guidance counselor's discouragement and resolve, on her own, to become a nurse in the first place. Her mother owns her home, and Jasmine lives with her to help keep costs down for both of them; she's paid rent to live in her childhood bedroom since turning eighteen. Once she became a full RN, family began asking for help: paying for food at graduation parties, helping out when bills were tight. She regularly helps out her father, who worked mostly odd jobs and has no retirement plan beyond social security. Now a new mother, Jasmine is figuring out how to balance her responsibilities to her son with those she has to her family.

I suppose I could look at how Jasmine and Katrina are each doing fine and think: No harm, no foul. And yet, it seems obvious to me that Katrina's current stability and pending homeownership came in part because of the impact that racism, from people and from institutions, has had on her life. Jasmine, on the other hand, has done the inverse: She's succeeded *despite* it.

3

MY PARENTS' CHILDHOODS

SOUTHEAST MICHIGAN

1944–1974

Kate and Don Weddle, my grandparents, brought baby Charyl home to their rented house on North Marshall Street. It was a tiny two-bedroom with a bay window jutting out from the front room, so newly built that it sat without shrubbery in a shadeless yard. My grandfather worked at his father's welding shop, while my grandmother raised my mother and the two sons who followed. Most welders at the time earned incomes that would have put their family squarely into the rapidly expanding white middle class; I think that likely describes them, too. Just as my mother neared school age, the family moved again. This time, they bought their home, a clapboard ranch on Oneida Street across town. It was 1952.

Their second home was one of the smallest houses in Seminole Hills, a subdivision full of stately homes. Like many white, middle-class homes of the era, the Oneida house's property deed prohibited anyone "other than a person of the Caucasian race" from living there. This was part of what had led HOLC to categorize Seminole Hills as the "most desirable home location in the city" fifteen years earlier.

By the time the Weddles moved in, covenants were no longer enforceable by law. In 1948, the Supreme Court had ruled that government could
not enforce racist covenants—a ruling that stood as the culmination of
a battle the NAACP had waged since filing its first case in 1909. It took
another twenty years before covenants became illegal—under the Fair
Housing Act of 1968—and still longer before integration came to Seminole
Hills. My grandparents' census tract there remained more than 90 percent
white through much of the 1970s.

* * * * *

It is hard for me, in 2023, to fathom the investments my government
made in straight, white families—and especially its white men—after
World War II. The rewards organized under the G.I. Bill were legion. Veterans could get their full tuition and living expenses at a college, university, or vocational education program covered by the government. Vets
who wanted to apprentice, rather than study, could earn a subsistence
wage while completing on-the-job training. Vets who wanted to buy a
home could get plenty of help: No down payments, modest interest rates,
and thirty-year terms combined to make it possible for veterans from the
working class to own a home. If you were a veteran who wanted to build
a mid-century American Dream, the G.I. Bill had the tools you needed.

And yet, as Ira Katznelson details at length in his book *When Affirmative Action Was White*, few of the bill's resources went to Black vets.
This was not an accident but part of the design of the Servicemen's Read-
justment Act, the formal name of the G.I. Bill. One of the bill's initial
cosponsors in the House, white supremacist and sixteen-term Mississippi
Democrat John Rankin, insisted that the G.I. Bill be administered locally.
This structure ensured that the new raft of benefits would be subject to
local law and custom—particularly Jim Crow, which was deeply ingrained
in Rankin's home state. "We are in favor of maintaining the rights of the
States and keeping as many bureaucrats' fingers out of [G.I. Bill programs]
as we possibly can," he said during a debate over the bill.

Local administration meant that the G.I. Bill delivered new funding to a preexisting, already discriminatory system, and did little to close the gap between white and Black America. Take, for instance, the Veterans Administration mortgages, which funded nearly one million homes from 1946 to 1951. While the government would back the mortgage and offer favorable terms, the actual financing had to go through a private bank. To buy a home, a Black vet would need to find a bank willing to give a loan—for a house in a neighborhood the VA, which used FHA standards to assess homes, would approve. (The FHA, in turn, had long equated racial covenants with insurability.) Homeownership grew for all Americans in the postwar years, but while white families had ready access to federal aid, Black families largely achieved homeownership without government help. One organization estimates that fewer than 2 percent of FHA mortgages went to Black homebuyers. Even as the ranks of homeowners grew, it remained far more common for white Americans to be among them. In 1940, 46 percent of white Americans owned their homes, compared to 23 percent of Black Americans. In 1960, after nearly twenty years of federal subsidy for homeownership, 64 percent of white Americans were homeowners, compared to 38 percent of Black Americans. Over the last sixty-four years, the rate of white homeownership has crept over the 70 percent mark, while the rate of Black homeownership has yet to break 50 percent.*

Educational benefits in the G.I. Bill were little different. To use the grant, Black vets needed to get approval from local bureaucrats, who typically harbored prejudices that could pose barriers to access. Once approved, they would need to find a college that would accept them. In 1940, three-quarters of Black Americans lived in the South, where racial

---

* Data from the Federal Reserve of St. Louis shows that Black homeownership in America reached its peak in April 2004, with 49.7 percent of Black households owning their homes. A 1994 report from the Bureau of the Census tracking homeownership from 1940 to 1990 suggests that white homeownership has not been that *low* since sometime between 1940 and 1950, when white homeownership grew from 45.7 percent of white households to 57.0 percent.

segregation was mandated by law—and where historically Black colleges and universities were fewer in number, smaller, and had less money than white schools. In the North, schools did not ban Black students but often used quotas to limit nonwhite student admissions.

One scholar estimates that twenty thousand Black veterans were turned away from Black colleges in the 1946 to 1947 school year alone. Another found that twenty-one Black southern colleges, combined, had to turn away 55 percent of veteran applicants for lack of space. Before the war, three times as many young white men went to college as Black men—11 percent, compared to 3 percent. By 1960, the ratio had narrowed—to double, with 19 percent of white men completing at least a year of college, compared to 8 percent of Black men. This is why, Katznelson writes, "the G.I. Bill did create a more middle-class society, but almost exclusively for whites."

I cannot prove that Grandpa Don was among the eight million veterans who paid for college or training with the G.I. Bill, or that he bought the house on Oneida with its help. There are no records, public or private, that remain to answer this question. But the mortgage company my grandparents used to buy the house on Oneida, the Greater Detroit Mortgage Corporation, advertised itself as a leader in loans insured by the FHA and VA, which by the late 1940s were attached to nearly half of all new homes. The university he attended tells me they no longer have my grandfather's files from the 1940s, but a representative assured me that the G.I. Bill boosted enrollment significantly after the war. It seems extremely unlikely to me that my grandfather, supporting a family of five, could have saved a down payment or covered the cost of classes without help from somewhere.

If help did not come from his government, it would likely have come from Grandpa Don's parents. They were stable by then, their middle-class wealth cemented by the purchase of a home built with a restrictive covenant, itself built by a member of the white supremacist terrorist group the Black Legion. Don's father's wages had risen since his arrival in Pontiac three decades earlier. He'd gotten training that took him out of the foundry—while Black workers were almost always left to work in it. As is true of so many things that have helped my family, our race ends up underpinning it all.

*   *   *   *   *

Shortly after the move to Oneida Street, my grandmother received a frantic phone call: Her father, Harley, had been in an accident at work. By then he had worked his way up to a machinist position, placing him in the tier of "skilled trades" at the factory, where he operated a turret lathe carving moldings out of blocks of steel. The machine, six tons of steel torque and drill, caught my great-grandfather's back with its spinning auger.

My grandmother would tell me her father broke his back, but this was a generality obscuring the violence of his death: "Crushed in machine" reads his death certificate under "How did injury occur?" Under "Condition Leading to Death": "Fractured spine, ruptured liver, shock." He died within nine hours of the accident, which was gruesome enough to earn a news story in the local paper. Three days later, H. H. Savage, a Baptist pastor who had vocally defended the Black Legion in the 1930s, presided over my great-grandfather's funeral.

This was a loss for my grandmother and her family, but it was eased by Harley's membership in his factory's union, United Auto Workers Local 594. I remember Grandma Kate telling me that Harley had been a vocal critic of unions, resentful of being forced to join with other workers. But two years earlier, the union Harley complained about had won pensions, health coverage, life insurance up to $5,000, and accidental death coverage up to $7,500 for its members. When my grandmother would recount her father's death, she would shake her head and say, *"He always said you shouldn't have to join the union."* Then she would pause and add, flatly, *"But it helped us out that he did."**

*   *   *   *   *

---

* According to the Bureau of Labor Statistics, $5,000 and $7,500 in January 1953 were the equivalent of $56,235 and $84,352, respectively.

By Mother's Day in 1953, my grandmother was twenty-five years old with three children. To celebrate the occasion, she wore a pale felted trapeze jacket and matching skirt; gloves; a lampshade hat balanced on the crown of her head; and dark, clunky heels. My mother's younger brothers, two-year-old Tim and infant Chip, would have needed my grandmother at all hours then. But my mother, who turned five that June, would start school in the fall.

I don't know if my grandparents paid close attention when the Supreme Court heard arguments for a docket of cases challenging racial segregation of public schools in five districts across the South. They could not have avoided hearing, in May 1954, that the Supreme Court had ruled that such segregation was unconstitutional in *Brown v. Board of Education of Topeka, Kansas*. Public opinion polls that year showed that most white northerners agreed with the court's decision, which noted that separate educational facilities were "inherently unequal." Polls also showed that many northern whites balked at the prospect of integrated schools for their own children.

In Pontiac, demographics were shifting as the second wave of the Great Migration began to hit its stride. When my grandparents had been toddlers in 1930, 94.8 percent of Pontiac's 64,900 residents were white, while 3.9 percent were Black. By 1960, the white share of the population was dropping and the Black share was growing. That year, Pontiac was 83.0 percent white and 16.7 percent Black.

As the share of Black residents grew, school integration must have begun to feel like a concrete possibility for my grandparents. In 1958, the *Detroit Free Press* told its readers to "accept what is beginning to look like the inevitable," and to prepare for integrated schools. Their understanding of integration would have been shaped by the news coverage about the process in the South, too. In the late 1950s alone, Georgia's governor prepared to shut public schools entirely before allowing desegregation, opponents of integration in Tennessee set off three bombs in the state's first integrated high school, and President Eisenhower sent federal troops to enforce desegregation at Little Rock's Central High School for nine

months. It would not take much imagination to look at what was unfolding in the South, then at the disparity between what white and Black
students received in the North, and know that change would soon come
to Pontiac. In the summer of 1960, my grandparents sold the house on
Oneida, and moved into a rental in a poorer—but 99.3 percent white—
part of the city.

My grandparents had bought the Oneida house for $9,450, so its
sale for $12,550 yielded $3,100 in profit. Presumably, this gave them a
nest egg. My grandfather was still working for his father then, and he
had graduated from welder to purchasing agent—a step toward taking
over the business. Whatever their mix of savings and help from family
may have been, by 1961, my grandparents had signed a $21,500 mort-
gage to build a new, much larger home near Orchard Lake, in West
Bloomfield Township, fifteen miles west. Two years later, the NAACP
organized a sit-in against the lender they used for their second home,
First Federal Savings and Loan Association of Detroit; one of the complaints was that the bank discriminated against Black homebuyers in
mortgage lending.

Developers were transforming the landscape, which was mostly
farmland, into suburbia. Pine Lake Estates, the subdivision that held
my grandparents' home, was advertised with a brochure that I imagine
my grandmother found alluring. The cover is a line-art illustration,
depicting a white couple in cocktail attire, behind them a trilevel and
trees. "Pine Lake Estates," it reads. "For people going places who require
the 'right' address."

My grandparents sank time and care into the home. It was open and
airy, with a primary suite, two more bedrooms and a den; two and a half
baths; an eat-in kitchen and a dining room for entertaining; a brick patio
off the back, with redwood slats overhead for shade. Under the foyer's
vaulted ceiling was a floor of irregular polished slate, overlooked by a stair-
case lined with elegant supports my grandfather had welded himself, then
topped with a custom-made banister ordered from Chicago.

They moved to the new house in 1962. My mother was fourteen, starting her first year of high school. Instead of attending Pontiac's high school, where Black enrollment was on the rise, she began classes at Bloomfield Hills High. The building had been remodeled recently, its size nearly doubled to accommodate all the newcomers, with a track and ball fields cut out from the still-wooded lots next door. The yearbooks back then only show the junior and senior students, so my mother and her classmates are not pictured; I cannot tell you anything about her class's racial makeup. Instead, I can observe that the 449 faces of the school's upperclassmen that year reflect what my grandparents had likely been seeking: 446 of them, or 99.3 percent, were white.

* * * * *

I know less about my father's childhood than my mother's. The photographic record is thinner, the public records sparser. I can tell you that as a boy he resembled Beaver Cleaver, the poster child for mid-century, middle-class white America. He played baseball and football, dressed up in his dad's army jacket to play at war one day, wore a cowskin-print shirt to play cowboys and Indians the next. I imagine many of the white Baby Boomers, as boys, did the same. My father's parents were doing what many of the other postwar middle-class families were doing: Grandmar stayed home to care for my father, and Grandpa Mac climbed the professional ladder.

In 1957, Ann Arbor Bank announced that Grandpa Mac would become a branch manager. There is no mention of the job being racially restricted, but being white would have been an assumed requirement for the promotion. To get the job, Grandpa Mac would have needed to appeal to his predecessor at the bank, Norman Ottmar, who was retiring—and also was a leader in the National Order of Elks, which restricted membership to white men until 1972. His annual income would have been around $15,000 at the start of the decade, placing my father's family well into the upper-middle class.

Meanwhile, my father attended Catholic school, which he hated. His parents had him serve as an altar boy and acolyte in the church until he graduated high school, but instead of a spiritual faith he developed an unwavering anger at the church. In my twenties, I asked him about his objections to the church. He told me, with noticeable anger, that the church was full of hypocrites, offering, as an example, that he had to pay an entrance fee to the Vatican despite having contributed to the collection plate all his life. The intensity of his reaction did not seem to match the stated offense, and I have since wondered if there was more to his anger than he shared. When I asked him in 2022, on record, about his opposition to the church, his reaction had softened: "Things just kept building up that didn't make sense to me."

By high school, my father displayed an athleticism of which both he and his parents were proud. He played varsity football and baseball; both teams won league championships, and he was comfortable with girls. He also had a reputation for being a bit of a wild man; one story of his high school years involved a stripping and drinking game that my father was losing. Eventually, he was clothed only in a blanket, and when he lost the final round, my father threw the blanket in the air.* To hear him tell it, this gesture prompted uproarious laughter from all. As a teenager, I laughed at this story as my father did when he told it. As an adult woman, more familiar with what excesses of alcohol and privilege can lead young men to do—and what it may mean for the young women around them—it gives me pause.

Even in his youth, my father thought a lot about what people deserved. When he wrote notes on his senior photos to his friends, he often ended by telling them they deserved wonderful things; later, he would do the same in a letter to my sister on her first birthday. I wonder how often he has told himself similar things about just what he deserves.

---

* I have a clear memory of hearing this story at a house party of a friend of my father's when I was fourteen. When I asked my father about this in 2022, he said it was vaguely familiar, but he did not remember.

My father will not talk to me about this, so I examine the facts. He grew up in 1950s America as a boy with affluent, white parents who had prayed for a child, and he had been the answer to those prayers. I can see how, coming of age in this way, he would assume he deserved what he had. How, in his shoes, I might have floated along, mindless of whether I had earned what I had, and whether it had been given to me for reasons beyond my control or comprehension. How it might not even occur to me to object to the ways in which it was unfair; how I would be compelled to defend what I had, worried that it might be taken away. I can see how, in my father's shoes, I would do no better.

I tell myself these things because it is less disappointing than the truth: My father had choices. He could have done better. He did not.

★ ★ ★ ★ ★

Both my parents went to college immediately after high school—less out of an ardent desire for education, more because it was what they felt they should do. My father, being older, left home first. In fall of 1964, just after Congress authorized the use of force in Vietnam, he hitchhiked to John Carroll University, a then all-male Catholic school outside of Cleveland; he had won a football scholarship. In pictures he looks like a preppy party guy, dressed in V-neck sweaters and jeans, fit from football, face still plump with youth. One photo from my father's college years shows him piled with six other boys on the floor of a dorm room. His eyes are half closed, and he holds a liquor bottle and a beer can in his hands. Another shows him asleep on a bottom bunk, sneakers and a beer bottle next to him on the floor. The draft expanded a year later, but my father was safe, thanks to his status as a full-time college student. In school and outside of it, he was learning which rules he could disregard and which ones he would have to manage.

My father was not a good student. He spent two years on academic probation and then went home. He worked shoveling gravel and paid for a few college classes with his parents' help, but he no longer had the safety guaranteed by full-time studies. In 1968, Richard Nixon won the presidency with a populist appeal to the white working class. The campaign hinged on racist subtext, but it relied, also, on promises to make the draft more "equitable." That word was code for limiting student deferments, which protected students who had the money to pay for school; reducing the discretion of local draft boards, who, critics argued, were inclined to protect the sons of local elites; and instituting a random lottery.

As my father remembers it, his number got called in early 1969, drafting him into the army. In hopes of avoiding infantry in Vietnam, my father volunteered for the navy, reasoning that he would be safer on a ship than on land. At graduation for basic training, he listened in shock as his classmates were assigned to riverboats in Vietnam—a possibility he had not considered. When his name came up, he was sent to a ship in the Mediterranean, a hemisphere away from harm. He visited ports all over Europe; his favorite was in Mallorca, Spain, where he went with my mother on their honeymoon. I grew up admiring his favorite souvenir of that time: a massive globe that hinges open on a hip-height equator to reveal decanters of liquor under sketches of the constellations.

After my father finished his active service, in early 1973, he came home. He stayed with his folks for a while, then visited friends out west. That fall, he started classes at Eastern Michigan University, a state school in Ypsilanti, a working-class town near Ann Arbor. He covered tuition with his G.I. Bill and part-time jobs to cover living expenses, but he could count on his parents for emergencies. In both situations, his race eased his path. Because he was white, he was more likely to have used the G.I. Bill for education than if he had not been white; because he was white, he was likely to earn more money when he worked; because his parents were white, they were more likely to have more wealth to share with him.

He was in his late twenties, nearly a decade older than incoming freshmen, driving a blue Fiat 850 Spider that rode so low he could graze the ground with his fingertips from the driver's seat. He no longer went by John, preferring instead the same nickname his father used: Mac. He'd retained his teenage comfort with women and could be funny and charming. When student clubs advertised for members in the fall, he didn't see much that appealed to him, not even—and given his penchant for drinking I am surprised by this—Greek life. ("A bunch of spoiled rich kids," he'd tell me later.) Other than the softball league, he found one group that seemed promising: the Vets Club, for guys coming back from the war. He took note of their next meeting, and went.

★ ★ ★ ★ ★

My mother graduated high school in 1966, a well-liked but middling student. She enrolled at Central Michigan University for the fall. She was still in love with her high school sweetheart, Tom, who stayed in Orchard Lake; her first-year notebooks are peppered with doodles of his name. She took classes in English literature and French and a home economics class on courtship and marriage. After three years, she dropped out.

It was 1969, the height of the 1960s counterculture. I imagine that my mother, like a lot of her white, middle-class peers, felt hemmed in by the conventions of her parents and the steady path to which college seemed to lead. She took a semester off, then resurfaced at a community college near her parents' house. She followed a new boyfriend to Rhode Island for a year, but they broke up and she came home just in time for the funeral of her last remaining grandparent, Don's father, Bert, who died in 1971. By 1972 she was sticking close to home, bouncing between living on her own and staying with her parents. To make money, she picked up temp work through an agency, American Girl. At one of her assignments, she befriended Bonnie Huston, a blond girl from another Detroit suburb, whom she would know the rest of her life. In early 1973, my mother enrolled at Eastern Michigan University. Tuition was $17 per credit hour—about $510 a year.*

She rented an apartment in a low-slung brick building off an avenue

---

* According to the Bureau of Labor Statistics, $510 in January 1973 was equivalent to $3,582 in January 2023.

leading into Ypsi. Her friends tell me she was reserved but friendly, ready
to join in fun but never an organizer of it. This made her appealing to the
instigators of the world. Among them was Barb Stevens, a fellow English
major whose background contradicted my mother's in every way: The
daughter of a single mother who'd worked as an anesthesiologist since the
1950s, Barb had lived in cities and at boarding schools; she had decidedly
not taken any classes in courtship. She took a liking to my mother and
made a project of drawing her out of her shell. In service of this, Barb
invited my mother to join a club she was helping to run. An antisorority
sorority, Barb said.

The group existed, mostly, to poke fun at the seriousness with which
Greek organizations took themselves. They were registered with the Greek
Council, but similarities with the official sororities ended there. Their
motto was "If you can't shit on it, piss on it," their colors the correspond-
ing brown and yellow, their flower the dandelion. The pledge books were
spiral-bound notebooks with felt pasted to the cover, and "rush" consisted
of showing up at bar nights and paying house visits to existing members.
There were no requirements to buy outfits or perform rituals, their song
referenced being "good for a lay," and the only criteria for membership,
claims Barb, was an interest in joining. Like all the sororities pictured in the
yearbook, all of its members were the same race. They called themselves
the Beavers.

* * * * *

My parents graduated high school in 1964 and 1966, part of the first
generation to attend college after the massive expansion of higher education prompted by the G.I. Bill. Tuition, still heavily subsidized by
both federal and state government, was low enough that many middle-
class students and their families could afford it. In 1970 to 1971, when
both my parents were working on their degrees, the average "sticker
price" for a year of public university tuition was $478—the equivalent in
2023 of $3,593. By the time I headed to college in 1994, it had increased

by two-thirds after adjusting for inflation. By 2020, it had more than tripled.

Researchers are clear that the biggest reason for that change has been a drop in state funding. "It's not that colleges are spending more money to educate students," Sandy Baum, a researcher at the Urban Institute, told NPR in 2014. "It's that they have to get that money from someplace to replace their lost state funding—and that's from tuition and fees from students and families." From the mid-1970s to 2020, state educational funding for college dropped from two-thirds of its cost to one-third.

That drop in state funding tracks with two other significant changes: an *increase* in the share of students who are not white, and an *increase* in student debt. In my grandparents' era, universities swelled with students whose G.I. Bill benefits largely covered the cost of classes. Roughly 96 percent of college students were white back then—and about 5 percent of them needed loans to cover the cost of school. That is different from the world of my parents, who went to school when 84 percent of college students were white—and about one-quarter of students needed loans. That is different from my world as a student, when 74 percent of college students were white—and half of students needed loans. In today's world, when just over half of college students are white, paying for college out of pocket without family wealth is unthinkable. By 2010, nearly two-thirds of white, public college students needed loans to graduate school—as did more than 80 percent of nonwhite students.

These changes in support for public education mirrored a broader political shift that had begun unfolding in national politics during the 1950s and 1960s. During that era, writes Ian Haney López, the legal scholar, Republican presidential candidates began to strategically deploy coded racial language in order to win political power. Most had begun their political careers as racial moderates—then moved decisively toward racism as its political power became clear. The most iconic of these may have been George Wallace, a four-term governor of Alabama and three-time presidential hopeful. When he first ran for governor in 1958, he was known for being a fair and evenhanded judge. His initial gubernatorial campaign barely mentioned race at all, and he was endorsed by the NAACP. Four years later, he ran as an avid segregationist and won, ending his 1963 inaugural address—written by a member of the Ku Klux Klan—with, "Segregation now, segregation today, segregation forever." Like Barry Goldwater in the 1964 Republican primaries, and Richard Nixon in that party's primaries in 1968, Wallace leveraged racism for his own political gain—what Haney López calls "strategic racism."

Combined, the rise of overtly racist campaigns also fueled a shift in how Americans saw the role of government and its programs.

Before the 1960s and the gains of the civil rights movement, white America saw public spending as something that benefited "everyone." (The implicit assumption was that everyone was white, and that other people could be excluded.) But starting in the 1960s, Republicans began to talk about public spending as "welfare"—something that benefited only people of color, and for which taxpayers should not have to pay. They did not mention that Black and brown Americans had long been paying taxes that funded programs overwhelmingly designed to benefit white people far more than themselves, such as FHA mortgages and the G.I. Bill. They mentioned only that Black and brown people, who they did not believe deserved help, were receiving it.

Within a decade, white Americans' support for government ensuring a basic standard of living for its citizens plummeted. In 1960, before these campaigns took off, 56 percent of white Americans believed that government should guarantee jobs or a decent standard of living to everyone, and 29 percent believed the opposite—that everyone was on their own. By 1968, the numbers had nearly flipped: 26 percent of whites believed that government should help—and 51 percent believed that everyone was on their own. In less than a decade, the majority of whites disavowed government as a source of help, even though so many of them had benefited from it themselves. They also began to disavow the very thing that had made all that help possible in the first place: taxes.

This was the world that welcomed my parents to adulthood.

★ ★ ★ ★ ★

My parents met at the Bell Bar, a student hangout in downtown Ypsilanti, half a block off the main drag. Outside, there were a porthole door and glass block windows beneath helix-patterned brick that reached to the second floor. Soul, rock, and funk would have been playing inside: the Isley Brothers and the Rolling Stones, Stevie Wonder and Eddie Kendricks and the Allman Brothers Band. The bar has switched hands five times since my parents were visiting it, but every owner has kept the curved, wooden behemoth of a bar that was there when they met.

I do not know much about my parents' meeting; there's no family story handed down, and when I ask my father about it, he tells me he doesn't remember. I know that when they met, they were young but older than most college kids, trying to make friends in a new town as they both reentered college after stretches away from it. And I know that, on some night in October, the Vets Club and the Beavers had a joint meeting, which is to say that they went to the same bar and drank together. There was no plan beyond that.

My mother wore her hair short, in a shag, and its fringe framed her heart-shaped face, pale, unblemished skin, and full mouth. I imagine her leaning on the bar, a cheap, sweet drink next to her elbow—a 7 and 7, maybe—a lit cigarette in her other hand. She was reserved but beautiful, and this combination would have drawn my father, who was outgoing. He wore his hair long then, in thick black waves to his shoulders, and had a warm smile. Maybe she was talking with friends when he sidled up and ribbed her gently, insulting her with good humor to get her attention. Or, maybe she smiled at him as the wah-wah riffs of "Higher Ground" played in the background, and watched him come to her. Or maybe they didn't talk at all, just noticed each other across the room, said nothing until the next time they found themselves at the same bar together, or the time after that. But, eventually, at some party or another, they started talking.

On December 7, they went on their first date. By December 22, they had decided to marry each other.

★ ★ ★ ★ ★

My mother's family was uneasy about my father. A few days after their initial engagement, my mother took Mac to her family Christmas. Grandpa Don took one look at Mac's long hair, grunted, and walked away. Don's sister Roberta, who was hosting, turned to my father and offered him a scotch, a kindness he would remember for decades. The couple spent the night together at the apartment my father shared with a friend, picking up Burger King on the way home.

Years later, my father would expand the story of that first Christmas to include a more difficult moment. Sometime after the presents that night, but sometime before dessert, Grandpa Don pulled my father aside. I remember my father telling me, indignant, that Grandpa Don warned him that his daughter needed to be cared for in the manner to which she was accustomed. As a child, I thought my father was indignant because he has always taught me to value people's character more than their pedigree. As an adult, I wonder if my father—who now tells me he does not remember this—also found the warning unsettling because he had been raised the son of a successful white banker, and was not used to being found unworthy of praise and respect. I wonder what it took to convince Grandpa Don that he was. I know only that this convincing took a couple months, until February, when my parents' engagement notice appeared in the local paper.

My parents' friends approved of the match more easily. My parents' personalities were opposite—my father outgoing and temperamental; my mother verging on shy—but they complemented each other. And they had other things in common. Both had been raised in conventional 1950s families and absorbed their families' lessons and aspirations. They shared the 1960s countercultural skepticism of convention even as their families' material stability meant they could acquire a conventional life if they chose.

Even back then, my father's temper was no small thing. It was unpredictable rather than constant, erupting over seemingly small things: a broken object, teasing that went further than he liked, a mishap of scheduling. He could be belittling and cruel, laying enraged disappointment at his target's feet: *I would not be this upset,* went the thinking, *if you had not made me so.* When these outbursts happened, he would rarely apologize or discuss them afterward; it was as if they had never happened.

There is a term for that kind of behavior, well-known among psychologists who study trauma and abuse: deflection. If abusive behavior is met with objection, the abuser will turn their attention to what their victim was doing. Often, the abuser will suggest they had no choice but to be abusive, given the circumstances. The abuser may imply that they themselves are the true victim. This is typically understood as a hallmark of interpersonal abuse, but I see parallels here with larger-scale abuses. It echoes the argument of white officials that they could not outlaw housing discrimination, since the entry of Black families into white neighborhoods so quickly led to a drop in housing value. As if the drop in value had nothing to do with white officials' willingness to overlook white violence. As if they had no power to stop it.

Once, before they were married, my father unleashed a tirade at my mother while they were at a bar among friends. Barb remembers comforting my mother as she cried, the two of them sitting low on a curb, their feet in the gutter, their knees nearly touching their chests. Barb does not remember what the argument was about, if my father apologized, or how my mother came to forgive him. But when Barb told me this story, she remembered clearly that my father was blaming my mother for something beyond her control. I know only that my mother and her friends knew he had this in him, and that my mother had loved—and married—him anyway.

* * * * *

My parents were happy on their wedding day. To hear my father tell it, his primary responsibility was to show up on time, and to buy the booze for the reception. The rest was up to my mother and Grandma Kate. My parents' wedding album, rich brown leather with gilded edges, suggests they outdid themselves.

They held the ceremony in a historical clapboard church on the shore of Orchard Lake, overseen by both a Catholic priest and a Methodist minister, and celebrated in a wood-paneled reception hall in Detroit. There were hooded, floor-length bridesmaids' dresses, pale yellow and green, and matching gingham tuxes for the groomsmen. My father wore a rented white tuxedo, with a checked, black-and-white jacket. My mother borrowed a sleeveless satin gown and a veil that pooled on the floor from a friend. It was 1974, and tradition required that Grandpa Don, who by then was working as a union millwright at a Ford factory, pay for the wedding.

In every photo from that day, my parents radiate joy. They beam as they walk out of the church into a shower of rice. My mother laughs as my father helps her into a white Mercury Cougar with a JUST MARRIED sign affixed to the trunk above a string of cans. At the reception, they smile while stuffing each other's faces with slices of a tiered cake and performing a garter dance.

The honeymoon looks joyous, too. Two days after the wedding, my parents flew to Portugal, then Spain. My mother smiled coyly at my father as he photographed her: wearing sundresses in the hotel room, modeling a cover-up at the beach, posing in a new white fur coat, hair up, looking like a movie star. My father returned the favor, posing on a balcony overlooking the Mediterranean.

When my family talked of the wedding, it was in terms of its thrift: How my mother borrowed her dress. How she kept the bridesmaids to three. How her engagement ring had just one diamond. They did not talk of the expense of the church and the hall, the engraved invitations and the tuxes, the cocktail napkins embossed with my parents' names. They did not note that flying to Europe was a luxury back then, unaffordable without help from my father's parents. They spoke of the wedding as special, but if they understood it as an extravagance, it was one they believed they had earned with hard work and careful spending. There was no mention, in my family, as there rarely is in white families, of the ways that our race had made the church and the gowns, the booze and the honeymoon, possible.

Three months before my parents' wedding, Grandpa Don and Aunt Roberta sold their father's house in Waterford. By 1974, the racial covenant on that house had been unenforceable for twenty-six years and illegal for eight. The subdivision's developer's membership in the Black Legion had been forgotten. And yet, the Waterford subdivision remained all-white. Enough Black people had moved to the Pontiac area by then that, however Waterford residents managed it, preserving segregation would have required effort—whether codified in law or not. For whites, that effort, in turn, offered financial advantages. Then, as now, a home in a white neighborhood fetched a higher price than the same home would in a mixed-race neighborhood. The house sold for $40,000, the equivalent of $256,798 in 2023. By the end of the year, Don and his sister, Roberta, had split the proceeds down the middle. My grandfather would not have had that money without being white.

Nor, I suspect, would my parents have had as nice of a wedding. At the time, my grandfather's annual income was likely around $8,320 a year, the national median for a millwright in 1970. By then only one child, my mother's youngest brother, might've still depended on my grandparents. For a household of three, the Weddles in 1970 would have been at the edge of lower-middle and middle class, still paying off their mortgage. Stable, but without much wiggle room for splurges like lakeside churches and engraved napkins.

I do not know if my mother understood that the trappings of her wedding were as much a product of racist housing policy as of her parents' hard work or of their generosity. My father tells me that, inasmuch as he thought about it, having that nice of a wedding was "normal." He tells me that race "wouldn't've even entered my mind." Little wonder that, when I looked through my parents' wedding album as a child, I understood the middle-class extravagances of their wedding as the natural way of the world.

But before I could understand any of this, my parents had to make me. They ended their honeymoon in Barcelona and flew back to Detroit, and began their life together.

LINDSEY AND MARYANN BECKER: SCHOOL
B. 1989 AND 1994
HATTIESBURG, MISSISSIPPI

It probably smelled like pine that first day of school, back in 1999, when Lindsey Becker looked around her fourth-grade math class in surprise. It would have been late summer, the humidity hanging heavy in the Pine Belt forests out of which Hattiesburg has been carved. The woods in this part of Mississippi have always been thick, and pine trees edge nearly every development, waiting for a chance to reclaim territory. There were pines around the grounds of Thames Elementary, where Lindsey went to school, and whole woodlands full of them out west, where the city stretched out of Forrest County and into Lamar. Pine trees lined the avenues and shaded bungalows, and they edged toward the riverbank downtown. The economy in Hattiesburg had changed since the city was founded, back after the Civil War, evolving from lumber and railroads to health care and education and services. By the 2020s, the depot and a Coca-Cola bottling plant downtown had become event spaces well-suited to Instagram. Still, whatever year it was, the smell of pine remained: sharp but diffuse, something that seemed to disappear if you tried to name it.*

---

* All names of the "Becker" family have been changed.

It would have been strong that morning in 1999 at Thames Elementary, then the newest school building in town, even though it was more than thirty years old. In most ways, the school had looked the same the first time Lindsey Becker walked through its doors on Jamestown Road: Long wings of tan brick, interrupted by aluminum-framed windows, still faced the parking spots for visitors. Flat-roofed breezeways with round metal pillars still protected students from the Mississippi sun and rain. Wooden cubbies still greeted first graders after the double doors swung open. And the grounds, acres of coarse grass ringed by subdivisions, were still massive, dotted with play areas. But as Lindsey went through her first day of fourth-grade classes, with little-kid pudge and a haircut from her mom, she noticed something had changed: Her math class was almost entirely made up of white children.

A mostly white class, in any subject, was new for Lindsey. Nearly all the students who attended the Hattiesburg Public Schools were Black, making Lindsey—and the three siblings who followed her—unusual in the grand scheme of American public education. All of Lindsey's classes before that math class had been mostly Black children and only a few white ones. The pattern was so consistent that Lindsey's mother, Rosie, pictured administrators at Hattiesburg Public Schools setting up all the chairs in a classroom, placing a folder for a Black student on each chair—then swapping in just enough folders for white students to give each classroom the same demographic mix. So when Lindsey noticed her advanced math class was almost all white, Rosie and Lewis, Lindsey's father, noticed, too.

The Beckers noticed race, of course, but it was hard to separate from economic class. If Lindsey's math class had mostly white students, that was probably because so many white children lived near Thames. Their parents were professors and doctors, mostly, with generous incomes. Most children seemed to have two parents at home; with that much support at home, the Beckers assumed, any kid would do well at school. The Beckers did not stop and seek to understand why their daughter's math class was now so much whiter; the school, after all, was majority Black. And they did not think much about why Black students made up 84 percent of public school students, when only half of city residents were Black. They did not ask these questions then because their kids were in school and doing well. And they did not ask them later, as their kids graduated from the district, just as Hattiesburg schools began to fail most of the students who remained.

★ ★ ★ ★ ★

Because they did not stop and wonder, the Beckers did not realize that they were living through what scholars now refer to as "resegregation": the steady reemergence of racially homogenous schools after a few decades of progress toward racial integration. The trend began to develop in the late 1980s, as school desegregation orders from the civil rights era expired—and it was not unique to Hattiesburg, or even to Mississippi. Across the country, North and South, East and West, the same pattern repeated, leaving nearly all American public schools as segregated today as they were in the 1960s.

There are many stories that have been told about resegregation. One of the first is about the harm it has done, the loss it has generated: loss of education, loss of potential, loss of opportunity for the students integration was supposed to help. That story is mostly about people who are not white; usually it is about people who are Black. A second story is about the families who fled. That story is overwhelmingly about white people. At first, white people openly admitted they left the schools to avoid Black people. As time passed, though, norms changed, and the public schools tried to lure white families back, and white people talked less about race. Instead, they spoke of the "quality of education" and "safety." But white people's actions—avoiding schools with noticeable populations of Black students—did not change much.*

The Beckers' story is different because they are among the few white families who did not flee public schools that had large numbers of Black students. For the Beckers, this was a practical decision. Both Rosie and Lewis had gone to public schools in the 1960s and 1970s—she in Ohio, he in Mississippi—and that had worked out fine. They weren't political people,

---

* Although it is not directly cited here, the excellent coverage of segregation in public schools by Nikole Hannah-Jones's work for the *New York Times Magazine* and by ProPublica is crucial reading on this topic, and was important to the work done in this chapter.

choosing to engage with community mostly through their church, which was integrated, nondenominational, and Christian. When their children were little, they'd approached the public schools as a bit of an experiment: They'd try it out, and revisit the decision if it wasn't working for them or their kids.

Lindsey started school just as that district, and the country, largely abandoned the project of integrating public schools and began resegregating by both race and class. The next two Becker children, brothers, were there as resegregation progressed. But the youngest Becker, Maryann, was there as it bottomed out. As a white girl from the middle class, she carried many advantages with her to school that were not shared by most of her classmates, who were mostly Black and mostly poor. In the end, both she and her family got a lesson in what their white advantage could, and could not, do for them.

★ ★ ★ ★ ★

The Becker family came into the district forty-two years after the Supreme Court's landmark decision in *Brown v. Board of Education*, which declared school segregation unconstitutional, but Hattiesburg's public schools had only been integrated for a decade. This sort of heel-dragging does not simply happen: All of it was by local officials' design. After *Brown*, which the local newspaper, the *Hattiesburg American*, called the Supreme Court's "most stupid decision," Hattiesburg did nothing to integrate. They had a lot of company. While the Supreme Court had ruled that segregated schools were unconstitutional, the justices had no way to directly enforce their own mandate. It was up to state and local officials to carry out the court's sweeping order. With very few exceptions, most southern school districts ignored the court's decision without consequences. The same was true for most, but not all, northern districts, where white officials and residents assumed that the segregation in their districts was not objectionable.*

---

* Notably, in 1968, the school district into which my parents' first home was zoned became the first northern school district sued by federal officials for maintaining a segregated school. See page 138.

In Mississippi, little changed at schools in the first decade after *Brown*. State leaders did amend the Mississippi constitution to allow for the dissolution of public schools in order to preserve racial segregation. They made no move to do so. Instead, education officials continued a strategy they'd begun even before *Brown* in hopes of fending off racial integration: beginning to "equalize" district spending on Black and white students. The thinking, observes historian Charles C. Bolton, was that Mississippi might be able to preserve "separate" facilities if they made even minimal efforts to provide "equal" ones. In 1939, Hattiesburg schools had spent more than six times as much on each white student as on each Black student. One year after the *Brown* decision, the district "only" spent a third more per white student than per Black student.

Whites' conviction that integration could be avoided was so profound that white enrollment in Hattiesburg schools grew in the wake of *Brown*. White enrollment in the district had peaked in 1963, at nearly 4,700 white students—about half the student body.* But Black students were entering the district at a faster rate than white students, and the share of white students in Hattiesburg schools began its first, if modest, decline.

White flight from the schools intensified with passage of the Civil Rights Act of 1964, which made segregation illegal. This gave federal officials the power to enforce integration, rather than leaving it to state officials. Hattiesburg followed the lead of most districts in the South and shifted from ignoring the desegregation mandate to making only a token attempt to meet it. The most popular model was called "freedom of choice," which gave students the option to apply to attend any school within a district; Hattiesburg adopted it in 1965. In response, several white community leaders in Hattiesburg founded a private school that would

---

* This is true insofar as data tells us, but there is no public source of data for the racial composition of Hattiesburg Public Schools between 1965 and 1968. Under segregation, racial demographics could be tracked by enrollment at individual school buildings—the unit by which segregation worked. After passage of the Civil Rights Act of 1964, the district did not track race again until mandated by federal officials looking to assess racial segregation in the district.

take only white students, enrolling twenty students that year. The same approach, which relied on so-called segregation academies, was unrolling across the South.

In principle, freedom of choice worked both ways: It opened the formerly white schools to Black students, and the formerly Black schools to white ones. In practice, it was a sham: Administrators carefully controlled the process to make sure that little changed in the schools' racial makeup. By the end of 1965, less than 1 percent of Mississippi's Black students attended previously all-white schools. "In actual operation," writes Bolton, "freedom of choice was just another effective manifestation of massive resistance." It was also broadly used across the South until federal court rulings effectively ended the practice by 1970.

Most districts did not integrate voluntarily. It took the Supreme Court's 1969 decision in *Alexander v. Holmes,* which ordered immediate desegregation nationwide, before Hattiesburg began to integrate a few of its schools. When classes began in the fall of 1970, three of Hattiesburg's elementaries and one of its junior high schools had student bodies that approached the district's roughly half-and-half mix of Black and white students. But the other twelve schools in the district—eight more elementaries, another two junior highs, and two high schools—remained segregated. In all twelve of those schools, the student body was either more than 90 percent Black or more than 80 percent white.

Throughout the 1970s, Hattiesburg displayed little urgency when it came to further integrating its schools. Mostly, the district had tried to "integrate without really integrating," as Tracy Williams, a former administrator who'd also grown up in the district, put it to me. Shortly after *Alexander v. Holmes* was decided, the Department of Justice sued school districts all over Mississippi and obtained consent decrees that required districts—including Hattiesburg—to submit demographic reports, down to the classroom level, each semester. Those reports show that administrators combined students of the same grade across the two high schools in 1971. They also show that, within a few years, the district introduced integration in its junior highs and a couple more elementaries. Yet while the district remained roughly half-Black and half-white in 1980, only a handful of schools reflected that mix. It stayed that way until 1987, the year the Beckers married.

★ ★ ★ ★ ★

The Beckers tell me they didn't think about schools much when they bought their homes. Not when they used an FHA down payment program to facilitate a $50,239 mortgage on their first house, a three-bedroom bungalow, putting down just $1,500. It sat outside the city limits and was zoned into Lamar County schools, a rapidly expanding white district. The Beckers also tell me they didn't think much about schools in 1992, after the birth of their third child, when they took out a mortgage for $59,400 and bought a larger home. The four-bedroom, two-bath just inside the city limits is where Lindsey and her siblings grew up. It was zoned into Hattiesburg schools.

Back then, the Beckers got used to hearing from white neighbors about wanting to leave the schools "for white flight reasons." Those neighbors might talk about how schools were getting bad, or about how they feared for their children's safety. Sometimes they vaguely talked about the "quality" of the school. Others talked about not wanting their child to be in the minority in their school.

Eventually, Rosie remembers, these people left Hattiesburg in favor of Lamar County to the west, or Petal to the east. But whichever direction they went, white flight had reached a new, final stage.

★ ★ ★ ★ ★

The collective power of other white parents' decision to leave had been draining the district for years. As white flight out of Hattiesburg built to a critical mass in the 1980s, the loss of students was just the start. Their departure began to drain public coffers, too. As families left, the property tax paid to the city by homeowners dropped. As businesses followed the families, commercial taxes dropped, too. New retail developments on the west side of town, like a 900,000-square-foot mall anchored by Sears and

JCPenney that opened in 1994, were within Hattiesburg's city limits—but in Lamar County. That meant the business taxes went to fund that county's schools, instead of the schools in Hattiesburg. This was true even though those businesses used the city's fire, police, transit, and sewer services—which made insurance rates for the businesses affordable.*

By the late 1980s, Hattiesburg officials were trying to recoup their losses. The city filed suit to annex adjacent parts of Lamar and Forrest Counties, hoping to bring tax revenues back into the district. In 1989, the school district joined in, arguing that taxes collected within any expanded city limits should fund the city's schools, too. In 1991, the Mississippi Supreme Court approved the annexation of part of Forrest County, south of the city—but rejected the request to annex the part of Lamar County, west of the city, where the emerging commercial district and its revenues sat.

The decision, says then superintendent Gordon Walker, "effectively locked the Hattiesburg school district into its boundaries that existed at that time, so it never could reach out and recoup students who had moved." Segregation *within* the district was slowly being erased, largely because there were so few non-Black students left, but white flight meant that segregation *between* districts—the pattern that northern whites had long used to keep their children from having any significant number of Black classmates—had grown. The decision in the annexation case did not affect only Hattiesburg. It set precedent for the entire state, removing Mississippi school districts' ability to challenge white flight when it crossed county lines. At least seven Mississippi cities had filed a petition in support of Hattiesburg in the case, all of them facing the same problem.

Closing the borders to the district in this way added yet another source

---

* To clarify: Hattiesburg was founded in Forrest County. As the city grew, it crossed the line into Lamar County, to the west. This puts the city in the vexing position of being situated in two counties at once. Notably, Forrest County takes its name from Nathan Bedford Forrest, a Confederate general and the first Grand Wizard of the Ku Klux Klan.

of segregation by enticing members of the middle class to cluster in more-affluent school districts. Without a guarantee of well-resourced public schools within the city limits, any family who sought that sort of school had to move out of the city. This was technically true for families of any race, but moving was easiest for white families, who were overrepresented in the middle class, who didn't face discrimination from Realtors or residents, and who, with help from the government, had built wealth for generations longer than their Black peers.*

* * * * *

Rosie and Lewis, who married in June 1987, don't remember the headlines that year about a new attendance policy for Hattiesburg schools. In 1985, after decades of court orders, eight of its eleven elementary schools were at least 80 percent white or 80 percent Black. In spring of 1987, a federal judge issued a consent decree: Integrate *now.* The Hattiesburg school district suggested magnet schools, to attract students of all races, but Black parents objected; there was no guarantee of equalizing resources across the district. The district suggested a busing program, but a judge struck it down on the grounds that it would spur white flight. The Black parents won on appeal, and a federal judge issued a new consent decree: No school building could be more than 80 percent of a single race.

To change those segregated patterns, Hattiesburg had to radically restructure both its schools and the attendance zones that assigned students to them. Rather than continuing to run multiple school buildings serving many grades, the district began to consolidate each grade into fewer buildings. This structure meant fewer options to move kids around. This would keep white families from doing what they had tended to do elsewhere: clustering into—and taking disproportionate advantage of—the best schools.

Still, Jimmy Hopkins, the district's first Black assistant superintendent, lamented to me how much the Black community had to give up in hopes

---

* For a discussion of racial discrimination in housing, see pages 21–29.

of getting access to equal resources. "Usually the Black schools had to give up a lot," Hopkins told me. The neighborhood schools may have been underfunded, but they were still a source of pride and a center for the community. "People want to see kids moving around the neighborhood. It suggests life and not death," he told me.

Local leaders had understood the restructuring would be controversial, particularly among white families, but they underestimated the scale of the backlash. They were prepared for white parents' complaints about the district's use of buses—which had been an effective, if controversial, method of integrating schools in the North's residentially segregated cities. And they were ready, too, for white residents to lament the loss of "neighborhood schools"—a term used in the North to justify schools having students that were mostly the same race. But even during the furor over *Brown* and the Civil Rights Act in previous decades, white enrollment in Hattiesburg had only slightly dipped each year. Leaders assumed the same pattern would continue; in a 1984 desegregation court appearance, an expert suggested increasing integration would spur about 10 percent of white students to leave Hattiesburg schools in the first year.

This was a significant underestimate: In the first year after integration, white enrollment dropped by 16.6 percent. The raw number of students who fled in the late 1980s was smaller than the losses in the 1960s, but it still marked the steepest decline in white enrollment in the district's history.

There's no way to know for sure where all those students went, but everyone I talked to in Hattiesburg pointed to two places: the private schools in Hattiesburg and the public schools in the counties outside of the city. Some families stayed in Hattiesburg and paid for private schools. Otherwise, people moved: east across the river to Petal, or west to Oak Grove in Lamar County. Indeed, in the first decade after integration, Hattiesburg lost 1,438 white students. Meanwhile enrollment in Oak Grove jumped by 1,666 and Petal's grew by 626. In both of those districts, nearly all the new students were white. It wasn't just that white people were leaving Hattiesburg; white families who came to the area now sought the county schools instead of the schools in the city.

The Beckers listened to their departing neighbors talk about the Hattiesburg schools going downhill and dismissed the griping with a shake of their heads. "They moved out west because they wanted to be away from these schools," Rosie said. She shrugged. She was happy with the education her children had gotten, which had started with Thames Elementary.

★ ★ ★ ★ ★

Rosie and Lewis describe white flight as moving from a city to an outlying county, and this was part of how I'd grown up thinking of it, too. But that's not the whole story: There had been another, initial wave of white flight that laid the groundwork for the one that Rosie, Lewis, and I discussed. This earlier wave had a much smaller radius, entailing only a move from public schools to new private ones in the same town—the segregation academies.*

Hattiesburg's segregation academy was founded in 1965 as the Forrest County Foundation School, and renamed as Beeson Academy two years later. Segregation schools were opening all across the South then, made affordable by a web of subsidies ranging from government vouchers to tax-exempt status. By 1976, some 750,000 white students across the South attended private schools that would admit only whites. In Mississippi, roughly one-fifth of white school children went to new private schools in 1970. One of those schools was in Simpson County, Mississippi—where Lewis grew up.

---

* The idea of building a system of separate, private, white schools took root as soon as *Brown* was decided. According to Bolton, in *The Hardest Deal of All*, in June 1954, Walter Sillers Jr., then the Speaker of the House for the Mississippi legislature, consulted with a Jackson attorney about establishing private schools to avoid *Brown's* integration mandate. Sillers even wanted to directly fund the new schools with public money. Attorneys advised that funding private schools with public money would never pass constitutional muster. Mississippi officials nonetheless continued to explore this idea until 1970.

Lewis had all the markers I'd expect of someone who attended a segregation academy. His extended family showed up among the list of faculty for Simpson Academy; in news reports about the school's founders—even among the leadership of Mississippi's statewide association of segregation schools. Lindsey and Maryann both remember Lina, Lewis's mother, using the N-word freely, as if it were a neutral description and not a racial slur. Martin, Lewis's father, was a strict military veteran who'd been raised on the same family farm he moved his family to in the 1970s—including Lewis. This path, moving from a rural life to a more stable position in the middle class thanks to military service, was a common one for white men of Martin's generation in the South, and one that often correlated with opposition to integration. It would not have surprised me if Lewis's parents had put their children into an all-white school. But they had not.

Lewis is not sure why his parents kept him in public school, but his best guess as to why has three parts. The first is an optimistic tale of fading prejudice. Lewis believes that Martin—who he remembered had commanded integrated units in Korea and Vietnam during his military career—had set aside most of the personal prejudice with which he had been raised. "Twenty years in the army, he didn't see Black and white anymore," says Lewis, who doesn't remember his father using racial slurs the way his mother did. "He just saw people."

The second and third guesses are more mundane: cost and quality. Segregation academies came with a price tag—although state governments across the South initially subsidized tuition with tuition vouchers, funneling public education money into private schools. But even the notion of paying for education would have been anathema to Martin, whose frugality was legendary. What's more, says Lewis, everyone knew that the new academies weren't very good at teaching, which mattered to his parents. "Daddy told me . . . 'You'll never make anything unless you get a sheepskin,'" says Lewis—a college degree.

It's almost impossible, so many years after the death of Lewis's parents, to know for certain why they kept Lewis and his sisters in public schools in the 1970s—at the height of controversy around desegregation. It is easier, given the work of historians, to know why so many others fled.

★ ★ ★ ★ ★

I have found myself tempted to assume that segregation academies were a haphazard response to *Brown*: uneducated white parents fleeing the schools out of fear and prejudice. That is a dangerously naive assumption. The move to segregation academies was the product of a white-led grassroots movement against integration, headed by well-off community leaders and explicitly designed to preserve white supremacy. For most of my life, "white supremacy" felt like a loaded term: a phrase used to antagonize. It also is the accurate one to use here, given the movement that emerged after the *Brown* decision was announced in May of 1954.

It started with Robert "Tut" Patterson, a one-time football star turned plantation manager who'd already been urging whites in Indianola to "stand together forever firm against communism and mongrelization" when the decision came down. He organized a meeting of community leaders to strategize about a response—lawyers and cotton administrators, mayors and bankers. By July, Patterson had held a rally with nearly a hundred attendees and founded the first chapter of the white Citizens' Council. That fall, a Mississippi judge named Thomas Pickens Brady declared a call to arms in a speech he titled "Black Monday." Although the speech began with white supremacist pseudoscience—one passage observed, somewhat incoherently, that "the jungle, the black blood swallows up, and with it goes this deterioration. It blows out the light within a white man's brain"—its historic significance comes from its call for organized resistance to school integration. Brady turned the speech into a booklet that quickly became a phenomenon; Patterson later cited it as an inspirational guide. By 1956, estimates of the Council's membership sat at more than eighty thousand members—with chapters springing up across the country.

As Council leaders mounted opposition to integration, they styled

themselves as a more respectable alternative to the Ku Klux Klan.* The
ruling in *Brown* declared segregation unconstitutional, but it did not provide for enforcement. After the *Brown* ruling, the Council vowed to fight it
without spilling blood, waging what Brady called an economic "cold war"
against Black people who supported integration. They did this mostly
by intimidating Black activists who filed desegregation suits—the only
path toward integration provided by *Brown* alone.† The war was effective:
From 1955 to 1958, membership in Mississippi's NAACP dropped by nearly
two-thirds.

Still, it was white moderates—many of them moving, like Martin,
from laboring on farms to a more stable position in the middle class—who
worried the Council the most, says historian Stephanie Rolph, whose book
Resisting Equality follows the group from inception to dissolution. Poor,
uneducated whites were easy recruits to a white supremacist organization.
The upper class had a vested interest in keeping the system as it was. The
only allegiance in question was that of the anxious middle class—the white
moderates that Martin Luther King, Jr., decried in his famous "Letter from
Birmingham Jail." The middle class's material stability, at least compared
to the poor, gave them breathing room to question the racial order. Their
precarity, at least compared to the wealthy, meant they might question the

---

* As historian Stephanie Rolph points out in *Resisting Equality*, although comparison to the KKK served the Council's aim of recruiting white moderates
   to their cause, it is of dubious relevance, given that the KKK was dormant in
   Mississippi in the 1950s. Council chapters have been tied to racial intimidation
   and other violence throughout mid-century in Mississippi and other southern
   states, and a Council member murdered the civil rights activist Medgar Evers.

† To access the constitutional right declared in *Brown,* citizens had to sue the
   district to integrate—and put their names on public documents. Among the
   intimidation strategies documented by Bolton and Rolph in their books are
   a white bank president calling Black customers who'd signed a petition and
   telling them to get their money out of his bank; a Black plumber who signed a
   petition and in turn lost customers and his wholesale supplier, and was charged
   higher prices for food by the grocer; and a signee who looked out their front
   window and saw a hearse looming out front.

economic order. The Council knew this and strategized about using social and political pressure to create white unity across class lines by disciplining "members of the white race who fail[ed] to cooperate."

Council chapters also ginned up racial hysteria with their newsletters. Some were formal, text-only pamphlets, neatly typeset and bearing titles like "How to Keep Schools Open," and "How to Save Our Public Schools." Others were more crude. A chapter in Little Rock, Arkansas, sent out sixteen pages of collaged newspaper crime stories and images of Black and white couples together with captions like "mixing means racial suicide," and "their parents didn't think it could happen, either." This was the hysteria spreading in 1955, when Emmett Till was murdered.

"Their rhetoric . . . [was] really aimed at keeping people upset all the time," says Rolph. "When you first encounter something new and different that seems threatening, if it stays stable, eventually you acclimate to it," she says. "The Citizens' Council [was] committed to not allowing people to acclimate to this idea of desegregation."

Instead, in the 1970s, many of those who could afford it fled the public schools for segregation academies. A steady attrition of white students began to drain integrating districts like Hattiesburg. School integration in the United States peaked in 1988, when fewer than one-third of Black students attended schools that were 90 percent or more Black. Then, just as the Beckers began their life in Hattiesburg, the first wave of white flight began to give way to the next.

★ ★ ★ ★ ★

Instead of fleeing, the Beckers stayed in Hattiesburg's schools. When Lindsey began first grade at Thames Elementary, the schools were still under a court order to integrate. With the help of a busing program and careful attention to attendance zones, every *school,* including Thames, had a racial makeup close to that of the district. That was the standard set by the court. Yet if the district followed the letter of the law, it did little to follow the spirit of it; few individual *classrooms* met the court's standard. Then, in 1997, the courts declared that the district was "unitary" and released it from oversight. The district had proven it was desegregated. Now administrators could assign students to schools however they liked.

In the fall of 1999, Hattiesburg's public schools ended the busing program that had ensured that each school in the district was integrated. In its place, the district adopted a "neighborhood schools" model, assigning students to the school closest to their home. For the Beckers, this meant their children stayed at Thames. This was a relief for Rosie, who had been observing the differences among schools as she became more familiar with them. "I was glad we ended up at Thames and not some of the other schools, because some of the other schools really were awful," Rosie told me. If they had landed at any other school, says Rosie, "We would've moved. I would have made sure that happened."

While "neighborhood schools" can sound innocuous, it began as an anti-integration term, deployed by white parents trying to prevent school desegregation, says historian Matthew Delmont, whose book *Why Busing Failed* tracks battles over school integration from mid-century through the 1970s. The term first entered broad public use after white parents in Glendale-Ridgewood, Queens, objected to the prospect of students from Bedford-Stuyvesant, Brooklyn—a Black neighborhood—being bused to their schools in order to relieve overcrowding. "The white parents started saying they want to protect their 'neighborhood schools' and that they were opposed to 'forced busing,'" says Delmont; the terms were "two sides of the same coin." Neither term addressed the problem that civil rights activists had hoped *Brown* would address: the concentration of public education spending on white students at the expense of Black students, a practice driven as much by housing segregation—itself fueled by private practice and public policy—as by Jim Crow laws.

When Hattiesburg schools returned to a neighborhood assignment model, the demographics of each elementary shifted. Instead of approaching the racial composition of the *district* overall—about 15 percent white and 84 percent Black—each school now reflected the race and class makeup of the public school students who remained nearby. Under the court-approved integration plan, every elementary had been around 10 to 20 percent white—just like the district overall. When neighborhood schools opened in 1999, more than three-quarters of the district's white students were clustered in just two schools: Woodley and Thames. Indeed, in a district with 306 white elementary kids to spread across six schools, more than half of them, 173 students, attended Thames.*

That was the year when Lindsey walked into her math class and saw, for the first time in her life as a student, mostly white faces. Her homeroom that year remained mostly Black, as did most homerooms at the school; the school was still only one-third white, after all. It was only Lindsey's math class, an advanced one, that seemed so much whiter. But as time went on, Rosie says, the pattern was clear: "The white kids would end up in all the smart classes. There'd be Black kids there, too, but almost every white kid would [be in the advanced classes]."

Indeed, as school administrators at the time remember it, Thames was considered the best elementary—and was particularly prized by affluent white parents, wherever they lived. A former Thames principal and assistant principal tell me they remember a district practice in the 2000s called a "special visa," granting students permission to attend schools outside of their neighborhood. The district administrator who managed attendance zones in that era remembered the "special visa," too. These people remembered it as an informal policy—openly discussed but never codified as a written rule—that affluent white families living in the city's historic district used in order to send their children to Thames. The superintendent and assistant superintendent at the time,

---

* The reemergence of effectively all-Black schools was no surprise to the district. Under integration, white students made up between 9 and 19 percent of the students at each of its six elementaries. According to articles published in the *Hattiesburg American* at the time, when the district announced its plan to return to neighborhood schools in 1998, administrators expected the share of white students at three of the city's six elementaries to drop to between 1 and 4 percent. White enrollment at Woodley was expected to jump to 21 percent, and to 35 percent at Thames. The district also converted one elementary into a junior high, which it expected to be 2 percent white under the neighborhood schools model.

who would have been privy to—and, ultimately accountable for—those visas, tell me they do not remember the practice in that way, or by that name.

At Thames, seeing white kids so heavily represented in advanced classes made a certain kind of sense to both Rosie and Lewis. So many of the town's white professionals—doctors at the medical center and clinic, professors at the universities—lived near Thames. They had good jobs, which made it easier for them to take the time to be involved with their kids. No wonder so many white kids wound up in the advanced classes, they thought; no wonder all four of theirs did. It did not occur to them, as it would not occur to many parents, to wonder whether—maybe—their children had been given something they might not deserve.

* * * * *

Rosie and Lewis hadn't known about Reach, Hattiesburg's gifted and talented program, before their children started school. Although a 1989 state law required every district to provide classes for "gifted" youth in grades two through six, Hattiesburg had introduced a program in 1986, in the midst of consent decree battles to integrate the district. When the Beckers registered Lindsey for first grade—they'd paid for her to attend a Montessori kindergarten—the school had tested her abilities as a matter of course. They were happy with the assessment that came back: Lindsey was gifted.

As each of their children entered school, the Beckers hoped for the same designation for each of their children. For children who'd started kindergarten at Thames, getting into Reach required a referral. Anyone could suggest one: a parent, a teacher, a counselor, the child themself. The Beckers were so happy with Thames that they skipped Montessori for the rest of their children, sending them to kindergarten at the public school. Rosie tells me she did not make referrals for Lindsey's brothers and sister—but she might have if the same news hadn't come back about all three: Martin was gifted like Lindsey, and so was Isaac, and so was Maryann.

For the gifted and talented students at Thames, classes worked a little differently than for regular students. Lindsey remembers getting called out of class several times a week to work with a teacher who specialized in working with gifted and talented students. The lessons, according to program paperwork, were intended to boost creative thinking and "meta-cognition," the ability to deconstruct one's own thought processes.

By their very nature, gifted and talented programs divide students into those who deserve extra attention—the "gifted"—and those who do not: everyone else.* Few are found to deserve that attention—and the likelihood that a student will be found "gifted," and gain access to additional educational resources, differs dramatically by race. In the 2000s, the share of all white students in gifted and talented programs was around 8 percent, while the share of all Black students did not exceed 4 percent. A 2016 study found that the odds of a white student being assigned to gifted and talented classes was triple that of Black students; other studies have documented similar trends.

In a district that was more than 80 percent Black, only one part of the schools was consistently whiter than the district as a whole: the gifted and talented programs. This was particularly true at Thames, which ran the district's largest elementary gifted and talented program and, by 2002, taught two-thirds of the district's white elementary students. At Thames, 41 percent of its white students were found to be gifted and talented, according to state records. That was more than five times the national average for whites and nearly triple the share of Black students designated gifted at the school. The district's funneling of resources to white students in this way seems to have intensified in the upper grades. By the time Maryann, the youngest Becker child, started classes at the high school, more than 40 percent of white students there took AP classes—compared to fewer than 4 percent of Black students.

It is difficult to see how that lopsided support for white students could happen by accident. It is easier to see how the politics of desegregation

---

* "Gifted education" was popularized in 1916 by Stanford University psychologist Lewis Terman. He was an advocate of eugenics, a pseudoscientific movement whose adherents—including, later, Adolf Hitler—believed, in part, that differences in intelligence and other traits could be traced to race and nationality.

kept district leaders from addressing it. As white flight intensified under the integration orders in the 1980s, the district doubled down on quality of education to keep whites from leaving the district: gifted and talented programs, a string orchestra, speech and debate, theater programs. "We tried to make our district's curriculum the best in the area, so the only reason you would have to not go there would be maybe you didn't like the demographics," says Gordon Walker, the superintendent who oversaw the district during the years of court-ordered integration.

After speaking with Walker and other administrators, and reading news accounts, I got the sense that the district had made a certain kind of peace with the demands of white parents: If white parents insisted—subtly or otherwise—that their children were smarter than Black children, and if they insisted on access to specialized resources in order to stay, well, that was better than the district losing them. The district could still afford it then; stable real estate values, combined with a vibrant downtown commercial district, gave the schools sufficient tax revenue to pay for the extras.

Offering more educational opportunities did not persuade many white families to stay. Indeed, white enrollment in Hattiesburg schools continued to drop. But it persuaded the Beckers.

* * * * *

In high school, Lindsey dug into speech and debate, as well as her studies. Inspired by the promise of scholarship money, she competed in the local Junior Miss pageant, winning first runner-up her junior year. She had a trim figure and her mother's pale eyes and dark hair, and a natural competitive drive, preparing for debates on weekends instead of goofing off. She made all As with ease, ranking in the top ten of her class. More than once, her sister, Maryann, referred to Lindsey, in a way more admiring than resentful, as "the golden child."

Lindsey had friends at school, from classes and the speech and debate team, but those relationships stopped at school. She socialized more with friends from her church, which was substantially integrated, and from a junior sorority, which was not. In middle school, the sorority was called the Independent Club of Hattiesburg; at the high school, it was called "Deb," a residual term from the days of debutante balls. As Lindsey remembers it, by the time she joined Deb, it had become a way to enjoy school dances and other purported rites of American teenagedom she'd watched in movies.

Partly this was her own inclination toward the conventions of the middle class, but it was shaped by the school system, too. Tracy Williams, a former principal at Thames who'd grown up in the district herself, told me that Hattiesburg's high school, like many schools in the South, initially suspended dances in 1972, when the high school integrated. Lindsey remembers the high school putting on a prom, but none of the other dances, like homecoming and winter formals. Lindsey wanted those "typical" high school experiences, and ICH and Deb offered them. She was grateful for that. She also noticed that both groups were overwhelmingly—if not only—white.

The sorority drew most of its members from the private schools, and this meant that Lindsey had a circle of friends from families wealthier than her own. As a teenager, she noticed how her friends wore UGGs and North Face windbreakers to fend off the chill in winter, while she had off-brand versions. She went to sorority meetings at other girls' homes, which were usually bigger and newer than her family's; sometime they were grand, restored Victorians in the historic district. If she'd been asked to host a meeting, she says, she would have hesitated, worried about how the girls would judge her family's cluttered 1970s ranch.

The comparisons felt endless: Her friends' families flew to Disney World for spring break; her parents drove the family van to a cheap motel outside Six Flags Over Georgia. Many of her friends got cars as gifts from their parents, some of them brand-new; her parents split the cost of a $2,000 overhauled "junker" with her—and pranked her by saying, inaccurately, that the backseat was upholstered in orange.

Lindsey remembers her friends from Deb, many of whom went to Hattiesburg's private schools, and church, where most of the kids went to Oak Grove schools, telling her what they thought about Hattiesburg's public schools—especially the high school. They said Hattiesburg was the dangerous school. That drugs were rampant. That there were no school dances because of the threat of violence. One year, at the annual football game between Oak Grove and Hattiesburg, Oak Grove visibly amped up its security. "They felt like they weren't safe, which I thought was so stupid and offensive," Lindsey told me. When other kids talked about Hattiesburg as a school with a drug problem, she had a ready reply: "You may have some kids [at Hattiesburg] who, like, smoke weed, but the rich kids at Oak Grove were blowing coke and worse," she says. "I'd kind of shrug it off as 'Your school's not any better. You have your own problems.'"

Lindsey's friends were repeating a long-documented habit of white Americans to equate Black youth with crime and violence. There is no evidence that Hattiesburg was particularly violent in those years; in 2000, the city's violent crime rate was noticeably lower than that of the state and nation. It also suggests, I think, that her friends equated their own white, rural school with safety. Given Mississippi's history of racial violence and lynchings, it would have been harder for Black people to see those schools the same way.

Even so, Oak Grove began to draw more Black families in the 2000s. In 1990, Oak Grove schools had been 7 percent Black. By 2010, Black students made up one-third of Oak Grove's enrollment. Some of these families were new to the area, but some of them were middle-class Hattiesburgers who noticed city schools' struggles and wanted more for their kids. Felicia Johnson, a Black educator who was an elementary principal in Hattiesburg during the early 2000s, was one of them.

Johnson told me she moved to Oak Grove in 2006, as soon as she decided to finish out her term as principal. When Hattiesburg's superintendent heard Johnson was leaving, she called to object. She was offended that a principal was taking her kids out of the district in which she still taught, says Johnson. "It sounds horrible," she told me more than fifteen years later. "[But] my kids are the first thing that God gave me to steward. And I wanted to make sure that they had every opportunity," she said.

It wasn't until the early 2010s, as Maryann neared the end of high school, that any of the Beckers had any reason to wonder if they should have left the district, too.

* * * * *

Maryann was the last Becker kid to go through Hattiesburg schools, and in many ways she followed in her siblings' footsteps. She did speech and debate like Lindsey and her brother Isaac; one of her monologue performances put her into national rankings. She did strings, like Isaac and Martin, her other brother, had. And she picked up volleyball and soccer, less out of passion for athletics than a way to stay busy with her friends.

Still, Maryann was living in a social world that was far less white than the one her siblings—especially Lindsey—had come up in. When Lindsey started ninth grade, the student body was about 13 percent white, making white students a small but significant share of the population. By the time Maryann graduated from the high school, white students made up just 3.5 percent of the school. Maryann was one of two white girls enrolled in her grade.

The social world that Lindsey had embraced, albeit with some hesitation, felt unbearable to Maryann. She tried joining the junior high sorority, and noticed the same class differences as Lindsey had. When there was a semiformal dance with the theme "fictional characters," Maryann dressed as Nancy Drew, in a pleated skirt and blouse, carrying a magnifying glass from a thrift store, her hair in pigtails. She remembers feeling embarrassingly underdressed; a girl in a silver prom dress said she was Cinderella, while one in a red ball gown declared herself Pocahontas. "Every time I went to any meeting, every time I went to any formal, I felt [like] I could not connect to these humans in front of me," says Maryann. "I was the only one from Hattiesburg. We just didn't have similar interests."

Her understanding of race was different, too. By the time Maryann was a teenager, there were no longer enough white students in the Hattiesburg schools to dominate anything—not even the advanced classes into which she'd been placed. Maryann's best friend was Black; so was her boyfriend; so were nearly all the other kids in strings, speech and debate, and the sports teams. Whatever prejudices Maryann may have held, she could not have survived in school if she had clung to them. And she was a sensitive-enough kid that she didn't just resist her own biases; she learned to spot them in others. This made it harder for her to relate to most of the white girls her age.

Maryann struggled to pinpoint the disconnect at first. When she first joined ICH, in junior high, she'd attributed her discomfort to class and social awkwardness. When the spring casual dance came up, she invited her boyfriend Bobby, who was Black, to come as her date. The couple spent the entire dance alone together, ignored by the other kids. At some point in the dance, likely when Bobby was using the restroom, a group of girls approached her. Maryann could tell that they were trying to include her. It went sideways when they began to speak. "What they really did was just ask me, 'So, like, what's it like dating a black guy?'" says Maryann.

She remembers hedging politely in response, saying something like, "*Yeah, it's, you know, it's just like dating anyone else.*" An uncomfortable tension grew and the other girls excused themselves. Maryann told Bobby about the exchange, and apologized profusely for having taken him to the dance. "I was like, 'Uh, [I'm] sorry. I just didn't want to be alone,'" says Maryann, who was embarrassed by her own cluelessness. She remembers being more upset by it than Bobby, who had not been clueless at all. He told her it wasn't that bad. He'd experienced worse.

As Maryann got older, she got better at spotting and refuting the racist things other white kids said to her. She met them at church, at debate competitions, at soccer matches. And they always said the same, coded things, as if drawn from a script: "We were the dumb school, we're the poor kids, we're the ones that don't care at all about our education. We don't want to do better," Maryann says. The same stories about violence and gangs that Lindsey had heard persisted, too.

The worst, for Maryann, was when other white kids made vague, racist pronouncements about her school. "They always use that stupid word, 'dark,' and it pissed me off," she says.

She learned to respond with a feigned obliviousness: "Like, I don't get it. What do you mean? That side of Hattiesburg is darker . . . Is the sun setting? I just don't understand," she says. "It's a 'little too dark' for your taste? I mean, I don't know. I like the gray walls at the school. I really like that deep gray color; I think it's nice." Once, she says, a boy from church called Hattiesburg the "shadow realm"—a reference, she knew, to the Nintendo game, *Legend of Zelda*. "I was like, 'That can go back into video games,'" she says.

Maryann, Lindsey, and their parents all speak so affectionately of Hattiesburg that it would be easy to write off other whites' disparagement of it as nothing more than personal prejudice. It would be easy to stop short and not look at the ways those prejudices, and the flight they had spurred, had begun to weaken the education Hattiesburg schools could offer. It would be easy to ignore what Maryann came to learn firsthand: how poorly Hattiesburg was preparing most of its students for college.

★ ★ ★ ★ ★

The first time Maryann really wondered if she was getting a good education at Hattiesburg High came in the spring of her senior year. She had thought about transferring to a school with a better reputation after tenth grade, but as she and her parents compared Hattiesburg to Oak Grove and even to the Mississippi School of the Arts, they had felt drawn back to Hattiesburg. Oak Grove was massive; it'd be so easy to get lost there. And it felt unfair to take a limited spot at the performing arts school when Hattiesburg already had such a strong program. And Maryann was already thriving there, excelling at speech and debate, and among the top students in her class.

Indeed, Maryann's prospects for college looked good. With the help of tutors her parents paid for, Maryann had slowly raised her ACT score. Her first score had been 23, putting her in the 68th percentile, and just slightly above the average for white students. By the sixth and final time Maryann took the test, her score had climbed to 28, ranking her in the 90th percentile nationwide. Most high school students at Hattiesburg, where 89 percent qualified for free or reduced lunch in 2012 when Maryann was graduating, did not have the economic padding that allowed Maryann's parents to spend so freely on the test.

The Beckers understood how to use a little strategic spending to boost their kids' likelihood of staying in the middle class. Spending hundreds of dollars to boost their children's test scores was a work-around to avoid the declining quality of public education. They spent the money because they knew the public schools were unlikely to prepare them well for college aptitude tests—and spending money on test prep was far cheaper than private school. This was especially true for Rosie, who'd grown up with educated parents, including a preacher mother, and gone to a liberal arts college in the 1970s because of a tuition discount for the children of clergy. She now worked as an accountant. Because the Beckers had both material resources and a familiarity with the path to the middle class, their daughter's score went from a respectable one to one that outranked 90 percent of students nationwide. This is a significant jump in the competitive landscape of college admissions

As much as the Beckers loved Hattiesburg's schools, even they had to admit there had been worrying signs about school quality in Maryann's last couple years. The yearbook stopped publishing. Classrooms didn't have enough desks, so teachers took to pushing any unoccupied ones into the hall between periods so others could grab them. And there was the semester when Maryann's schedule had forced her into a regular biology class instead of the advanced one; she remembers the teacher opening the semester by telling the students he believed in creation, not evolution, and would be teaching them the latter only because it was required—not because it was right. Still, for Maryann, it was a government test that would have earned her credits from the local college that really made her wonder about what kind of education she was really getting.

In the spring of Maryann's senior year, she and a few dozen other students filed into the "dome," an old gym repurposed for classes that perpetually smelled of stale sweat. They put their book bags on the floor along the perimeter and climbed onto the benches of lunch tables that had been wheeled in. Cardboard dividers kept the students from being able to see each other's test booklets and answer sheets. The proctor gave the signal, and there was a rustling across the room as students opened their test booklets.

A mix of anxiety and dread began to settle over the room, pages turning at an unusual pace. Maryann found herself looking up, making eye contact with her best friend, Ashley, across the room, as if to say, *Is this really happening?*

Maryann paged through the booklet more rapidly as she panicked. The government class, she and Ashley remember, was some kind of partnership with a local college—something for which they could get college credit. But the test before them asked about history and policy and theories Maryann had never heard of; she didn't know anything on the test. As she looked around, she realized nobody else did, either. Slowly, students began to put down their pencils and walk out. Soon, only a handful remained.

"Almost everyone walked out," Maryann said. "They started reading some of the questions and they were like, 'Nope, I don't know any of this.' I mean, I was even sitting there like: 'Mr. Fairchild didn't teach us anything.' Like: 'We watched movies.'" Instead of lessons about the Vietnam War, she says, they watched *Apocalypse Now*. Maryann grimaced when she talked about it. The same teacher had called her "Smurfette"—because she was the only blond white girl in her grade. Maryann remembers only a few students, including herself, even finishing the test. Nobody, as Maryann remembers it, passed.

Ashley remembers the test much as Maryann does; it left her wondering what the teachers thought of their students. The class, she said, was "just thrown together. I don't know if maybe they did care or if they didn't care. . . . But it wasn't a good experience at all. It was just a waste of time."

In some ways the test didn't matter for Maryann. She already had a debate scholarship to a small college in Minnesota; the next step in her future was set. A test wouldn't change that. But, in other ways, the test did matter, because it made Maryann question her school. It marked the first time Maryann really wondered if her school was as good as she thought.

* * * * *

The Beckers felt comfortable covering modest and incidental expenses for all four kids—but they didn't feel prepared to commit to college tuition for them. They could pay for ACT tutors, hoping to increase their kids' chances of winning not only admission but *scholarships*. They could pay for half of a car for each child, so that they would have the ability to find paid work of their own—and, importantly, to relieve their parents of the duty of transport. The same logic caused them to pay for the kids' car insurance and cell phone bills—at least until each kid got a job after college. When Lindsey had a car accident that damaged both her car and the laptop her parents had given her as a present, for instance, the insurance kicked in to cover the repairs. This let her focus on her studies, rather than manage the debt she'd have incurred by paying for the repairs herself.

Rosie had started preparing her children for college early—and with a rigor that is rare. As each child approached the end of high school, Rosie sat down with them in the breakfast nook under wallpaper covered in fuchsia carnations. Hunched over the kitchen table, Rosie, an accountant, talked each kid through the calculations they needed to make. Which college was the right fit for their interests—academically, but socially, too? How much would it cost? How much would they need in loans? Could they cover the rest of their costs by working and still maintain their grades? Would the degree they picked lead to a job that paid enough to cover their debt?

When Lindsey decided on a small liberal arts college in the South, she plotted her budget carefully with Rosie—whose careful planning had paid off. Lindsey's academic successes had yielded a scholarship that would cover three-quarters of her tuition, room, and board, leaving loans and work to cover everything else. Lindsey decided she could work twenty hours or so a week. She'd take out about $42,000, in loans, over four years, to cover the remaining costs.

Maryann seemed to be on the same track, winning a debate scholarship to a liberal arts college in Minnesota. She remembers that the debate team offered a small scholarship—but the team leaders had also helped her get a much larger scholarship for which she was dubiously qualified; it usually required an ACT score of 30, two points higher than Maryann's score. After counting the scholarships, Maryann and her parents needed to come up with $6,000 a year. It wasn't as cheap as community college, which Maryann had considered as a way to keep costs down, but it felt affordable.

Maryann was the last child the Beckers had to worry about shepherding into adulthood. Martin and Lindsey had both gotten enough scholarships to be able to afford their college degrees without calling on their parents for tuition, and without taking on unmanageable debt. Isaac had dropped out of college after a year but had landed on his feet, working a good-paying job. If the Beckers' plan worked—and they felt confident it would—Maryann, like all their kids, would become a financially independent adult, without Rosie and Lewis having paid any tuition at all.

* * * * *

Even when their children were young, the Beckers had understood that Hattiesburg schools weren't perfect. But they also had faith, one I sometimes notice in myself and other white Americans, that things would probably turn out okay. In any event, most of their children's education had been in a district that remained strong—and, optimistically, believed it might annex adjoining county land, bringing the students and tax revenues that had fled the district back within its bounds. When the annexation failed, all of Hattiesburg's students paid a price for it.

Between the school year ending in 2012, when the state introduced letter grades to rank schools and districts, and the year ending in 2016, Hattiesburg's schools floundered. In 2012, with 4,600 students enrolled, the district was graded as a C. In 2016, it dropped to a D, where it stayed until the 2020 pandemic paused rankings. The high school fared even worse. Its ranking began in 2012 as a D and dropped to an F by 2018.* Thousands of students stayed in the district as it floundered, their lives and futures shaped by the lessons they learned. More than 90 percent of those students were Black, and nearly all of them came from low-income homes. These numbers do not reflect Hattiesburg's population as a whole. In 2020, Hattiesburg's population was 54.6 percent Black and 39.1 percent white, with a poverty rate of 32.0 percent.

The Becker girls, in attending Hattiesburg, were extraordinarily unusual. During their school years, less than 1 percent of white students in America attended a school that, like Hattiesburg, was 90 percent or more Black. Having low-income classmates—whatever their racial demographics—is far less likely for white students than for Black students. Civil rights experts estimate that the average white kid goes to a school that is 40 percent low-income, while the average Black student goes to a school that is 68 percent low-income. And when those white students enter the competitive world of college admissions, their education at a poor, Black public school can even become an advantage, marking them as unusual— while a Black student from Hattiebsurg, even with stunning grades, would struggle to be seen as such.

Scholars have several phrases for the two prongs of school segregation: "racial economic segregation" is one; "double segregation" is another. Double segregation can lock students out of the stability that comes with a middle-class job in several ways. For one, researchers have found that racial economic segregation largely explains the fact that white student achievement grows much faster between third and eighth grade than does the achievement of Black students. For another, achieving at least a stable middle-class income in America—something far more people achieved

---

* According to Mississippi Department of Education data for the school year ending in 2022, the district rose to an A ranking, and the high school to a B that year.

with a free, public high school diploma, of which government covered the cost, throughout the mid- to late twentieth century—is now most readily guaranteed by a college degree. Getting into college requires good test scores and the funds to pay for it; successfully completing it is also much easier with a fluency in middle-class rules and norms.

Rosie and Lewis didn't know any of that research, of course. They were making the most of the advantages they'd been given, in hopes of helping their kids succeed. The families that came into Hattiesburg's public schools after them did the same, but they faced much starker choices: They could send their kid to a failing school, or they could leave. In the public school system, at least, there was no middle ground left.

* * * * *

Lindsey had needed to adjust to life at college, but it was nothing compared to what Maryann faced in Minnesota. Both girls attended small liberal arts schools of comparable rigor, but the similarities ended there. In college, Lindsey could fit in easily if she was willing to pass for wealthy—a trick made almost effortless by being white, feminine, and slender in a wealthy space. And while Lindsey's scholarship had required her to maintain good grades, it wasn't contingent on any other school commitments. In Minnesota, Maryann wasn't just less wealthy—she was southern. (An acquaintance, she remembers, took to adopting a singsong drawl and calling her "MISS-uh-SIP-ee MARE-ee-YANN.") What's more, the debate team expected her to pay for most of the related expenses to competitions, like suits and shoes; show up to practices; and make it to every competition. The combination was overwhelming.

She might have pulled through all of that if it hadn't been for the history class. Maryann had been silent for most of the semester, too worried about sounding stupid to participate in class. The professor had pulled her aside and encouraged her to participate more. Maryann tried to explain how unprepared she was for the rigor of the school; how she felt, deeply, that she did not belong. The instructor encouraged Maryann to contribute in class anyway; nobody was going to laugh.

The encouragement backfired. When Maryann tried to participate in class, weighing in on a myth they'd read—she thinks it was Persephone, but is not sure—she mistook a metaphor for fact. "It turns out the whole chapter is metaphorical . . . he's just trying to erase her from his mind. And it just went right over my head. I just felt so stupid," Maryann says. A decade later, it still stung. "And I was like, 'This is why I don't do this . . . I am an idiot and I do not understand like half of what I'm reading.' I will never forget that. I'll never forget how horrible that felt."

Her mental health began to suffer. Some of it was culture shock and homesickness, but those were slow-burning fires she could manage with calls home. The academic disconnect was another level, says Maryann. There was an early morning class she'd stopped attending, not because she disliked it or couldn't get up, but because she hated how stupid she felt sitting there, barely able to comprehend the discussion in class.

At the student union, she confided in one of her new friends about how stupid she felt, how completely incapable of keeping up. The term she uses to describe it today is "drowning." Before Maryann even understood what was happening, she says, her friend had brought over a crisis counselor. She ended up being admitted to a hospital for suicide watch. When she was released, Maryann was disoriented by the new medications she'd been prescribed. Still, she remembers clearly that the debate coaches were firm when she returned to practice: The incident suggested to them that she was unreliable. A letter on university letterhead arrived, says Maryann, flagging concerns about their liability.

Rosie and Lewis weren't sure how to respond. This had not been part of the plan. In any event, they believed in letting their daughter make mistakes. They told her to focus on her studies and forget about the debate team. They could help her make up that share of tuition for now, and at the end of the year they could reassess.

★ ★ ★ ★ ★

Back in 2013, when Maryann came home after her first year at college, her parents did what they could to help. Rosie dove back into her daughter's college application files and helped her apply to the University of Southern Mississippi in town. Once Maryann was accepted, Rosie helped her withdraw from the school up north. It felt as if there'd simply been a hiccup, a bad fit. Closer to home, Rosie reasoned, her daughter could get her footing again.

It did not really work out that way. Although Maryann had been a dedicated high school student, she was less directed at college and had a streak that could be interpreted as either free-spirited or impractical. She wasn't interested in the core curriculum that the university required, so she did not go to class. She didn't want to live with her parents, and she didn't like the dorms, so she moved into a shared house with friends. She completed degree requirements at a local community college, but got frustrated by bureaucracy and still hasn't technically graduated. Through all of it, she had racked up about $30,000 of debt, most of it college loans—a mix of federal loans and a private loan she says Rosie helped her secure from Wells Fargo. Even today, Maryann can't explain how the debt got so big. She's not sure. Rosie had handled all of that for her. When it became clear that the debt was too big for Maryann to get out from under it herself, Rosie and Lewis intervened in a way that few parents can. Without telling their other children, Lewis and Rosie paid it off as a Christmas gift for Maryann.

This is the kind of investment that many middle-class parents make all the time in their children: supporting a child now in hopes of putting them on the path to independence. For the Beckers, part of it was guilt, too. From their perspective, the Beckers felt they should have intervened sooner, maybe made her come home midyear. "Even though we knew what she ought to do, we didn't make her do the right things," says Rosie. "I don't know that we *should* have made her, but, anyway, we wanted to give her that gift."

It was a generous gift, but also a savvy one. In the modern United States, far fewer jobs provide the good wages and benefits that expanded the middle-class in the decades after World War II. Meanwhile, the cost of making up for the lack of those benefits has risen steeply—particularly health care costs and saving for retirement without the help of an employer. Without one of those far-rarer good jobs, staying in the middle class is *possible*, but it's akin to walking a tightrope with a long drop looming below.

If the Beckers want Maryann to stay housed and healthy in the long run, her surest bet is one of those jobs. To get one of those jobs, rather than the low-wage jobs she's held in restaurants and stores since returning to Mississippi, she'll likely need more education. And to get more education, she'll need some stability as well as more money. The Beckers' decision to pay off her debt was a bid at this last—but actually first—step, giving her the breathing room to get on her feet. In the words of policy experts, helping Maryann now would boost her chances of social mobility—of staying in, or rising above, the economic class into which she'd been born.

When I visited Maryann in 2022, she had settled in with a boyfriend who details cars. The couple splits a tiny, aging bungalow: a kitchen, a living room, and two bedrooms. Maryann had the day off from working at the retail store where Lewis, her father, is her manager.

We talked for a while about what college had been like, and where she felt she had gotten off the track her mother had so carefully laid out for her: Was it the education she'd had in Hattiesburg? The college classes she'd signed up for? The difference between Minnesota and Mississippi? "It had to do with a big ol' bundle of all of that," she said. "I definitely think if I had been academically prepared . . . I could've at least made it through the four years without withdrawing or going to the hospital," she said. "I think it played a big role."

* * * * *

When talking about their financial strategies, the first thing the Beckers talk about is their thrift and diligence. (And, often, the brash, evangelical Christian financial planning personality Dave Ramsey.) But as we talked more, Rosie pointed out an advantage that many families overlook: She and Lewis had few obligations to their own parents.

On Rosie's side, they'd had almost no obligations at all. Her mother and stepfather had both died young, excusing her from needing to care for—or financially support—them in old age. She had been estranged from her father since her parents had split up when she was ten or eleven. And because Lewis's father had had a military career, there'd been a pension and full, free medical coverage for both his parents—including several years in a Veterans Administration nursing home.

Until we spoke, Rosie and Lewis hadn't ever really thought about whether these advantages had anything to do with their race. When I asked about it, they were not defensive so much as curious: Why would that have anything to do with them?'

"If there's a certain portion of our success that is solely because we are white, there's another portion of our success [that] is because we didn't buy new cars and go into debt," says Rosie. "We didn't buy furniture on time. We didn't go to Disney World with our kids every year and then pay for it all year long on a credit card. We just didn't."

That's all true, insofar as it goes. But it is also true that Rosie and Lewis were not facing many bad choices. Even outside any help they'd gotten from their families, they'd both had good luck with jobs. Much as being white had tilted the odds in favor of Katrina's construction worker father in Pittsburgh, the Beckers' race meant they were more likely to be called for a job interview than an otherwise comparable Black person—and to be paid more if they were hired. Their financial discipline and savvy, after all, would not have been of much use if they couldn't afford basic living expenses in the first place.

★ ★ ★ ★ ★

The first time I met Rosie and Lewis, I was visiting the family farm in Simpson County with Lindsey. She'd come in from Texas, where she now lives, with her daughters. The whole family had gathered to eat and talk and see the land. There was sausage and gravy over biscuits for breakfast, followed by a walk past the goats to the fish pond. Lunch was Mississippi caviar and barbecue, then a ride in the MULE 4x4 to see the pond where all the Becker kids had learned to swim.

The farm came from Lewis's parents, who transferred about 125 acres to Lewis for ten dollars as they neared the end of their lives. Lewis and Rosie tell me they had paid his parents for fifty of those acres—$200 or $300 an acre, paid off slowly over time in an off-books, between-family deal. The Beckers tell me they do not rely on the farm for income, but it has been a welcome safety net. "It's a place to go [if] things get bad, you know," says Lewis. "I've got a place for a garden and everything like that. So it's kind of a security in that way."

Today, the Beckers use the land to generate income that can cover the cost of owning it—the taxes, keeping up buildings. There are three houses on the property, one that they keep for their own use, and two that they rent out, grossing a couple grand a month. The Beckers also regularly plant timber as crops, generating income at harvest. In 2022, they told me, they harvested eighty acres or so of hardwoods, split the profits with Lewis's two living sisters, and funneled their share into the property. This setup allows them to keep the farm as an asset, which they can use to access more money if they need it—through using the land to leverage debt, through the crops it can generate, or even by selling some of it for profit. They plan to leave it to family in the end, transferring some wealth to the next generation.

The land has been a source of stability and wealth for more than a century. At the county deeds office, the family's ties to Simpson begin appearing in the 1870s—though the family has been in the South longer than that. Marcus Becker had immigrated to the United States from Germany in the 1790s, settling first in South Carolina, then moving on to Georgia, and then, finally, landing in Mississippi by the 1810s. Their white bonus is right there in the census: By 1850, three generations of Beckers lived in Jones County, southeast of Simpson, and held twenty-six enslaved people as property among them. In 1860, the year before the Civil War broke out, their land was not worth much—adding up all of the family's holdings, the Beckers' collective land was only worth $1,550—but their personal estates, which included the people they owned, came to nearly $23,725. Their total capital, which was available to them because of their own race and the race of the people they enslaved, was the equivalent of nearly $875,000 today.

For Rosie and Lewis, owning the land feels a little like bowling with bumpers in the gutters: probably unnecessary, but a good guarantee, just in case. Rosie told me about a Ramsey Group study profiling millionaires. Most of them, she said, got there by paying off their mortgages as quickly as they could, and regularly putting funds into a retirement account. "We're millionaires now, technically—on paper," Rosie told me. She said it matter-of-factly, not bragging. "If you own more than what you owe, and the difference is over one million dollars, then . . ." She paused mid-sentence, a little reluctant to repeat the figure aloud. "It sounds really big."

This wealth ranks the Beckers solidly in America's upper class, with more wealth than 88 percent of Americans. Like most Americans, the Beckers tend to deflect attention from their advantages. Researchers have documented this habit most clearly among white people discussing racial advantage; faced with the reality of racial advantage, white people generally counter with a description of economic hardship—their own or that of their parents or grandparents. I've observed myself doing this same thing, under the same circumstances. I've noticed I also do it when I'm faced with the suggestion that I enjoy any kind of unearned benefits, or that I have advantages I do not believe I deserve.

As Rosie, Lewis, and I discussed their advantages—racial and otherwise—I asked them how they planned to handle medical care in retirement. Rosie explained, "Everyone who is sixty-five does Medicare—even if you're rich, mostly, unless you're super rich. Because, millionaires, that's not the same thing as a billionaire. You might have an eight-hundred-thousand-dollar house and two hundred thousand dollars in retirement," she said—house rich, but with much less cash to handle expenses.

The Beckers' house is not worth $800,000. In early 2023, the real estate site Zillow estimated its worth at $215,000. Indeed, it doesn't look like the home of millionaires at all. They'd gotten it for a steal; desperate sellers had taken their offer—yielding, Lewis tells me, a "disgustingly cheap price on the house." The mortgage had been, after all, just $59,400. The low price—and relatively low mortgage payments—had allowed them to funnel cash into retirement accounts. It also left them with an asset worth more than $200,000.

That increase in value is a reflection of a historic rise in home prices more than sweat equity. The Beckers have changed little about the house since moving in. The same beige carpet is underfoot in the parlor and dining room; the same wood beams, chalet-style, decorate the family room ceilings; the same dark parquet floor sits in the entryway. They'd prioritized paying it off quickly, and in 2013, both fifty-two, the Beckers owned their home outright, something less than a quarter of Americans can say.

However Rosie and Lewis feel about their wealth or its source, it has allowed them to compensate for the failures of the Hattiesburg Public Schools in the 2000s and 2010s. They could pay for ACT prep, which helped with their children's college admissions and scholarships. They paid for half of each child's first car, which also made it easier for the kids to work. They paid for each kid's insurance, cell phones, and monthly phone bills throughout college and until that kid got a real job. When Maryann began to veer away from the middle class, they had the money to keep her from experiencing the strain of poverty.

They gave her, in other words, a custom safety net. This net made up for low wages in restaurant jobs, and put limits on the student debt that entering the middle class practically requires. And it had saved her the trouble of learning how to use public aid at all. Hard work and financial prudence were the tools they used to weave it, but white advantage was the material of which it was made.

5

MY PARENTS AS PARENTS

SOUTHEAST MICHIGAN

1974–1983

My parents began acquiring the trappings of a middle-class, midwestern family. They adopted a puppy, a black Lab mutt, and named him Barcelona Stroh's, commemorating their honeymoon and my father's favorite beer. At first, they lived in low-income housing, proving how little they earned to qualify. My father had worked for a moving company in college, but after the wedding he got a job selling shoes at Baker Shoes, a chain store. My mother worked as a secretary. It's hard to say how much they earned; the early years of a salesperson's career often pay little, and my mother would have been inexperienced, too. My best guess, based on labor department estimates, is they would have been earning around $10,000 or so a year—an amount that would have put them in the lower-middle class. After my father got promoted to management at a store outside Detroit, they bought their first home.

My parents did not have money for a down payment. So, Grandpa Mac loaned them money for one, interest free; my father remembers it being about $8,000. He could do this because he was a banker: He earned a generous living, knew how to invest, and, crucially, owned his home. He had these things because he was white, and so my parents had their home because of that, too.

Their three-bedroom bungalow cost $26,500 and landed them in Oak Park, a suburb across Detroit's northern border.* They liked that the new house was convenient, cutting my father's commute to ten minutes. But it was also small and out-of-date; they planned to make improvements themselves, trading sweat equity for financial gain. My parents had heard from friends that the schools there were good. They liked, too, that it was considered diverse.

This diversity was mostly of religious and ethnic backgrounds, not of race. My parents' new subdivision, built in the early 1950s after covenants had become unenforceable, had never formally barred Black, immigrant, or Jewish people from living there. Oak Park was home to a large Jewish community and Middle Eastern immigrants, many of them Christian Iraqis. Still, both groups usually checked off "white" in the census. In 1970, Oak Park was 99 percent white. Over the next decade, whites born in the United States began to leave, while more Black families arrived and immigrant families stayed.

My father tells me moving to Oak Park was mostly a practical decision based on a coworker's recommendation. "He said, 'You should look in Oak Park: The taxes are good. Nice houses. You should look,'" says my father. "And so, we started looking for a house, and we found one." That, my father says, is all there was to it.

★ ★ ★ ★ ★

The racial and ethnic changes emerging in Oak Park were taking place all over the country. The passage of the Fair Housing Act in 1968 and the Equal Credit Opportunity and Community Reinvestment Acts in the 1970s changed housing discrimination, especially in the North. Once formal discrimination became illegal, Black people with means began to

---

* According to the Bureau of Labor Statistics, $26,500 in 1975 was equivalent to $152,169 in January 2023.

leave segregated neighborhoods in cities, seeking the better housing and schools that so many white communities had built—with government help—a generation before. Just as the barriers came down, a catch materialized: the suburban homes that had been so affordable for whites now came with a much higher price tag.

In Oak Park, just across Eight Mile Road from Detroit and with relatively affordable homes, Black residents began to arrive throughout the 1980s. While the suburb had been more than 99 percent white in 1970, by 1980 it was 86 percent white and 12 percent Black. (Over the same period, the Pontiac neighborhood my grandparents had left behind went from 1 percent Black to 25 percent Black.) Many other suburbs followed the same pattern as Oak Park, and gained Black residents. This "racial transition," to borrow the language of scholars, came from two things. One was the arrival of Black people seeking a better life. The other was white people fleeing as the Black neighbors arrived.

Often, this transition was accelerated by opportunistic Realtors and investors. If covenants had been the poster child for housing discrimination before 1948, blockbusting claimed that title after it. Both methods profited from racism. Covenants generated profit by building a fence around white communities and declaring everything inside more valuable than what lay outside. Blockbusting was different. It profited from the tensions that arrived as the fence came down.

In a classic blockbusting scenario, Realtors reached out to white residents in a mostly white neighborhood, usually once Black residents were about 15 percent of the population. The Realtor might make phone calls, or send out letters, or even knock on doors with one question in mind: Did they want to sell their house? Blockbusters would mention the changing neighborhood, imply that property values would soon drop, and say the best thing to do was to sell—quickly and cheaply. They might even offer the prospect of a cash buyer. The Realtor would then broker a sale to a speculator, who'd buy the house from the white family at a low price—then quickly sell it to an incoming Black family for a high price. In an analysis of eleven home sales to Black buyers through blockbusting in 1960s Brooklyn, nine paid significantly more than market value. Six had paid 60 to 65 percent above market value for their homes. Three paid more than double.

Blockbusting took many forms. Realtors attempting blockbusting left prominent FOR SALE signs in front of homes white people had sold long after a contract was signed. The more signs there were, the more whites would worry that they might miss the opportunity to sell before the neighborhood integrated; observers at the time called this "panic peddling." More flagrant blockbusters would pay young Black men to come into neighborhoods, walk the block, and cause minor mischief like turning over garbage cans, as researchers documented in Brooklyn.

In the end, the only people who really benefited were the brokers of the sales: "By acting on racial prejudices, the white community hurts itself economically," observed a 1971 law review article. "Blockbusting creates large profits for the broker at the expense of the panicked sellers and the desperate minority buyers," wrote the authors.

In Oak Park, blockbusting was such a problem that the city passed an ordinance in 1973 outlawing FOR SALE signs. Cities and suburbs across the country did the same, going to battle with Realtors and each other. In 1977, the Supreme Court struck down ordinances banning FOR SALE signs, holding that they violated free speech. Oak Park tried again, passing a law banning all signs; supporters of the ordinance began to float concerns about "sign pollution." *CBS Evening News* came to cover the story, highlighting the opposition led by a truculent white Realtor, Shirley Cash, who declared of city officials: "They can't make their own rules." In the end, a federal judge struck down Oak Park's rule. In the decades that followed, Oak Park's white population largely decamped. Today, the community that was 99 percent white in 1970 has become 36 percent white.

My father tells me he does not remember much about this, either. "I remember that happening, but that's about it," he says. He did not pay much attention.

★ ★ ★ ★ ★

As my parents settled into their new home, they were updating but not departing from the paths their parents had taken. I imagine they avoided noticing this similarity; they liked to dismiss convention and scoff at formalities. It would have been hard to ignore it, though, once children arrived. And here I came, six weeks early, jaundiced and with a thick fuzz of brown hair on my scalp.

I came home in October 1976, wrapped in a pink sweater set, still wrinkly and pinched. From the hospital in Pontiac, we stopped at Grandma Kate's, then continued to Oak Park. Our house was practical, intended for veterans starting families after World War II. An aluminum awning hovered over a front picture window. The yard held a magnolia tree that rained pink petals in the spring, but when I came home, the lawn would have been carpeted with its brown leaves, adding to those from the oaks and maples along the sidewalk. When I returned to the block in the 2010s, the street was canopied with soaring trees.

The house was laid out like a short, sideways T. The entry opened into the living room, which gave way to the dining room, then kitchen, then family room, then patio. A hallway with three bedrooms and two bathrooms branched off the dining room. In the backyard sat a small, above-ground pool, a stretch of concrete, and a shed at the driveway's end.

One of my earliest memories is in the family room, which always felt dark: brown carpet patterned with cream-colored hexagons, wood paneling, windows too high for me to see out of. I am three or four and have just had my first beesting. I am scared and crying, and my mother sits on the floor, cradling me in the watery sunlight passing through the side door. A little boy from the neighborhood, Frankie, is trying to explain, worried he will be in trouble. We were playing together in the backyard, unsupervised, when I was stung.

This is my first memory of my mother. It is as watery as the light, the focus softened by time. Still, even today, I can feel her hand gently stroking my hair; hear her speaking softly to Frankie. I remember her taking care of us.

This is the only memory I have where she is caring for me, instead of the other way around.

* * * * *

My father was earning enough in retail management that my parents decided my mother would raise me while my father worked. This echoed the way my mother's parents had raised her. But whereas my grandmother had been a motherless nineteen-year-old when she became a mother herself, my mother, like my father, had a robust social life and strong family. My parents drew on both circles for support.

This afforded my parents a degree of leisure that would have been difficult if they were farther from home or poorer. They threw parties at the house, carted me to friends' homes, and took me to the drive-in. They went on a two-week vacation, leaving me and the dog with my grandparents, who delighted in showing me off to their friends.

My parents were particularly lucky when it came to my four grandparents. Only Grandpa Don still worked, now with two decades of seniority at Ford. Both sets were happily married, relatively nearby, and financially stable, with no need for their children to support them as they aged. Decades of discrimination in employment and housing had made it easier for my grandparents to achieve this stability than if they had been Black. My grandparents' stability, in turn, freed my parents from needing to spend money on any family other than themselves.

My parents' changes to their home reflected middle-class comfort. On one wall of the living room, my mother pasted a photo mural of trees in fall, all gold leaves and black silhouettes. She added two armless chairs upholstered in an orange palm frond print. They replaced one sofa, of scratchy blue plaid, with a boxy, button-tufted blue velvet couch. In the kitchen, my father chipped tile off the wall and remudded the drywall, installed new cabinets and countertops; my mother hung wallpaper with elegant flowers in psychedelic colors.

In the backyard, my father and his friend Gene, who'd married my mother's friend Bonnie, broke up the concrete with sledgehammers and hauled it away. Then they put in soil and sod. Here, my mother could have a garden—and I could have a soft place to play with the new brother or sister set to arrive in the fall of 1978. The family was growing, and they had the resources to meet the challenge.

★ ★ ★ ★ ★

My memories of Oak Park begin after the arrival of my sisters, Johanna, who we called Jodie, and Shana, in August 1978. Because ultrasounds were not yet commonplace, and because my sisters arrived six weeks early, my parents had only learned they were expecting twins the month before. Shana was roundly built with tawny skin and thick black hair; Jodie was fine-boned and blond. But whatever variations there were between them, my sisters, like me, had my mother's eyes: so dark the pupils disappear, eyebrows slightly asymmetrical, eyes that narrow to slits when we smile.

My mother kept notes about our family in a calendar. She tracked her children's diet and weight, and the small joys of parenthood: when my sisters recognized her voice, when they began to crawl, when she found one of them, inexplicably, atop a table. She noted, too, my response to becoming a big sister. In her telling, I was enamored of my sisters and eager to help care for them, hugging them with such enthusiasm that my mother worried for their safety. There is only one note about sisterly tensions: I demanded—unsuccessfully—that my father feed me like my sisters, with a bottle.

My grandmother liked to tell a story of visiting us during this time. She walked into our kitchen to see the twins in baby bouncers on the table, my mother seated before them. I sat on my mother's lap and turned the pages of a storybook on the table as she read to me, each of her hands holding a bottle in a twin's mouth. I looked up and said hello. My mother would have smiled. She would have been glad to see her mother.

Family began to dominate my mother's life in a new way. There was no more hopping to friends' parties or taking in a movie. Instead, friends came to us. Bonnie brought clothes for my sisters, and Debbie, a childhood friend and bridesmaid, visited with her sons. My father took a new job, trading shoe sales for lawn equipment distribution. The latter offered a regular, nine-to-five schedule instead of retail's late nights. My parents pared their vacation from two weeks a year to one, and now our grandmothers cared for us at our house, instead of at theirs.

As the family grew, my parents' house sprouted shortcomings. Three bedrooms now felt too small. The yard too cramped for children to play in. The houses too close together. One afternoon, my parents sat on the patio and wondered if they had made a mistake.

My father remembers hearing "five loud, loud discussions going on, and they were every language but English." Talking about it now, he sounds bewildered by being unable to understand anything being said. "You know, the idea of having integration is great and it's not something we're against," he says. "But they ought to be able to speak English if they live here. So, we ended up moving."

My father says that one of the neighboring families was Black, and he had no problem with that. "It was language, as far as I was concerned," he says. My father said a xenophobic thing to avoid looking racist. Instead, to me, he sounds like he is probably both.

Whatever their reasons, my parents began to think about leaving Oak Park. They started looking for houses in the new year.

★ ★ ★ ★ ★

My family doesn't tell many stories of these early years, when things were good. For a long time, I believed this was because my family is not much for storytelling—my father in particular. Today, I wonder what secrets my family has chosen to keep from me. I wonder if the reason I have not heard stories of the good old days is that so few of the days were good.

There is a story that my grandmother told me, long after my mother died, that makes me wonder. As I remember my grandmother telling it, my mother arrived unannounced at her house, with my sisters and me, seeking refuge. My father had been drinking, my grandmother said, and he was stumbling around when he fell at Jodie's feet. This scared my mother. She wondered if she should leave my father.

"She came to me, with the three of you," I remember my grandmother saying. *"I told her, 'You can't stay here. You made your bed, and you're going to have to lie in it,'"* my grandmother told me. *"I couldn't fix everything for her. She needed to figure it out on her own."*

Many young marriages struggle, and three little ones would test even the strongest partnership; my grandmother knew this. And how would my mother survive if she left? That would be a mighty struggle; my grandmother knew this, too. My grandmother did not tell me if she regretted not offering the four of us refuge. I was too dumbstruck to ask.

I did not know how to tell my grandmother the empty panic I felt as she spoke. How it shocked me to learn that my father's drinking and temper were not hidden from the rest of my family. How it angered me that they knew these things, knew that it could be turned on his children, and did nothing. I listened for regret in my grandmother's voice. I heard only resignation.

My grandmother's life had taught her to endure abuse rather than challenge it. This was the lesson she passed on to my mother. Later, she would pass it on to me.

★ ★ ★ ★ ★

By the 1970s, most of my mother's family had left Pontiac, and moved to whiter communities. Grandpa Don's sister, an elementary teacher who eventually got her PhD, had moved with her husband and children to an affluent suburb nearby. Grandma Kate's sister and brothers were poorer, and several moved to neighboring Waterford Township. In 1980, that community was 97.5 percent white. Other cousins went farther, moving into the rural reaches of the county.

My family never shared the reasons for this migration with me. For a long time, it did not occur to me to ask. Because I was not taught, and I did not ask, I did not know that Pontiac had hosted one of America's most notorious battles over school integration, or that it predated the controversy in Boston by four years.

I did not know that Pontiac's schools had been segregated by neighborhood, and so by race. I did not know that its Black schools were overcrowded, with leaking roofs and rats and roaches. I did not know that its Black schools lacked chalk, pencils, and books, or that its white schools were so well supplied that a teacher who transferred between the two talked about going "from hell to heaven." I did not know that the school district acknowledged that its Black students received an inferior education, and then said it had no obligation to fix that. I did not know that the Ku Klux Klan blew up ten unoccupied school buses—an act, in today's language, of terrorism—to delay integration there. I did not learn that white mothers chained themselves to the bus depot on the first day of integrated school to protest—they said—the use of buses to transport children, or that the police association sent them $300 for the fines they incurred, or that factory workers walked off the line in solidarity with them, temporarily closing two GM plants. I did not learn that the self-proclaimed "colorblind" white housewife from Pontiac, Irene McCabe, became a national celebrity for protesting "forced busing"—and championing neighborhood schools.

I did learn, through mindless absorption, that journalists called "busing" the cause of the protests. This was an unhelpful euphemism that obscured the truth. In a congressional hearing on equal educational opportunity, Senator Walter Mondale asked Mr. Lacy of the Pontiac School Board whether "when they picket against busing, it is a certain kind of business that they have in mind . . . They direct the objection at the bus rather than, sometimes, the thing that is really bothering them." Mr. Lacy replied, "That is my personal feeling." Carole Sweeney, a Black mother in Pontiac who also testified, was more direct: "Busing is a red herring, a euphemism. My white friends at the bus depot on the first day of school were not called bus lovers. They were called n—lovers."

Because I did not know this history, I did not understand the racism that lay beneath my family's migration. I had only to ask to learn.

I asked one of my mother's bridesmaids Peggy (not her real name) about her move from Pontiac to Waterford. She told me she left Pontiac because it had gotten *"bad,"* and she and her husband wanted to live somewhere *"nice."* When I asked her what she meant by *"bad,"* she said it was *"the people."* When I asked what she meant, she mentioned people on welfare. When I commented that poor people weren't necessarily bad, she looked down and said, *"Black people."*

I also asked my mother's cousin Elaine how she ended up in Holly, my hometown. She told me that under school integration her daughter, Dawn, was assigned to a mostly Black school in Pontiac. Elaine remembers Dawn being the only white student in her teacher's class. On Sunday nights before returning to school, Dawn complained of migraine headaches. She had no friends at school, only in her neighborhood, which was white.

By then, Elaine tells me, she had left a violent husband and was a single mother. She worked morning shifts at a nonunion factory; same wages as at UAW jobs, says Elaine, and there were even benefits at first—though, over time, the company took those away, including retirement. Most of the workers were white, she remembers, and women earned less than men. Dawn spent a lot of time with a babysitter or with her mother, Eleanor. There just wasn't much time to talk to Dawn about anything—let alone why her school had changed, or how to feel about it.

And, besides, Elaine, who'd gotten married soon after high school, didn't really know what to say Dawn. As a kid, Eleanor had made Elaine send home the first Black girl she'd brought over to play, which had ended the friendship. Eleanor told her it was because of what the neighbors would think, and Elaine learned her lesson. "I still liked Black people at school," she says. "But I knew it had to stop at school."

Then there had been the uprisings—riots, the newspapers called them—down in Detroit a few years before. And those buses that got blown up in Pontiac. The one time Elaine had driven to Dawn's new elementary across town, some Black men on the corner had gestured at her at a stoplight. It scared her.

It was easier to just move away. "I thought, 'No, they're going to be moving to Waterford next,'" Elaine said. "So, I thought Holly was far enough away that they wouldn't do it. I didn't really check out the schools or anything. I just wanted to get [Dawn] out of a situation she shouldn't have had to be in."

I get stuck on this—the situation that Dawn "shouldn't have had to be in." I believe that it was hard for Dawn to be the only person of her race in a classroom. I believe Elaine thought it was harder to stay than to move. I also believe that these hard things were products of racism: Of a white child, raised in a racist family, thrown into a hotly contested integration battle without guidance or context. Of a white mother who preferred to uproot her children rather than teach her children—and, likely, herself— how to live as equals with Black people in all spheres of life. I feel for my cousins, who are loving people and who had so few tools to see the world in any other way. That does not make their actions any less racist.

Black families were in a situation they shouldn't have had to be in, too: white adults blocking buses, shouting slurs, and sometimes hurling rocks at them. Black parents had been paying taxes into the school system, and their children got little in return. That was hard, too.

White people like my family did not see it this way. We saw only the costs. The bombings, the pickets, the angry parents. The mess of it all. We wondered: *Why should we have to share?* If we had the option to move— something that, in this country, people who are white have had more access to than people who are Black—why put up with it? So, we did a selfish, racist thing: We left.

* * * * *

It took my parents a couple of years to sell the bungalow in Oak Park. After a few false starts, they found a Colonial in Rose Township, five miles outside of Holly. The property was a half-mile from a farmhouse the Black Legion had burned down five decades earlier, but they did not know this. They saw the rolling lot, the tree-lined dirt road, and barns leaning along the roadside. They imagined us under open sky, swimming in lakes, growing a garden. They saw the quaint downtown, heard about the downtown Christmas festival. They were smitten.

Because my parents were born early in the baby boom, the bulk of their generation—and its consumer demand—followed behind them. By the time they sold their first home in 1981, there were fewer homes to sell than middle-class people to buy them. Home prices, pushed even higher by inflation, had skyrocketed. A Black couple from Detroit paid $48,900 for the house my parents had bought for $26,500 six years earlier. These profits meant my parents could repay my grandfather for their first down payment, and get an $81,000 mortgage for their new house.

They bought a Chevy van, striped chocolate brown and vanilla, and got ready to cart us long distances. We moved in June, and my mother enrolled me in Holly Schools.

★ ★ ★ ★ ★

Today, my father tells me that he didn't really think about the schools in Oak Park—not when they moved there, and not even when they left. He tells me, instead, that he had heard Holly schools were "good," but this was based on word of mouth. If he'd gone looking for test scores or other data, there was little to find. In the 1980s, Michigan tested students every three years to check for basic skills, and school scores were inaccessible apart from mundane newspaper reports. Parents without the drive—or time—to pay more attention were left with the stories they passed on to each other, in Michigan and elsewhere. Like any gossip, school reputations reflected the experiences and prejudices of those doing the passing.

By the time my parents were angling to sell the Oak Park house, they would have realized their house was zoned into the schools for Ferndale, the next suburb east.* Ferndale had less money than Oak Park, where the schools benefited from the taxes at a busy shopping mall in its bounds. Ferndale's schools spent about one-third less than Oak Park did on each student. Still, Ferndale's spending ranked it in the top quintile of schools statewide. The earliest test scores I can find for Ferndale, from the year we left, rank around the state average.

I'd grown up thinking that Holly's schools had lured my parents, but there was little to recommend the district in the early 1980s. Student test

---

* In 2023, my father told me that he did not know that the house, which is only a half-block within the Ferndale Schools boundary, was not in Oak Park Schools.

scores were average, and the schools were in dire financial straits. In 1981, the year we moved, Holly's spending per student ranked 366th out of 529 districts in the state. The next year, the high school's accreditation status was at risk because—among other shortcomings—it had shortened school days to five hours instead of six due to lack of funds. The superintendent of Holly Schools told the local paper that "if your [sic] situated in a really poor area [accreditation] may just be out of reach." My elementary principal says the district had "exceptional teachers who did an awful lot with many fewer resources than teachers in other districts." Still, you wouldn't have moved there for the public education.

As a teenager, I remember talking with my father about why we had moved. Back then, he talked only about the schools. I remember him saying that if we'd stayed in Oak Park, he would have had to pay for private school. Today, he says he does not remember anything so specific. He just remembers worrying that "the schools were becoming less and less of a priority in the city." This concern is too vague to refute or deny.

Many white parents in the Ferndale district, however, had a more specific concern back then. Starting in 1968, this concern had showed up regularly on the front pages of newspapers and in federal court transcripts. It is the story of Ferndale Schools, the first northern school district to be sued by the federal government, and to lose federal education funding, for failing to desegregate its elementary schools.

My father tells me he never heard about that, either.

* * * * *

Ferndale resisted integration with the same strategies used by schools in the South, as if from a playbook. When federal officials first filed a complaint against Ferndale Schools in 1969, the school board's attorney, Burton R. Shifman, objected and did nothing to address the concern. "Ferndale has never . . . segregated its pupils by race," he wrote; the district was colorblind. By then officials had documented that 262 of the district's 278 Black elementary students attended Ulysses S. Grant Elementary School, with almost no white classmates—in a district with 3,500 elementary students overall. The schools, Shifman wrote, echoing the Pontiac School Board, had not caused the problem; it was the fault of housing practices. Why would they have to fix a problem they had not caused? Attorneys were called. Appeals were filed.

In 1973, the case wound up in the Supreme Court. The district lost its appeal. This left the district with two options: integrate or lose federal funding. The district chose the latter. In 1974, Ferndale officials adopted the equivalent of "freedom of choice" and invited white families to voluntarily send their children to Grant Elementary. White parents did not take them up on the offer. The school remained overwhelmingly Black. That August, Congress passed the Equal Educational Opportunity Act, and the Department of Justice sued Ferndale under the new law. Students who had been in kindergarten when the case began were now in sixth grade.

In fall 1975, Ferndale opened a magnet school program within Grant, the Black school. The magnet program brought 200 students to the school—31 Black, 169 white—but kept them segregated in nearly all-white classes, on a separate floor and with a separate lunch from the 230 other students, all Black, in the traditional school. In response, the Department of Justice filed suit. The DOJ's attorney, Thomas Keeling, noted that program would not be acceptable unless it "in fact desegregate[s] the Grant school." The new program, he said, "clearly does not do that." Judge Cornelia Kennedy, a Nixon appointee to the United States District Court for the Eastern District of Michigan, rejected the case. She argued that neither the Department of Justice nor the Department of Health, Education, and Welfare had proper standing for the suit. The DOJ appealed to the Sixth Circuit Court of Appeals.

The schools stayed in limbo as the case went through the courts. The Grant school had been overcrowded since the 1940s, and the district continued to refuse to send Black children to empty desks in white schools. Instead, classes at Grant were taught in shifts, its regular Black students forced to make do with half-days of education while the case moved forward. Federal funding continued to be withheld. In 1978, Judge Kennedy held that leaving Black students to half-days did not affect their education. In 1980, the Sixth Circuit overturned her decision, saying it found "no logic at all" in her ruling. The 1969 kindergarteners were now in eleventh grade.

In the summer of 1980, Ferndale Schools began to offer earnest proposals for integrating its elementaries. The first plan required Black students to be bused to white schools. By then, Kennedy had left that bench, and the judge who took her place, Horace Gilmore, rejected that plan. He also rejected the second, which required Black students to be bused across the district until sixth grade, at which point all sixth graders would take classes at Grant. "The Constitution will not tolerate a desegregation plan that places a five-to-one burden on black students as compared to white students," wrote Gilmore. That fall, the judge approved Ferndale's third proposal, which combined three of the district's elementary schools so that students attended school with all the other kids in their grade. (Structurally, this was similar to how Hattiesburg public schools integrated their elementaries six years later.) In January 1981, with the 1969 kindergarteners now seniors in high school, Ferndale integrated its elementary schools.

It had been nearly twelve years since the original complaint had been filed. Journalists estimated that the district had gone without $2 million in funding to resist integration. In June 1981, the kindergarteners of 1969 graduated high school from a district that had become fully integrated. The *Detroit Free Press* declared: "Busing Gets an A: Integration Is a Success in Ferndale." If we had stayed in my parents' first home, I would have started kindergarten in Ferndale's integrated schools.

We moved to Holly instead.

★ ★ ★ ★ ★

On June 13, 1981, the day after I graduated nursery school, my parents followed an orange moving truck to Rose Township. The drive took nearly an hour. Our house was deep into Oakland County, the roads narrowing from interstate to four-lane highway to two-lane blacktop to gravel.

The truck turned onto our road, West Rose Center, and coasted down a spit of asphalt, past a low-slung subdivision of small, modest houses, before hitting dirt. They drove past a gray shack surrounded by rusting cars up on blocks and policed by goats, between a set of cornfields, and then passed Bloom Hill Drive, a subdivision of larger, newer homes. They powered up a small, blind incline with a farmhouse at its peak. Just past the farmhouse, they turned into our driveway, a long, doublewide stretch of concrete.

The house, set back fifty feet from the road, was clad in pale yellow aluminum siding, with a brown roof and shutters. The flowerbeds were empty in front, and a small deck overlooked an acre and a half of treeless backyard. My parents also took out a $6,650 land contract for a lot beside the house, and Grandpa Mac agreed to cover its monthly payments of $70. This gave us two and a half acres, shaped like Oklahoma: a two-acre square of property with a skinny panhandle of black walnut trees and blackberry brambles at one end.*

Although the house's property backed up to the subdivision on Bloom Hill, we saw no evidence of that from the house. We saw only the farmhouse next door, and a small red barn that sheltered chickens and a lethargic gray horse named Justin. There was little noise aside from what the trees and meadows and the critters in them made. There were no streetlights or sidewalks. At night the silent dark would envelop us like a blanket. We were country people now.

* * * * *

When my family moved to Holly, we were taking part in a largely unspoken migration of white Americans, who in the 1980s began to trade integrating suburbs for whiter ones—or even for once far-flung rural towns. By the early 1990s, the interstate highway system launched under Eisenhower had completed its farthest reaches. This made it affordable for middle-income families to live in the countryside and work in a suburb.

---

* According to the Bureau of Labor Statistics, $6,650 in January 1981 was the equivalent in January 2023 of $22,868, and $70.00 the equivalent of $240.71.

The spread of the white middle class into rural areas goes by several names: "suburban fringe" is one; "sprawl" and "exurbs" are others. From 1960 to the late 2010s, fringe communities increasingly became woven into metropolitan areas. Indeed, by 2010, the majority of rural Americans lived in counties that, technically, were suburban.

Although formal rules restricting homeownership and financing to whites were gone by the 1980s, fringe communities have remained overwhelmingly white—far more than cities or even suburbs. They are also the most segregated communities in the country. A 2022 study of residential segregation found that exurbs, a designation that would include Holly, were the most segregated of any residential category. While about two-thirds of city residents are likely to live near people of another race, only about one-third of exurbanites could say the same. The trend of white isolation on the fringe is so strong that researchers noted it "raises questions about whether White populations are fleeing diversifying metro areas for outlying areas."

This migration of whites outward changed the nature of segregation. In the mid-twentieth century, segregation happened by neighborhoods *within* cities. In Oak Park, for instance, white families lived on the east side, Black families on the south, and Jewish families on the north. But whites' ongoing flight from integrated places turned segregation into a function of whole cities or suburbs.

This is what happened in Oak Park, which, by 2010, had become majority Black. Many of the whites who left landed in exurban places like Holly. When I discussed my family's move from Oak Park to Holly with Daniel Lichter, a sociologist who studies segregation, he said we were "following the racial script." That script, he said, has changed little in the forty years since my parents followed it.

And yet, my family and the white families we knew never discussed race openly. As a child, I had a vague sense that Holly was more diverse than neighboring towns. White residents seeking to refute charges of racism in the community often echoed a 1987 letter to the editor from the local paper: "For generations we have a racially mixed population with Black, White, Hispanic, Asian and others living side by side." This was not really true. Across the five townships that fed into my school district, the collective population in 1960 was 98 percent white. By 1980, the number of residents had more than doubled, going from 19,384 to 47,230—but the racial mix remained 98 percent white. I never heard white adults mention that people moving to Holly were often trying to avoid the integrating schools, in Pontiac and Flint and Detroit, despite that fact being widely understood. I never heard white adults acknowledge the longstanding presence of a Black community in Holly. I never heard white adults discuss the fact that Fenton, the next town north, was known as a "sundown town"—a place where white people felt entitled to intimidate and attack Black people who stayed there after dark.

My parents and the other white people who followed a similar path didn't need to believe that race was essential and whites were genetically superior in order to do racist things. They did not need to believe in separate schools and drinking fountains. They did not need to casually use the N-word, as Grandpa Don did, or to be so convinced of their racial superiority that they dressed in blackface for Halloween as an adult, the way my mother's brother did in 1981. To do a racist thing, all my parents had to do was look around their neighborhood and schools, see Black and immigrant people, and decide to leave as a result.

* * * * *

My parents set about making the house in Rose Township their own. My father had an hourlong commute to his offices, though mostly he drove to independent lawn and garden stores across Oakland County. This meant he had a company car, a station wagon. A bottle of mouthwash sat, perpetually, between the front seats; he used it to freshen up between sales calls. My parents did not have wealth of their own then. They were in the first years of a thirty-year mortgage, and so did not have much equity. My father's income was probably around $23,000 a year, placing us near the bottom of the middle class.

Outside of work, much of my parents' energy went into their home. My father bought a tiny tractor, and mowed down thick weeds until they

resembled a lawn. On this newly reclaimed yard, they carved out a vegetable garden, and set up a metal swing set with a slide. As children, my
sisters and I clamored to be pulled behind the tractor: in a two-wheeled
trailer, sometimes, or atop a large plastic disc.

When they weren't fixing up the house, both my parents tended to our
family. My father could be silly and warm, and I loved it when it was his turn
to help me after a bath. Sometimes, when it was time to dry my hair, he
threw a towel over my head, loose, and said, *"Where's the dog?"* I giggled and
barked as he rubbed the towel over my hair. *"I don't see the dog,"* he said. I giggled more and forgot to bark. *"I don't hear the dog,"* he said. I began barking
again, and my father began to tickle me, the towel still over my head. I was
a pile of damp giggles under the towel. I pulled the towel off my head and
looked up at him. *"Dad, it's me!"* He looked surprised: *"I was looking for you!"*

My parents' friends came to visit frequently. In summer, my parents
and their friends spent daylight hours admiring the yard and tipsily trying
and failing to set up a kid-size teepee someone had brought for us. After
the sun set over the trees, painting the sky pink and periwinkle, they lit
a towering bonfire of yard waste in the middle of the mowed weeds and
ringed it with folding lawn chairs. Sometimes, my mother teetered as she
stood, but it was easy to chalk it up to the cocktails. In the fall, we piled
into the van with friends to go to a cider mill, eat apples, and buy pump-
kins. In every photo of this time, my parents are happy and eager, laughing
and young.

By the summer of 1981, my mother began to teeter more frequently.
Her hands were stiff. She began to see double and had piercing headaches.
She saw one doctor, who ordered a CT scan, which he judged "negative;"
nothing to see here. Yet the symptoms persisted.

On Christmas afternoon, at Aunt Roberta's Christmas dinner, my
mother tried to stand up from the cream brocade sofa and could not keep
her balance. My father held her arm tightly, bearing much of her weight,
as they walked to the car. In the morning, my father drove her to the
emergency room. Doctors admitted her for observation and testing, and
sent her home on New Year's Day with a diagnosis of multiple sclerosis, a

degenerative neurological disease. She was thirty-three. My sisters were three. I was five.

I remember my father explaining this illness to me in terms I could understand. Our bodies, he said, had an electrical system that let us do things like walk and breathe and draw. Our brains were the power in the wall, the lamps our hands and our feet and our limbs. MS was a disease that attacked the cords.

I nodded and tried to be brave. When I was alone, I began to stare at my hands, wondering when and if they would start to quiver, too.

* * * * *

Sometime after my mother's MS diagnosis, my parents began to fight. I did not sleep easily, and so I listened to them raise their voices in the kitchen downstairs. I do not remember what they shouted at each other, just a volley of anger back and forth followed by quick, heavy footsteps on the stairs. Their bedroom door would shut, and silence took over. I hated it. I was scared. I wanted it to stop. I made a plan to try and stop them.

By then I was already reading, drawn to drama and simple stories I could understand, in which love and goodness battled cruelty and evil. My plan reflected the simple morals of children's stories. When my parents argued, I envisioned myself running downstairs and planting myself between them. I would yell at them to stop. They would look down at me, as if waking from a dream, and they would be saddened by the fact that their own daughter had to bring them to their senses. Then they would look at each other and remember they loved each other. They would thank me for helping them. And they would never fight again. I would save the day.

That was the idea, anyway. Instead, I remember my mother's surprised face, my father's pause midsentence, both of them shaking their heads and telling me, with frustration, to go to bed. I remember the splotchy brick-patterned linoleum, and the black mirror of the sliding door at night. But this is a fuzzy memory. The documents I can find—intermittent journaling, medical records—say nothing of this. If anything, they suggest the

fighting came later, after my mother's accident, when they would have
both been struggling to adjust to the new life emerging in its wake.

My mother was sick. My parents were fighting. I wanted to help. I
wanted to fix it.

I couldn't.

* * * * *

My mother had her accident on the way home from the grocery store. She
had wanted brownie mix, to make treats for a Valentine's Day party the
next day. Jodie fussed in the parking lot about putting on the seat belt; my
mother, worried she'd be late to meet me after school, almost relented,
but did not. It was 1984, and the rules about children and cars were lax.
My mother pulled out of the parking lot with Jodie in the front seat, and
Shana in the back. They both were wearing seat belts, though neither of
them—as per custom at the time—were in car seats.

She drove on one of the two-lane roads that cut through woodlands
and lakes and farm fields. The snow on the roofs of the trailers and trilev-
els was dingy; the season's three feet of snow had been melting under a
trace of rain. The sky was overcast, the clouds trapping heat below and
pushing the temperature up past fifty degrees. The roads were dry.

As my mother neared home, she drove north along a curve that
hugged the side of a small hill. On her left, there was a cemetery from the
1800s, flat and ringed with trees, leafless in winter. On her right, the hill
rolled down perhaps fifteen feet before flattening into meadow and creek,
cattails spiking out of the snow. In Michigan, this constitutes a view.

Not far ahead, Albert Tipolt was headed south on the same road in his
pickup. He was fifty-five, with a tenth-grade education. Like my grandfather, he worked in auto factories and served in the military. He had been
visiting a friend up north, where he'd gone through nearly a fifth of Black
Velvet whiskey the night before. He began driving home around ten thirty
that morning. He drove for an hour and stopped for a whiskey, then got
back on the freeway. He drove another hour, stopped again, drank another
whiskey. He stuck to local roads after that.

Maybe my mother was glancing at my sisters in the rearview mirror; maybe they were hungry and squabbling and she got distracted. Maybe that view down the vacant hill had caught her eye, a postcard of the rural life she had chosen. I imagine the accident as a complete surprise, an obliteration she didn't see coming. I don't want to imagine my mother's fear if she had seen Albert Tipolt's truck round the bend, cross the center line, and hit her.

There are no records of what precisely happened to the cars in the accident, no documentation of how close they came to tumbling downhill; whether they slammed together and stopped, or if the truck, a hulking 1977 Chevrolet pickup, glanced off and sent my mother's car spinning. When the vehicles came to rest, they had hit nothing of consequence but each other.

My mother's head broke through the windshield, leaving a hole ringed with shards. Airbags were not yet mandatory. If she had not worn her seat belt, she would have been thrown from the car. Glass sliced into her left eye, the bridge of her nose, her forehead, her cheek. She could not remember if she lost consciousness, but it would have been disorienting to go so quickly from running errands with her girls to bleeding in front of them, unable to open the door, unable to get to them as they cried and called for her. I do not know how long they sat there before someone found them.

Someone reported the accident. The call brought a fire truck and a volunteer ambulance, the local solution to too few people, and too little public money, to support better service. The firefighters pulled my mother from the wreck and began to assess the landscape of cuts across her face. Jodie was bleeding from her forehead, and both she and Shana had shallow, bleeding cuts across their bellies from the seat belts. The volunteers loaded the three of them, along with Tipolt, whose blood alcohol level was twice the legal limit, into the ambulance. My mother, still dazed, said she'd been going home to get me. One of the women from the volunteer ambulance drove the final five minutes to our home. Another turned on the ambulance's emergency lights and began the thirty-mile drive to the hospital in Pontiac.

When I stepped off the school bus, I saw a strange car in the drive and assumed my mother had a visitor. Before I could try the front door, I heard someone yelling my name. I turned around to see a woman, skinny and gray haired and plainly dressed, scrambling down the hill that led to our neighbor's house. Her voice was tight and breathless as she ran to me, then said my mother had been in an accident. She took me to the ambulance service's office, a refurbished farmhouse, where I stayed until family could get me.

My father and Grandma Kate went to the hospital. There, doctors ordered an X-ray of my mother's face and limbs. They referred her to a plastic surgeon to repair her beauty. They did not order a CT scan to assess her brain. It was the early 1980s, before the medical establishment had concluded, decisively, that concussions could cause serious injury.

The doctors told my mother to rest. They told my grandmother and father she would be fine. My mother and sisters had lived, and so my family thought we would be okay. We were wrong.

★ ★ ★ ★ ★

It was after dark when Grandpa Don finished his shift at Ford and retrieved me. Grandma Kate and my father were still at the hospital, so Grandpa Don took me to Big Boy for dinner, then put me to bed. In the morning, Grandma Kate took me to school and explained to my teacher why I did not have any valentines for my classmates. After school, my grandmother picked me up and took me to her house, where she cooked while we waited for my mother and sisters to come home.

I was in the kitchen when they arrived, my sisters scrambling through the door, my father and mother slowly coming in behind them. I stood in the kitchen, peering through a doorway, while my grandmother took my sisters' coats and shooed them in with me. While the adults talked, my sisters and I assessed each other in the kitchen.

"*Ow,*" Jodie said. She pointed at scabs on her forehead.

"*Tracie, look,*" said Shana. She pulled up her shirt.

Low across her belly, scabs formed rectangle outlines where the seat belt had held her in place.

"*Yeah*," said Jodie, showing her matching injury.

I stared. I did not know what to say.

Later, Jodie's refusal to buckle her seat belt became lore in our family: But for her refusal, went the story, my mother would have been safely home by the time Tipolt came around the curve, and there would have been no accident. The adults repeated this story mindlessly, used it to answer the question already haunting them: *Why did this happen?* As a child, I could not understand the adults' story as a pointless compulsion; I did not know enough to blame the adult man at fault, Albert Tipolt. Instead, I took the story we heard as truth. So did Jodie, who has been haunted by it ever since.

The adults came in from the foyer, then. The kitchen was warm and big and brightly lit, the table a white rectangle big enough for the seven of us. My mother sat down gingerly, a wall papered in pastel daisies behind her. My grandmother's china was set before her. At the setting next to her, I could see a child's cup, imprinted with SESAME STREET—my favorite. They wanted me to sit next to her.

I stared at my mother, whose face was crosshatched with black stitches. She had a two-and-a-half-inch cut across her left temple so deep it touched the skull. A two-inch cut sliced from her brow to her eyelid. The bridge of her nose was one large, stitched scab. Her left cheek was peppered with cuts. The flesh around her nose and eyes was swollen and purpled. She was looking down at her plate, her eyes unfocused.

"*Tracie, sit here,*" said my father. "*Next to Mom.*"

I balked. My grandparents had said my sisters and mother were in an accident, but they had also said they were okay. The scabby bellies and my mother's disfigured face were not okay. I did not yet understand what my grandparents had learned as white, working-class children in the Depression: "Okay" did not mean "the same," or "healthy," or "without problems." "Okay" did not mean "we can fix this." I was beginning to learn that "okay" meant "we take what we get, and we make it work."

I shook my head and ran out of the room and cowered in the family room. When my grandmother coaxed me back, I refused to sit next to my mother. I sat opposite her for the meal, too timid to correct the snub, too ashamed of myself to apologize. So many years later, my fear and confusion still feel like a failing, an omen of the failures I had ahead. Of every time I have failed those I love. I am ashamed that I did not look at my mother and overcome my fear. That I did not look at her wounds and say, *"It's all right, Mama."* That I did not tell her, *"I'm here, and I love you, and I'm not going anywhere."*

JARED BUNDE: CRIME
B. 1976
NAUGATUCK, CONNECTICUT; NEW YORK CITY;
VALLEJO, CALIFORNIA

Like many decisions that lead to felony charges, Jared Bunde's plan to sell acid had seemed like a good idea at the time. A friend's older sister had been selling off sheets of LSD for $200, a hundred hits each. Jared figured he could sell each hit for $5. "I had a good buddy who sold pot. It was kind of like, 'Well, he could be the weed guy and I could be the acid guy,'" says Jared.

So, one Friday a couple of weeks before Easter in 1994, Jared taped eight hits to the back of the flat buckle of his military-surplus belt. Short and muscular, he wore standard-issue skater clothes: big hoodies he could disappear into, loose jeans or cargo pants, low sneakers, half-inch circular plugs in his earlobes. He slid another twenty hits between seams he'd sliced open on an L.L. Bean backpack strap. Jared had been doing this for a week or two without incident when the school security guard caught one of his customers. The guard demanded to know who'd sold him the acid. The kid named Jared.

When the security officer approached Jared and said he knew Jared had acid on him, Jared paused. He wondered if he could lie successfully. The guard had harassed Jared before, telling Jared he knew he had drugs on him—even when he didn't. But Jared was seventeen, aware of the expectation that he should do as adults told him. He unlatched his army surplus web belt and peeled off the shiny foil packet he'd taped to the buckle. There were eight hits of acid inside.

The police came to the school, put handcuffs on Jared, and led him out of the school to a waiting cruiser. Jared ducked his head under the frame and settled into the backseat. At the police station, two miles away, Jared remembers the cops joking about him openly—"treated like shit by a bunch of good old boy cops," is how Jared remembers it—but otherwise left him alone.

They never found the tabs in the backpack strap. Even now, three decades later, this fact feels like an irony, a reminder that he might've gotten away with it entirely if he'd continued to deny his guilt. "In hindsight, I should have told the guy to fucking search me," says Jared. "He would have never found the shit."

★ ★ ★ ★ ★

Jared was living with his father then. The family had moved to Naugatuck, a working-class town outside Waterbury, Connecticut, about six years earlier, when his parents were still together. Jared had hated it as soon as they moved there from a small town outside Rochester, New York. He hated it more when his parents separated after the move. At first, Jared stayed with his mother and younger brother. Jared was just entering his teenage years, and mostly he felt angry: angry at having been moved away from his friends, angry about his parents' split. He fought with his mother constantly. Eventually, Jared says, she told him: *Go live with your father.*

Jared's father, Rick, wasn't around much, so after school and well into the evening Jared mostly did what he pleased. Sometimes he sketched and painted. Sometimes he went with friends to skateboard around Naugatuck's downtown, or hang out on the Green. Sometimes he hung out at other kids' homes. Eventually, someone introduced him to pot. Later, someone introduced him to acid.

Jared didn't get an allowance, and his father, a quality engineer, had a frugal streak. Jared remembers the heat staying off well into winter, the kitchen cupboards bare aside from flour, sugar, and coffee. Jared didn't really think about getting a job, but he felt keenly aware that money would make things easier. Acid was the first time he'd tried selling drugs. If he had not gotten caught, it would have been an easy, lucrative endeavor.

Rick had a dim understanding that Jared was misbehaving. But he assumed that Jared would figure things out on his own, just as he felt he had. Rick did not worry about teachers or the police punishing his son unfairly—an assumption that is much harder for the parents of Black children to make. If Jared was disciplined, Rick assumed he deserved it. Still, this was the first time Jared ended up with charges more serious than shoplifting.

Police had charged Jared with two drug felonies and, Jared remembers, released him to his father without requiring bail. At home, Jared remembers Rick yelling, saying he should search Jared's room, but he didn't even know what to look for. Jared, who had been suspended from school for a couple weeks, began making his way through the rest of the acid. He remembers taking a bunch of it on Good Friday.

"After that, I was pretty spun," Jared told me. "I was pretty disconnected from reality." He was still reconnecting when he went back to school. A friend suggested they confront the snitch. The two boys approached the third in the lunchroom. They told the kid that they knew what he'd said. They told him Jared had legal bills now. They told him he was going to pay: with money, or with physical pain. The kid handed over about five dollars, says Jared. Then the snitch snitched again. The police arrested Jared on felony charges of robbery and larceny.

This time, Jared remembers, the judge required bail before Jared would be released. This time, Jared spent the night in jail. Neither Jared nor his father is sure, but Jared thinks he walked home in the morning, alone. They were both at a loss. "I was, like, a seventeen-year-old kid, right? So I didn't think about the consequences of anything," Jared says. "That wasn't even on the radar."

★ ★ ★ ★ ★

It was 1994. Waterbury, the court where Jared was arraigned and charged and ultimately convicted, was known for being aggressive in policing crime. "I think it's fair to say Waterbury was the most sort of Trump-like place in the state," says Michael Lawlor, a Democrat who represented part of New Haven in the state legislature from 1987 to 2011. The state's governor then, John Rowland, who'd made cracking down on crime a campaign issue, was from Waterbury. "Just very tough on crime—prosecutors, police, a reputation for, like, being really 'If you do the crime you do the time,'" says Lawlor.

The attorney Jared's parents hired—a former cop, Rick remembers—was sober in his assessment. The prosecutor's case was strong; Jared had handed over eight tabs of LSD to a school safety officer, who reported it directly to the police. This worried his father. "My thought was, you know, plead guilty," said Rick, who remembers splitting the cost of the attorney with Jared's mom; recently unemployed at the time, he remembers covering his share with money pulled out of his retirement savings. "Plead mercy of the court. Beg forgiveness, you know, start that way." In exchange for a guilty plea, the prosecutor offered Jared a sentence of six years, with the possibility of parole after three. The lawyer offered another option, but it was a long shot: ask the judge to agree to "accelerated pretrial rehabilitation."

Pleading guilty is the most common response to criminal charges—even when someone has been wrongly accused. Researchers have found that more than 90 percent of convictions come through plea bargaining, where defendants plead guilty in exchange for less punishment than they'd risk at trial. This practice became even more common in the 1980s after Congress passed laws establishing significant mandatory minimum sentences for federal drug offenses.* From the 1960s through the early 1980s,

---

* The most notable of these are the Anti-Drug Abuse Acts of 1986 and 1988.

the average time served in federal prison for drug possession had steadily dropped from about three years to less than two. With passage of new sentencing guidelines in 1986, the average time served for drug offenses doubled within a decade.

The minimum federal sentence for distribution—i.e., sales—of hard drugs was five years: for 1 gram of LSD, popular with white teenagers; 5 grams of crack, most commonly used by Black people in cities; or for 500 grams of cocaine, more commonly used by white adults. In 1996, Hillary Clinton, then the first lady, would warn of the dangers of "kids that are called super-predators" adding that "we need to bring them to heel."

All of these changes were creating a harsher system of punishment than the one under which Jared's parents had grown up. By the late 1960s, the racial uprisings in cities fueled white support for stricter law enforcement. In 1971, the Nixon administration launched a War on Drugs, intended by its architects as a means of squashing challenges to Republican power. "We knew we couldn't make it illegal to be either against the war or Blacks, but by getting the public to associate the hippies with marijuana and blacks with heroin, and then criminalizing both heavily, we could disrupt those communities," Nixon staffer John Ehrlichman told a *Harper's* writer in 1994.

In the 1980s, Connecticut followed Congress's lead and passed mandatory minimums for drug sales or distribution—whether sharing or selling—of drugs other than marijuana. Then, in the 1990s, state lawmakers added penalties for selling within 1,500 feet of schools, childcare centers, or public housing. Under state law, Jared's charges required a minimum three-year prison sentence if he was convicted. Pale-faced boys like Jared had not been the target of the War on Drugs or the punishments it created. But the stricter rules, along with the law of averages, meant that at least a few of them would get caught up in it anyway.

Jared's lawyer said he'd do the best he could, but he warned that Jared and his family needed to be prepared for the worst. Even at seventeen, Jared was considered an adult insofar as the state was concerned. The lawyer told

Jared he expected the judge would refuse their request for rehabilitation, and that Jared would be going to prison.

★ ★ ★ ★ ★

After the second arrest, Jared kept his drugs to himself; he did not try to sell them again. But he remained enterprising. After he graduated high school, he stayed at his father's house, paying a few hundred dollars rent. He got a job landscaping, showed up on time, and worked hard until the day's work was done. He smoked a lot of weed. A friend went to a wild college party in Vermont and came back to Naugatuck, agape: "Dude, we gotta move to Vermont," he said. Jared and another friend went along. They got a three-bedroom apartment in Montpelier that cost $435 a month. After a month or two, the other two guys went back to Connecticut. Jared stayed in Vermont. He persuaded the landlord to use the initial deposit to cover one final month's rent, then started looking for a cheaper place to live.

By then, Jared had found another landscaping job. It was in Burlington, forty miles west. To get there, he hitchhiked. When he had to leave the Montpelier apartment, he found another in Plainfield, eight miles farther east. Hitchhiking to and from Plainfield was unreliable, so Jared would ride his bike to Montpelier, then hitchhike from there to his job in Burlington. He lived this way through to the following spring, making friends with the college kids in town.

In the meantime, his case was moving through the Connecticut courts. The advice from his lawyer had been clear: *Get your shit together.* Jared was trying. During his senior year of high school, he had gone to an open house for a prestigious art school, Parsons School of Design, in New York City. He hadn't applied, but now that the court was looking for signs of maturity he sent in an application for the school year starting in 1995. Jared won admission. When the next acceptance deadline came around, he had still not gone to trial. He deferred.

Jared saw the deferral as hedging his bets: There was no point in making a deposit on tuition if he might get sent to prison before classes began. If he got convicted with a suspended sentence, there was the issue of financial aid. The 1988 Anti-Drug Abuse Act had increased sentencing and spurred changes to the Higher Education Act that let judges bar people with felony convictions from receiving federal educational loans. This policy decimated prison education programs, but it also meant people with felony convictions couldn't get money for school after they'd done their time. "Actions have consequences, and using or selling drugs will ruin your future," said the bill's sponsor, Mark Souder. If Jared was convicted, the judge could keep him from accessing federal aid for as little as a year after his release—or as long as indefinitely.

* * * * *

Nobody remembers much about the hearings leading up to the decision in the case. Jared remembers going to court in June 1995. He didn't own a suit or dress shoes back then, so he figures he wore khakis and a button-down shirt with sneakers. Maybe a tie? He's not sure. The prosecutor would have talked about the things he had done: Multiple drug felonies. Robbery. Larceny. Threatening another student. What else might Jared do if he was not held accountable for his actions? His lawyer argued the other side: Here was a young man who had made mistakes. But he was now self-sufficient, supporting himself in Vermont, with admission to a prestigious school in New York. He deserved a chance.

Research about young people charged with crimes suggests that judges are substantially more inclined to give that kind of chance to young white people than to young Black people. Although there is no systematic study of accelerated rehabilitation programs, a study of juveniles convicted of drug charges in 1997 found a striking difference in how young drug defendants were sentenced, depending on race. The study showed that 59 percent of youth drug cases involved white defendants, and 39 percent involved Black defendants. But white kids were far more likely to be given the small mercy of staying in a juvenile system—where their records could be sealed, protecting future prospects—than were Black kids. Of those same cases in 1997, 63 percent of juveniles sent to adult court were Black defendants—and just 35 percent were white. The same study found that young Black defendants were six times as likely to be sent to state facilities as were white ones convicted of the same charges.

In the end, the judge listened to Jared's lawyer. She granted the accelerated rehabilitation program, and Jared walked out of the courtroom with his parents a free man. There were a few catches, of course: He would need to stay out of trouble for two years, submit to random drug tests, and do four hundred hours of community service. If he could do these three things, he would never be incarcerated. His records would be sealed. The files would be erased. The entire thing would disappear.

★ ★ ★ ★ ★

Jared's attorney didn't work magic: He knew how the system worked. But he also didn't work for free. Jared's father remembers spending about $3,000 on the case.* This was money Rick spent without expecting repayment. He saw it as his responsibility to look out for Jared in this way.

Because Rick was unemployed when Jared was first arrested, he remembers the difficulty of that period well. He speaks of being grateful that he was able to weather it. He had retirement funds to draw on, and he could have sold the house if he'd needed to. He had the house and the funds because he'd had good jobs; his position of quality engineer typically paid about $54,000 a year at the time, landing him well into the middle class. He had those jobs, by then, because he had a master's degree and a good work history. And he tells me he had the master's degree because his last employer in Rochester, Kodak, had paid for the tuition. He finished the degree in 1987.

It seems unlikely that Kodak's tuition assistance would have been as easy to access for Black people in the area. From the 1960s through the 2010s, Kodak battled charges about racism in its hiring and employment practices. In the 1960s, community activists argued that Kodak, then the largest employer in Rochester, did not hire enough Black workers, and

---

* According to the Bureau of Labor Statistics, $3,000 in January 1994 was equivalent to $6,139 in January 2023.

pushed for changes. In the 1990s, Black employees filed a complaint with the Equal Employment Opportunity Commission (EEOC) that listed pay disparities and harassment from supervisors that included use of language like "porch monkeys" and the N-word. In the 2000s, Black employees continued to document pay disparities and an overrepresentation of Black workers in the most dangerous jobs.

Because of this history, it is hard for me to see Kodak's generosity with Rick as the way he seems to: as an entitlement earned, and fairly given. Instead, it looks like a gift. Even, maybe, like a bonus.

* * * * *

Rick told me the story of Jared's case with an ambivalent pride. He feels guilt for not having grasped that Jared's experimentation had gone beyond weed, which he'd observed and let slide. But he feels good about how he and his ex-wife had handled the charges and the trial. They had shown up at every court appearance for Jared, dressed in their best, even when it meant missing work. Jared's parents did this not just to support their son but also because his attorney had explained that their presence would be important to Jared's sentencing.

In the language of criminal justice, Jared's parents were proving to the judge that their son had "community ties." If a judge considered community ties in sentencing, neat, respectable-looking parents could be an asset; people who showed up looking rough might not be.* Worst of all was if nobody—not your parents, not your friends, not your colleagues—showed up at all.

---

* At the time Jared was going through court, judges were required to follow federal sentencing guidelines, which considered it *inappropriate* for judges to consider community ties—or vocation, employment, education, or family. In a 2005 ruling in *U.S. v. Booker,* the U.S. Supreme Court held that these guidelines could only be considered advisory—and thus freed judges to consider criteria outside of the guidelines. I have found *Crook County,* by legal scholar and sociologist Nicole Gonzalez Van Cleve, to be an instructive portrait of how this discretion can open the door to disparate racial treatment of defendants by judges.

To Jared's parents, this was not a story about race. It was a story about overcoming their tension with each other to show up for their kid. To have both parents show up, even though they were divorced, sent a strong message of support for Jared, Rick told me. "That's different from a lot of the stories I hear about people that are going to court. It was something that we did as a priority in our lives," he says.

By then, Rick had gotten a new job. He was working at an aircraft company, a middle-class, salaried job with paid time off; Jared's mother worked for the post office. It was relatively easy for each of them to make it to court. "I could take time off from work. So is that a different luxury because of race?" says Rick. "I would beg to say no."

★ ★ ★ ★ ★

I can see what Rick is saying, but I think something larger is at work. Given what I know about race in my country, I can see how even neatly dressed, quiet Black parents might not be seen as proof of stability. How the constant association in news accounts of Blackness with dysfunction and hardship could lead a judge in Waterbury to see a Black family and assume they faced poverty and hardship and could not manage their child. How the fact that more than half of Black children grow up in single-parent homes, often with a single parent who works, often with the pressures of poverty despite that work, would make it so much harder for a parent to be in the courtroom for every hearing. How white people's compulsion to associate Black men and boys with crime has been proven in study after study after study. How heavy the pressure of history is; how it would have worn a deep, rutted path for Black families. How that pressure and that path would make it so much more likely for a white judge to look at a floundering Black boy and think: *Locking him up is the best I can do.*

It is not right, but I can see how being white, and particularly being white and middle class, is the biggest, easiest explanation for why Jared— caught red-handed on school grounds with narcotics at the height of punitive drug laws, then caught again threatening and stealing from a peer—was not locked up. I can see how he was given something most kids in that position would benefit from: a second chance.

Jared can see this, too. When I asked him if he thinks his court case would have gone differently if he hadn't been white, he nodded. "I do," he said. We were in the car, zooming down I-80 toward his job for the Alameda County health department in the East Bay, across from San Francisco. He looked blankly at the traffic before us, then flicked his gaze at the rearview mirror. "I think I would have probably went away, right?"

★ ★ ★ ★ ★

When Jared talks about his drug charges, he talks about how he managed to avoid having a felony on his record. This is for good reason: In the United States, felony convictions impose hardship long after the time has been served. The world of criminal justice has a phrase for the cascade of effects that follow arrest, conviction, and incarceration: "collateral consequences." Many of these come with price tags, so much so that scholars have developed a term for that, too: "legal financial obligations," or LFOs.★

When a person is arrested and charged, and goes through the court system, and ends up incarcerated, there are costs they must pay every step of the way. And while there is no way for me to prove, definitively, that Jared was spared a felony record and incarceration because he was white, the odds overwhelmingly suggest that is the case. I have paged through many statistics on this, but I'm most moved by one showing what happens

---

★ Among the less-tangible costs that reentering citizens face are lifetime bans on their receiving various forms of public aid, including educational loans, housing subsidies, cash welfare, and food assistance; housing and employment discrimination; and limits on their political rights. A 2018 study found that landlords considered apartment applications from 100 percent of white men without a criminal drug history—but just 17 percent of white men with one, and only 2 percent of Black men with the same. As of April 2023, the National Conference on State Legislatures reported that incarcerated people cannot vote in 48 states; in 25 states, people with felony convictions lose the right to vote for at least some time after they are released.

when Black and white men, of similar age and employment history, face similar drug charges: Black men are 30 percent more likely to be incarcerated. Because Jared did not go to jail, he did not have to pay the costs. In this instance, I think it is fair to consider the money Jared did not have to spend as a kind of white bonus.

In the long, slow build to trial there are court costs and fees. Defendants can be billed for a public defender in forty-two states, including Connecticut. If people who've been charged with crimes are allowed to go home before trial, they often must pay bail. Once released, they are almost always responsible for paying the cost of electronic monitoring.

Once a person is incarcerated, another series of costs begins to build. Often, you must pay for your shelter; a 2014 survey found that forty-one states, also including Connecticut, had laws providing for the state charging inmates for their room and board. The families of the incarcerated must also bear the costs of communication and visits. Prisons contract out phone services to for-profit companies, so Jared would have paid a connection fee and per-minute charges each time he called home. Commissary, where inmates buy snacks and shoes and postage stamps, cost an average of $947 a year in the late 2010s. It is commonplace for people to be incarcerated hours away from their families; the average distance is about a hundred miles. In this regard, Jared would have been lucky; the nearest state prison to his family was eleven miles away, a twenty-minute drive. But however far or near, families must spend the money required to make the visit: They pay in their time, in gas money, the wear and tear on the car if they have one, or on the transport and lodging the visit requires if they do not.

This is what they must do to keep their loved one sane, to let them know they have not been forgotten, to tell them that despite their mistakes they remain loved. This is one thing they can do to help make a loved one's stay in prison their last one. Reconviction rates are 13 to 25 percent lower for people who receive visitors while incarcerated when compared to those who are left in prison, alone.

The end of imprisonment is not the end of the fees. Once released, judges can also order people who've been convicted of crimes to pay the cost of probation and supervision. If they run afoul of their probation—if they live near a border and the electronic monitor falsely suggests they have fled the country, if they miss a meeting with their probation officer, if a police officer decides they are loitering too long in a place—they may end up back in jail and responsible for a new round of fees.

Jared's attorney had told him to prepare for three to five years of prison. One study, from 2015, put the average cost of incarceration, per family, at $13,600—about $17,400 in 2023. When I compiled the direct costs that Jared would have likely faced by spending three years in prison—the visitation, the commissary, the phone calls—I came up with a slightly higher number: $19,050 in 2023.*

★ ★ ★ ★ ★

Those are the immediate financial costs; there are indirect ones, too. While incarcerated, Jared would not have been able to work, so he would have lost at least three years of wages—just under $53,000 in 2023. His rent would have gone unpaid and his lease would have been broken, leading to dings on whatever credit score he had accumulated. If he'd had any other debt, he would have defaulted on that, too. Researchers have found that prison stays of up to two years reduce credit scores by an average of thirty-two points per year.†

Avoiding financial problems is especially difficult for people who leave prison, because getting a job becomes much harder. As a formerly incarcerated person, Jared would have been just over half as likely to be considered for a job as a white man without a criminal record. Even so, research

---

* The direct cost of being incarcerated in Connecticut is much higher today. Jared's case predated a 1997 Connecticut law that charges incarcerated people room and board for their time served. Initially, the state charged incarcerated people $31,755 a year for their room and board. By 2022, it was charging $90,885 a year.

† These drops in credit score only affect those who enter prison with a credit score already on record. The poorest Americans often have no credit score, and often pay double-digit interest on any debt they acquire.

suggests he would have been one-third more likely to be considered for a job than a Black man *without* a criminal record. After prison, Jared would have earned less; researchers put the initial income drop for reentering citizens of all races at 10 to 30 percent of preincarceration income. Another study found that incarceration on the cusp of adulthood correlates with earning 14 to 18 percent less for the first six years after leaving prison— mostly, the authors note, because it can be difficult to gain work experience while incarcerated.

Jared is a smart, adaptable, and self-directed person. I can see how, if Jared had found himself in prison, he would have shaped himself to his surroundings. How he would have developed the skills he needed to get by. Jared puts it more bluntly: "If I had had a felony conviction when I was seventeen, gainful employment would not have been my path forward. I would be a fucking thug."

If Jared is right about himself, he would have been likely to join the two-thirds of people who leave prison before the age of twenty-four only to be returned to prison again within ten years. Across all ages, this boomerang is remarkably equitable across race lines, hitting 59 percent of white released prisoners, 60 percent of Hispanic released prisoners, and 63 percent of Black released prisoners. Much of this boomerang, researchers point out, reflects the heightened police surveillance in low-income communities and communities of color, two groups that often—but not always—overlap with each other.

Jared showed up in court with a clean white face and two clean-cut, white parents in the gallery. He showed that he was trying to be an adult. This was enough for the judge to give him the benefit of the doubt. It was enough to keep him out of prison and to save him all the costs of going there. It was enough to give him time to reflect and to learn, and to correct his course.

This generosity has paid off for my country. Instead of spending tens of thousands of dollars each year to monitor or incarcerate a man cycling in and out of prisons, my government receives taxes from Jared and has a citizen living his life without hurting others. And the generosity has paid off for Jared, too. It let him build his life. It let him collect all the advantages that had been set up for a young white man looking to build his twenty-first-century version of the American Dream.

★ ★ ★ ★ ★

Jared stayed on in Vermont, and spent the summer after his sentencing living in a tent on an organic farm in Plainfield. He bargained with the farmer: He'd trade a day of hard work a week for a spot to pitch his tent and whatever produce he wanted. He did regular farm work a couple days a week at another farm outside town. For fun, he rode his bike and taught judo holds to a local tae kwon do teacher in exchange for lessons.

In August, Jared packed his tent and moved to New York to start at Parsons. One of his Vermont friends had family in Brooklyn and offered Jared a couch in their basement apartment. He walked to save on subway fare, and one day found himself on the Fulton Mall, a commercial strip in downtown Brooklyn lined with department stores, sneaker shops, and jewelry counters. He realized that he was the only white person around. The surprise he felt wasn't fear, but novelty: He'd never been the only white person somewhere before.

He was experiencing a different kind of shock at school, too. Even with financial aid, Jared owed about $10,000 a year for tuition.* He and his parents split it, with his dad paying $5,000, his mother paying $2,500, and Jared taking out an educational loan for the rest. This was different from most of his classmates, who went out to eat, bought new clothes at expensive shops in the Village, and went to concerts. Jared did little more than sleep, make art, and go to class; he was too broke for anything else. And the longer Jared spent in his classes, the more he understood the financial reality of life as an artist. "I had the realization that basically to be a successful fine artist, you've got to sell stuff to rich people," Jared told me. "To

---

* According to the Bureau of Labor Statistics, the $10,000 in tuition—calculated as $5,000 in January 1996 and $5,000 in January 1997—was the equivalent of $19,090 in January 2023.

be a successful artist, I have to sell stuff to people that I don't even want to talk to. I think I had some sort of psychic disconnect there," he said.

Jared was still adrift and unfocused, not sure what to do next. As the first year wound down, his hosts in Brooklyn asked him to leave; they had not intended their hospitality as an indefinite solution to the problem of his housing. He left without finding another place and began bathing at friends' apartments and sleeping on their couches. Other nights, Jared found unlocked classrooms and bedded down where he could not be seen from the door. One night, a security guard found him and told him to leave.

Jared went to the locker he kept at school. He stuffed his sleeping bag into a backpack and walked out onto Fifth Avenue. A few blocks away, buses lurched along Fourteenth Street. Solitary cabs reflected in dark storefront windows. The streets were mostly quiet, the sidewalks mostly empty. Jared wandered south. In SoHo, on some block of old warehouses turned into galleries and condos, he spied a roof deck. The building's fire escape dropped into a vacant lot surrounded by a rickety chain-link fence with a gap in it. Jared ducked into the lot, pulled the ladder down, and quietly climbed his way to the roof.

Jared can't say for sure if anyone ever noticed him—a small, lean, white teenager—trespass in this way. But nobody ever disturbed him there, on expensive lawn furniture several stories up. He still slept at friends' places some nights; on rainy nights when hospitality wore thin, a rare coincidence, he would ride the trains. But otherwise he made the roof deck his bed. On the coldest nights, he'd do jumping jacks to stay warm. He'd wake around dawn, the Twin Towers' steel columns glinting above in the early light, and steal out the way he'd come in.

★ ★ ★ ★ ★

I first met Jared in 2001 at a Halloween party put on by a bunch of bike riders. By then I'd begun using a bike to get around the city; for me, it had become a kind of therapy. But for Jared, bikes were his life.

He had left Parsons after that first year, fearful of the debt it would require, and entered a period of being unhoused. For a year or so, he bounced from the roofs into sublets that failed, then tried squatting in abandoned buildings with friends. He had also started working as a bike messenger and eventually landed in a single-room occupancy (SRO) hotel in Williamsburg. For about eighty-five dollars a week in cash, Jared remembers, he had a room with a bed and kitchenette, and shared the bathroom with other tenants on his floor. Most men in my cultural class, when they talk of the drugs they did in their twenties, laugh about it with bravado. *My misspent youth* is the vibe. The way Jared talks about doing drugs reminds me of how I now understand my heavy drinking in the same period: as a means to quiet the sense that nobody had my back, that I was alone in the world.

Jared's work as a bike messenger led to work as a bike mechanic and bike racing. That work led to a job managing a community bike shop and training its teenage interns to fix bikes. His experience there got him a job helping to run a parks program teaching teenagers how to race bikes in a velodrome. Jared's work in these circles meant he met and befriended many working-class men and teenage boys who were not white. It did not take long for him to notice that the police treated them differently from the way they had treated him.

When Jared smoked weed in Tompkins Square Park and a police officer approached, he flicked away the joint and smiled affably. The strategy, says Jared, was this: "If you were smoking a joint or something, just sort of tossing it away and being like, 'I don't know what you're talking about.'" He does not remember getting arrested or ticketed once. It wasn't like this for the Black and brown messengers he knew; they were lucky to catch only tickets. When they were not lucky, police took them on "rough rides," throwing them into vans handcuffed and unbuckled, then driving erratically to throw them around—the same practice alleged in the 2015 case of Freddie Gray, who died of spinal cord injuries sustained while in the custody of Baltimore police. Jared remembers a friend, who was brown, getting his front teeth knocked out in this way.

The stories from Jared's friends intensified under Mayor Michael Bloomberg, who took office in 2002, and ramped up use of "stop and frisk" policing. In 2009, Black and Latino residents were nine times as likely as whites to be stopped—even though, as Jared's experience suggests, whites were just as likely to be breaking the law.

Jared didn't see his ability to avoid punishment as a racial issue at first. It felt, to him, more like he was doing as he had been told and staying out of trouble. His perspective changed over time, as he continued to smoke weed and grin at officers, then hear stories of his buddies getting harassed and arrested for doing the same. "It's like, as a young white person you're given the benefit of the doubt. There's a lot of my life where . . . if the color of my skin were different, I just would not have been able to do the things that I did," he said.

We had been talking on the phone, disembodied voices separated by the continent. But when I remember this conversation, I picture him as I saw him later, looking for the words to explain difficult things. He placed his hands flat on the graying fuzz of hair on top of his head, then slid them down to cover his face. He groaned a sigh between his fingers and released his hands. This is how I picture him telling me about his ability to do as he liked without facing consequences: "That's the fucked-up part."

* * * * *

It took Jared almost a decade after leaving Parsons before he tried college again. Throughout his twenties, Jared's life centered on bikes, then: racing, repair, teaching. None of it paid well. At the bike repair project, many of his employees were kids living in the projects, their families getting by with a mix of work and public benefits. Because public benefits could be canceled if a household's income went too high—even if only by one dollar—Jared learned to schedule his kids for as many hours as they wanted beneath that threshold. These constant calculations made him think about how thin the margin between stable and stressed would be if he stayed in the same jobs—how he'd never make enough to own a house or a car. So he thought about what he was good at and what jobs might pay enough to cover the cost of student loans. He thought about what careers might let him travel. Nursing fit all three.

Jared had left Parsons to avoid taking on debt, but there was no avoiding it if he wanted a nursing degree. Even attending a public university in New York City required about $60,000 in loans—the beginning of what Jared calls the "shell game." Once he began classes, Jared was drawn to community health, which started to explain the differences he'd seen between his own opportunities and those of the city kids he worked with. He decided to dedicate himself to school, reducing his work hours as much as he could while still meeting the work requirements for food stamps. This was the first move of the shell: living on student loans to complete his bachelor's degree.

After finishing a community health degree in New York, Jared enrolled in an accelerated nursing degree at Johns Hopkins in Baltimore, the top public health school in the country. Hopkins is also a private university. In 2012, its tuition and fees were about $33,000 a year. Jared applied for scholarships, but he would not hear back from them until after he agreed to enroll. He had to be willing to take on $66,000 in debt and simply hope for a scholarship. By then, Jared had maxed out his student loans and needed a private loan to cover tuition. He had little income, so his father cosigned a loan.

While Rick had never given Jared much in the way of cash, he now offered what Jared calls "implicit security"—the feeling that he had enough support behind him to responsibly take on debt. In the end, the scholarship came through, and this became the second move of the shell: committing to more debt only to have the scholarship pay back most of it.

By then Jared had fallen in love with a woman named Merrin, five years his junior with thick, yellow-blond hair, bright blue eyes, and pale, freckled skin. Merrin grew up in towns along Florida's Gulf Coast. Her mother's parents were wealthy but her parents—"the black sheep of the family," says Merrin—were not. Like Jared, she'd tried college but left, returning several years later to finish a degree in education. She has mostly worked as a religious educator and administrator for Unitarian churches.

The two met while Jared was in school in New York, and Merrin was working for a congregation in New Jersey. Merrin followed Jared to Baltimore. As Jared was finishing his degree, she got hired by a church in

Berkeley. Now it was Jared's turn to follow. They lived in a two-bedroom apartment in El Cerrito, a middle-class neighborhood north of Berkeley. Merrin's mother knew the owner's sister through her book club. The rent, Jared remembers, was around $1,200 or $1,400; market rate at the time was around $2,000.

Jared, now a continent away from the professional network his schools had offered, began volunteering with harm reduction and homeless street outreach. Then, still struggling to find a full-time job, he began a master's program in public health. He found a job with a federal health clinic, which paid more than he'd ever made before: around $60,000 a year. He took out more student loans, which he and Merrin used for living expenses. They funneled most of her salary into savings. This was the third move of the shell: using a student loan to turn a salary into savings.

After Jared finished his master's degree in 2016, one of his professors helped him get a part-time job doing street nursing outreach in San Francisco. After two years, a he took a job in Alameda County, visiting Oakland's vast homeless encampments with another nurse. His job was to persuade people without homes to visit doctors, to consider moving into a shelter, to switch from shooting fentanyl to smoking it in order to lower the risk of infection. Sometimes, he ran into his clients when he was out for a drink and gave them a few bucks. Sometimes he drove past them sitting on a milk crate beneath an overpass, silent and puffy with infection, and circled back to give them five dollars, his card, and the unsolicited advice to visit a clinic. By 2020, state salary data put his earnings at more than $130,000 a year. Combined with Merrin's salary, and compared to the extreme cost of living in the Bay Area, that landed them safely in the middle class.

Jared had begun suggesting they buy a house as soon as they got to California, but Merrin had balked, wary of taking on more debt. Jared argued they'd be more stable by freezing their housing costs instead of watching their rent climb. It wouldn't be easy to buy. Housing prices were soaring. Neither of them had inherited any money from their families.

Neither family offered a down payment. But thanks to the last move of the shell—and everything that had led them there, from avoiding incarceration to maintaining good credit to living frugally—Jared and Merrin had savings. They began to look for a house to buy with it.

*　*　*　*　*

In 2015, the couple began using Merrin's Yaris, a present from wealthy relatives during a rough patch in her twenties, to visit smaller cities within commuting distance of Oakland. They liked Vallejo, about twenty miles north across the Carquinez Strait, and its historic homes. The town housed a shipyard from the 1850s until the yard closed in 1996. Vallejo went bankrupt twelve years later, in 2008. As Merrin remembers it, the residents that remained—or who had arrived since—were perfectly mixed: one-quarter white, one-quarter Black, one-quarter Asian, one-quarter Hispanic. They hoped to start a family, and the idea of raising a child in a place where integration was normal appealed to them.*

As they walked around Vallejo's neighborhoods, Merrin and Jared also looked for—and found—signs of friendliness and care. In El Cerrito, neighbors had mostly kept to themselves, so averse to chatting that Merrin wondered if people were scared of each other. "How many of the people that you pass on the sidewalk acknowledge your presence? Where they're like, *'I see you, you see me; have a good day,'*" says Jared. "It's not common for somebody to walk past you on the sidewalk [in Vallejo] without some degree of acknowledgment."

---

* Vallejo's racial demographics have made it a favorite among journalists. In 2001, the *New York Times* ran a story about Vallejo ("A Diverse City Exists Equal but Separate"), calling it "a nearly equally spiced racial stew." Vallejo's racial mix, the story said, owed in part to its "history of tolerance," evidenced by its home county, Solano, voting to integrate schools in the 1890s. It also cited, as evidence, Vallejo's status as the hometown of "the integrated rock band Sly and the Family Stone, whose appeal crossed racial lines." The *Times* ran another story about Vallejo in 2017 ("Does Race Matter in America's Most Diverse ZIP Codes?"), citing its 2001 piece and observing that integration remained a challenge: "Then, as now, racial and ethnic groups often stuck with their own."

After visiting a few open houses, Merrin told me, she and Jared noticed a pattern when they walked into an open house. "The Hispanic family or the Black family who would be talking with an agent just got dropped, and they [the Realtor] would gear toward us," says Merrin. She and Jared would smile politely and tell the agent to finish speaking with the Black or Hispanic family first.

Research on Realtors suggests that agents' inclination toward white clients is commonplace. Sociologist Elizabeth Korver-Glenn followed seven Houston-area real estate agents for a year and found that her subjects routinely provided more and better service to white buyers. They justified this by saying that white buyers would have more money to spend and would require less paperwork.

Still, Jared and Merrin liked the town, and they made an offer on a Victorian in need of repair. They didn't get the house, but they had noticed how the Realtor at the open house had not beelined for them; she seemed to treat everyone equally. They nursed their disappointment at losing the offer. Then they asked the Realtor whose client had turned them down to help them find a house.

★ ★ ★ ★ ★

In October 2016, Jared and Merrin made an offer on a two-building property on the gradual downslope of Vallejo's central hill, with a view of the hills to the north. An attractive two-bedroom Craftsman bungalow sat at the front of the lot, with a small courtyard and patio behind it. At the back of the lot was a two-bedroom apartment above a two-car garage. The block was stable but not fancy, and it was mixed-income: One neighbor told them she covered rent with federal subsidies, while a couple across the street had twin BMWs. And having two smaller buildings rather than one large house appealed to them: There would be room for visitors, for family to live with them, for them to take on tenants to cover costs as they aged.

Along with the offer, Jared and Merrin sent a letter to the owners at the suggestion of their Realtor. They talked about their hopes and their dreams, the family and life they hoped to build. Their Realtor also suggested sending a photo; they sent one of Merrin kissing Jared on the cheek.

For most of my adult life, these kinds of letters, framed as a way to make an emotional appeal to sellers, have been commonplace whenever the housing market booms. They are both mundane and powerful, so much so that, in 2013, the *Wall Street Journal*'s real estate section published a writing guide to such "love letters," advising buyers to include photos of themselves and to highlight experiences they have in common with the seller. There was no mention in the *Journal*'s guide of implicit bias.

In 2020, in the wake of the George Floyd protests, some Realtors began to speak up about this concern. That fall, the National Association of Realtors warned its agents that, though "seemingly harmless, these letters actually raise fair housing concerns, and could open real estate professionals and their clients to fair housing violations." Late that year, the association shared the story of a white woman in Florida who had agreed to sell her house to a couple, then retracted the offer when she realized the couple was Black. The NAR advised Realtors against using the letters at all, and to be vigilant about risks if clients insisted on them anyway.

In December 2016, Jared and Merrin signed a $413,000 mortgage for the two buildings, paying $43,507 in cash to cover the down payment and closing costs. They covered the expense almost entirely with the savings they had built by living on Jared's loans and saving much of Merrin's salary.

In the front house, Jared and Merrin began to replaster the walls themselves. In the back house, they hired workers to paint the walls and install a new kitchen floor. In 2018, they had a daughter, and Merrin's mother came to live above the garage, planning to exchange childcare for below-market rent. Eventually, they hired a painter to turn the exterior from faded yellow to lavender with navy trim. They had made it to the middle class.

* * * * *

For Jared and Merrin, having a child validated their decision to buy a house. Here, finally, was a way to give their daughter some of the stability they each felt they had missed. And California, they learned, is a good place to do that, because its property tax system encourages families to do just what they planned: stay in the house a long time, then pass it on to relatives.

In California, property taxes are based on the value of a home in the year the house is bought. Under a state law referred to as Proposition 13—the name of the 1978 ballot proposition that gave rise to it—property taxes are set at 1 percent of the home's assessed value, and they can never increase by more than 2 percent each year, no matter how much the home's value grows. They don't change again until the house is sold outside of the family.

California's proposition set off what historians now refer to as a "tax revolt"—a broad, white, middle-class opposition to taxes. Ronald Reagan heralded Prop 13 and the movement it sparked as the start of a "prairie fire" destined to shrink government. Before the proposition, property tax bills were reassessed each year. The rampant inflation in the late 1970s meant that, in competitive housing markets, some people saw their taxes double in just a few years. In Southern California's suburbs, older, white homeowners began to make the case against having property taxes at all. The problem, they argued, was not only that they were being taxed more; it was also that government was spending too much.

The revolt's leaders were clear about which government spending they opposed—and who they didn't think deserved to benefit from the spending itself. "Not life, liberty, and welfare," declared the proposition's most prominent champion, a real estate lobbyist named Howard Jarvis. "Not life, liberty, and food stamps. Not life, liberty, and illegal aliens." Jarvis found common cause with another movement active at the time: the one seeking to prevent school integration, ostensibly due to its use of "forced busing." Just as the racial implications of opposition to busing for schools had been clear to observers in 1971, the racial implications of the 1978 tax revolt were, too. "This was people who had their piece of the system," Willie

Brown Jr., then a state legislator, told filmmakers in a 2019 documentary. "And they wanted to erect a fence around their piece of the system."

And so they did. Government had thrown white Americans scraps of wood to help them in their crossing—things like racial covenants, which a 1927 study found were present on the deeds of 90 percent of California subdivisions; mortgage insurance; well-funded public schools—and they had arrived on the other side. Having finished their own journey, they saw no point in helping others make it across.

Why, they said, should they have to pay higher taxes just because their property was more valuable—when they didn't need the services the taxes paid for anyway? Why should they have to share, or pay back into the system? If taxes on property were going to be raised, then the new homeowners—who, as a group, were less likely to be white than the people who already owned homes—could pay them. It was these newcomers, went the thinking, who needed social programs anyway.

Proposition 13 didn't just lower taxes, though: It also shrank available funding for public programs, particularly those that helped the poor. In the fifteen years after Proposition 13 passed, school revenues drawn from local property tax plummeted by half. Even when leaders tried to plug the holes, overall public spending on schools still dropped by 14 percent. Spending on public assistance dropped by 6 percent. And with taxes now limited to just 1 percent of the assessed value, local governments could no longer generate much revenue from low- and moderate-cost housing.

To make up the shortfall, government needed to prioritize housing with higher assessed values, and raise development fees. This, in turn, pushed developers to focus on higher-priced projects that could cover the higher fees. The ripples extended further still: With such low property taxes, most tax revenue now came from sales and income, giving government a strong incentive to encourage retail and service businesses that generated sales tax, like shopping malls and restaurants. Property-intensive businesses that functioned far upstream from the point of sale, such as manufacturing, were no longer a good bet.

The changes overwhelmingly benefited property owners, especially corporate ones. Pacific Telephone and Telegraph saved $131 million in taxes, Standard Oil of California saved $13 million, and Southern Pacific Transportation Company—the railroad—saved $12 million. Longtime homeowners who stayed in their homes benefited, too. The family that built Jared's house, for example, saved an estimated $122,069 in taxes from the time Proposition 13 passed until they sold it in the year 2000—an average savings of $462 a month. But anyone who relied on public schools or libraries, or might need affordable housing, or might want a union factory job instead of waiting tables, lost out. The prairie fire took off in nearly every state. From 1978 to 1980, forty-three states adopted new property tax limitations or relief plans that cut taxes—and threatened public programs.

When Jared and Merrin bought their home, they joined the ranks of the owners. Just as Jared had planned, owning their home helped to freeze their housing costs—including their property tax. In the six years after they bought their home, its market value climbed by 65 percent. The value on which it was taxed, though, only went up by 9 percent. Because inflation skyrocketed over the same period, their annual tax bill—still pegged to the market value six years before—actually decreased over the same period if adjusted for inflation. Because of Prop 13, Jared and Merrin did not need an average of $11,472 a year, or $956 each month. The total costs avoided for six years came to more than $68,000.*

★ ★ ★ ★ ★

Once Merrin's mother moved into the back house, Jared and Merrin began building the life they had planned. They began to leave their daughter, then a toddler, with Merrin's mom. It was hectic: Jared commuting twenty-six miles through traffic to Oakland each way in a Chevy Volt they'd bought, Merrin doing consulting work at home while her mother watched the baby. They began to overhaul their courtyard, strategizing about fruit trees and vegetable beds. The plan had worked. They were settled.

---

* Readers can see these calculations in detail on whitebonus.com.

Then the plan began to fall apart. Merrin's mother lost track of the toddler, who wandered into the alley behind the garage. Merrin found her daughter quickly, but now she and Jared worried about relying on Merrin's mother for care. Within a year, in the middle of the pandemic, doctors delivered the news they had feared: Merrin's mother had early-stage dementia. With the pandemic, daycares didn't feel safe. Merrin began waking at 2:00 A.M. to complete remote work on her computer before her daughter and mother awoke and needed her.

Jared continued working throughout the pandemic. He spent the first six months working in homeless encampments. Then he switched to administering COVID tests and, when they became available, vaccines in homeless shelters. Work that had always been draining—he once described it to me as watching genocide, given how overwhelmingly his unhoused clients were Black and brown and in grave danger of death—had become even more so. He listened to news stories, and a rage would fill him: "There was a lot of media about how, like, inconvenient it was for people to fucking be at home," he says. "I was out here worried that, like, my folks weren't going to have water to drink." After each work week, Jared could not shake the feeling of shell shock. He arrived home barely able to speak, his temper quick and intense.

Merrin and Jared talked and retooled. Their housing costs were stable, and Jared's salary was generous. As they looked at the cost of childcare and eldercare, the financial calculation became clear. Merrin's career centered heavily on care and education and did not pay much. She would leave the workforce and become the caretaker for both their daughter and her mother. They did not have enough money to make up for the limits of the childcare system, or the cost of care for her mother—whose pension and Social Security, a caseworker explained, were about $100 over the income limit for public funding for care. But they had a home they could afford, and a salary they could live off of. That would be enough to make it work.

★ ★ ★ ★ ★

In 2022, the year their daughter was slated to start kindergarten, the plan changed again. Merrin and Jared had talked with each other, openly and extensively, about their commitment to public schools. Merrin, who grew up in the South and has taught in public schools, felt especially strongly about it.

"When we bought this house, we had friends like try to talk us out of it because of the school system. And I was like, 'I think even poor city schools have a lot of value, especially when you invest as a family in them,'" says Merrin. But if they'd stayed in the East Bay, they would have rented a small apartment indefinitely, never building any wealth for themselves or their daughter. And even if the schools were good, they worried about what their child would absorb unthinkingly from the increasingly affluent world around her. "It felt important that she has fundamental relationships with people from all walks of life, and that she not be scared of people who look different from her," says Merrin. Whatever the schools lacked, Merrin and Jared felt they could compensate for it with attention at home.

It felt different after the pandemic. The stories they heard from friends whose children were already in school made them wary. So many instant reversions to virtual school once a single kid got COVID. A friend's daughter went six months without a teacher. They began to realize that many of the families they knew in town, whatever their race, sent their children to private schools if they could afford it, or drove them to charter schools outside of town if they had the time to do it.

While Jared and Merrin had been drawn to Vallejo because it was mixed in terms of both income and race, they had assumed that the schools would share the city's demographics. They were wrong. In the Vallejo City Unified School District, half the students are Hispanic and another quarter are Black. About one-fifth are of Asian, Filipino, or Pacific Island heritage. In a city that is 32 percent white, just 6 percent of public school students are white. Whatever racial group students may belong to, they are most likely to be poor or working class. In 2022, officials classified nearly three-quarters of the students as being socioeconomically disadvantaged. Unsurprisingly, given the body of research showing a steady correlation between high concentrations of poverty in a school and low academic performance, every group within the school that year ranked as either "low" or "very low" in academic performance.

Because of these concerns with the school, and because Merrin is a trained teacher, and because Merrin agreed to stay out of the workforce, they opted to homeschool their daughter for kindergarten. But they are thinking, too, about what they will do as their daughter's educational needs outstrip what they can provide at home. Sending her to Vallejo's schools scares Jared, who is acutely aware that his daughter is sensitive and used to individual attention. Will she be damaged by the shift to being one of many? Will she be ignored? Will she become a target of other students' ire? Would it be fair to force her to endure that just because of his values? Merrin's concerns are milder. "Personally, I am not interested in putting her in private school. And I'm not excited about putting her in public school either," says Merrin. "We'll see what we do."

These conversations, as with all parents thinking about the schooling of their children, were an endless weighing of costs and benefits. Were the public schools so bad that it was worth driving a half hour each way to take their child to a charter school they believed would offer more academic rigor or more individualized attention? Could Merrin earn enough to cover the expense of private school? Were the private schools so much better that it was worth the cost of tuition, which in California averages $15,290 a year for elementary school and $20,942 a year for secondary? Which failings of a school could they most easily compensate for at home: the academic shortcomings they expected at a public school, or the elitism they expected at a private one?

When the state of California passed Proposition 13, voters were weighing costs against benefits, too. It is only now, with forty years of history gone by, that the stakes of the calculation have become clear. Jared and Merrin pay $11,500 less a year in taxes than they would have without Proposition 13. In part because of those savings, multiplied across all the homeowners in the state of California, the free public education in Vallejo is, by the state's measure, either low or very low quality. This is the tradeoff that was made, and which Jared and Merrin now face.

My country offers a solution, of course, to this problem of underfunded public services. They can pay for their daughter's education on the private market, at a price that far exceeds the taxes they've saved.

MY CHILDHOOD

SOUTHEAST MICHIGAN

1984–1994

In my memory, my mother got sick slowly. In her medical records, my mother's decline was rapid and relentless. Within a year of the accident, the woman who'd married my father when she was young and smiling and beautiful, who'd borne and begun to raise three girls, had slipped away. The doctors did not warn us what was coming; brain injuries were only newly considered a category of medicine of their own. We were left to discover it ourselves.

My parents fought more, and my mother continued to withdraw. Her world contracted to the end of the kitchen table, where she sat all day, chain-smoking and eating candy, watching soap operas and talk shows. When I think of my mother, I do not see her young and smiling and beautiful. Instead, I see her hunched over the kitchen table in tinted glasses framed by a dark, lank perm. She wears shabby velour sweats, reaches for her vinyl cigarette case, and sips ice water through a bent plastic straw.

The first mention of dementia in my mother's records came the December after the accident the previous February. By then, her speech was slurred and she was having suicidal thoughts. Her first brain scans since the accident showed "moderate degenerative changes." Doctors advised my father to provide twenty-four-hour care at home. They had little advice about how to pay for it.

By then, we had sued the drunk driver and won a settlement. My father took the money—around $20,000, he thinks—and put it into an annuity he still collects from today. My father's medical insurance would cover basic medical costs like occupational therapy, but none of the significant costs her emerging, and permanent, disability would require, such as modifying our home or hiring help. My father earned too much for my mother to qualify for Medicaid or disability. Michigan, though, had a generous no-fault insurance law that required auto insurers to cover the cost of injuries from car accidents—including the care at home it was increasingly clear my mother needed. My parents' lawyer began asking my family's auto insurer about covering my mother's care.

Although the no-fault insurance had paid for my mother's stitches and plastic surgery, they balked at this new, costly request. *Were these changes really from the accident?* the representative, a twenty-six-year-old woman from Waterford, asked. *Didn't she already have multiple sclerosis? Why should the insurer have to pay?*

Those were the questions the insurer asked directly. But they were asking something deeper, too: *Does she deserve medical care?* It was up to us to prove it.

* * * * *

Whatever the cause, my mother was deteriorating rapidly. She could no longer concentrate enough to read. Her hands trembled too much to write. She began asking me to take notes from her phone calls: who had called, what they had told her, and, if it was a referral for help, who to call next. She was too tired to cook meals, so I read cookbooks and Tuna Helper boxes, trying to learn. She threw a smoldering cigarette in the trash, where it caught fire, so I began watching ashtrays closely. She began falling in the house, so I watched her movements and called for my father if she tried to walk unaided. In those days, she often said things like: *"I didn't use to be like this."* She said, *"I don't understand what happened."*

None of us really did.

Because my mother had not died, we had no language for the loss that was unfolding. She had been an avid reader who wrote poetry; now, doctors put her verbal IQ at 88 and judged her as having "severe to profound impairment." The adults missed her personality, her jokes and conversation. It was different for my sisters and me. We were too young to know and miss our mother's personality. Instead, we nursed a feral hunger for mothering. We were adrift and unmoored, searching.

We began to behave badly. My father left for work a half hour before the school bus arrived. Technically, my mother was in charge, but even as children we understood she could not intervene. Our fights grew violent. We wielded chairs and walkers as weapons, locked each other outside, threw steak knives like daggers. I imagine these behaviors showed up in school, though I can't recall a specific instance. A therapist, engaged after my mother overdosed on pills, advised that "immediate steps need to be taken on [the children's] behalf." At school, we each began to get called out of class for visits with a counselor.

It was the first experience I had of considering my emotional life as important as my physical and academic one. For my family, it was an offering of help, made at no cost to us.

* * * * *

Schools worked differently for other students.

My sister Shana tells me of watching her fourth-grade teacher grab the collar of a Black boy in her class who was misbehaving and all but throw him into a corner. It was violent enough for her to remember it decades later and tell me about it in passing. Violent enough for me to remember it years after that.

Although our families were different in many ways, this boy's family was weathering a similar battle to the one my family faced. The year before, according to court documents, his father had been severely injured at his job in the paint shop of an auto plant.* Before the accident, their family—like my family—had survived on the father's income while the mother cared for the children. After the accident, worker's compensation benefits and a settlement were slow in coming. The mother tells me she tended a vegetable garden and relied on family to get by. Welfare, which at the time was available only to single mothers, was not an option.

I cannot say how the behavior of my sisters and I differed from my sister's classmate, but I can see a difference in how we were treated. My sisters and I, three white girls, and our effectively single father, a white man, were struggling and stumbling, and we were met with sympathy and help. This was true of our school, where our misbehavior was met with care, and it was true of our neighbors, who occasionally invited my sisters and me for sleepovers to give my parents a break. My sister's classmate, a Black boy in a family that faced pressures similar to mine—as well as the pressures of racism—had a different experience. At school, a teacher threw him. In the community, the family was met with indifference. His mother tells me she does not remember any of her white neighbors volunteering to help.

The difference in our experiences echoes research on the rationale given for school discipline. On average, difficult white students are considered "high-strung" and to have "had a hard day." Difficult Black children are described as "destructive" and "violent," and "cannot be managed."

Our experiences also echo extensive research showing that white students—and especially white girls—are far less likely to be disciplined or face corporal punishment for the same transgressions than are Black students—especially Black boys. In the 1970s, white elementary students were roughly one-third as likely as Black students to be suspended from school; by the 2010s, they were one-sixth as likely. When I was in high school, the chance of a white, female public-school student being hit by

---

* Historian Joyce Shaw Peterson's 1979 article in the *Journal of Negro History*, "Black Automobile Workers in Detroit: 1910–1930," documents clearly how Black auto workers were typically segregated into the most dangerous departments of auto factories: the foundry and the paint shop.

an adult in school was one-sixteenth that of a Black boy. No matter the gender, the income level, or the behavior being punished, Black students in American schools are consistently disciplined more, and more harshly, than their white counterparts.

That's another way of saying that white people have more patience, and give more benefit of the doubt—are kinder—to students who are not Black; that they are kinder to people like me. Given the difference between my sister's classmate's story and mine, I cannot see it any other way.

★ ★ ★ ★ ★

For years, I longed for a way to cure my mother. I wrote about it in school journal entries, which I knew teachers would read; in letters to Santa long after I knew he was fiction; in missives pleading with President Reagan. I think this is a common way people react when a loved one is snatched-away-but-still-there: We beg, plead, and bargain for a return to normal. We pray. We are desperate. And as with all desperate people in America, there are entrepreneurs offering to solve our need—for a price. The solution presented to my family—to my father—was of rehabilitation. He could send my mother to a home where specialists would help her regain what skills she could. Then she could return home.

My father did not find this solution himself. As I started fifth grade in 1986, my father switched attorneys, to one specializing in auto injury cases, Wayne Miller. Our new lawyer recommended a new doctor, who in turn recommended sending my mother to a home. My father had become my mother's conservator by then. He testified that he visited a few nursing homes. One, he said, "was a pit." Then Miller suggested my father contact a local chain of "cognitive rehabilitation" homes, Total Therapy Management.

Centers like Total Therapy were relatively new then. In 1981, there were just fourteen of them nationwide. Within three years, there were 266. States with no-fault insurance laws, which gave survivors of auto accidents medical care regardless of who caused the accident, fueled the industry's growth. Half of all brain injuries then were sustained in car crashes; anyone offering care for brain-injured patients could access a large market. Little wonder that rehabilitation centers, a growing share of them for-profit businesses, attracted investment capital.

Industry profits grew. In 1987, observers estimated annual revenue for the head-injury rehabilitation industry at $800 million, and predicted it would reach $1 billion by decade's end. They told the *New York Times* that it was the "fastest growing niche of the health-care industry," with "enormous growth potential." They did not say that medical research had yet to prove which treatments worked, and which did not. They did not say that the enormous potential for profit came from the prices they set, around $400 a day for residential care. If they noted brain rehab was five times as expensive as traditional nursing homes, I imagine they quickly added that it cost half of what hospital care did. The industry kept growing. By the early 1990s, more than seven hundred brain rehabilitation centers operated in the United States.

The industry was profitable, but it was flooded with abuses. Brain injury wasn't yet formalized as an injury within medical practice or health insurance. There were no codes in Medicaid or Medicare to correspond to it, no mandatory accreditation ensuring standards of care. It was broadly understood, back then, that nursing homes could be nightmarish places. Cognitive rehabilitation homes, said their managers, were a better option—and there was nobody to say what was fair and what was predatory. The combination of desperate patients and bottomless insurance coverage struck some entrepreneurs as an opportunity— and they took it. By 1992, enough patients and advocates complained about the industry that a congressional subcommittee held a hearing to parse them.

A month after the hearing, the *New York Times* ran a front-page investigation into the industry. The story included a Michigan family suing Total Therapy Management for overcharging for care of a brain-injured ten-year-old, done by untrained staff. My mother had left Total Therapy by then, and I remember hearing adults mention the news, but I did not ask about it. I understood, without anyone telling me, that we had no right to complain. This was America. We'd take what we got and make it work.

★ ★ ★ ★ ★

It was November, just after I turned eleven, when my father told me he might send my mother away. We were in the station wagon, puttering past tumbledown Victorians in town. I remember watching streetlights cast gingerbread shadows on porches, and hearing our wheels rumble over a series of railroad tracks, as my father told me his plan for my mother. There was a place to send her, he said. Like a hospital but smaller, where people could help her. She would go for three months. Then, maybe, she could come home.

I sat quietly and considered this. My father was offering a solution to the problem I'd been consumed by. I knew I should be grateful for it. I felt numb instead. I could barely speak. It was my job to care for her, and now it was being taken away. I had failed her.

"She might get better?"

My father nodded. "Yeah, she might."

I paused, unsure.

My father kept talking. There were special doctors to help my mother. I would like the home. But he would need my help. He still needed to tell my sisters. He wanted me to help him tell my sisters why my mother needed to go away.

My father and I told my sisters in my parents' room, just the four of us. I don't remember what my father said, but I remember my sisters' response: howling and crying and clinging to my father. They sobbed for our mother, who was not in the room with us. She must have been elsewhere in the house, listening. I watched, and I listened, and I did not cry. I tried to help.

My family's memories of this differ. My sisters do not remember being told at all. My father remembers telling us, but that we were calm. "There weren't any tears that I remember," he said. "Maybe you understood that it was best for her that she couldn't continue to live where she was." My mother, he says, was only confused. "She wasn't angry, like yelling and screaming. But she didn't understand why she couldn't take care of herself," he says.

On the first Monday in January, my sisters and I stayed home from school. My father put my mother's suitcases, then her wheelchair and walker, in the station wagon's trunk. Then we piled into the car and drove to Flint, parking in the drive of a ranch house with a long, wooden ramp leading to its front door.

I remember being surprised at how the house was so much smaller than ours. I remember going for burgers and fries afterward. But I do not remember what we said to my mother, what she said to us, or if we hugged or kissed her as we prepared to leave. I did not cry or make a scene, and today this feels like a failing.

We were leaving my mother in a home. The least I could have done was protest. But I did not. As far as I remember it, I did as my father had asked, and I endured without complaint.

★ ★ ★ ★ ★

My mother entered the rehabilitation home for "cognitive restructuring" in January 1988. Reports from Total Therapy indicate the goals set: to bring her reading comprehension to sixth-grade level; to bring her addition and subtraction to third-grade level; to teach her how to prepare a cold lunch "with cuing for safety only." To practice fine motor skills, my mother drew stars and wrote her name; both verged on illegible. After a month, staff reported that "Charyl now accepts that she needs to be here." They told her, as they must have told my father, "Only by trying to better herself will she be able to return to a quality of life that she previously enjoyed."

For my mother's care and lodging that first month, Total Therapy billed my family $15,400. They billed similar amounts in February and March. By the end of her first three months, we had bills totaling $45,265.

Nobody expected these bills to be paid until the lawsuit was settled—

and even then, only if the case went our way. Wayne Miller had helped my father broker an arrangement with the home to carry us through the trial. They accepted my mother in hopes that the trial with the insurer would find her eligible for no-fault coverage. If we won the lawsuit, the insurer would pay Total Therapy for her care—all the costs incurred before the trial, and all that came after. If we lost, Total Therapy agreed not to charge my father for the care they had given; he'd just have to find another way to care for her. This arrangement also removed Total Therapy from a normal competitive market, where customers would weigh price against benefit.

Even this, I think, reflects a grim aspect of our white advantage: Total Therapy had been willing to take on my mother despite the fact that she could not immediately pay. Given what I know about racism in my country, it's hard for me to envision the same offer being extended to a Black family who could not pay now, and would only ever be able to pay if a jury decided in their favor.

The costs were astronomical even by contemporary standards, but the price tag didn't matter to my father, who'd never have to pay the costs himself. The price mattered more to the lawyer, who'd deduct the cost of the trial from the settlement, and then get one-third of what remained; the larger the settlement, the more money he would make. The price also mattered for Total Therapy, which was a for-profit company—and which held a license, only, for providing adult foster care. The more they could charge, and the less they spent on care, the more they made.

After my mother's initial three months at Total Therapy, she had not improved. Without progress, the director told my father that "it is not advisable to return her to your home." Instead, the director suggested that my mother stay on at Total Therapy, where they would shift their focus to maintaining a quality of life. Costs, accordingly, dropped; that May, the company billed about $9,200 for her care.

At first, Total Therapy continued my mother's occupational and physical therapy, which my father's regular insurance covered. The company also began to provide therapeutic treatments, which—like any care not covered by my father's medical insurance—they provided for free at the time, with hopes of being repaid. Soon, though, Total Therapy stopped those treatments altogether, swapping them out for a simple daycare program. By late that year, the only care Total Therapy provided was essentially the same as adult foster care: hygiene, room and board, simple activities like visiting a museum or park.

As a child, I believed what my father told me: My mother had to go into a home because we could not afford to pay for her care at home. There is some truth to that. At the time, neither Medicaid nor private insurance would have paid for the at-home care my mother would have needed to stay in our house, which consultants estimated would cost $77,000 a year.* The coverage we were seeking in court would have covered at-home expenses for the duration of my mother's life. But there was no company offering to provide *that* for free while the case progressed.

And so, the lawyer and my father tell me, my mother went to Total Therapy. From May to November of that first year, the monthly cost of her stay at Total Therapy increased by 50 percent, to $13,440—while the scope of services had *decreased*. By the end of 1988, my mother's first year at Total Therapy, we had been billed $145,784. That was the equivalent, in January 2023, of $392,214.

★ ★ ★ ★ ★

From then on, I only saw my mother on weekends. Sometimes we packed picnic lunches and went to state parks; sometimes we visited my grandmother. But mostly we went to shopping malls, sheltered from rain or heat. We would eye things we could not afford to buy, daydream about toys and fashion and housewares. Then we would go eat.

One weekend, I remember, we visited the mall in Pontiac, Summit Place. In 2019, after its halls had been empty for a decade, the city demolished it, but in the 1980s it was booming: 160 stores, 1.4 million square feet, strip malls multiplying at its borders. The food court, just opened, was a

---

* According to the Bureau of Labor Statistics, $77,000 in January 1987, the year the estimate was made, was equivalent to $207,159 in January 2023.

novelty to us. We sat at tan Formica tables ringed with plastic benches and chairs. We ate Burger King and Sbarro.

As we finished eating, my mother said, *"I have to go to the bathroom."*

"Tracie, can you help her?" asked my father. I was already rising from my seat and walking to my mother's wheelchair, a donation from Easter Seals. I stood behind her and reached around to release each brake.

"Okay," I said. I reversed the chair and looked around until I spotted the bathroom sign, posted above a doorway between two restaurant counters. A line of women and girls reached into the dining area. My mother and I joined them. The line moved slowly. I noticed that the women in the line were looking at us, but I did not understand why.

"Tracie, I really have to go," my mother said, fidgeting. I was twelve, used to following the rules. Even though I knew that my mother might wet herself, it did not occur to me to ask to jump the line. *"You have to hold it, Mom,"* I said.

When the line reached the bathroom, my mother repeated herself. *"I really have to go,"* she said.

I got out of line and knocked on the door to the accessible stall. *"Hello?"* I said, timid. *"My mom needs to go. Can you hurry up?"* I said. There was no response. My mother fidgeted. *"I really need to go,"* she said.

"Should we try a regular stall?" I asked.

"OK," she said.

When the next stall door opened, I wheeled her chair to its door and locked the wheels. My mother stood shakily, grasping at the doorframe, the toilet paper fixture, anything to support her. I can picture her in the stall, turning, attempting to lower herself, still clothed, onto the toilet, then saying, helplessly, *"I can't."* She clambered, sweating, back into the chair.

I knocked on the accessible stall again. A few minutes later, a young woman, maybe twenty, emerged wordlessly, a change of clothes clutched in her arms, her hands going anxiously to her hair. She said nothing to us. I wheeled my mother's chair into the stall and positioned it so she could reach the bars.

For a long time, I remembered this by judging the young woman who'd been changing her clothes, heedless to my knocks: Why didn't she hurry up? As an adult, I wonder more about the people around us. I wonder why all those women watched us, a child and her mother struggling, and did nothing. I wonder why nobody helped us. Why silence was the best they could do.

I learned an ugly lesson that day. I learned to be silent. I learned to respond to suffering and injustice by observing and keeping my mouth shut. I learned that it was foolish to complain; that if I saw someone struggle, it was not my place to help. I was wrong, of course, but I had little way to know it. I was a child, looking for answers, and absorbed the one in front of me: If nobody was looking out for me and my mom, it was silly for me to look out for anyone else.

That was the first time I learned that lesson. It would not be my last.

★ ★ ★ ★ ★

In August 1989, five years after the accident, we went to court. The lawyers ran through twenty-three jurors before seating eight. Of the fifteen jurors excused, four were excluded after saying they had argued with insurers to cover care. A fifth was excluded after calling insurers' denial of claims "standard procedure."

Because my mother had multiple sclerosis at the time of the accident, doctors argued about why she had gotten so bad, so quick: Was it the car accident, or was it the MS? The insurance company said it was the MS; in the accident, they said, "the bang to her head wasn't hard enough to knock her out." It was 1989, seven years before brain injury would even be recognized in federal policy. My family's lawyer argued that my mother's mild head injury in the car accident—"quite a wallop," he told the jury—had made her MS worse.

This left the jury with two questions. The first was whether the car accident had contributed to my mother's current condition. If the jury decided the car accident hadn't made my mother worse, the case was over. But if the jury thought the accident *had* made things worse, that meant my mother would get no-fault coverage—and medical care for the rest of her life. Then, the jury would decide whether the money we were asking for was reasonable repayment for the cost of her care so far.

We were asking the insurer for more than $300,000. About $125,000 of that was for my family, to cover the years of care we had provided at home. The rest of it, about $177,000, was for Total Therapy. The case was important for other families, too, because it would settle a question about whether car accident injuries that *worsened* a preexisting condition—a condition like multiple sclerosis, or, more commonly, back pain—could be covered by no-fault insurance.

My compulsion, in reading the transcripts of the month-long trial, is to answer the questions posed to the jury: Was my mother sicker because of the MS alone, or because of the brain injury, too? Is MS made worse by head injuries? How severe was the head injury? Did the lawyer miss a 1981 peer-reviewed study, found by me in 2021, showing that one-third of patients with "minor head trauma" were unable to return to work within three months? Am I being emotional when I want to believe the four caregivers who testified for my mother? Is it unreasonable to reject the three paid expert witnesses, called by the insurer, who'd never met my mother before the trial? Can I prove, all these years later, that it was the "wallop" that did her in, not the MS?

These are the wrong questions, though. They are the wrong questions because beneath them lies another: *Did my mother really deserve care?* That question, in turn, begged another: *Was my mother milking the system, trying to take something to which she was not entitled?* We were consumed with proving what my mother deserved. There was no room to even consider what my mother needed: decent care.

★ ★ ★ ★ ★

The jury delivered its verdict the same day that argumentation ended. *Yes,* said jurors, *the accident had made my mother worse.* But our victory largely ended there. The jury awarded Total Therapy only $60,000 of the $177,000 they had billed for her care. The jurors did this, the judge later suggested, because my mother would have become debilitated by the MS, car accident or no. The jury did not give my family anything for the care we had provided at home. The jurors did this because my family's lawyer—still early in his career, and learning the ins and outs of going to trial—had not submitted the figure to the jury with the case's exhibits.

My family's lawyer insisted that the decision meant we had "prevailed," which meant my mother would have no-fault coverage, and be able to stay on at Total Therapy; this also meant his fees would be covered by the insurer.

The insurer disagreed. Since the jury hadn't awarded all the money requested, the insurer's lawyer said, nobody had prevailed—and the insurer had no obligation to cover my mother's care. The insurer took my family back to court, seeking a declaration that they would not have to pay for ongoing care.

Total Therapy, which had spent the last two years caring for my mother for free in hopes of receiving no-fault insurance payments, would no longer wait. They sent a letter to the attorney, thanking him for connecting them with our family and urging him to consider them for future cases. They told my father that, without no-fault payments coming, he would soon be responsible for the cost of my mother's care. If he couldn't pay the $9,000 a month Total Therapy charged for my mother's care, he would need to send her somewhere else. They were a business, after all.*

★ ★ ★ ★ ★

When the lawsuit failed, my father says, he followed Wayne Miller's advice. "The attorney came and sat down and said, you're probably going to last about six months and then you'll be out on the street to pay for her care. And if you get divorced, then Medicaid will take over. The

---

* In order of ascending value, $9,000 was equivalent to $22,234 in January 2023; $60,000 to $148,226; $125,000 to $308,805; and $177,000 to $437,267, according to the Bureau of Labor Statistics.

outcome for her is going to be the same," my father says. "So, we went along with that."

Wayne Miller told me he does not remember whether he offered this advice or not. "I really don't remember that," he told me. "I would generally be loath to give that kind of advice because of my feelings about the importance of marriage. It's possible I referred him to another attorney who made that recommendation."

My father must have been traumatized and exhausted. He testified at trial that it was impossible to have my mother in the home—"not only physically but mentally." In trial, his attorney asked him, "From whose point of view, yours or hers?" He responded, "From ours, everybody but hers. It's a terrible strain on the kids to have to be in charge of their own mother." The case files include the psychological assessment of my sisters and me from several years before, urging immediate steps be taken on our behalf, but he did not mention it at the trial.

After the trial, my father went to Grandma Kate and Grandpa Don, and told them he was filing for divorce. Years later, my grandmother told me about this conversation and others like it. She shared what she remembered my father telling her and Grandpa Don, that the stress in his life was making him sick, putting his life in danger. As she remembered it to me, he said he needed to divorce my mother if he wanted to live. My grandmother told me my father said that my mother was dead to him.

My father's memories differ from mine, from the record, and from what my grandmother told me while she was alive. Today, my father says he remembers my sisters and me as "normal kids," largely unaffected by the loss unfolding before us. He remembers Grandma Kate being supportive of his choices, including the divorce. He does not remember mentioning stress or saying that my mother was dead to him. He remembers that we all endured without complaint.

This is striking to me, particularly given what was left unsaid. When my father broached the topic of divorce, he did not tell my grandparents—although they had already heard through family—that he was dating. After he placed my mother in the home, my father began spending time with Bonnie, my mother's friend, whose marriage was faltering. Bonnie says her first husband felt distant, uninterested in her and their daughter. My father, who still managed to run my sisters and me to play practices and softball leagues, who struggled so much to care for my mother, was a welcome counterpart. Here, she says, was someone who needed her, someone she could help.

* * * * *

My grandparents became my mother's guardians in February 1990. Total Therapy did not accept Medicaid and they set a deadline for my mother to move out. My grandparents found a nursing home near their house, in a suburb called Novi, and hoped for the best. "The care isn't very good," my grandmother wrote in her journal shortly after my mother moved in. "And it's going to take its toll on her. Time will tell." The divorce papers had come a couple weeks before.

The nursing home was full of poor and elderly people. Even that place, I remember, was segregated; the only nonwhite faces I remember were of the aides in the halls. But whatever white bonus these people carried, its material benefit had faded by the time they ended up here. Now they, and my mother, were subject to the punishing rules at the bottom of our economy, in the bottom reaches of our health care system. These were rules that many white people had assumed would only ever be applied to people who were *not* white.

After a month in the Novi home, my mother developed pneumonia, which develops rapidly when a patient spends most of their time lying down. My mother could not move between her bed and wheelchair without help, and the nursing home did not have enough staff to help her do so daily. Soon, she was in the hospital. Within two weeks, doctors performed a tracheotomy, puncturing her windpipe beneath her vocal cords and installing a plastic cuff to keep the wound open. The procedure eased her breathing and made it easier for doctors to keep her on a ventilator. It also removed her ability to speak.

For the next two months, my mother swung between life and death. We would get urgent calls asking us to rush to the hospital, forty-five minutes away, and we would arrive breathless to find my mother sweating in her sleep, machines beeping around her. On one of these calls, someone told my father that my mother was going to die that night.

At the hospital that night, we gathered around her bed and took turns holding her hand. Her palm was clammy when I grasped it. I looked at her closed eyes, the curled baby hairs damply plastered to her forehead, and thought, *My mother is going to die.* I waited for tears to come but they did not. Instead, I thought something I remember overhearing my father say, privately, to friends: *It would have been better if she'd died in the accident.*

* * * * *

The doctors were wrong, and my mother did not die then. She spent four months in the hospital, and then doctors moved her to a rehabilitation facility. She was weaker, and more disabled, than she had been before the pneumonia. Before, my mother could tell us what she had done that day and ask us questions when we told her about our lives at home. Before, she could walk or use her wheelchair, and we could take her places with us, driving our regular cars. When she transferred to the rehabilitation facility in July, she could not talk, and had to be transported on a stretcher. That month, my parents' divorce became final.

I think the divorce papers had been signed when Dad and Bonnie called my sisters and me to the kitchen table after dinner one night. I remember a bottle of Korbel on the table alongside juice glasses we'd had since I was small.

"Bonnie and I have something to tell you," said my father.

"We're getting married!" said Bonnie. They were both smiling.

My father popped the cork and poured champagne into my mother's juice glasses. We each took one.

"Cheers!" said my father, looking at Bonnie.

"*Cheers,*" my sisters and I repeated. We clinked our glasses and took little sips.

By then, Bonnie was coming to our house most nights. She would help with dinner and eat with us. My sisters and I would watch TV as they played games of rummy that ended long after my sisters and I had gone to bed. My father didn't explain to my sisters and me what was happening. I was too young to understand it as courtship.

My father encouraged us to be as excited about Bonnie as he was, and so I told myself that she would make things in our family better. My father's temper had been getting worse ever since he had sent my mother away. I was in junior high, and I remember him shoving me as he yelled, and once pulling my hair. I remember being called a bitch. I remember telling the social worker I saw at school that my father had cornered me under a couch cushion, then pulled me half-upside down to spank me. She was sympathetic, and said he seemed to need a lot of control, but she did not make a report. I thought Bonnie could solve this problem: There'd be someone to stand up for us.

And I was hungry, too, for mothering. Bonnie, I thought, would do the things my mother no longer could: help me, guide me, care for me. With Bonnie, I could have the things I'd kept writing for, and wishing for, in journals and letters: a normal, happy family. A mother. This was a fantasy, borrowed from my father and *Brady Bunch* reruns. Believing it required only one thing: that I let my hunger for mothering supersede my loyalty to my mother.

I am ashamed that I believed it.

I wonder if I'd be ashamed if I'd gotten what I wanted.

* * * * *

Nobody told me that I needed to earn my keep. But when my father sent my mother away because it was too expensive to keep her home, that is the lesson I took. As a kid, I'd sold food I'd made and babysat for family. Once I turned fourteen and could legally work, I looked for a real job.

Being young and female shunted me into the worst-paid corners of the job market: domestic and agricultural labor. When I babysat for neighbors, I earned one or two or three dollars an hour.* At fourteen, the youngest legal age for children to work, I made caramel apples at an orchard two miles from my house—close enough that I could walk or ride my bike.

I no longer have my pay stubs for that job, but I remember the boss explaining that our wages might look low, but that was because we worked at an agricultural business; they had different rules than other jobs. As I remember it, for every hour I coated apples in caramel, I earned less than if I'd been selling clothes in a department store, which would have paid $3.35 an hour.

If I was paid less than the regular minimum wage, it was only because farmworkers had been excluded from the country's first labor laws in the 1930s. And those exclusions had been allowed, in turn, because some white men decades before me hadn't wanted to pay Black workers fairly.

My wages mattered, deeply, to me. The less safe I felt at home, the more that paying for college became my obsession. Every penny counted. What I could not earn by working, I tried to make up for in scholarships. After I read an article in *Sassy* magazine mentioning a National Merit Scholarship that required high scores on a test called the preliminary SAT, I realized that every grade and test counted, too. I worked harder at school and used some of my earnings to buy a study guide. I planned to buy a cheap car, so I could get an after-school job, so I could save money for college.

I had intuited, dimly, that a job would make me less of a burden to my family. As I began to earn money, I understood that it gave me independence from them, too. My father understood that, too, and I think it scared him. I cannot think of another reason for him to have begun telling me, regularly but especially in anger, that he was named on my bank account. My money was his, he told me. He was entitled to everything I had.

★ ★ ★ ★ ★

---

* According to the Bureau of Labor Statistics, $1 in January 1990 was the equivalent of $2.35 in January 2023; similarly, $3 was equivalent to $7.04.

In February 1991, my mother moved into a second nursing home, called the Greenery.* Before my mother moved to the Greenery, Grandma Kate lamented her losses: "We feel Charyl slipping away from us more and more. She is not as alert as she was and doesn't pay much attention when we are there," she wrote. Within a few weeks of the move, Grandma Kate saw improvements in her daughter: "Charyl is doing beautifully. She had a permanent today."

If my mother liked her new home, she couldn't tell anyone because she still had an open tracheostomy. Nobody at the main hospital or the recovery facility had asked about closing it off so she could speak. It took a speech therapist at the Greenery a few months to ask my grandparents if my mother's vocal cords were paralyzed. The question surprised my grandmother. "To our knowledge they are not," she wrote in her journal.

A few weeks later, doctors replaced my mother's tracheostomy tube with one that could easily be plugged, finally allowing air to move past her vocal cords. She had been voiceless for twenty months by then.

My mother spoke, haltingly, with the nurses, but she did not speak to her parents for several days. I wonder if she could not fathom how to express her rage: *How could you let me live like that for so long?*

* * * * *

My mother died on February 24, 1993. I didn't know it was coming, except for the fact that it was always coming, a tragedy and a relief just out of sight. I do not remember my father saying anything to me about it. Shana remembers him inviting her to come with him to the nursing home the night before, but Shana declined. She regrets this.

---

* Advocates had begun asking the state to close her prior home, in Novi, the summer before she moved there. It did not pause admissions until five months after my mother left with pneumonia—and then only after one patient sued for being beaten and another choked to death at lunch, unnoticed by a twenty-six-year-old aide tasked with feeding twelve patients with dementia. The *Detroit Free Press* featured that home in a series of articles in 1990 investigating suspicious deaths in nursing homes, including the one my mother was in.

It was early morning, the sky still dark outside, when the phone rang. I was washing my face in the bathroom. I heard my father pick up the receiver, say hello, and sigh. I heard my sisters, who had picked up the phone in the hall, begin to sob. Without anyone saying anything, I knew what had happened. I looked in the mirror and thought, *I can't.* At home, my job would be to care for everyone else—to comfort my sisters and my grandparents, to absolve my father, to navigate my stepmother. I thought: *I cannot be here.* I went into my room and began getting ready for school. The bus was coming soon.

I walked out of my room, fully dressed and with my backpack. I remember Shana coming into the hall and looking at me with wide eyes. She said, *"You're going to school?"*

I did not reply. I walked downstairs, where my father and stepmother sat at the kitchen table in their pajamas.

"I'm going to school," I said. *"The bus is coming right now."*

My father blinked at me. *"Okay."*

I put on my coat and my boots and walked out the door, my feet sinking into a thick blanket of snow. When the bus arrived at our driveway, I climbed wordlessly aboard.

★ ★ ★ ★ ★

Forty days later, the Michigan Court of Appeals issued a final ruling on my mother's insurance case. It had been bouncing between judges for more than two years. The court ruled that my mother was entitled to no-fault benefits.

That meant my mother could have stayed at the first home, Total Therapy, after all. It meant she could have moved to a better one, or maybe, even, gotten funding to stay at home with us. It meant she never needed to go to that first nursing home, where they beat the patients and she got pneumonia and needed a tracheostomy and lost the ability to speak. It meant the last two years never needed to happen.

During the era in which my mother became sick, people with power in America were beginning to use economics to analyze health care in a new way. When my mother was a child, in the 1960s, it was unusual to talk about "cost-benefit" and "cost-effectiveness" in health care; only six or seven journal studies a year used that phrasing. In 1990, more than 250 studies used that language. This makes some sense: With the creation of Medicaid and Medicare in 1965, the government needed to ensure it was paying reasonable rates for the health care it now covered. But "cost-benefit" has come to warp care, with insurers and medical groups increasingly measuring success not by care given but money made. It has made it easier to think of human bodies as costs, and to forget that they belong to people. It has made it easier to be cruel.

This sleight of hand has a long history in America. Its taproot stretches back to the enslavement era, where intricate data tables scribbled in ledgers chart how much value a human, worked until ragged, can create from a cotton field, and how little they can be fed to create it. In studying the records of enslavement-era hospitals in the South, historians Jonathan Pritchett and Kevin Lander found that plantation owners withheld care from enslaved children and the elderly enslaved, who, as commodities, were considered the least valuable. The same enslavers spent money freely to cure prime-age enslaved males, who commanded higher prices. "Owners cared for slaves when it paid to do so," they write. Enslavers only sent the enslaved to doctors, in other words, when the financial benefit outweighed the cost.

The suffering and health of the enslaved were not part of the calculation. My country has learned to feel moral outrage about one man claiming ownership of another. We don't yet acknowledge this "practical" rationale of cost and benefit, which American society increasingly applies to almost everything, for what it usually is: apathy and cruelty justified with numbers.

In the end, the two-year delay in my mother's insurance case benefited the lawyer, whose fees were covered by the settlement—and who, by winning the legal argument, broadened the pool of viable cases in the area of law in which he practiced. It benefited the families who came after us, because it set a precedent for coverage in future cases. It benefited the insurer who ran out the clock on my mother's life and had no future obligations.

It did not benefit me. I do not think it was worth the cost.

* * * * *

After my mother died, things got worse at home. My father and Bonnie had started fighting soon after they married, but I remember it intensifying after the funeral. I withdrew from my family, burying myself in school and work. My sisters clung to each other. We were all grieving, and I do not remember any of us turning to each other. I do not remember anyone suggesting that we should.

Despite all that, my plan to use college as an escape hatch seemed to be working. I'd done well enough on the PSAT to be a finalist for a National Merit Scholarship, which led to a deluge of marketing materials from colleges all over the country. I don't remember meeting with a guidance counselor at my high school, where most kids went to community colleges and state schools. In the fall, I applied to University of Michigan because that was the good state school near Grandpa Mac. I applied to Northwestern, outside Chicago, because I was considering journalism. I applied to Illinois Wesleyan and Northeast Missouri State because their applications were free. I was paying for my own application fees—for each one, I'd hand my father wads of dollar bills I'd earned waiting tables at Big Boy, a job I'd started the summer before, and he'd write the check—so I was careful about where I applied.

I would've stopped with those four schools, but in December I'd had an intense fight with my father. With a panic, I'd realized that if I went to school within a day's drive of home, I'd be expected to come back regularly. I remembered the packet that had arrived from New York University, and fished the application out of the pile. I filled it in by hand, attached an essay from English class, and sent it in just before the deadline.

I got into every school, but I remember that the cheapest schools out-of-pocket were NYU and the University of Michigan. I'd visited U-M, Northwestern, and NYU with my parents, who even paid to fly the three of us to New York. I'd liked NYU the most. My dad surprised me when he suggested I go there, before I said a word. *"I can see you there,"* he said.

It must have been so hard for him to see that I belonged somewhere that he did not. It must have been so hard for him to say that to me; to give me permission to just *go*. It is the most selfless, generous thing I have seen him do for me, and I am grateful for it.

★ ★ ★ ★ ★

That July, I used one of my father's beer figurines to kill a roach in the basement, which he'd renovated into a bar. The figurine's base broke in half. Fearful of my father's temper, I put it back on the shelf and pushed the halves back together. When he found it, he told my sisters and me that we could not leave the house until someone admitted to the damage. Nobody had spoken. The next afternoon, he called from work, asking who'd broken the figurine. I sighed and told him it was me.

"I am getting ready to go to work. We can talk about it later," I said.

"I'm coming home now," he said.

I was in the family room, standing near the sliding door when he arrived. I wore my uniform: a polyester pencil skirt the color of wet cement, a sheer, short-sleeved blouse imprinted with outlines of Big Boy and a bow at the neck. Drugstore pantyhose and black flats.

"Where are you going?"

"I'm going to work, Dad."

"You're not going to work."

"I'm going to work." I looked at the sliding door, tried to calculate what would happen if I got through it and ran to my car. The pull of my father kept me from trying.

"I have to pay for college." I remember how he looked at me, the distinct flutter of panic in my chest. I felt like prey.

"You're not going to college."

"Dad, I—"

"Give me your keys."

"No," I said, surprising myself. *"I'm going to work. We'll talk about this later."*

"You're not going to work."

"You bastard, leave me alone."

By then he was facing me, with six inches and fifty pounds on me. He reared back his right arm and smacked my face with such force I saw stars. Then his hands ringed my neck, lifting my skull up without squeezing.

"Dad, I have to go to work."

"You're not going to work."

"Give me your keys." His teeth were clenched.

I would not. I stood on my tiptoes to match his grip on my throat.

"No, I'm going to work, Dad. I need money for college."

"You're not going to college. Give me your keys! You will do what I say!"

I must have wrested myself away from him. Something had to have changed for me to end up where I next remember: On my stomach on the floor, pinned beneath my father, who now straddled my back.

"Give me your keys!"

I clutched my hands under my chest.

"No." I was sobbing. *"I have to go to work to get money for college."*

"You're not going to college. That's my money."

He grabbed and pulled my head up by my ponytail. Then he pushed my head into the carpet.

"Give."

He pulled my head up, then slammed it down.

"Me. Your. Keys."

With each syllable, my face met the carpet. I screamed for help. Jodie was upstairs. There was the farm family next door, or the new house across the vacant lots. *"Help,"* I screamed. *"Help me."*

People were home. People could hear me. Nobody came. When I

realized nobody was coming, I let my arms go limp beneath me. I learned the wrong, ugly lesson again: To speak up was to invite *this*.

My father wrestled my arms out from under me, took my keys, and walked out of the room. I was too disoriented to stand. I crawled from the family room and through the kitchen, down the hall, and up the stairs. When I got to my bedroom and stood, shakily, I stared at myself in the mirror. My face, blotchy and swollen from crying, was covered in rug burn. A purple bruise bloomed along the length of my right forearm. I remember Jodie in my doorway and the sound of neighbors chatting, a hundred yards away. Downstairs, my father went out the front door. I went into Jodie's room and watched out her window.

My father went to my car and popped the hood. He leaned over, pulled out two cables, and closed the hood. He came back into the house and picked up the phone. *"Hello, I need to speak to the manager,"* he said calmly. *"Hello, this is Tracie's dad. She's not going to make it to work today. She's had some car trouble."*

A wave of panic washed over me. I eyed the roof of the porch outside Jodie's window and wondered if my father would hear me pop out a screen, creep down the roof; wondered if I could lower myself enough that the drop would be safe. I went back to my room and looked out my room's windows. One was above a walk-out basement, three stories high. The other was five feet over from the lattice that shaded our deck; I wondered if I could leap, superwoman like, to it and escape. I could not. I was trapped.

When Bonnie came home, she found me in the bathroom, staring at my bruises. She led me to the kitchen table and called for my father. My forearm was already mottled with violet. Bonnie said, *"Mac, this can't happen."* My father smoked a cigarette and looked vacantly at the kitchen cabinets. *"She needs to learn,"* he said. *"She can't talk to me that way."* He had long since stopped apologizing for calling me a bitch. He did not apologize for hurting me. He never has.*

---

* When I interviewed my father and Bonnie in May 2023, he confirmed that he and I had had a physical fight the summer before I left for college. In July, he sent a letter stating, "I never choked you or beat your head into the floor."

★ ★ ★ ★ ★

The ugly lesson continued. After the attack, I remember talking about it in the basement with Jodie, Shana, and Shana's boyfriend, Jason, and considered my options. My sisters were fifteen, then, and scared. They didn't want me to say anything to anybody. *"You're leaving—if you say something you'll just make it worse for us,"* said Shana. I didn't know how to counter her.*

I remember Jason saying that if we did nothing, my father's abuse would only get worse. I remember agreeing with him. I remember knowing, also, that my sisters were right, and that we were stuck. The abuse was going to get worse either way.

When I went to work the day after the attack, I called the police on my break. I was young and white and female, and I had been told my whole life the police were there to protect me.

"What happens if I report that my father is hurting me?" I asked. My voice shook. I prayed they wouldn't ask my name.

The officer said they would have to talk to my father. I began crying. I was at the pay phone in the entryway, customers filing in and out of the restaurant behind me

"But he'll take all my money and I won't go to college," I said. My voice cracked. The police officer, his voice soft, repeated they had to talk to my father. *"If I tell you, he'll kill me,"* I said. Then I hung up the phone.

I asked my best friend, Mandy, if her parents would let me stay with them until I went to school. We were close, but they did not want to get into it with my father. *"They don't think it's a good idea,"* Mandy said. *"I'm sorry. It's just another month, right?"*

Last, I called Grandma Kate from the basement phone while my father was at work. It smelled of new carpet and tobacco smoke. I stared at the rack of pool cues as I asked if I could stay with her.

---

* Today, my sisters' recollections of this conversation is vague. They remember only that there was a fight that upset me.

"*It's really bad here, Grandma. I don't want to be here,*" I said. She asked me what I meant a few times before sighing and lowering her voice.

"*Did he hit you?*" she asked.

"Yes," I said. I started to cry. "*He said if I told anyone, I wouldn't go to college and he'd take all of my money.*"

There was a long pause. My grandmother's voice grew small. She advised me as she had advised my mother, as her mother had advised her, as scared people have long advised each other.

"*You better stay there, Tracie. You know, it hasn't been easy for him. You're lucky he didn't leave you,*" she said. "*Just stay out of his way.*"

★ ★ ★ ★ ★

For most of the time that my father was abusing us, I told myself that nobody knew it was happening. I convinced myself of this because I did not want to confront the truth: people knew and did nothing.

The truth sent me spiraling into a powerless rage. At my family, but also at that school counselor I'd told about my father chasing me. And, later, at the high school English teacher I visited the year after I graduated, who asked me if my father hit my sisters and me. When I told her yes, she nodded and said she could tell. Nobody said anything to the authorities or to my father. They said very little to me, and nothing that suggested the abuse was wrong.

For a long time, I assumed that the reason people said nothing was that I was worth nothing; that I was worthless. Eventually, I came to understand something related but different. People did nothing because they believed my father, a white, middle-class man doing the feminized work of raising children alone, was worth their respect. I see this as a cousin of implicit bias. Rather than the presence of an active favoring, though, it is the absence of oversight and correction—a kind of implicit deference. When the people who knew my father was abusive and did nothing to intervene, the worth of me and my sisters, of his first and second wives, never entered the picture. It was the deference to my father that mattered.

There is good reason to believe that this deference comes from the fact that he was male, and also because he was white.* White families with a child welfare case in the 1990s were far more likely to be allowed to keep their children at home than similar Black or Hispanic families. In 1994, white families on welfare who had open child protective services cases were twice as likely to be left intact as similar Black families.

When the state takes children from their family, it exacts a devastating emotional cost on child and parent alike. In America, it often exacts a financial one, too. In 1984, federal officials, citing concerns that parents might "shirk their parental responsibilities and abandon their children to welfare," began to require that states charge low-income parents, who were disproportionately Black and Hispanic, for the cost of placing their children into foster care. Federal guidelines did not require states to collect these costs from more-affluent families—but it offered guidance for any state interested in doing so. Michigan was interested.

Ever since, Michigan has billed parents with children in foster care for this "service," basing the fee on parents' income rather than on the cost of care. If the ongoing violence in our home had been reported, and if it had resulted in even just one of us being taken into foster care with strangers, my father could have faced a new monthly bill. I remember that, when I was applying for college, my father's income was around $45,000. At that income, if one of his children had been placed in foster

---

* The child welfare system's involvement in Black families is fraught and difficult. While recent studies have documented that there is a higher rate of child maltreatment in Black and Native families than in white ones, researchers have been clear that this is the direct product of the higher rates of poverty among those groups. In a chapter of *Child Maltreatment*, published in 2021, leading researchers shared that "the research is generally consistent in showing that the nearly two to one disproportionality in overreporting of Black children compared to White children disappears or even reverses when income and other risk factors are controlled for."

care with strangers for six months, it would have likely cost my family nearly $8,000.*

That is money that we would have been less likely to have if we were not white. If it had been charged to my family, I can see how—given my father's mindset at the time—he might have taken that money out of my accounts to repay himself. Or he might not have. It's hard to say.

Take, for instance, the social security checks that began to arrive for each of my sisters and me after my mother's death. We each got a few hundred dollars a month, I think, until we turned eighteen. This was yet another dollar amount that was greater because of our race: Our mother had earned enough to generate these benefits; her earnings had been higher because she went to college; she could afford college because of her parents' middle-class wealth, which they had largely gained because they were white. When the checks arrived, my father deposited them in each of our savings accounts. He could have, he has reminded me, used these benefits to cover the costs of our shelter and food and free up his own income for himself.

In exchange, my father expects loyalty—including, I am sure, the kind that would have kept me from telling anyone about his attack. There's a long line of "ifs" in this calculation of the money my family saved when our community deferred to my father—if I'd told the police; if they'd called child welfare; if they'd faulted my father; if they'd put me into foster care; if they'd charged him the money. At the end of that line, I can see how he would have felt justified in taking the money I'd saved for college.

If he'd taken it, I can see how, seventeen years old and bruised and afraid, I would have been at a loss. I would have decided he had won and

---

* According to the Bureau of Labor Statistics, the rough estimate for the cost of a year of foster care in 1994, $7,707, was the equivalent of $15,771 in January 2023.

that it was no longer worth the fight. I can see how I would never have gotten to college at all.

★ ★ ★ ★ ★

In the end, I endured, and so I got an education. The scholarship at NYU was generous, and I qualified for just under $7,000 a year in federal loans, which Grandpa Mac offered to pay off each year, leaving me with a $28,000 debt to him instead of the government. I remember that the remainder of the bill was about $9,000 a year, making NYU the cheapest school for me to attend—cheaper, even, than University of Michigan, which had lower tuition but offered less scholarship. We planned for my parents to pay $3,000 a year.* I would make up the difference by working part-time during school and full-time every summer.

At the end of August, my father and Bonnie drove me to the Detroit airport. They hugged me at the gate. They told me they loved me. I must have hugged them back and said I loved them, too.

When my flight landed at John F. Kennedy Airport in New York, I did not think, *I'm scared.* I did not think, *I'm excited.* I did not even think, *What about my sisters?* I thought only: *I'm safe.*

---

* While my journal entries note clearly that my father and stepmother had promised to contribute $3,000 a year to my college costs, my father told me in May 2023 that "what sticks in my mind is $5,000, but I'm not sure that's right."

8

BARBARA NATHAN KATZ: POVERTY

B. 1944

HOUSTON, DALLAS, AND CARROLLTON, TEXAS

Nobody saw Barb's death coming: not her husband and not her coworkers at the International House of Pancakes. Not the manager at the senior apartments and not the girl at the front desk. Not her cousin, who invited her to family gatherings. And definitely not her three sisters. If anything, the sisters figured it would be Barb's husband, Mike, who'd go first.

Barb and Mike had been married more than thirty years by then. When the couple had first married, back in 1983, nobody had liked Mike much. He seemed crabby and materialistic, and generally obnoxious, but these objections felt small. They were the kinds of things you'd make do with—not big enough to make anyone suggest calling off the wedding. Mostly, the family was just glad Barb, who'd had an especially challenging childhood, had found someone.

They began to worry more after the wedding. Mike began calling Barb's father, asking for money. Then Barb started calling to ask. Anita, the oldest of the four sisters, remembers her father saying that Mike would be startlingly direct. He would say things like, *"I married your daughter, so you should send me money."* Once sent, the money vanished. Then another call came. Mike and Barb also asked her cousins for money, and they asked her sisters. Eventually, the sisters tried to persuade Barb to leave Mike, but she would not. So here they were: Anita, Debbie, and Miriam—all well into middle age, all worrying over Barb.

They told themselves that the only thing left to do was wait. At first, they hoped for a crisis, wanted Barb to lose her patience and finally accept Miriam's invitation to come live in Rochester, New York. Then, more grimly—and more honestly—they settled in to wait for Mike to die. It wasn't a crazy thought; he'd told them he had diabetes and heart failure. Once he passed on, they could reclaim Barb. Maybe she could even have some joy in these last decades of her life. They assumed she had more time.

Then someone from the senior apartments called Miriam and said that Barb was gone. The sisters hadn't realized that to have more time, you had to have a stable life; you had to have health insurance and see doctors regularly. The three sisters, who'd done all right for themselves, same as their parents had, were the kind of people who had more time. Barb was not.

It was a couple of months before the sisters knew how Barb had died. What the last days and weeks had been like. Why she hadn't been to the doctor. How the abuses she endured from Mike mixed with trauma and poverty and the fear of medical bills, all of it metastasizing into a paralyzing fear that kept them from calling an ambulance. The story they learned was so grim that, when Mike died three years later, it took a conscious effort to feel relieved instead of avenged.

After Barb was gone, their loss was breathtaking. So was the guilt they felt.

★ ★ ★ ★ ★

Barb and her sisters grew up in a middle-class Jewish family that was spread across Houston and its suburbs. This was the world of their father, Charles, the eldest of four children born to William Max Nathan, a well-to-do attorney, and his wife, Erma. The Nathan men were dark-haired and worked as studious professionals—merchants and lawyers—and the women were mostly blond and worked as housewives. Every weekend, the Nathan family attended services at the reform congregation Emanu El, which William had helped found in a controversial split from Beth Israel in the 1940s.* Anita, who goes by Nina, remembers women wearing furs in its soaring, Frank Lloyd Wright–styled sanctuary, their Arpège perfume scenting the air, Schubert drifting from the organ. To outsiders, Texas is largely understood as a land of cowboys and roughnecks, border towns and football. This image reflects diligent work on the part of state officials and governors, from Oscar Colquitt in the 1910s to George W. Bush in the late 1990s. When the state's centennial approached in the 1930s, Texas commissioned more than a thousand inscriptions, plaques, and historical markers across the state for the occasion; only two mentioned southern heritage. Yet, the Nathan sisters remember their childhoods not as western but as southern. They lived in a state that once belonged to the Confederacy, and in a city that was much closer to New Orleans than to El Paso, its landscape shot through with tree-lined bayous that drained to the Gulf. It was hardly cowboy country.

Houston was southern in another important way: It was segregated by public law. The Nathan sisters attended segregated schools, grew up riding in the front of segregated buses, and sat at segregated lunch counters in the Woolworth's downtown, eating questionable pizza. According to most people's perceptions—and, importantly, according to Jim Crow laws—the Nathan family was white.

Still, the Nathans' Jewishness limited their access to benefits freely offered to whites who were elite and Protestant. After Charles finished his undergraduate degree, at Rice, he hoped to attend an Ivy League graduate school. Many Ivies—including Columbia, Harvard, and Yale—had quotas to limit Jewish enrollment. It was the first time Charles had felt the sting

---

* The split, which became national news, exemplified a push among American Jews to assimilate—and ensure that they were not relegated to a position similar to Black Americans, writes Allison E. Schottenstein in *Changing Perspectives*. In service of this, Beth Israel issued a declaration titled "The Basic Principles." Principle 2 declared, "Our religion is Judaism. Our nation is the United States of America. Our nationality is American. Our flag is 'the Stars and Stripes.' Our race is Caucasian."

of exclusion, says Debbie. "I don't think that he felt [discriminated against] until he tried to go to college, and he realized he couldn't get into a grad school," she says. "He talked about it for the rest of his life." He ended up studying chemical engineering at the University of Pittsburgh instead, graduating in 1948.

The threat of anti-Semitic violence was in the background then, a low hum that never went silent—still loud enough to compel silence among many Jews on the issue of civil rights throughout the 1950s and 1960s, Joshua Furman, founder of the Houston Jewish History Archive at Rice University, told me. There had been the lynching of Leo Frank, a Jewish factory superintendent in Atlanta who'd been accused of raping and murdering a teenage girl, in 1915. The Nazi government's execution of six million Jewish people in accordance with a population policy intended to "strengthen Germanic Ethnic stock" and eradicate the Jewish race was fresh in people's minds in the postwar years. In the late 1950s, in the wake of McCarthyism and as the civil rights movement gained steam, attacks on synagogues in the South happened with startling frequency; Jewish communities were understood to harbor sympathizers with both Communism and civil rights. (Indeed, Sylvia regularly attended civil rights meetings.) There were four completed bombings of synagogues, and another three attempted ones, in a twelve-month period between 1957 and 1958. Growing up, the Nathan girls only ever heard jokes about cheap Jews, or sometimes felt the sting of teachers calling them "shifty-eyed," but this did not erase the threat.

★ ★ ★ ★ ★

The Nathans led comfortable lives. Charles had met his wife, Sylvia, in Pittsburgh. He was in graduate school at the University of Pittsburgh. She was the daughter of Russian Jewish immigrants who ran a grocery in a glass town outside the city. Charles told Nina he was drawn to Sylvia's beauty—she had a passing resemblance to Elizabeth Taylor—and her "vulnerability." They married in 1948, and Charles brought his bride back to Houston.

Charles got a job working for an oil company, and the couple began to build a mid-century, middle-class life. They began by joining the whites fleeing central Houston. From 1950 to 1960, the residents in the neighborhood Charles had grown up in went from 76 percent white to 29 percent white. With the help of Charles's father, Debbie thinks, the couple purchased a small but new ranch home in Bellaire, a nearby suburb that was 99.5 percent white. They began to have children: Nina came in 1949, Debbie in 1950, Barb in 1953, and Miriam in 1957. They hired a Black maid, just as Charles's parents, aunts and uncles, and sister had, just as white, middle-class families did wherever Black women sought work and could find it only in the unregulated workplace of white women's homes—doing work their earlier kin had been forced to do for free and against their will under threat of bodily harm.

Much of this life was enabled by the Nathans' standing as a white family. Maids, whose labor cost half what minimum wage would pay, were affordable because Congress had exempted all service workers, including domestic workers, from minimum wage, Social Security, and labor law protections.* Those exemptions had been granted to pacify segregationists seeking to preserve white dominance in the South. The Bellaire house, on Evergreen Street, had a racial covenant, as did the one Charles's parents soon bought a few blocks away. Both documents provided that "no lot or part of lot shall be sold or conveyed to or occupied by any person not a member of the Caucasian race." For these purposes, "Caucasian" included the Nathans. Covenants had been overruled by the Supreme Court the year before, but, as was the case with my family's homes in Michigan, this did little to change the demographics of the neighborhood. Bellaire stayed more than 90 percent white until the end of the century.

★ ★ ★ ★ ★

---

* For a more detailed discussion of the exclusion of domestic, service, and agricultural workers from labor protections, see page 56.

All three sisters are haunted by regret about what happened to Barb. Miriam is haunted by what more she could have done to prevent Barb's death. Nina and Debbie are haunted by how unkind they were to Barb as children, and how that shaped their sister's life. But these two hauntings, of Barb's life and her death, are entwined: Her descent into the poverty that led to her death seems incomprehensible until you understand her childhood.

For all the middle-class comfort of the Nathan family, the house on Evergreen was an incredibly difficult place for children. The Nathans, affluent and assimilated, did not welcome Sylvia, who was "an immigrant from the shtetl," as far as they were concerned. The first two sisters, Nina and Debbie, were bright and sociable, but Barb seemed different. She was slower to walk and talk than her sisters, and avoided eye contact. Today, the sisters believe that Barb had a mild form of autism spectrum disorder, but there was no language for that then. All three of Barb's sisters remember, clearly, that Sylvia took it upon herself to make Barb "normal," drilling her on spelling and vocabulary that Barb struggled to comprehend.* Sylvia's frustrations during those lessons could boil over into rages. Nina remembers once phoning her grandfather as a teen, asking for help, terrified at the way Sylvia was beating Barb.

And there were signs, too, of mental illness in Sylvia. When her temper snapped, she'd chase her daughters through the house wielding a hairbrush. Other days, she spent hours staring into space, picking at her lips. But in that era, there was little discussion of mental illness other than the threat of sending a loved one to an asylum. The Nathans, like most families of the era,

* While it is beyond the scope of this book to interrogate notions of able-bodied, disabled, and "normal," readers looking for more on those topics may want to start with *The Disability Studies Reader*. In that book's introduction, editor Lennard J. Davis observes, "So much of writing about disability has focused on the disabled person as the object of study, just as the study of race has focused on the person of color. . . . I would like to focus not so much on the construction of disability as on the construction of normalcy. I do this because the 'problem' is not the person with disabilities; the problem is the way that normalcy is constructed to create the 'problem' of the disabled person."

simply endured—but, eventually, Sylvia could no longer bear it. In 1986, all her children grown, she took her own life.

The consequences of such unsettled childhoods are no secret; they are certainly no secret to me. Children who grapple with a parent's mental illness or violence invariably struggle with their relationships to trust and responsibility, to love and acceptance. Some kids bond together and carry each other through it. Others become isolated and splinter off, struggling to feel close to anyone at all.

* * * * *

In the early 1980s, Barb moved to Dallas. She'd finished college, which her parents paid for, and she had lived with them off and on ever since. Now in her late twenties, Barb was chafing at her parents' oversight—and at life in the small town of Socorro, New Mexico, where Charles had taken a teaching position at the university. When a family member died unexpectedly, each Nathan girl received a small inheritance—around $3,000, the sisters remember.

Barb took her money and headed for Dallas. Her sisters remember her sharing an apartment with a friend from elementary school at first, and she connected with a cousin, Bonnie, who had moved to North Dallas. Barb joined a synagogue, waited tables, and started going to Jewish singles events. At one of these, she met Mike Katz, a high school classmate of Bonnie's husband. They married in 1983.

There was little about Mike that worried Barb's family at first. "It seemed really normal," says Debbie. "He would make fun of our car because we never had a new car—we didn't want a new car, you know. And we have some of that in my family. So, I thought, 'Oh, he's just another one of these people.'" But the promise of the wedding, the ineffable sense it gave that Barb was moving toward the life every American was supposed to seek, overwhelmed those concerns. Maybe this was Barb's chance to have a normal life.

It did not occur to anyone yet that, in choosing Mike, Barb was setting on a dangerous path. That her habit of keeping to herself, of rarely calling family to check in, might be isolating rather than freeing. That Mike's instinct upon seeing Barb's tendency toward isolation might not be to care for her, but to capitalize on an opportunity for himself. "I would tell people this Camelot tale of how I knew she was okay finally," says Miriam. "I thought she was happy. And it gave me comfort to think that she was fine without us. I said, 'I have a third sister and she doesn't need us anymore.'" Barb had grown up and gotten married, and they were glad for her.

★ ★ ★ ★ ★

Barb's parents and grandparents probably didn't think too much about safety nets—the policy term for public antipoverty programs. The Nathans' ancestors were white immigrants and entrepreneurs who'd managed to clamber into the middle class at a time when government did little for its poor. Safety nets as a public responsibility first emerged in the United States in the 1930s, during the Great Depression. Poverty, hunger, and homelessness had become so common that the federal government began to pass round after round of legislation to address those problems. (Many historians also note that the reforms of the 1930s, in pragmatic terms, quieted a workforce that was increasingly critical of capitalism, minimized concessions from capital, and in the process created a relatively complacent workforce.) Taken together, those laws constitute the New Deal.

"The New Deal" does not refer to a single policy but to a series of laws passed from 1933 to 1939. Among them were the Social Security Act, which promised money for workers in old age, unemployment insurance, and cash aid for the widows and dependents of covered workers, and the National Labor Relations Act, which gave workers the right to organize, and unions to collectively bargain on behalf of workers. The Fair Labor Standards Act limited child labor and established minimum wages and overtime pay for covered workers. Public health insurance, for which few advocated but both unions and the American Medical Association vehemently opposed, was absent from the list.

Racism determined the weft and warp of the safety net, stitching together a patchwork where those kept safe were mostly white, while those allowed to fall through were mostly Black. Southern senators and representatives held powerful positions in committees that allowed them to dictate how generous or stingy new policies would be, writes labor historian Ira Katznelson; they were "pivotal" figures without whose support legislation could not pass. With great consistency, southern legislators "assessed New Deal policies for compatibility with organized white supremacy." It was a delicate balance: northern progressives would not support legislation that discriminated by race explicitly, and southern legislators wouldn't sign off on programs that could not discriminate in practice. In order to get the New Deal passed at all, legislators designed its policies to be *technically* colorblind but with enough flexibility that they could be used in a racist way. This drive to ensure that new benefits would rarely go to Black Americans, without ever saying anything about race, led to two different, but related, structures in the new programs.

The first structure affected programs that set rules for workers or employers. When legislators created new rights—either rules about how to treat people, or the promise of government support without having to prove you deserved it—they set them behind the equivalent of a velvet rope in front of a nightclub. Like a bouncer granting access to a club, legislators only granted rights—to organize, to a minimum wage, to Social Security payments in old age—to jobs held by white men. They left most of the jobs held by women of all races, as well as men of color, outside the protection of these rights.

The second structure emerged when legislators created programs that offered temporary, tangible help: unemployment insurance, welfare, food stamps. For these programs, federal legislators barely limited access at all. Instead, they allowed states to limit access to help as they saw fit— the equivalent of the velvet rope disappearing, only to have the bartender inside ignore you all night. This gave southern states and public administrations the power to effectively deny help to people without ever naming race, or any other prejudice, aloud.

The result has been a safety net that is of far less use to our citizens than the nets that other Western and northern European countries offer to theirs—such an outlier, in fact, that policy experts sometimes call it American exceptionalism. Many European countries adopted pensions, unemployment insurance, and family allowances years—even generations—earlier than the United States introduced social benefits of any kind. By the late 1980s, the majority of European Union countries provided free preschool to more than half their children. By the late 1990s, the majority of residents in all fifteen countries of the European Union had universal health insurance or national health care.

It's tempting to say that the difference between social supports in Europe and the United States is that Europe is generous, and the United States is not. Indeed, comparable European Union countries spend anywhere from 10 to 44 percent more (as a share of GDP) than the United States on safety net programs. But the truth is more subtle, and more insidious, than dollars and cents alone will show.

It's not as if, in the United States, we do not offer *any* benefits. There are welfare checks, albeit tiny when they exist at all. There is some limited childcare for the working poor and, increasingly, health insurance for the poor through the lower middle class. The difference is that to get help here, you must do something that is rarely required across much of Europe: Prove you deserve it. Get past the velvet rope, or ingratiate yourself with the stingy bartender inside.

* * * * *

There are many theories and explanations for why America spends so little.* They can be found in histories and sociological studies, in analyses

---

* Although opponents of social spending often point out that Americans typically give far more to private charity than do citizens in Europe, the scale of private donation is minuscule compared to scale of social need. "Anyone who thinks that private charity will make up for lowered government budgets is whistling Dixie," Elizabeth Boris, director of the Center on Nonprofits and Philanthropy at the Urban Institute, told reporters in 2013. As an example, the largest anti-hunger charity, Feeding America, spent $5 billion to feed the

based on economics and politics. But one of the most widely accepted threads running through all of these explanations for our lack of safety net is this: White racism has so contorted American politics and institutions of government that broad redistribution has faltered badly here.

One well-documented study of racism's central role in shaping America's safety net was published by Harvard economists Alberto Alesina and Edward Glaeser in 2004. The pair used economic analysis to assess what accounted for the difference in European and American social programs. Was it the economic model? The political structure? Racial diversity? Economics didn't account for much, they found. But they could trace about half of the difference in social spending between America and comparably wealthy European nations to "racial fractionalization" and the other half to political institutions.

Racial fractionalization, they wrote, explained why white hostility to cash welfare programs tracked with an increase in hostility to Black people, and it explained the political success of President Reagan's campaign against "welfare queens." It explained why, across the fifty states, the increase in Black residents was so clearly correlated with a drop in welfare benefits that they could write a formula for it: For every 20 percent increase in Black residents, welfare benefits for a family of three in 1990 declined an average of $138.

Alesina and Glaeser's work on how racism limited and policed access to America's safety net also lines up with the work of Katznelson, as well as the work of sociologists like Jill Quadagno and Cybelle Fox. All of these scholars, and more, have documented how legislators designed the safety net of the 1930s to preserve white advantage: to boost white wages while keeping Black wages low, to offer white families help with affordable mortgages but to refuse loans in Black neighborhoods. If white Americans noticed the ways this redistribution of money was unfair— how it took taxes from everyone, then spent it almost exclusively on white

---

hungry that year, compared to the U.S. government's spending of $105 billion on food assistance.

American men and their families, whose wages and working conditions rapidly eclipsed those of men of other races—few said anything about it. We learned that ugly lesson and took our money, and we kept our mouths shut.

* * * * *

It took a while for it to become clear that Barb and Mike might be in need of a net. At first, the marriage had seemed to follow a typical pattern. A few months before Barb and Mike married, they had bought a condo near a freeway interchange on Dallas's northwest border. None of the sisters were in regular touch with Barb then, so they don't know how the couple afforded the down payment—Debbie thinks Mike's father probably helped out but cannot say for sure. They stayed in the apartment for nearly a decade. Friends and family remember them renewing a lease on a Cadillac each year. Then, in 1993, they defaulted on the condo's mortgage. They kept leasing the Cadillac and moved into a North Dallas duplex that Mike had inherited from his father.

The duplex was a nice house. Mike's father had bought it in the early 1970s, just after it had been built as part of a new, upscale subdivision. Almost as soon as Mike and Barb moved in, they began taking out loans against it, although they did not explain this to Barb's family. So far as the Nathans knew, Barb was living comfortably in a nice house she and Mike had gotten for free. In any event, the sisters rarely saw the house, all of them in the middle of careers and raising children, all of them far away: Nina in California, Miriam in upstate New York, Debbie a nine-hour drive away in El Paso.

When the sisters did come, they learned little about Barb. Mike would point to stacks of collectible dolls and sports memorabilia and talk about how it would all be worth money someday. Sometimes, he would talk about how Barb had been given an Employee of the Month award from IHOP, and brag about how she could work in the best hotel restaurants if only she'd try. Other times, he'd tell the sisters how horrible they had been to Barb, how the family had given her nothing. I imagine it sounded to Barb like he was standing up for her—that he was taking her side—in a way that no one had during her childhood. On these visits Barb rarely spoke at all.

By the end of the 1990s, it had also become apparent to the sisters that Mike did not work—if he ever had at all. He claimed that he worked at home, but the details were vague. In any event, there was no evidence of that work yielding earnings. The sisters knew he gambled. Now they wondered how much. If Mike ever talked about work, it was to talk about Barb: how she needed to work more, how unfair it all was, how they just needed a lucky break. Sometimes, Miriam remembers, he said racist things, complaining about being evicted by a "dirty Arab" just because he was Jewish—not because, for instance, he had not paid the rent.

Mostly, though, the Nathans kept tabs on Barb by phone. Nearly all the calls were about money. The calls that had begun after the wedding persisted, always with a story about a bill Barb and Mike needed help with, a check they were waiting on. It was "a few hundred here, a few thou there," remembers Nina. Neither she nor her sisters could suggest how much, over the years, Charles had given the couple. They know only that the money was never paid back, and another call always came.

★ ★ ★ ★ ★

So far as Barb's sisters know, she never worked at steak houses or other high-end restaurants where servers can approach a middle-class income. It was always national chains: Red Lobster or Big Boy or, starting around 1999, at the IHOP in Carrollton, a first-ring suburb twenty minutes from the house Barb and Mike shared in North Dallas. The job put Barb among the 7.9 million restaurant workers in the country at the time, a number that's grown by more than 50 percent in the years since. Although restaurant staff gained labor protections along with hospital workers in 1966, industry leaders fought for—and won—an exemption to minimum wage for tipped workers like servers. Under this new rule, employers only needed to pay half the minimum wage to tipped workers, who were expected to make up the rest with tips. Servers' wages got even worse under President Clinton, when a Republican congress set servers' wages at a flat rate of $2.13 an hour, no longer tying it to minimum wage at all. During Barb's time at IHOP, the federal minimum wage for servers remained exactly where it had been set in 1996: $2.13 an hour. It remained there still in 2023, when the median income for servers across the country was around $26,000 a year.

Barb worked the breakfast shift, so she'd rise at 4:30 or 5:00 A.M. and dress in her uniform: black polyester slacks, white short-sleeved oxford shirt, and a black necktie. She'd roll the Cadillac down the highway and park in front of the restaurant, duck inside, tuck her purse under the register in the lobby, and punch her code into the sales system to sign in. Back in those early days, Barb could be fun, says Irma Perez, who worked alongside her. Some days, Barb would sing Elvis Presley songs as they started the vats of coffee and pulled the three-pound tubs of butter—from which they would scoop balls to place on top of pancakes—from the walk-in. Irma was only a few years younger than Barb. She and her husband, a construction worker, supported a family of five; they'd both come to the United States from Mexico as teenagers. Both women preferred the shift that started at 6:00 A.M. and ended by 2:00 P.M. They worked together almost daily and became friends, and prided themselves on making it through their shift without ever dirtying their ties.

Although Barb worked hard, she and Mike remained poor. Mike got around $800 a month from Social Security in those days, according to the manager of the senior apartment complex where they lived. I have no records for Barb's income, but Irma tells me she and Barb worked the same shifts, both of them full-time; they likely earned about the same. In Irma's best years, she says, she earned $15,000. Other years, she earned less.* If

---

* Servers often get paychecks for zero dollars, since taxes for their full income, including tips, are taken out of their formal paycheck—which is based on $2.13 an hour. Additionally, hours worked can vary widely, with full-time employees working a range of thirty to forty hours a week or more. The most generous calculation of Irma's hourly wage would be to assume thirty hours a week, and that the $2.13/hour comes on top of her stated income. If Irma earned $15,000

Irma's experience is any clue, Barb and Mike's household income rarely got above $25,000—a figure that would have landed them among the nation's lowest-income households.

Their life would have been hard. Researchers suggest that Barb and Mike's income was roughly half the cost of food and shelter, transportation and food in Carrollton. At that time, households there with two adults, only one of whom worked, would have needed about $49,000 a year to cover basic expenses.

★ ★ ★ ★ ★

As Charles aged, he agonized over how to provide for Barb in his will. He would be splitting his estate among the four daughters. For Nina, Debbie, and Miriam, he planned to simply leave a lump sum for each of them, to use as they liked. But a direct bequest to Barb was clearly a bad idea: Mike would commandeer it, and Barb would see none of it. For Barb, Charles instead set up a trust of around $100,000 with Nina as its executor. The trust would pay out 10 percent each year for a decade, after which Barb would get the lump sum of whatever remained.

Charles's health began to fail in the early 2000s. He had moved back to Houston by then, and the sisters took turns flying in to help manage his care. Barb did not come to visit him in Houston, though she was only four hours away. When the sisters called to update Barb on their father, they'd have a minute on the phone with Barb before Mike grabbed the receiver from her. He'd ask, *"Why aren't you telling us anything?"* If the sister explained that she *was*, in fact, calling to tell them Charles was dying and Barb needed to come if she wanted to see him, Mike said, *"No, she can't go, she has to work."* Both Mike and Barb repeated these excuses when the sisters called after Charles died in 2001. Barb did not go to her father's funeral.

The death of Charles had brought Nina, Debbie, and Miriam

---

in tips by working fifty-two thirty-hour weeks, she would have earned $9.62 an hour in tips. Combined with $2.13 an hour, that puts her hourly wage at $11.75.

together in a way that hadn't happened since their mother had died fifteen years before. Miriam, the only sister younger than Barb—and in far less regular touch with her than the older sisters—had been struck by the calls with Mike. In the next few years, as he directed his calls to the sisters, a worry began to grow. Miriam began to question whether the happy story she and her sisters had told themselves about Barb was true.

"I just thought, 'This is crazy. She's out there all alone, and I don't even know her, really,'" says Miriam. "I decided I needed to have eyes on it. Someone's got to see what's going on down there."

* * * * *

The first time Miriam went down to visit Barb and Mike, in 2005, she had shock after shock. At the house, she found their newspapers stacked so high they created corridors within rooms. Magazines lined the walls and towered on tables. Boxes of collectible dolls took up an entire bedroom, their glassy eyes staring out through the cellophane packaging. The refrigerator smelled of rot. The term that came to mind was "hoarders."

At Mike's request, Miriam took the couple to dinner at Dunston's, a steakhouse that had been open since 1955. The place looked its age: windowless and trimmed in rough wood, the dining room perfumed by mesquite burning under a massive grill open to the dining room. They sat in a button-tufted booth upholstered in oxblood vinyl, in view of the salad bar, and watched the cooks grill steaks for Barb and Mike. Miriam, a vegetarian, opted for a salad.

At dinner, what had been a vague concern began to take shape in Miriam's mind: "I just realized that [Barb] was completely, you know, under this guy's thumb." The sisters were sitting on the same side of the booth and Miriam put her arm around Barb, as if she could protect her sister from the man across the table.

Before Miriam left town, she stopped at IHOP and asked Barb to talk with her after her shift. Barb was quiet and terse: She could stay for ten minutes, but Mike would be mad if she didn't get home on time. Miriam ordered a piece of pie and and watched her sister ferry sandwiches and pancakes to early-afternoon customers.

When Barb sat down, Miriam steered the conversation to health care: How was she feeling? Barb said she hadn't been to a doctor for years—not a primary care physician and not a gynecologist. She had had a prescription for high blood pressure medication, but it had run out.

Miriam was floored. They had a family history of high blood pressure, thyroid problems, and diabetes. As middle-aged women, all the Nathan women needed to be going to the doctor regularly.

"So, you haven't had anything like that?"

"No." Barb shook her head. *"I can't."*

The more Miriam asked, the more worried she became. Barb told her that Mike wouldn't let her go to the doctor because of the cost. He wouldn't let her apply for Medicaid, either, because they weren't "like those welfare people," a sentiment with which Barb—distressingly, to Miriam, given its racist undertone—seemed to agree.

Miriam had not had much contact with the working poor. She didn't know, as Barb may have, that even if Mike hadn't objected, pursuing Medicaid would have been pointless. Still several years out from the passage of the Affordable Care Act, Medicaid would not cover any working adult unless they were disabled or a parent. For able-bodied, childless adults, there were no public options for health care, no matter how poor they were.

By then their ten minutes was up. The sisters stood up from the beige IHOP booth. Miriam hugged Barb and left her sister to finish her side work and gather her things. The entryway door chimed as Miriam walked into the Texas heat, worry fluttering in her chest. In the car, safely out of view, Miriam burst into tears.

* * * * *

Barb wasn't from a family that depended on, or believed it would ever need, a safety net, least of all for health care. In a way that made sense: Charles's job for big oil companies provided a stable income and came with generous health care benefits. His parents had plenty of money to offer in times of need. But while that stability felt normal to the Nathans of the 1950s, it was a dramatic innovation—less than a generation old.

Much of the stability reflected the fact that the Nathans were white. In the 1800s, Charles's grandparents and great-grandparents had lived in Texas and Mississippi—and, further back on his mother's side, had owned enslaved people. The American government had taken the land by force—a euphemism for theft. The American government had protected the institution of slavery in its founding documents. And then the American government had ensured that the wealth this land, and these people, generated was far more available to whites than anyone else.

That stolen land and labor, in turn, generated sufficient wealth to launch Charles's parents into the upper reaches of the middle class. William Max graduated from Rice in 1916, its first Jewish graduate, and Charles did the same in 1940; the university did not admit Black students until 1962. Those degrees in turn allowed the men to attain well-paid careers that were nearly impossible for nonwhite Americans to achieve, which in turn allowed them to buy homes—with racial covenants—which gave them wealth. They also gained wealth, in part, because their private medical insurance would keep them from running into debt if anyone got sick. Because of all this, Barb and her sisters grew up knowing that they would be housed and fed comfortably, and that if they needed medical care, they could get it.

Having health insurance was standard for white, middle-class families by the 1940s and 1950s. During the wage controls of World War II, employers had begun offering medical insurance as a fringe benefit to stand in for wages. Unions did the same. As a result, insurance was almost exclusively tied to having a union job or a job with benefits. Everyone else either paid out of pocket, or prayed for health. But by the 1960s, the limited access to medical care for both the nation's poor and the elderly—even workers who'd been covered by Social Security—had become a central political concern.

In 1965, President Lyndon B. Johnson signed bills creating two new public health insurance programs, Medicare and Medicaid. But while LBJ is broadly given credit for this legislation, many historians consider Wilbur Mills, a conservative Arkansas congressman, and chair of the House Ways and Means Committee, just as important to the creation of public health insurance in the United States. Known as a fiscal conservative, Mills pushed for Medicare to be limited to workers already covered by social security, whose taxes helped pay for the program. The people who were not covered—most of whom were not covered because their jobs had been excluded from legal protections in order to keep Black labor cheap—didn't deserve the help, he said. They could stay uninsured, or try their luck with Medicaid, where admission to the program echoed the rules for cash welfare.

When it came to cash welfare, Mills was clear on who he suspected did not deserve help at all: single mothers, particularly if they were Black. An aide to President Johnson recalled that in 1967, Mills proposed limiting welfare benefits—and justified it with a story about a Black mother: "Across town from my mother in Arkansas a Negro woman has a baby every year . . . My proposal will stop this," he said.

At the same time, a white backlash was brewing in response to policy changes that expanded Black Americans' access to mainstream institutions and resources. There were civil rights legislation outlawing segregation and housing discrimination, new efforts to equalize spending across public schools, even an incremental boost in welfare benefits won by Black women in New York City. White suspicion about people using any public program began to mount: Did the people benefiting from schools, libraries, and public parks deserve it? Were all those doctor visits Medicaid paid for really necessary? Why did wages need to be raised when people could just learn to live within their means instead?

Those questions drove the tax revolt in California, and they fueled Ronald Reagan's rise to the White House. They also helped a willing white public believe that poverty among Black people was the product of bad choices, a belief already embedded in mainstream journalism. One study found that from 1950 to 1992, African Americans were used as subjects in news magazine stories about poverty 53 percent of the time, while constituting just 29 percent of the nation's poor. Stories about the Black poor almost always focused on pathology and dysfunction—and nearly always portrayed their Black subjects as dysfunctional.

Meanwhile, journalism about poverty rarely depicted white people, who even today remain the largest share of the poor by race. When stories about the white poor did get published, it was almost always during economic downturns, when they served as examples of how blameless they were for their poverty. Whether it was Reagan or well-intentioned journalists, the narrative about who did and did not deserve help remained the same: White people were considered blameless and deserving of help. Black people were seen as responsible for their poverty and suspected of lying about their need; they were not deserving of help.

I do not know how directly Barb and Mike discussed these things. They weren't civically minded people, engaged in the issues of the day. They figured that the safety net wasn't for people like them. For a long time, it didn't really matter that they were wrong. Their families had the resources to shelter them from the harshest realities of American life. Eventually, though, even that could not protect them.

* * * * *

Miriam returned to Texas within a few months of that first visit and took Barb to the doctor. Barb didn't have insurance, and Miriam worried her sister would refuse the appointment if it seemed like there was any threat of expense. Miriam told Barb she had found a voucher that would cover the cost, when, in fact, she paid the bill. Just as Miriam had worried, Barb needed medication for her blood pressure and thyroid. Debbie's husband, a physician, began to write Barb's prescriptions, order the meds from Canada, then mail them to her in Texas.

Barb and Mike had left the duplex by then, bouncing around in extended-stay motels before landing in a studio at a senior retirement complex called the Corinthians, a couple miles up the road from IHOP. The manager took a liking to Mike, who he'd talk with about sports, and cut the couple a deal on rent. He charged them $800 a month for a tiny studio that listed, he said, for at least $1,700 a month. Miriam and her sisters had so far assumed that Barb wanted to stay with Mike; it had not occurred to them that she could leave. Then Miriam was saying goodbye to Barb at IHOP after another visit, and the idea hit her: Barb could just leave. Without thinking, Miriam suggested it.

"Barb, come with me now," said Miriam. *"You can just leave. Let's go. Get on the plane."*

Barb paused and looked at her sister and said, *"Wouldn't he be able to find me?"*

Miriam's mind raced. Medicaid has expanded in New York, which meant Barb could be insured there; maybe she'd even qualify for disability. The sisters had enough accumulated advantages from their family—from their whiteness—to help Barb do this. They could not support Barb forever. But the sisters could get her to a place with enough of a public safety net that family could make up for the rest.

Barb just needed to do one thing: say yes to Miriam.

Before Miriam even realized what was happening, the opening closed. Barb shook her head. "I'm not ready yet," Miriam remembers her saying. When women seek to leave abusive partners, it often takes more than one attempt to leave for good; the average number of attempts made by women who do succeed in leaving abusive partners, say advocates, is seven. When Barb said no that time, Miriam resolved to ask again. She'd just keep asking. Eventually, she was sure, one of two things would happen: Barb would say yes, or Mike would die. Either way, she only needed to be patient and wait for her sister to come to her.

* * * * *

For years after Barb's death, Debbie believed that her sister had fallen into what policy experts call the "coverage gap" for health insurance. People in the gap earn too little to get insurance subsidies under the Affordable

Care Act, which are for households above the poverty line, but they do not qualify for Medicaid under their state's rules, either.*

As initially written, the Affordable Care Act did not have a gap. In addition to creating new public health insurance exchanges and subsidies, the act offered states funding to expand "original" Medicaid—which has very low income limits that vary by state, and which excludes all childless adults—to cover more people. The federal funding could be used to insure anyone earning up to one-third more than the poverty line, even childless adults like Barb. (After two years, states would be expected to begin chipping in, reaching 10 percent by 2020.) But there was a catch in the ACA as passed: If states didn't expand Medicaid, the federal government could withhold funding for *everybody* on Medicaid in the state—even people who had been covered without the expansion.

The day that President Obama signed the ACA into law, Florida officials filed suit to stop the ACA. Twenty-five other states, including Texas, joined as plaintiffs. So did the National Federation of Independent Business, a lobbying group; and two plaintiffs identified by law firms working the case. They argued that the act transformed public health insurance from a safety net into a "federally-imposed universal health care regime" that violated the principles of federalism. They argued that government could not compel citizens to buy goods or services, and called the Medicaid expansion program "an unprecedented encroachment on the sovereignty of the Plaintiff States and on the rights of their citizens."

That case made it to the Supreme Court. In 2012, two years before

---

* The federal poverty line is $15,930 for a two-person household, putting 400 percent at $63,720. As for Medicaid, ten states (including Texas) had not yet expanded Medicaid under the ACA in August 2023, according to KFF, a health care information organization. Veteran advocate Anne Dunkelberg of Every Texan explained that adults in her state can only qualify for Medicaid if they are pregnant, disabled, elderly, or parenting, and also live in households earning less than the program's income limits—which can be as low as $4,008 a year for a parent of two.

the Medicaid provision was slated to go into effect, the court upheld most of the ACA, but it prohibited federal officials from withholding pre-existing Medicaid funding from states who did not expand the program. Kaj Ahlburg, one of the named plaintiffs (both of whom were white), told a reporter he was disappointed with the result: "The federal government should not have the power to make us buy health insurance or any other product," he said, blurring the line between paying for access to health care and buying, say, sneakers or cupcakes.

The coverage gap emerged as a result. The number of Americans caught in it was vast. It swallowed over three million people that Congress had intended to cover. More than half of them were Black or Hispanic.

Throughout all of it, few voters or politicians talked about race directly when it came to the ACA—either in positive or negative ways. Some of this silence about race reflected a difference in how Americans differentiate between cash assistance and health care. Reagan had turned aid to the poor into a question only about race: *Were undeserving, lazy Black people getting money unfairly?* For a while, white Americans didn't see public investment in health care as a question of race—and they broadly supported it. That changed after Barack Obama became president, and sought to expand health care. Soon, racial resentment began to correlate with opposition to public health care. After the introduction of the Affordable Care Act, that opposition—rarely articulated in overt racial language—became a central feature of the Republican party.

Since the 1980s, social science has consistently shown that supporters of the Republican Party, as a group, carry more racial resentment than supporters of Democrats. Indeed, one study found that a state's level of racial resentment was one of the strongest predictors of opposition to Medicaid expansion under the ACA. In 2018, social psychologists described opposition to the ACA as a "three-legged stool" comprising racist hatred of President Obama, the GOP's adamant opposition to him, and "the emergence of open racism in America."

After Donald Trump took office, the administrator of the Centers for Medicare and Medicaid Services, Seema Verma, began making the case that

Medicaid was a handout that trafficked in the "soft bigotry of low expectations." Although work, as an activity, has no clear relationship to the program's stated goal of using public funds to offer health insurance to the poor,
Verma invited states to come up with plans to impose work requirements for
Medicaid clients. She spoke like a true believer, but before going to Washington, D.C., Verma had worked as a consultant for a corporation, Maximus
Inc., that makes its profits off the paperwork the poor must manage in order
to prove they deserve public help. After Verma's announcement, executives
dedicated part of a 2017 quarterly earnings call with investors to the wind-
fall they could see from Medicaid work requirements. Federal judges struck
down these requirements with such consistency that Texas didn't get in a
proposal before it became clear the point was moot.

Texas legislators do not openly discuss the race of Medicaid enroll-
ees, says veteran advocate Anne Dunkelberg, but there has long been an
assumption that "if the people in charge think a problem is a problem
of people of color, nobody will do anything about it." In Texas, three-
quarters of clients in the Medicaid coverage gap are people of color. Failing to expand the program has left 5.2 million Texans without health
insurance—a full 18 percent of its population, more than any other state.
Part of the problem, says Dunkelberg, is that eligibility can be so complex and daunting that people without the time or patience with bureaucracy to run, endlessly, after paperwork simply forgo insurance. The
same pattern exists on a smaller scale in the nine other states that, by
early 2023, still had not expanded Medicaid. The consequences of these
decisions are clear: People die. More than fifteen thousand Americans
could have avoided death in the first four years of the ACA, estimate
researchers, if Medicaid had been expanded in every state.

Debbie, who works as a journalist, knew much of this. She knew, and
so her sisters also knew, that people die in America all the time because
they cannot afford health care. When Barb died, Debbie remembered how
her sister would complain about needing more hours at work, and about
the cost of insurance. She remembered that Texas hadn't expanded Medicaid, and she put the pieces together.

"She wasn't insured," says Debbie. "I blame that on the government of Texas."

★ ★ ★ ★ ★

My best guess is that Barb did not, contrary to Debbie's hypothesis, fall into the coverage gap. The franchise that runs the IHOPs at which Barb worked, AFD Group, declined to answer inquiries about Barb's work or insurance options with the company, so I don't have any documentation of the plans they have offered.* Irma remembers the insurance offered by IHOP costing around $50 per two-week pay period. Even at Irma and Barb's low income, this would have been within the bounds of what the Affordable Care Act deemed affordable. Still, Irma never paid for it. Her paychecks, based on $2.13 an hour but taxed for both wages and tips, were tiny enough as it was.

Because IHOP offered this plan, policy experts would not consider Barb to have been in the "coverage gap," but this feels like a technicality. My best guess is that, if IHOP was charging $1,300 a year for health insurance, the quality was closer to the low-coverage plans referred to as "bronze" on the health insurance marketplace. These plans offer relatively low financial obligations each month; in 2015, the last year Barb was alive, bronze plans in Texas cost roughly $2,300 a year, which works out to a $167 monthly premium.† But the deductibles, which must be paid in full before insurance covers *any* cost other than the doctor's fee for annual checkups, as well as the out-of-pocket maximum for the year, are much higher.

It seems more likely to me that Barb was so focused on avoiding costs

---

* AFD Group staff indicated, over six calls made during the course of two weeks in May 2023, that nobody was available to speak, and no message could be taken.

† Because Barb was offered a plan by her employer, she could not access subsidies to reduce the cost of her premium to as low as 2 percent of her household income. The IHOP plan, for comparison, likely cost 5 percent of her household income.

that she could not see the point in taking on a new one. The massive medical costs she might face in the future were abstract and far off, while paying premiums and co-pays would have immediate effects: less money for food, more harassment from Mike. This kind of perversely intense focus on immediate need has a name in the world of behavioral economics: tunneling. In the tunnel, Barb had only one goal: to take as much money home to Mike as she could. She could see nothing else.

★ ★ ★ ★ ★

When Miriam's cell phone buzzed early on September 7, 2015, she remembers answering the call without thinking as she puttered around her kitchen. It was the start of the semester, and she was distracted, getting ready to head to her job at a local college.

The voice on the other end of the line was female. *"Is this Miriam?"*

"Yes, this is she," Miriam said, fiddling with her purse, only half-paying attention.

"This is Alexandra from the Corinthians," she said. There was a pause, maybe; a tension in her voice. Alexandra continued: *"I'm calling because Barb is dead."*

Miriam heard the word "dead," and she thought: *It's Mike. Mike died.*

Her heart leapt into her throat. This was the call she had been waiting for. The plan had worked. Barb could come and live in Rochester and join the choir and wait tables at Denny's. All the ways the family had failed Barb before wouldn't matter.

"Mike died?" Miriam asked.

There was a pause.

"No, no. Barbara."

The world slowed. It narrowed to the yellow Formica counter Miriam was leaning on, the mug of tea she grasped in her hand, the spice rack over the stove.

"My sister?"

"Yeah . . . your sister. She's . . . she's dead."

Miriam's heart fell, then, dropped through her throat and her gut and her feet to the floor. She pressed the phone to her cheek, her eyes wide.

"What are you talking about?" she said, her voice breaking. *"What are you talking about? What happened?"* What happened to my sister?

★ ★ ★ ★ ★

Two days before, on Saturday, September 5, Barb rose in the dark, let Mike's caretaker, Elena, into the tiny studio apartment, and left for work. It was just before six o'clock, birds chirping in the damp, dark air as dawn broke. She drove her car down Old Denton Road, went through the traffic light, and slid into the parking lot IHOP now shared with an H Mart. Irma wasn't working but she stopped by that day, and remembers Barb—uncharacteristically—hugging her and thanking her for being a good friend. Around ten o'clock, the manager told Barb to go home; she looked that sick.

When Barb got home, Mike was upset to see her. They needed the money. Barb slumped in a chair at the tiny kitchen table. Elena noticed how all the blood seemed drained out of Barb's face, now a pallid white. Elena had no medical training, but she was in her fifties and had raised two children back in Russia; she knew sick when she saw it. Elena warmed some soup in the microwave and joined Barb at the table. Barb would have been breathing deep and fast, almost panting. There would have been a sweet, almost rotten, smell. As Elena began feeding Barb, Mike began yelling.

"No! Not her! You're supposed to take care of me!" Elena remembers him saying.

"This your wife. She needs doctor," she said back.

"Go home! She'll take care of me! Not you!" he said.

"She needs doctor," Elena said again. Mike yelled that it wasn't her business, and they couldn't afford doctors. This quieted Elena. "Medicine here, it's like a business," Elena told me later. It had been different in Russia, where the state health care system offered, at least, the promise of easy access to care—however basic—for free. She didn't know

what kind of insurance they had, what cost she might create for them. She paused.*

As Elena and Mike had begun to argue, Barb went into the bathroom and put on her nightgown. Now she sat listlessly on the bed, panting, watching them. Elena gave up and helped Barb into bed. "I tell Mike, 'Leave her alone, she needs rest,'" Elena told me. She told Barb to rest and said she'd call before coming in the morning.

On September 6, a little after five in the morning, Elena called the apartment. Barb answered, her voice soft. She told Elena she planned to stay in bed that day. Elena should come tomorrow. Nobody knows when, or how insistently, but Barb did tell Mike she wanted to go to the emergency room. Mike told her no. It was too expensive, and she'd feel better in the morning. Barb settled into her side of the bed, near the window. Her view, at the end of the bed, was the backside of the television. The front of the TV lit up the couch on the opposite side. Mike sat there, staring at the screen, his features lit up by its glow.

There had been so much enduring: of a family and a society that could not see and help her as a child, of a husband that could not see and help her as an adult, of a country that proclaimed it saw everyone as equal, then drew hard lines separating who it would help from who it would not. Barb had been born white and middle-class, into the group said to deserve help, and over time fell outside of its bounds. If she'd had time to think about it, maybe she could have seen what those born on the outside already knew: The lines were arbitrary, justified by greed and selfishness masquerading as reason, that they mattered only because people treated them as real. She had been headed outside of them since she was a child, always needing help that was not on offer. For so long, her only choice had been to endure.

Barb did not know that endurance could not save her. She did not

---

* Elena, born in 1960, tells me she came to the United States in 2008. Although she is very happy here, the medical system alarms her. We talked in a mix of English and, with her daughter translating, Russian. She said she was willing to talk to me—a strange woman who knocked on her door—because, "Medicine here, it's like big corporation for money, money, money, money."

know that her body, straining against genetics and stress and a diet supplemented by the free meals and soda she got with each shift, had begun
to struggle to use the insulin it produced. She did not know her thirst
came because her kidneys were trying to flush out glucose her body could
not process; that the slightly sweet, rotten taste in her mouth came from
unusually high levels of ketones, acids her body released into her blood as
it turned fat into energy, since it could not process glucose; that she was
panting as her body tried desperately to reduce the acids by expelling more
carbon dioxide, itself an acid. She did not know that she was diabetic, and
she was going through ketoacidosis.

Sometime in the night, Barb's body reached its limit. Help was so maddeningly close: There was insulin in the refrigerator for Mike. There were
emergency rooms, where a nurse or doctor could have caught the problem
with a basic blood test. None of the help was close enough. The acids building up in Barb's stomach had begun to erode and weaken her esophagus.
It is impossible to know the progression, but a likely scenario is that these
acids kept building until Barb began to vomit, and during one, final retch
her esophagus tore and that was the end.

* * * * *

It's easy, with Barb's story, to dwell on all the things she and her family
could have done differently. What if she'd had a mother who knew how
to help her learn, or who didn't lapse into rages? What if her sisters had
gathered around her and lifted her up from the beginning? What if she'd
married a different man? What if Mike hadn't been so irrationally obsessed
with money and status? What if, what if, what if.

There are other things we in America could dwell on. What if Wilbur
Mills and LBJ had ignored the employers, health insurers, and medical
systems and built a public health care system in the interest of America's
people, instead of brokering a deal with companies looking to profit?
What if Congress had ignored the demands of the National Restaurant
Association in the 1990s and had instituted a living wage for everyone,
even for servers, instead of freezing the tipped minimum at $2.13? What

if Texas had expanded Medicaid instead of fighting it? What if, what if, what if.

For Barb, what ended up mattering was not what if, but what was: a life without health insurance because she could not fathom paying its cost. Given the contorted obsession both Barb and Mike had with money by the end of their lives, I am not sure that if Barb had been insured, she would have gone to the hospital. She would have needed insurance that was both good and affordable for that.

Even for the insured, medical decisions are often a thinly veiled calculation between the risk of bankruptcy and the risk of death. Plans that are affordable insure us only against full bankruptcy each year, not that we can afford the care we need. In the end, the only unmitigated beneficiaries are the companies selling the "product" of health insurance and the providers—medical groups and hospitals—who are paid for the care insurance is intended to cover. By 2018, health insurance stocks had outperformed the S&P 500 by 106 percent, largely because so much government spending had increased their profits.

My best guess is that even if Barb had bought the insurance that IHOP offered, health care could have cost her nearly $9,000 a year. Jobs like Barb's usually come with insurance plans similar to the bronze plans on the affordable care marketplace. Using that as a ballpark figure, if Barb had been insured, her annual premium bill would likely have been around $2,300, given her household income and the affordability standards of the ACA. She would have paid that in monthly installments, and she would have paid pay full price for care beyond an annual checkup until she met her deductible—a figure that, in 2015, was around $5,300 for the cheapest marketplace plans. After that, insurance would have reduced the per-item cost of her care, but she likely would have another thousand dollars in bills before she hit her out-of-pocket maximum and no longer had to pay. At the end of each year, the calculator would reset, and she'd begin to pay again.

There are only three ways out of this nightmare of unpredictable insurance in America. You can be wealthy enough to pay for medical care entirely out of pocket, confident that you can afford any bill that arrives.

You can age into Medicare, where costs to patients are modest and predictable. Or you can prove you are poor enough to get Medicaid, where
federal law typically limits clients' total health care costs to 5 percent of
household income. These are not perfect systems, but they offer something our privately run plans do not: care without the panic of debt. That
is probably why a survey of 149,290 Americans found that people who
use Medicaid and Medicare report more consistent access to care, and less
medical debt, than do people insured through private plans. Being insured
through IHOP or the marketplace, with private insurance, then, would
not have saved Barb from the panic.

To escape the panic, Barb's best bet would have been Medicaid. Yet
even that would have been fraught. To stay insured, she would have
needed to prove she *deserved* care, again and again, through paperwork
that was nearly endless and rarely intelligible. She would not have had
time to look at the bigger picture.

Most white Americans of all classes, I think, do not look at the bigger picture. If we did, we might see this obsession with *deserving* for the
distraction that it is. We might see that when we fight over who deserves
what, we often make assumptions about race. We assume that we, as white
people, deserve our government's help without question. We assume that
Black and brown Americans need to prove they deserve that same help.
If we looked at the bigger picture, we might see how our willingness to
subject Black and brown people to this test has morphed into a culture so
accustomed to it that, now, we are increasingly subjected to it ourselves.
We might see how much we lose by picking a fight over who deserves
what, again and again, instead of fighting, together, to say we all deserve
to have enough.

That's another way of saying that racism here has never been about
color. It has always been about power.

But white Americans have held tight to the myth of *deserving*, reflecting that ugly lesson we have learned. We have listened to leaders who said
the safety net was not for us. We have dismissed the fact that these leaders
are often bankrolled by the same companies who benefit, massively, from

this fractured, punitive, and expensive system. We believed that asking the poor to prove their worth was reasonable because we assumed they would mostly be Black. We told ourselves it was reasonable because we did not believe it would happen to *us*. Our error has become easier to see as the safety net, made thin and flimsy by racism from the start, has turned to raggedy threads beneath us. That companies turn a profit at every step along the way only adds insult to this injury.

Nobody with a body that needs care can claim to be an impartial observer of this problem. I certainly cannot. My mother had a body once, and when her country asked her to prove she deserved the help that would keep her alive in it, she failed. So my country took her, and so my family, and so my heart. America took and it took, and it took.

I would be a fool to think it is done.

So would you.

9

MY YOUNG ADULTHOOD

NEW YORK CITY

1994–2009

Before I arrived in New York, I hadn't thought much about NYU being a private school. The class difference between me and my classmates surprised me. When I told one of my roommates, the white daughter of a Manhattan doctor, that my father sold lawn mowers, she said *"Really?"* and giggled. *"That's funny."* When another, the daughter of a movie producer, bought a throw pillow for fifty dollars, I thought: *I'd have to work for a day to pay for that.**

I started looking for work as soon as I got to campus. I picked up work as a tutor and babysitter, and got a community service job with a new federal program, AmeriCorps. I remember taking home around $40 or $50 a week for helping teachers at a public high school for ten hours, with the promise of a small educational grant at the end. I helped teachers at Seward Park, a public high school on the Lower East Side, with their classes, walking the half hour downtown to save on subway fare. As classes got under way that

---

* According to the Bureau of Labor Statistics, $50 in January 1994 was equivalent to $102 in January 2023.

first year, I was working fifteen or twenty hours a week, the same as I had during high school.

The balance of work and school was the only thing in college that felt familiar to me. At Holly, I'd been second in my class without much effort at all. At NYU, I was embarrassed by how impenetrable Foucault seemed, how little American history I knew. What's more, my rural public high school—overcrowded and underfunded, where I'd taken what I got and made it work—hadn't prepared me for an elite school full of resources and helpful staff. I knew, vaguely, that there were professors and deans and office hours, but I assumed they came with the same strings attached to public benefits and help from my father: I would have to prove I deserved it, and it would require enduring humiliation.

It was hard for me to see, then, how much more advantage I had compared to other kids who talked about culture shock, or about not having parents who helped them, or about feeling out of place. I did not meet many white, middle-class students at NYU who talked about a disconnect between themselves and the school. So, when I heard first-generation students talk about how they didn't ask for help because they didn't know how to seek it out, I thought: *I know what that's like.* When I heard Black students talk about feeling like they were not treated fairly, I thought I knew what that was like, too. When I heard anyone at all talk about feeling dumb, like an imposter, in this wealthy, white place, I thought I knew what that was like, too. In crucial ways, though, I knew nothing at all.

I didn't understand, yet, that none of us were really talking about the specifics of the university. We were talking about how readily we could access the power and social mobility the university could grant us. And while I *thought* I had an experience similar to those other students, there were hard limits on the overlap. I was white and familiar enough with middle-class dress and diction that all I would have had to do to fit in was dress and speak the part. With a costume change and a tweak of dialect, nobody would have looked at me and thought, *She doesn't belong.* I couldn't see that, though. My father's abuse had convinced me I was powerless. Other adults' overlooking of it had convinced me I was worthless. I was scared, and I did not look up, and so I did not see the bigger picture.

I couldn't see that the kinship I felt was one of abuse—a term, I think, that describes pretty well the way my country has treated Black people, and how so many institutions treat people without money. And because I could not name the root of this imagined kinship, I could not see how vastly my experiences differed from racism and poverty. At that point in my life, most of the oppression I'd endured was personal and individual. The oppression that other kids faced—first-generation students, middle-class kids who weren't white, any kid whose family had been poor for generations—was bigger than one troubled dad. It was the whole society in which they lived.

* * * * *

In the fall of my sophomore year, a wealthy white family who lived in walking distance of my dorm hired me to work with their two children, aged eleven and fourteen. It was more money than I'd ever made before: $200 a week in cash to show up four nights a week and help with homework and meals. Their apartment covered an entire floor of a converted factory, and it was beautiful. Windows bigger than the twin mattress I slept on flooded the place with light. The kitchen held a six-burner range and bottles of vinegar that cost more than my books for class. Paintings and gallery-framed photos covered the walls, and a leafy ficus arced over the living room sofa, the biggest I'd seen outside shopping malls.

The girls' mother, Maggie (not her real name), was about the age my mother would have been. She was beautiful and worldly, an artist married to an attorney, and she spoke kindly to me. When she talked about going to social dinners with her husband, she rolled her eyes, as if to say, *I'd so much rather be home.* I liked her immediately.

When Maggie interviewed me in September 1995, she asked about my family. I remember talking a lot, almost unable to stop; Maggie just seemed so kind. I told her that my mom had died a couple years ago, and my dad was abusive, and now I was here. I think she was the first adult I'd told about my father's abuse in that way: as a statement of fact instead a cry for help. It felt liberating to admit it had happened, then to preempt pity by showing that it didn't even hurt. *"Whatever,"* I said. *"I'm here now. I love college. I love learning. And I need to pay for school."* Maggie nodded and smiled. Her younger kid, who had done their homework at the table where Maggie and I talked, took a liking to me.

I started working for them in October. It was a good job, and I remember having a general sense that Maggie wanted me to feel at home. I'd never had a job that easy before. I'd show up at six thirty in the evening and ask the two kids, who I adored, if they needed help with their homework. They rarely did. If Maggie was home, I'd help with dinner, or order takeout and pay from the household's petty cash—kept in a change purse in the kitchen. If Maggie wasn't home, or if she was busy, I'd cook dinner. I ate with them, then cleaned up. Afterward, I would study until nine thirty, when I went home.

There was an emotional component to it for me, too, though I did not see it then. My upbringing had left me anxious and starved for care and affection. When Maggie implied that I was one of the family, I believed her fully—another small way, I think, that being white benefited me. I did not carry any of the history that a young Black woman would have carried into that job; I was not doing a job for low pay that my ancestors had been forced to do against their will. Instead, I compared my job to my own history—to the orchard where I'd earned less than minimum wage, to the Big Boy manager who'd warned me about missing work after the fight with my father. And I compared Maggie, who seemed interested in the things I learned and thought, to my father and stepmother, who did not.

On the days when I worked at AmeriCorps, I spent my mornings helping New York City public school kids—mostly immigrants and city-born Black kids, mostly working-class—with their homework. Then I went to class with the children of professionals at a private university. At Maggie's, I helped out in the home of some of the wealthiest people in the world. In a single day, I would walk the entire American spectrum of race and class, and I took all of it in.

* * * * *

I dreaded going home for Christmas, where things had been getting worse. The past summer, between waitressing shifts and interning at Detroit's alternative newsweekly, I'd noticed that Bonnie had begun hiding a change of clothes and her purse in the upstairs hall. I assumed this was to make for an easy exit in case of a fight. In September, after I'd gone back to school, my sisters told me my father had slapped one of them, emptied and thrown bureau drawers, swept belongings off desks and dresser tops. I tried to talk to him about it, but I only angered him; he told me that if it was important to me, I would come home. Late that fall, my sisters told me he threw one of them with sufficient violence that Bonnie called the police. My father drove off. When the police arrived, Bonnie did not file a report.

Even so, my father bought me a flight home for Christmas, as if everything was fine. My parents, sisters, and I celebrated the holiday exchanging presents until late on Christmas Eve, playing pool and darts in my father's basement bar, Bob Seger on the stereo. On Christmas Day, we visited grandparents and exchanged more presents. Surrounded by family and distracted by the holiday, it was easy to tell myself that maybe things would work out okay. That maybe, finally, I could have the family I wanted: one that supported me, and each other.

The day after Christmas, I went to get my car's brakes checked. When I learned they needed to be replaced, costing a few hundred dollars, I shook my head and drove home carefully. Most of my savings had been spent on tuition. As I remember it, my father, who'd been jobless for a few months of the year I started college, had not contributed to my first year at NYU, and promised to double up the second year. At the start of my sophomore year, I remember him contributing $3,000 as promised. Then, in December he told me he would only pay half that in the spring; Christmas bills were coming due. Making up the difference would all but empty my savings, and I needed tuition more than I needed a car with brakes.

Both my sisters' cars were gone when I got back to the house. Inside, Bonnie was alone in the bedroom she shared with my father. She ignored me when I said hello and continued packing a suitcase on the bed.

My father came home soon after. I listened to their voices rise.

"*I'm leaving,*" Bonnie said. "*I have had enough of this.*"

"*Don't leave, I'll fix them,*" he said. "*Don't leave. I'll talk to them. Just don't leave.*"

Bonnie tells me that Jodie was blaring music and refused to turn it down. When Bonnie protested, Jodie called her names, so Bonnie hit her. "It started with me slapping her face," Bonnie told me. "I'll admit that. But it was her defying me. . . . She said, 'I don't have to do what you say,' and I was tired of being treated like that." Shana jumped into the fight, scratching Bonnie. When the fight was over, my sisters left. A little while later, I walked in the door.

★ ★ ★ ★ ★

In the evening, I eavesdropped on the upstairs phone when each sister called. Shana agreed in a shaky voice to come home. But I remember admiring how Jodie spoke to my father, calm and firm. "*I want you to know that I'm all right,*" she said. "*But I need some time to think. I am not coming home tonight.*"

My father spoke in the same icy tone he'd used with me when Bonnie made him look at my arm. "*Just remember there are privileges that can be taken away from you if you don't come home,*" he said. "*Things like a car. And a bank account. Get your ass home.*"

"*I don't think that's a good idea,*" she said. My father said her bank account was his and he would empty it, and he said he would report her car stolen. Still, she would not agree to come home. My father hung up the phone.

I began to shake. I turned on my radio and started doing jumping jacks to keep from screaming. I didn't hear my father until he stood in the doorway. He told me to turn down the music.

I glared at him and turned it down. He was already angry.

"*If you don't like the rules of this house, you can go somewhere else,*" he said.

"*Maybe it's other things,*" I said, backing up. I turned, but there was nowhere to go.

My father came into the room, yelling things he had said before: I was a brat and a bitch. I was spoiled and ungrateful. I was driving Bonnie away. If they got a divorce, it would be my fault.

"*Bonnie was hitting Shana,*" I said.

"*Your sisters are lying sacks of shit,*" he said.

"*You can't do this!*" I screamed. "*You can't hit your family! You can't hit peo-ple.*" I was watching myself from outside of my body: the two of us facing off in the corner of my room, my hands shaking. My father looming over me. Then Bonnie was at the door.

She looked at me, and then my father.

"*You're a spoiled brat,*" she yelled. "*All your father's done is love you and give you everything! All you do is lie about him.*"

"*He hits us,*" I said. "*He hits us.*" I was muttering to myself by then.

"*No, he doesn't!*" Bonnie said. "*You just make that up to get our money. You're a liar!*"

"*You are sick, sicker than a lot of people out there,*" my father yelled. "*Get out of my house! Get out! Get out!*"

A friend came to get me. The next day, I called my grandparents to ask for help and advice. They each told me my father had called them. He had told them I had lost my mind; that I was delusional. I do not know if they believed him. I do not think they contradicted him. I do not remember what advice they gave me. I know they did not offer me a place to stay. I spent a couple more nights in Michigan, at friends' houses, then went back to New York early.

My family has changed so little. In the last conversation I had with my father and stepmother for this book, they both remembered most of the violence I had noted in my journals. My father stayed close to silent in that conversation, staring into the middle distance, uttering responses so short they were monosyllabic. Bonnie wanted to talk more. She spoke, mostly, about how hard it was for her to come into a family where her husband did not support her and the children neither welcomed nor obeyed her. When we talked about the violence and the call she made to the police, the attack that I endured, she nodded sympathetically. She wished we'd talked about this more, and earlier. Then she told me, "You were never in danger."

In the 2010s, when the verb "gaslight" entered common language, I felt a thud of recognition. I knew what it felt like to be abused, and then watch as bystanders excused my abuser. I knew what it felt like to complain about abuse, then watch as concern swirled toward my abuser, as effortlessly as water rushing down a drain, while blame puddled at my feet. I knew how it felt to object to abuse, and to be told I was crazy because it had not happened at all. And by then I knew, shamefully, that I was so used to having abuse of me denied and excused that I had denied and excused the abuse of others.

To do that denying and excusing, I'd had to tell myself it was the way of the world. But when I read books and articles and social media posts where Black people explained what happened when they tried to challenge racism, how they were told by white people that they were imagining the racist treatment—that they were, perhaps, imagining the racism itself—my subconscious flickered with recognition. It began as *I know what that's like,* before my intellect kicked in, before the difference between the abuse of my father and the organized abuse of an entire government and culture, came into focus. I could not say, *I know what that's like.* But I could say, *I believe you.*

I suppose that's useful, insofar as it goes. I don't know that it matters much unless I do something about it.

* * * * *

When I got back to New York, I told Maggie everything. I had only been working for her for a couple months, but I'd fallen a little bit in love with the family by then. On evenings when Maggie stayed home, I would help her cook, and she'd ask me about myself and tell me her own stories. I told her how relieved I was to be free of my father. She nodded and smiled like she understood.

One night, when I was at work with Maggie, she cooked dinner while

I loitered around awkwardly. I knew I was at work but had no tasks before me. Didn't she need me to do something? Maggie saw me fidget and asked me to set the table. I went to a custom cabinet and opened its doors. I pulled out earthenware plates curved so deeply they were nearly bowls. Placemats made of linen, instead of the paper and plastic I'd grown up with, were already on the table.

"I know this is a weird job, Tracie," Maggie said. *"I know you don't have to work much when you come here."*

"That's okay," I said.

"But my kids are never going to have to work, and they need to know some-how that people do," she said.

I nodded as I carried plates to the table, and felt shame spread through my chest. I thought I'd been hired because I was smart, or a good tutor. I didn't understand how different the lives of the wealthy were from my own, so I didn't understand why she'd pay me $200 a week to show her kids that people worked.

Later, I'd realize that the kids already saw people who "had to work" all the time. A Hispanic woman worked in the house daily as Maggie's assistant. Other women cleaned the house. There were workers at the corner bodega, in the subway clerk's tollbooth, in the cafeterias of their private schools. The only thing that really separated me from those work-ers, I thought, was that I could be mistaken for kin: a student at a private university who was white.

Maggie tells me she didn't really think about my race when she hired me. She had recently remarried, and the relationship came with social obligations. She needed help in the most basic way: someone to provide a stable evening presence at home as her kids grew into young adults. As best as Maggie can remember, she hired me because I was smart and reliable; clearly liked kids; and came from a small town in Michigan, as had some of her family. If I'd shown up, but with dark brown skin, she'd have hired me just the same. And yet, it seems incredibly unlikely to me that Maggie is so colorblind that my race did not matter at all. It seems unlikely because of my own cynicism about the existence of colorblindness in my country. It also seems unlikely because of my own racism.

For a long time, I understood Maggie's explanation of my job as one of kinship: *Of course a white family would need to hire a white college student to model work to their children,* I thought. *How else would their children see themselves in me?* It took time before I understood how my assumption—that white people could not be kin to Black people—is as deep as racism has ever run.

Being able to appear as kin to people with power and money helped me. Being able to *see myself* as kin to the powerful—to believe, however tenuously, that I might belong among them, at a time when I had no sense of belonging or being wanted anywhere at all—helped me, too. As I began swimming in the world of work and school, the color of my skin was a kind of flotation device. It wouldn't get me from place to place, but it helped me keep my head above water. It was just enough to keep me afloat.

* * * * *

When the semester ended, I loaded my things into the wheeled plastic bins most students used to move belongings from their dorm room to the curb. I pushed them a mile each way down the sidewalk, unloading them at Maggie's building, then returned for more until my dorm room was empty. She was letting me stay there while I looked for an apartment with my best friend, Oscar.

Neither of us had much money, and even Oscar's parents, who paid his tuition, weren't going to pay his rent. For two months, we loitered around drop boxes for the *Village Voice* every Tuesday to check classifieds. Our budget was around $800 a month, which pushed us deep into Brooklyn. Most landlords ignored us once they realized how young we were; I was still a teenager. When landlords for a rent-stabilized apartment in Sunset Park, forty-five minutes from NYU on the train, offered us a lease, they asked for an adult to cosign. I complained to Maggie about this, frustrated. She offered a solution. She or her husband could cosign for us—just as Jared's dad had cosigned for the loans supporting Jared's nursing degree.

"I know you're responsible, so I'll sign it. I'm happy to help you out," her law-yer husband said to me later as he pulled out his pen. He sat on a European leather sofa, watching TV with work papers in his lap. He read the paper closely, then pointed at a clause and shook his head. *"But I'm not giving them my Social Security number. They can call me if that's a problem."*

I nodded and thought, *I didn't know you could just ignore a rule like that.* I wondered what other rules I followed that I didn't have to. I didn't yet grasp that the rules would almost always be different for him than they were for me. I thanked him and took the form he'd signed to the landlord. By August, I was living in Brooklyn.

★ ★ ★ ★ ★

Almost as soon as I started working for Maggie, she was asking me for a copy of my résumé. She told me her husband loved opening doors for young people. I nodded and thanked her, and thought, *I don't want their charity because I don't want to owe them anything.* And then, *It's not like it will do any good, anyway.*

Even before I parted from my parents, I'd started feeling a resentment and bitterness I could not shake. I believed that things were much easier for other people. I envied my friends, nearly all of whose parents paid their tuition. I envied the other waitresses if I thought they were prettier than me, because I thought it was easier for them to get tips. I loved Maggie's kids and thought of them almost like siblings, but I envied them, too, for their attentive mother and the ease their wealth brought them.

"The more I put into things, the less I get," I wrote to myself one day. "God hates me," I added—and part of me believed it. I would have told you then that my father's abuse was the reason I was bitter. Today, I know that was only part of the truth. I was also bitter because the abuse came even after I'd done everything my father had asked: I had cared for my mother and justified sending her away; I had left her and not complained. I thought my silence would keep me safe. It did not.

I also felt bitter because I had assumed, blindly, that college would be the same for me as for my father: fun, carefree, lots of parties. I did not understand that college being easy and fun was a product of it being affordable, whether that derived from parental wealth or social policy. I was lucky in that I'd gotten a sufficient scholarship that a fancy private school was affordable. NYU's financial aid package was generous enough that the cost to my family, after suggested loans, was within a thousand dollars of the cost to attend the University of Michigan, my home state's flagship university. That was partly a function of NYU being generous. It was also a reflection of how stingy the public system in Michigan had become.

At NYU, I remember needing to pay about $9,000 a year out of pocket.* I still feared my father, and assumed he would claim me on his tax return, so I didn't get myself declared independent—a bureaucratic task that intimidated me, but would have likely boosted my financial aid. I remember Maggie paying me $200 a week. AmeriCorps was paying me around $140 every two weeks. Over the four summer months between semesters, I'd earn around $10,000 by waiting tables and patching together part-time office jobs I found with help from Maggie or activists I knew. The first year I was independent of my parents, I held eight part-time jobs over twelve months. My income would've been around $18,900—a figure that put me just shy of the lower-middle class. If I deducted what I paid for tuition, though, I was squarely within functional poverty.

It took me until the end of my junior year to hand Maggie a résumé crowded with part-time jobs and campus groups. I was conflicted about internships. I'd learned in a journalism class about this strange practice of working for free while also paying the university for credit. I was personally offended that the university would charge me $3,000 to go work

---

* As noted earlier, I had an unusual arrangement with Grandpa Mac. Each year, he loaned me the full amount for which I qualified from a Stafford loan and a Perkins loan, interest-free, on the condition that I did not take out additional loans. My records indicate this was just under $7,000 a year, leaving me with an informal debt after graduation of roughly $27,500.

somewhere without getting paid. But as I neared completion of my degree, I could appreciate what a boon it would be to have less coursework to complete—and how useful it would be to have experience. I asked Maggie if her husband might be willing to send my résumé to the *Village Voice*. She said it was no problem; her husband knew the publisher. By summer's end, I was hired.

★ ★ ★ ★ ★

In September, I walked into the *Village Voice* offices on Cooper Square to start apprenticing with an investigative journalist, Wayne Barrett. I sat down with the internship director, Frank Ruscitti, a barrel-chested, long-haired man with a gravelly voice and a black concert T-shirt taut over his belly. *"Wayne's a yeller, you know,"* said Frank. *"But his bark is worse than his bite."* He didn't tell me about Wayne Barrett's reputation, presumably because he figured I knew that Wayne had been the first to investigate Donald Trump, was investigating Mayor Rudolph Giuliani, and was known for being a crusader on behalf of the public—he called himself a "detective for the people." I didn't know any of that, though; I was still too timid, and too inexperienced, to think about work strategically—as a portal and a stepping-stone to other jobs. I just knew that Maggie's husband had opened a door, and I should be grateful. Beyond that, I understood only that I was being hired for a job, for which I needed to show up and do as I was told.

"Wayne can be a real handful," said Frank. I nodded and pictured my father. *"But if you can take it, you're in luck,"* said Frank. *"It's the best internship at the paper."*

Barrett took a liking to me, fueled by a paternal concern for how hard I worked and how little my family helped. The internship went well. Barrett sent me across the city: tracking down obscure land records, copying campaign filing records by hand, interviewing Black mothers whose children died when police declined to intervene in a stampede at a concert, investigating sweatshops in Chinatown. Contrary to Frank's warnings, Barrett never raised his voice at me. Instead, he gave me work that taught me I had a right to know what was done in my name or with my tax dollars. And, because Barrett coupled my training with kindness, I began to stop worrying so much about myself. I started to realize I could stand up for people who were being abused—just as I'd wished people would have stood up for me.

When I graduated college in the spring, my plans were vague. I wanted to be a journalist and make the world better. But I was also exhausted from the last four years and scared of failing. When journalists—even Barrett— offered to open doors, I made up excuses and did not follow up. I worried about what they'd want from me later, or their anger at me if I failed. It paralyzed me.

Maggie's kids were now too big to need me, so I got a tutoring job with another family and started volunteering, unpaid, as the editor of the youth magazine for the Democratic Socialists of America. It didn't feel like I was shunning advantages or lowering my goals. It felt safe, because I was asking for nothing, and doing it all myself, just as I always felt I had.

* * * * *

I had been dangerously naïve about the implications of severing my relationship with my father before I had wealth of my own. My father and stepmother had encouraged this naïveté, accusing me of only wanting their money—as if the food, shelter, and education I sought from them were compulsions of greed. On my own in New York, a low-grade panic had set in: I had nothing to catch me if I fell. And yet I could not bring myself to return to them. I'd do my best to make it. If I failed I knew, with a conviction that scared me, that my next step would be to head to a homeless shelter. I was that scared.

By 2000, five years had gone by without me talking to my father and Bonnie. I had kept in touch with my sisters and grandparents, but I was not honest with them about my life in New York. In college I survived, mostly, on Nutrament shakes, free food at campus events, and dinner at Maggie's. I did not talk about how I'd begun to have spells of vertigo so intense that I'd vomit, or how, some nights, I'd be so overcome with anxiety that I could only stare at the wall, unable to even answer Oscar's questions about what was wrong. Instead, I told my family the stories I thought they expected of a young woman in New York: young men I had met, reporting trips to the Bronx, dance parties on the subway, watching the sun rise on my way home after dancing all night. My sisters and grandparents heard these happy stories, and told themselves, *Tracie is doing great.* I gave them no reason to believe otherwise.

They began to lose patience with me. They said things like *"You can't break up with family,"* and asked me what more I wanted from my father. They told me how much I hurt my father, and how he had already suffered so much with my mother. I was exhausted by fighting this battle alone. So, I went back to them.

That year, Shana was graduating from Michigan State, and I went to the family dinner at a steak house. I felt self-conscious as I approached the tables where all my grandparents, my sisters, and my father and Bonnie sat. When my father turned to me, my stomach seized. I wanted to run away. I know today that this is a trauma response, a gut instinct to protect myself from harm, but I dismissed it. Instead, I smiled and let my father give me a long hug. When he stepped away, I saw everyone beaming at me. I had returned and made the family whole. It made me uneasy, but I would make it work.

★ ★ ★ ★ ★

When I moved to Brooklyn, I didn't know anything about renting an apartment—least of all the details of the city's rent stabilization law, which limits rent increases. Once a tenant gets into a stabilized apartment, landlords can't refuse to renew a lease unless the tenant breaks the rules of the lease. Just as importantly, they can't jack up the rent, either; rent increases set by a public board of representatives for both tenants and landlords, are modest. Since 1970, the rent increases on one-year lease renewals have exceeded 10 percent just three times.

I hadn't understood my extraordinary fortune to land in a rent-stabilized apartment. My first apartment, which Oscar and I had found in the ads of the *Village Voice*, was a two-bedroom for $700, which Oscar and I split down the middle: $350 each.* I remember paying twice that in the dorm I'd left, an "apartment-style" one-bedroom that I split with three other women. The apartment was an hour from campus, in Sunset Park, Brooklyn, a working-class neighborhood of Puerto Ricans and immigrants from China and Poland. The move, even with the added expenses of utilities and commuting, cut my living expenses in half.

Today, rent regulation is only found in New York and a few other cities, but it wasn't always so rare. In the 1940s, rent regulation was a national program. The economic boom generated by World War II pushed housing prices up severely. To keep housing affordable for workers so they could support the war effort, President Roosevelt's administration set "rent controls" in 1942. Federal rent control ended in the early 1950s, and most local rent regulations went with it as federal priorities—and funding—shifted toward making suburbs affordable to the middle class, like my mother's parents, rather than supporting city housing.

It would have been easy for New York City to follow the same path as cities like Detroit, where the end of federal rent controls was the end of rent controls, period. But in New York City, a multiracial alliance of tenants had been organizing since the 1920s. Because tenants' primary interest is in maintaining affordable rent—not boosting property values—urban renters had no financial reason to seek segregation. Instead, observes the scholar Roberta Gold, tenant power came from sheer numbers, which encouraged racial inclusion instead of exclusion.

---

* According to the Bureau of Labor Statistics, $700 in 1996 was equivalent to $1,356 in January 2023.

As the expiration date for federal control loomed, New York City's activists began to lobby and protest. In 1951, two years before federal protections expired, tenants succeeded in getting the state to pass a rent control law for the city. The new law set the rent for more than two million apartments back to 1943 levels, then set rules for how and when it could increase. By the late 1960s, intensive lobbying by landlords, the fissuring of the radical left in New York, and other political pressures would force a virtual end to rent control. But tenants managed to hang on to what is now one of the strongest rent protections in the country: rent stabilization.

I didn't know it as I signed that first lease in 1996, but state officials had weakened the laws governing rent stabilization two years before. Originally, rents in stabilized apartments were just reflections of annually improved increases. The base rent did not change—ever. And if a tenant didn't renew their lease, the next tenant's rent was adjusted for the annual increase, same as it would have been under the previous tenant. And on it went, without limits. For tenants, this created the same kind of stability that homeowners get from mortgages: Affordable, stable prices for housing.

In 1994, the real estate industry won two concessions that—if left unchecked—would have eventually deregulated every apartment in the city. The first, "vacancy decontrol," allowed landlords to increase rent by 20 percent every time a new lease was signed with new tenants. Under the second change, "luxury decontrol" allowed landlords to charge whatever rent they wanted once an apartment's rent went over $2,000. Both of these changes made tenant turnover profitable for landlords. White NYU students with out-of-state IDs, likely to leave in a year or two, offered the promise of a 20 percent rent hike in the near future—instead of the modest ones set by the public board.

For as long as I've been in New York, I have had government—and the tenants who lobbied and protested—to thank for my affordable rent. When I moved to Brooklyn in 1996, the program covered 52 percent of the city's rentals, including mine in Sunset Park. My second apartment was also stabilized, as is my third and current one. In my nearly three decades as a New Yorker, I have never paid market rent. Without that affordable rent I doubt I would have been able to finish college—at least not within the five years it took me. I would certainly not have been able to survive on what I earned as an independent writer.

Rent stabilization is an example of what the writer Heather McGhee calls a "solidarity dividend"—the benefits that result from cross-racial alliances that work in service of the common good. In the end, I could pursue a lower-income career because other people had worked together, across race lines, to make it possible. Today, the nearly one million stabilized households in New York, most of us making well below the city's median income, benefit from that.

Just not, it's worth noting, anyone living in either of my first two apartments. By 2009, the legal rent for both of my first two apartments in Brooklyn had gone so high that the units had become unregulated. Landlords have been able to charge whatever the market will bear for them ever since.

★ ★ ★ ★ ★

After a year in Sunset Park, I moved into a three-bedroom apartment in a neighborhood that Realtors called Clinton Hill, but my neighbors still called Bed-Stuy. I split the $1,080 rent three ways with two guys I had met at NYU, Sam and Andrew. They drank frequently, both at bars and at home with friends. Nina, another student who'd previously rented the room I now had, came by most nights to drink at our kitchen table, sometimes passing out surrounded by beer bottles. Eventually, my roommates invited me to the bar with them.

I'd never really drunk alcohol before then. In high school I'd been keenly aware that my mother's accident had been with a drunk driver, and would not touch it. In college, I was too broke and too focused on my studies to bother. As soon as I became accustomed to the taste, I realized I loved the way it felt to be drunk: as if I didn't have a care in the world. This was how my father had talked about college, and it was how college looked in movies. I felt, finally, that I was getting to be a kid.

By the summer of 1999, I was spending most nights with a tight circle of drinkers: Sam and Andrew; the women they dated, Sara and Katherine; and Nina. (I have changed all their names.) I thought that because we stayed up late and got sloppy together, we were friends. I did not understand that a shared interest in drinking was no guarantee of care. I did not understand that to be drunk and young, female and broke, was to be vulnerable.

That summer, Andrew and Sara both went to Europe, traveling. I spent Labor Day drinking with Sam, Nina, and Katherine, willingly ceding a whole day to blurry memories, and passed out on a couch in Nina's apartment. I woke up with Sam on top of me, grunting and shoving my underwear aside. Nina and Katherine were giggling on the floor. I could not tell if this was a dream or if it was real. It did not occur to me that I could object. I got up to use the bathroom, then returned, and let Sam continue. Then I passed out again.

A few days later, I asked Sam what had happened.

"Did we. . . . ?"

"I don't know. I don't remember."

"Oh, okay."

For all the feminist theory I'd read in class, I hadn't learned anything about what actually constituted sexual assault. I wondered if this meant Sam liked me. I wondered if Sam thought this meant we were dating. I did not ask him any of these things, because I was terrified that the answer would be yes.

★ ★ ★ ★ ★

That thing with Sam, as I began to think of it, created tension in my drinking circle. *"Slut!"* Katherine yelled at me after a night of drinking. *"How dare you do that to Sara?"* I told her that Sara and Sam weren't exclusive; that I had done nothing wrong.

Neither of us thought to yell at Sam.

* * * * *

It would be years before I wondered why I didn't object. I had not wanted to have sex with Sam. But it had not even occurred to me that I could say no: I awoke with a man, whom I did not want to have sex with, on top of and inside of me, and I submitted without saying a word. I'd had a far more innocent version of the experience a couple years earlier, when a male friend offered me a place to crash after a night out—by which he meant we could share his futon. He threw his arm over me—to cuddle, he later explained—and I remember freezing in place. I could not bring myself to speak.

I have long read about being "broken" by something, but I did not really understand what that meant until I considered the long tail of the attack from my father. I think that abuse, combined with the silent acceptance of it by every adult around me, broke the piece of me that would have said no to Sam; the piece of me that would have shoved him off of me and stumbled drunkenly out of the room instead of complying. My body had already learned the consequences that it would face if I did not yield. When danger presented itself, my body overrode my mouth and tried to keep me safe.

It makes sense to me, then, that the researchers who've documented this way that people shut down have also found a striking correlation between childhood abuse and sexual assault in adulthood. Women who experience significant hardship in childhood are seven times as likely to be sexually assaulted as adults. Judging from my experience, at least part of that is because they've learned that it is safer to submit than to fight.

After the assault, I behaved as if nothing had happened, just as my family had with my father's attacks. I thought, without thinking, that this would keep me safe.

* * * * *

In the months after that thing with Sam, I told myself that my roommate having sex with me while I was passed out was a predictable, acceptable series of events. There was comfort in this story. If the thing with Sam happened because I'd drunk too much, I could believe it was a choice—of a kind—that I had made. To call it "rape," or even the milder "assault," meant I had no choice, and so no power. This was terrifying.

And so, for the first year, I did not call it anything at all. I let it recede from my mind. When I made a new friend, Jessie, in 2001, I brought it up casually, as if it were a story about dating.

"We had a thing," I said, *"but it was a mess."* I explained how Sam had had sex with me while I was passed out, and how I'd gone along with it. I shrugged.

Jessie took a deep breath.

"Tracie, that's not sex," she said quietly. *"It's assault."*

Over the next few weeks, I talked about this idea with another friend, a political organizer who'd done work around sexual violence. When she heard my story, she called it "rape." She suggested I report it to the police. I was angry by then—at myself for the submission I didn't yet understand, at Sam for having seen my body as his to do with as he liked.

I had no faith in the police. I remembered that call to Big Boy several years before . The brutal abuse of Abner Louima in a Brooklyn jail in 1997 had angered me, and I had been haunted by the police killing of Amadou Diallo in a Bronx doorway earlier that year. But what my friend told me made sense, too: Sam had done something wrong, and there should be consequences for it. Maybe I was being cynical, I told myself. I decided to report it.

★ ★ ★ ★ ★

I rode my bike to the police precinct a few nights later. I went alone because I did not want to be a bother to anyone; because I wanted to do it myself. The station was in Crown Heights, deep enough into Brooklyn that the slow encroachment of white college kids and artists hadn't really reached it yet. I had never been in a police precinct before. The only other time I had tried to speak to an officer about a problem was when I had called to ask about reporting my father.

I remember little about the experience, which was very quick. I must have said I wanted to report a sexual assault. Maybe I said "rape." I remember two officers coming to the entryway of the precinct, brightly lit with fluorescent lights. I do not remember their race or their age. I remember they were both men.

They asked why I'd waited so long. Why didn't I file a report when it happened?

I said nothing. Somewhere in my mind, still too amorphous for me to articulate, I thought: *If I had objected, I would have had to move, and I can't afford that.*

They asked if something else was going on: Was I mad at Sam about something? The implication, I understood, was that I might be making up the assault to punish Sam for something else.

It didn't occur to me to say, *"I am mad at him because he raped me."* I withdrew and began to panic. My mind searched for ways to return control of the situation to me.

I remembered, then, an argument I'd had with Sam a few nights before. Andrew had moved out and we were looking for a new roommate. We couldn't agree on one.

"I was here first," Sam said; he should get to pick the roommate.

We argued more.

"I'm on the lease," I said; I had a legal right to the apartment and deserved a say, too.

Sam suggested I move out; I said I couldn't afford to live anywhere else.

Irrationally, I equated moving with having to return to my father, and this made me deeply stubborn. Sam and I talked in circles. The assault lurked beneath our argument, unspoken.

"I'm going to win, Sam," I said, narrowing my eyes.

"Yeah? Why?" he asked.

"I'm smarter than you, and I can take more," I said.

Sam looked at me silently and walked out of the room.

In the precinct, I wondered if this argument meant the officers were right: Maybe I was making this up. Maybe the officers were seeing through me. Maybe I had wanted to have sex with Sam, and now I regretted it, and I was wasting their time. Maybe nothing objectionable had happened at all.

I left without filing a report, embarrassed for having tried. I felt like a fool. *What did I expect?*

Sam and I would be stuck until one of us decided to budge.

★ ★ ★ ★ ★

Years later, I'd read research from scholars of sexual violence—people whose work required them to study police reports and interview detectives and prosecutors about rape cases—and see myself in that work. I would recognize my story in a study by Cassia Spohn, who interviewed Los Angeles police and found that officers were more likely to believe what they called "a righteous victim": someone who fought back, who had not been drinking, who didn't know her attacker. I'd recognize it in an *Atlantic* cover story about police departments' overwhelming failure to pursue rape cases and what the reporter called "a subterranean river of chauvinism" among police who investigated sexual violence. I had been drinking, I knew Sam, and I did not fight back. I walked into the precinct young, broke, female, and traumatized, leery of power instead of fighting to have it act on my behalf. So, the police turned me away.

For a long time, when I heard people talk about the privileges of white women, I remembered my assault and how I was dismissed by police, and I felt resentment stir up in me. What did being white get me? Nothing useful from the police, that is for certain. I did not understand that while I was white, I was also female and broke—facing off against a white man, albeit a relatively broke one as well. His whiteness would protect him from police action; mine did little more than give me the false hope that I'd be taken seriously.

This, it seems, is the way men with power have usually treated white women: as secondary to white men, our protection only of interest insofar as it justifies their violence against other men. This is how it was with lynching in the early twentieth century. The common understanding among whites back then, especially those in the South, was that lynching was a justifiable response to Black men raping white women.

The rape of white women by Black men was not common, but white journalists did little to dispel this notion. Some knowingly published stories that claimed to document rape of which there was no evidence. As the early twentieth century investigative journalist Ida B. Wells showed in her reporting, only one-third of Black men who were lynched had even been charged with rape—let alone convicted of it. Nor, argued Wells, was lynching an honest reflection of white men's desire to protect white women: "The cowardly lyncher revels in murder, then seeks to shield himself from public execration by claiming devotion to woman." Protecting white women was never really the point; terrorizing Black people was.

This history still echoes today. In the 1990s, feminists won inclusion of the Violence Against Women Act as part of President Clinton's 1994 crime bill. The act expanded the range of punishments for sexual assault and other gender crimes, and increased the funding available to prosecute them. Some women called this a victory. Some scholars began to call this use of the state's criminal justice system to achieve arguably feminist goals "carceral feminism."

Yet, these vast new punishments have done little to protect women from violence. In 2005, in consideration of a case where three girls were killed by their father, against whom their mother had a restraining order, the Supreme Court ruled that police have no constitutional obligation to protect any person from harm. Criminal justice data suggest that while *sentences* for sexual assault have nearly doubled in length since 1994, the *likelihood* of a sexual assault leading to conviction of a crime is minuscule. Victim advocates estimate that only 5 percent of sexual assaults even result in an arrest, while less than 3 percent of perpetrators are ever convicted.

The most significant change achieved by criminalizing sexual assault has been to lengthen the time spent in jail by the tiny proportion of assailants who are caught, charged, and convicted. The most significant change, in other words, has been to increase the power of the state to incarcerate citizens for much of the rest of their lives. Where rape convictions in the early 1990s typically saw a ten-year sentence, they now result in sentences longer than eighteen years. And as with so many things in American society, that power to punish hits hardest upon people who are not white. There are no contemporary numbers documenting the racial demographics of people convicted of sexual assault, but figures from the late 1990s offer a clue. From 1994 to 1998, criminal justice researchers estimated that 70 percent of sexual assailants were white—but only 60 percent of people charged with rape were white. Meanwhile, Black men made up 18 percent of sexual assailants—but Black people constituted 38 percent of arrests for rape.

It is hard for me to look at this history and believe that either lynching or modern criminal justice have ever been about creating a society that is safer for anyone at all. To me, it looks like powerful people justifying their own abuses—first vigilante violence by white men, and then mass incarceration by the state. In both cases, most white women bought into the idea that aligning themselves with those who promised protection— whether they needed it or not; whether it was delivered it or not—would keep them safe. But white women are no safer because of lynching or mass incarceration, not that those things would be justified if we were safer. The ugly lesson that silently watching oppression—even joining in on the oppression itself—is the only way we'll survive was always a lie. But it is a lie with which my country and I are familiar.

It is the lie Grandma Kate told herself when she said I should stay in a home where I was abused, and it is the one Bonnie echoes when she gaslights me. It is the lie my father believed when he attacked me, then implied I'd never go to college if I complained. My family treats that ugly lesson like it is gospel, and believes the lie like it is scripture.

I do not think we are the only ones.

* * * * *

In the end, it was Sam who budged. A few months after I went to the precinct, my new friend, Jessie, moved into the empty bedroom while Sam was out of town. Sam stopped paying rent and began sleeping elsewhere; eventually he moved out. The day that he took all his things, Jessie and I sat on the floor of a near-empty living room.

"You did it," she said. *"It's yours."*

"We did it," I said. *"What the fuck was that?"* I laughed and fell back on the floor and looked at the ceiling. Enduring, for once, had produced a reward: a home that would be mine as long as I paid the rent. I would not have to go to back to my father. I was safe.

* * * * *

By then, I'd gotten hired to help run an independent magazine, *City Limits*, with a starting salary of $32,000. I began to treat the apartment in Brooklyn as my home. Jessie and I painted the rooms and bought furnishings at flea markets, things I could now afford because of my job, which I had because I had learned how to be a journalist from Wayne, for whom I'd worked because of Maggie. And I'd met Maggie, after all, because I went to NYU, where I'd enrolled because my grandfather could loan me money, and he'd had the money to lend because he was white. And all of this had combined to give me an extraordinary gift: I had graduated college debt-free.

Grandpa Mac did not mention my college loans after graduation. I was ashamed to be in debt and felt a compulsion to build up my savings, so I did not mention them, either. I treated all the money I earned as mine to spend. I believed that this would be my path in life: to get a job, to save

carefully, to singlehandedly build stability dollar by dollar. I assumed I'd
pay back the loan eventually, when I was more stable. Then, at the start of
2004, Grandpa Mac died.

I flew home for the funeral, staying in my parents' home with my sisters and their partners. After the funeral and wake, my father and Bonnie
gathered all of us in the basement bar to toast Grandpa Mac. I remember
my father standing in front of the bar, a custom-made neon sign reading
MAC'S BAR in blue and yellow neon glowing behind him. Then he began
to speak.

Grandpa Mac had taken care of everything, he said. Grandpa Mac had
left each of us $25,000, he said, and I gasped at the amount. The six of us,
I calculated, would inherit $150,000, a sum I could barely comprehend.
Then my father went on to say that, as the only child, he had not inherited
$25,000. He had inherited *the rest* of "it." My father did not say how much.
But I remember him joking that, although he did not vote for George W.
Bush, he was grateful for that president's tax policies.

I had not understood that there might be an inheritance coming to me.
When I was a child, the only discussion my father had with me and my
sisters about money was that we did not have enough of it. We could not
afford to keep my mother at home. We could not afford dance lessons or
gymnastics lessons. We could not have more than one outfit at the start
of the school year. I had never thought to question the way my father discussed our finances. I had never considered whether anyone in our family
had the kind of money to leave behind an inheritance.

I don't know how much Grandpa Mac left my father, but I believe
it was seven figures. In 2001, the Bush administration passed a round of
tax cuts that slowly reduced the estate tax; in 2003, Congress sped up
the reduction. Before those tax cuts, my father would have paid taxes
on any inheritance over $675,000. In 2004, he could collect up to $1.5
million tax-free.

Six months later, my father paid off the mortgage for his house, four
years early. Within a few years, he and Bonnie had stopped working, both
of them retiring before they were old enough to draw Social Security.

They began to spend three, four, even five weeks a year at a resort in Aruba.

Today, my parents talk about their inheritance much the same way the Beckers talk about the family farm: as an appreciated, but wholly unnecessary cushion. "When your dad inherited that money, it went into an account and it's pretty much stayed there," Bonnie told me during my last conversation with her and my father for this book. "We still live the same way we have always [lived]." she said. During the 2008 financial crisis, my parents told me, they panicked and pulled money out of the market—a decision that they say cost them $800,000. Even with that mistake, they tell me their wealth is around $1.5 million today, including the condo they live in, for which they paid cash. This ranks their wealth just above the Beckers', in the 90th percentile of household wealth in the country.

"And you don't think you're rich?" I asked.

"No, I don't think we're rich," she said.

She turned to my father: "Do you think we're rich?"

"No."

She turned back to me: "We're comfortable."

Like the Beckers, my parents talk about their wealth by mentioning their generosity with what they have, and how they've earned it—if not through work, then through their thrift and financial savvy. For my parents, this means mentioning a family vacation to Cancún they paid for in 2004; sending all the sisters to their Aruba timeshare with a guest around 2007; and gifting each of us $10,000 apiece around that time. They believe they have wealth, they say, because of their financial philosophy: "You don't spend more than what you've got; you don't go into debt. You earn it," said Bonnie.

If I push—if I say it doesn't feel to me as if they've earned it—Bonnie nods in agreement. "I didn't mean to say that we earned everything that we have," she says. "But I don't think that our lifestyle would be any different if we hadn't inherited the money."

I know she and my father believe this.

I do not.

I spent about a decade living without a net—far less time, to be sure, than do the generationally poor. It was long enough to learn that the net, really, is everything.

★ ★ ★ ★ ★

I loved the journalism I did at *City Limits*. I spent months following single mothers struggling to either get by on welfare or leave it behind, at-home childcare providers filling in the gaps left by welfare reform, and teenagers trying to eat healthfully in neighborhoods without supermarkets—what people were beginning to call "food deserts." When our editor left in early 2005, and there was no replacement lined up, I felt a responsibility to stay and make sure the magazine—which had been founded in the 1970s as a tenants' rights newsletter—survived. And, by then, a colleague had given me a piece of advice about working at such a tiny publication: At a little place like *City Limits*, I could do big, ambitious work that might win awards and help me get hired somewhere bigger. So I stayed.

There was nobody to teach me, so I tried to teach myself. Left to my own devices, I began to model my work after prominent magazines: *Newsweek*, the *New York Times Magazine*, the *New Yorker*. I still believed in the mission I'd learned under Barrett: to hold the powerful to account by reporting rigorously and telling full, honest stories about the poor. I did not understand, then, that the magazines I was now trying to mimic rarely published those kinds of stories—especially in the early 2000s.

There was another misunderstanding at work, too. I told myself that if I wrote well enough, and treated my subjects as full humans, government might fix the problems I wrote about. But I did not question—and nobody prompted me to question—whether that approach was based on a fundamental misunderstanding of my government. Even though I could be cynical, questioning the motives and capabilities of my professors and employers and the institutions they worked for, I still fundamentally believed that America meant what it said: that we were all equal. When the American government hurt its citizens, I believed that it was by mistake; one that would be corrected if only the people in power had better information—information that I, as a journalist, could provide.

I did not question whether my experience, as a white woman, might be different from that of my friends and neighbors who were not white. I did not wonder whether, as a white reporter, I might misunderstand my subjects who were not white, and render them inaccurately. I did not question why I needed to prove to the powerful, who were nearly always white and wealthy, that New York City's poor, more than 90 percent of whom were Black or brown, were human. I followed an unspoken instinct as if it were a rule: Never talk about race. I believed that if I mentioned race directly, the people in power who read *City Limits*—government leaders, foundation officers, and philanthropists—would not listen, and nothing would ever change.

I wanted to write *about* the poor, but I knew implicitly that I wrote *to* the powerful. This was not new in America or unique to me. In 1967, President Johnson convened a commission to study the causes of that year's racial rebellions in cities across the country. The Kerner Commission's report, written three decades before I became a journalist, held that "the press has too long basked in a white world looking out of it, if at all, with white men's eyes and white perspective." If I am honest, my work reflected that same perspective, and was weaker for it. Even today, I read a lot of journalism that does the same.

When I wrote a story about a six-year-old Black boy who lived with his grandmother during the week, because his mother could not find affordable childcare, I did not protest my editor's cover line, "She's Not a Bad Parent." When I wrote about city teenagers learning to cook and garden, I wrote that a Hispanic girl in tight jeans and a bomber jacket "doesn't look like the type of girl to contemplate the aesthetics of legumes." I edited a cover story, about a troubling public access show where the host highlighted teenagers in need of adoption, and put one of the teens on the cover with the headline, "Will You Adopt Me?" I told myself that my job was to humanize my subjects for my readers, but I failed to treat them as fully human myself.

Later, I'd realize how deeply this ran in me, how my upbringing had taught me to squelch my impulses toward kindness because it seemed so unlikely to be offered by anyone else. The *world* was callous, I told myself; I didn't help anyone by behaving otherwise. I could be empathetic in my writing, but when I felt hemmed in—by a lack of resources or limited time, by the suggestion that I was screwing up—I reverted to callousness instead of introspection.

And, in any event, I was right about my audience. My callousness, refracted through racism, did not prevent me from succeeding. My work began to win awards. Finalist nods at first, then the awards themselves. When I did the first analysis of food access in New York City, judges chose to reward my work for tiny *City Limits* alongside stories from the *New York Times* and the *Washington Post*. These were not journalism's marquee awards—the Pulitzers, the Polks, the National Magazine Awards—but they were niche and respected. The awards told me that my work was good and that I could build a journalism career if I wanted, and I would not need to understand anything more about race to do it.

★ ★ ★ ★ ★

In late 2005, *City Limits*, which was having financial problems, laid me off. I used the unemployment, along with the inheritance from Grandpa Mac, to buy myself some time to think. I'd been diagnosed with multiple sclerosis that year and had begun crying almost daily, terrified of ending up in a home like my mother. The neurologist told me the best chance I had of staying mobile was to take a daily injection that, at the time, cost $35,000 a year—although my insurance, which I could extend with COBRA, covered it.* A therapist I'd begun seeing told me, gently, that I spoke about the diagnosis as if it were terminal. I did not answer her, then, because all I could think was: *That's because it is.* I felt as if my life was over; as if I had nothing to lose.

I could barely admit it to myself, but I needed to grieve. For my mother most of all, but for the active life I'd had—which seemed so likely to disappear. I understood that I was now facing a brutal job market, where the kinds of stories I wanted to write were not necessarily what editors wanted to publish. Was I really *sure* I wanted to fight for that—especially when health insurance would be so important to me? Could I be happy doing something else? I didn't know. And I knew I'd never have enough time to think about any of it if I just dove desperately into another job.

So, I did something foolish: I spent my inheritance on time to grieve. I went traveling for six months, visiting friends and their families in Europe, Asia, the Middle East, and even Oceania. It was the first time in my life, I think, where I answered only to myself, instead of to other people. It was the most luxurious, frivolous thing I have ever done, and it is something only the tiniest fraction of the people on this planet get the chance to do. It was also one of the most educational experiences I have had. I would make the same choice, every time. It's easy to say that, though, since it has turned out okay.

By the time I went home to Brooklyn, I was humbled to admit that what I wanted was the life I'd already been building: To use journalism to make the world a better place, to ride bikes and hear music, to see art and cook good food, to be healthy, to love and be loved. I didn't want a *Sex and the City* life, where trends and social status were a daily concern. Instead, I

---

* By 2013, the cost of my medication, glatiramer acetate, had climbed to $59,158, according to a 2015 study published in the journal *Neurology*. Researchers attributed the price increases to the fact that "companies raise prices of [drug therapies] in the United States to increase profits, and our health care system puts no limits on these increases."

wanted a life I'd always be able to afford, one where I'd feel safe, and one where I thought my work did something good in the world. I wanted a life, in other words, that had meaning.

★ ★ ★ ★ ★

I started freelancing in the summer of 2006. It was much harder than I'd expected. As I struggled to place stories about welfare and poverty, I began to look for another topic—any topic—that might let me talk about equity without having to say the word "poor." I remembered a conversation I'd had with journalist friends. Maybe there was something to the food access story. Maybe I could write a book about food that would trick people into letting me write about poverty.

It took me a year before I really considered writing a book. And another six months, probably, before I asked my friends who were writing books how they had started. I soon learned that having a good idea was only the first of many steps. The next step was to get an agent—which I'd need to get meetings with publishing houses big enough to pay a useful advance. The agent, in turn, would help me write a proposal. I tried sending queries to a few I admired, but nobody ever responded, no matter how many times I followed up. I started asking my friends who had agents for introductions. Sometime in early 2008, I met Rebecca Friedman, a young, white agent at a prestigious agency, who represented a friend. She invited me to lunch.

I spent most of the meal talking about how, throughout all my reporting in New York—with home health aides and unemployed teenagers in Brooklyn, childcare providers in the Bronx, welfare mothers and security guards in Harlem, gang members in Queens—I'd noticed how important food was to everyone I met. The people I reported about *cared* about their food, and their families, and their health. So did *my* family, even if we had depended, in my childhood, on industrial staples like Tuna Helper, and used bottled Italian dressing to marinate chicken. And yet, I could barely open a newspaper or magazine without reading about the white chef Alice Waters or the white journalist Michael Pollan—whose massive bestseller

The Omnivore's Dilemma opened a discussion of local and sustainable food by observing that, "Many people today seem perfectly content eating at the end of an industrial food chain, without a thought in the world; this book is probably not for them. There are things in it that will ruin their appetites." I told Rebecca: *"He's wrong. Most people care about their food, and their families. Mostly people eat that stuff because it's easy and affordable. How do I write a book that shows that?"*

I was surprised when Rebecca didn't blanch at my frustration with the foodies. I hadn't grown up poor but I carried a noticeable chip on my shoulder about class—some of it earnest, and some of it, I now see, a resentment of how my father's abuse forced me into financial hardship I could have otherwise avoided. And yet, I had spent enough time in low-wage jobs, and seen enough as a reporter, to feel a visceral ire at how so much journalism, and so many books, seemed to be disconnected from reality. They were always written as if the readers were wealthy and white—as if those were the only people who mattered. It was ridiculous! Outrageous, even! I hadn't had much luck with this line of conversation at the few writer parties I'd gone to.

If I'd had the social grace to keep my mouth shut, I would have. As I finished my lunch I had the sinking feeling that I'd complained too much. Instead, Rebecca looked me in the eye over the table. *"Let me think about what we could do,"* she said.

That summer, Rebecca called me with an idea. What did I think about combining undercover first-person reporting, like Barbara Ehrenreich's *Nickel and Dimed*, with food systems reporting, like Pollan? No publisher was going to pay much money for a book about the lives of farm workers or supermarket clerks, said Rebecca, but publishers might pay for a reporter going undercover—and that story would let me write about the structural issues I was so interested in. I was uneasy about the premise that these stories would only be marketable if a white reporter went undercover to tell them. But I did not have a better idea, either. For six months, in between copyediting shifts and freelance pieces, I worked up a proposal.

Most reported, narrative nonfiction books are paid in installments: You get a portion up front, called the advance. Then another payment once the book has been written and sent to the printer, and another when it's published. After talking with friends, I felt like a contract of $70,000 or $80,000 was a realistic goal—and it was in the ballpark of most debut-author proposals bought by major publishing houses. I had not considered how the economic crash the year before would change my prospects. In March 2009, I met with four editors. The one I liked best offered the largest contract: $35,000. I'd get $17,500 up front, from which I would pay my agent 15 percent. This was the only money I'd get until I finalized the manuscript, when I'd get another $7,500, again minus agent fees. The final $10,000 would come with publication.

Here was the open secret of publishing, so ingrained in the industry it did not merit comment: Even authors who get advances are rarely paid enough to survive on that contract alone. The result is that only the wealthy can afford to write books. I was not that, but I still had about $15,000 from Grandpa Mac in my bank accounts. If I was frugal, I thought, the advance plus my savings might last a year. That seemed like enough time to write a book.

My contract was so modest that it took time before I understood how unusual it was for me to get it in the first place. Since 1950, 95 percent of the people that major publishers paid to write fiction were white. When L.L. McKinney launched #PublishingPaidMe in 2020, she inspired the authors of more than 2,800 books to share their publishing deals in a spreadsheet. Although the data is self-selected, reflecting only the people who voluntarily shared their contract information, it is the only public source of information on publishing deals. By 2023, it showed that of 218 debut nonfiction authors since 2000, myself among them, 178 were white—about 82 percent.

I cannot look at these numbers and believe that my contract came solely because of my merit as a writer. It is harder still to believe in my merit when the story I sold depended on my being white in order for publishers to believe it would sell. And it is hardest of all, I think, to believe that I could have written that book without another gift that came because of my race: the $15,000 in my savings account that remained from the inheritance from Grandpa Mac.

I knew these things, dimly and shapelessly, even then. I did not dwell on them long enough to let them take form. I saw only that I had a chance to write a book I cared about; that it might help me earn a living while doing work that mattered. I pushed aside my unease and took the deal.

MY ADULTHOOD

NEW YORK CITY

DETROIT

2010–2023

Since the mid-1990s, when I began living on my own in New York, I had been terrified of losing my housing. It had started off as the gut fear of a near-child suddenly on her own. Working at *City Limits*, where we covered the intricacies of city housing policy for poor and middle-class New Yorkers, I learned that housing in the city was almost impossibly expensive for someone with my income. Even my family's wealth—at least, the share to which I had access—was not enough to close the gap. When I'd eagerly told my accountant, whom I'd needed to navigate the complexities of freelance income, about my inheritance from Grandpa Mac, she'd smiled politely. *"That's nice, honey,"* she said. *"But that's not even a down payment."*

The accountant was right—at least in New York. I realize, now, that I could have left the city for somewhere cheaper. But by then I'd built a community of friends and colleagues, the kind that could stand in for the family I felt I could not count on; that support was priceless to me. By then, I had figured out how to live cheaply in the city: I biked more often than I paid for the subway. I belonged to a food co-op and cooked much of my own food, which I enjoyed. I used the city's parks and beaches and streets for affordable entertainment. Buying property in New York was beyond my reach; so was paying market-rate rent. But with rent-stabilized housing, l could squeak by on the $25,000 or so that I earned as an independent writer and live a life that made me happy.

By then, I was considering leaving my second apartment. Around the time I went freelance, my landlord had begun raising the rent by exploiting loopholes in rent stabilization law. I'd hoped to stay there indefinitely, but the rent would soon pass the "vacancy decontrol" threshold, which would let the landlord charge as high a price as the market would bear. And that, I knew, was more than I'd be able to afford. I loved the neighborhood and didn't really want to leave. But, I was tired of navigating roommates and a poorly maintained apartment, too.

My work at *City Limits* had taught me about an option I hadn't known to consider before: new housing made affordable by government subsidy. Back then, I didn't understand that my own family's arrival into the middle class had been formed, in part, by government subsidy. There had been the G.I. Bill and FHA mortgages for my grandparents, as well as my parents' ability to save by living in low-income housing when they were first married. The Bloomberg administration began pushing homeownership for lower- and middle-income residents in the 2000s, and I tried sending in applications to *buy* apartments, but they never amounted to anything. When I saw an affordable apartment listing for a new rental building just a few blocks north of my apartment, I figured it was worth applying.

In May 2008, I got called for an interview about my application. To qualify for the apartment, I needed to prove with documentation that my income was between $23,960 to $29,588—30 and 50 percent of the city's median income, which is considered "poor" by most researchers. Provided I could do that, I would be offered one of the forty-seven apartments. That first year, a one-bedroom, 700-square-foot, newly constructed apartment had a starting rent of $599. The rent was equal to roughly 30 percent of the incomes required to qualify that year—what housing experts consider an "affordable" rent. Once I signed a lease, it would be rent-stabilized. I'd have affordable housing for decades.

We all "deserved" that rent according to the rules of the program, but it seems obvious to me that when policymakers pictured "low-income" New Yorkers, they did not have me in mind. Indeed, many of my neighbors came to the building with the help of social workers and city housing programs that aid the poor. And yet, as someone who'd lived in the neighborhood for more than a decade by then, I counted as a community member—a demographic for which half the units in the building were designated. At the time, there were no rules disqualifying tenants who had assets. I was months away from selling my first book, and still had that $15,000 left from Grandpa Mac.

When I went in to submit my documentation for my apartment, I remember asking the caseworker, a Black woman, if she was sure I qualified. What I wanted to say but did not was: *Are you sure I'm the sort of person this is for? I have an education. I could get a better paying job if I really had to. I have some savings.* She answered me warmly, and in strictly economic terms. *Your income is low enough,* she said. *This apartment, it's like winning the lottery.* What she did not say, but I heard, was: *Don't be a fool.*

I thought about the gap between what I could afford and what the market would bear. It was vast—more than I'd ever be able to cover working as a journalist. And, anyway, we *all* deserved affordable housing, from the poor on up through the middle class. Who would I help by turning down the apartment? There was no way to know if someone more "deserving" than me would get it, or if someone even further afield from the assumed residents would be brought in.

I moved into the apartment in August 2008, and I have not left. I landed there because of the things I learned from Maggie and Barrett and *City Limits*, all of which were partly contingent on my race. Their lessons and help could not give me a down payment, but they brought me to a similar place: Stable, affordable housing that I won't lose unless

I stop paying. It doesn't show up on ledgers as wealth, but it is much the same thing.

★ ★ ★ ★ ★

My building is modest, built by a developer who financed it in exchange for permission to build an oversized luxury building downtown, the Toren. Of the 240 units in the Toren, 198 are market-rate condos, going for as much as $1.8 million. There are also forty-two "moderate" income rentals, available to households earning up to $208,065 for a family of four. That building has a multilevel rooftop deck, a doorman, a yoga studio, and a lap pool. My building, when I moved in, had windows overlooking a Salvation Army warehouse and garage, where dump trucks and semis belched noise and soot from early morning to late at night.★ There is no lap pool or rooftop deck, which my neighbors and I do not mind much. Mostly we notice that the rich are over *there*—1.8 miles over there, to be exact, near transit centers and business districts—while we are over *here*.

The distance between the Toren and me—in miles, and in income—is not a product of personal preference. It is a predictable outcome of public policy from the last fifty years. In the 1970s, New York City began offering developers tax breaks if they built market-rate, residential housing in the city. Then, in the late 1980s, the Koch administration expanded the tax breaks, helping developers build more market-rate housing in central Manhattan—provided they also built affordable housing, which could be anywhere in the city. This made it profitable to put high-end housing in neighborhoods that were already expensive, and low-income units in cheaper parts of the city. That same logic is reflected in a zoning program called inclusionary zoning, which lets developers build bigger buildings than zoning rules allow if they also build affordable housing—again, anywhere in the city. That is the program the developer used when he built

---

★ The same block, circa 2004, is depicted in the 2005 film *Dave Chappelle's Block Party*, which documents a hip-hop concert held on the block.

our forty-eight affordable apartments, as encouraged by city policy, safely out of sight of the rich.

Neither program said anything about race, but both encouraged developers to segregate by income—and in New York City, segregating by income almost inevitably segregates by race. Four-fifths of New York's wealthy residents are white. Little wonder that the residents of new luxury buildings, so often built in convenient locations and with ample amenities, appear to be overwhelmingly white, too. Meanwhile, four-fifths of the city's poor are *not* white.* These are the people expected to live on blocks like mine when I first moved there: a handful of brownstones owned by longtime residents, the rest boarded-up warehouses and dirty trucks.

My block is different now. From 2000 to 2020, the share of white residents in Clinton Hill more than doubled, while the share of Black residents dropped by more than half. These are not the demographics of my building, where forty-seven of its forty-eight units are occupied by Black, Hispanic, or immigrant tenants. In my fifteen years there, I have been the only white, non-Hispanic tenant I have seen living in my building. That means our building is less white than the city's poor, and less white, even, than our neighborhood.

I know I have skills and time that many of my neighbors do not, so I try to be of use. I volunteer for the tenant association, doing rent history research for neighbors or calling management on their behalf in hopes of getting repairs made quickly. (Responses are always slow, but they seem to come faster when I—a white woman who has learned some patience with bureaucracy—make the call rather than when most of my neighbors do.) I work with tenants and management to find ways of avoiding calling the police when, as is common in many of the city's larger buildings, unhoused people come into the building and sleep in the stairwells. Partly, I help out in my building because of my compulsion to help, ingrained since childhood.

---

* The demographics of poverty in New York City do not reflect those of the country as a whole. In 2010, 42.4 percent of America's poor were white, 23.1 percent were Black and 28.7 percent were Hispanic (of any race, including white), according to U.S. Census data on income and poverty.

And partly I help out because it's in my self-interest: when my neighbors' complaints are addressed quickly, it keeps my home safer and nicer, too. It's not charity. It's sharing.

Whatever work I do in my building, there's no way I could live there—or anywhere in New York City, for that matter—without my affordable rent. I get as frustrated as anyone else—by the noise, by my neighbor's grandson using my air conditioner vent as a backboard, by the occasional puddle of pee in the stairwell. When these things frustrate me, I shrug. Even if I found a better-paid career, it's unlikely I'd earn enough to make market rent affordable. In February 2023, the median rent for a one-bedroom in Clinton Hill was $3,700 a month. In my experience, the housing market in New York can either be affordable or impossible.

★ ★ ★ ★ ★

After I agreed to my first book contract in April 2009, I left New York for Spanish-language school in Guatemala, reasoning that I'd need to speak Spanish to find farmwork. I spent five weeks there, then spent a month on a friend's couch in Los Angeles while I did research and bought a $1,200 used car—a gold 1994 Ford Escort. I had already spent three months and one-third of my advance before I even started reporting—but at least I had the cash to float me, preserving my savings and allowing me to forgo finding other work.

I had thought of the book contract as a salary to cover my regular living expenses, and reporting stints like business trips. In my imagination, I'd head to California, find work, spend two months as a farm laborer, then go home and write. I imagined I'd repeat that process in Michigan at a Walmart and again in New York City at an Applebee's. If I'd known any better, I would have seen how profoundly unprepared I was for the financial reality of writing a book. My advance—about $14,500 in hand after paying my agent and taxes—was gone quickly, eaten up by food, shelter, and health insurance.

For the next year and a half, I earned little beyond what I earned in the jobs I took, undercover, to report the book. I split my apartment with a friend, so that it wouldn't sit empty for months at a time, and stayed there when I could get back to the city. Meanwhile, the network of friends from private universities, and my work in journalism, yielded in-kind benefits that made living off very little money possible. I'd pick up shifts copy-editing in New York, then go stay with friends and spend the days writing undisturbed. I spent one summer living with a friend's retired hippie parents in New Mexico. I spent six months taking care of a town house in Detroit while its owner, who took a liking to me after learning I'd written about food for the *New York Times,* was abroad. I cobbled together an existence where my only nonnegotiable monthly bills were food, liability insurance for my car, and good medical coverage. I prioritized the latter because my neurologist said that if I stayed on the prescribed drug therapy, my multiple sclerosis might stay mild.

Initially, I covered these expenses with my savings, still left from Grandpa Mac's inheritance. As those shrank, I began to use the zero-interest balance transfers that the three or four credit cards I held had begun sending. I paid bills with one credit card, then paid a small fee to transfer the balance each month to a different card, which offered zero percent interest for a year or so. This let me borrow money nearly interest free until I reached the next book payment.

Still, I felt increasingly aware of how readily I could fall from the avoidable hardship in which I'd landed and end up facing hardship I had no idea how to escape: an MS exacerbation, a significant car repair, an unexpected end to the house-sitting gig. In Detroit, when I declined a round of drinks by saying I had no business buying beer when I couldn't afford more than rice, beans, and cabbage at home, a guy at the bar suggested I apply for food stamps.

I waved him off. "Those aren't for people like me," I said.

"You're not broke?" he said.

He had a point.

When I applied, I was surprised to qualify for my sixteen dollars a month. Six months later, I was so broke I qualified for two hundred dollars a month.

There were so many things I could not yet see.

I could not yet see how my assumption that *I* was not supposed to get food stamps came from racism and other forms of cruelty I'd internalized, things that ran so deeply I could not have told you they were there. I had unthinkingly assumed that food stamps were not for "people like me." I would have *told* you that they were not for me because I was educated and had options. But the shameful truth is that I did not think food stamps were for people like me because I *felt* material need was something that only "really" happened to people who were not white; that it was natural for them, but not for me.

This was not a clear thought, but an instinctive—and racist—assumption drawn from social norms and media coverage, from my parents and teachers and then later my colleagues. It was also a profound misunderstanding of capitalism and the pressures it exerts on all but the wealthiest among us. If I was white, went the logic I could not name, how could I possibly be suffering from needs I could not meet myself? If I was white and in need, continued the logic, there was something terribly wrong with me—something I needed to hide. This was a kind of self-gaslighting; an instinct to direct frustration toward myself instead of the powerful, who were so unlikely to help. Growing up in a home where my suffering was considered not only unavoidable but not worth mentioning had given me plenty of practice.

I could not yet see that, for all my lofty talk about wanting to do work that mattered, my options for building a career in journalism—any kind of journalism—were shrinking rapidly. When I left *City Limits* in 2006, there had been 75,000 jobs in newsrooms across the country. But the internet was blowing up the industry's economic model—and decimating it as a source of employment. By 2021, there were only 31,500 jobs left in newsrooms. I had prided myself on going to college, on not falling for the promises of the auto factories that began to disappear in the late 1990s. And yet, in the end, the industry I'd thought could employ me into old age—journalism—hasn't fared much better. Journalism garners more respect, I think, from the political leaders who've watched the demise of both—but that doesn't pay my bills.

And I could not yet see how, even amid this difficult and fearful period in my life, the advantages I'd mindlessly accumulated through my race and my family's race were much of what had pulled me through. My access to credit facilitated my survival—and I'd had that access because I had a credit history. I had that credit history because, during my freshman year at NYU, when the campus was thick with flyers advertising cards to students, a friend had persuaded me to get a credit card. I had been leery of debt, almost irrationally so, because my father had so openly used money as a cudgel. My friend, the white son of professionals in New Jersey, explained there was a way to use debt wisely: Never spend more than you could pay in cash, and pay it off in full each month. I do not remember the terms of the card when I signed up, but there is a broad body of research documenting that borrowers in white, affluent places—like lower Manhattan, where my dorm was located—are offered more generous and forgiving terms than borrowers in places that are majority Black (of any income) or poor.

I could only follow that strategy, in turn, because I had been taught to manage money using banks. My family had opened a savings account for me when I was a toddler, where I'd funneled birthday checks and my wages and tips from waiting tables. And I was only in a position to worry about managing savings, of course, because my banker-grandfather had covered enough of my tuition that I could pay for my share of it, along with living expenses, by working twenty hours a week. I think this is what researchers mean when they observe that "using debt as a tool for social mobility is much easier for individuals who already have some wealth." In the world of the wealthy, I had comparatively little. But in the world of America, writ large, I had a lot.

But all of that was hard for me to see then. I was edging my way along a precipice, terrified of falling: into poverty, into disability, into depending on my father. Beneath even my racism and cruelty lay the deepest fear of all: what had happened to my mother would happen to me, that I'd be left behind, unwanted, if I failed to be of use. I had no plan to avoid that fate other than the one I'd always used: prove my worth with my work, and figure the rest out later.

★ ★ ★ ★ ★

Throughout all of this, I had avoided considering one significant resource: my parents. I resisted turning to them, suspicious that it would open the door to new abuse from my father and stepmother. The same gut fear that had made me consider a homeless shelter preferable to their home was quieter now, but it was not gone. And yet, now safely into their early retirement after the inheritance from Grandpa Mac, there was the steady allure of *Maybe they've changed*. And the truth was that, more than anyone else I knew, my parents had so much to give.

By the time I called my parents to ask for money, I'd finished writing my first book's manuscript and returned to New York. I worked part-time as a copyeditor for twenty dollars an hour and landed a few freelance assignments, but I spent most of my time working on what I now realize was book publicity. I could sense how easy it would be for the book to come out and simply disappear, a pebble dropped into a lake. I was convinced that, if I wanted the book to have any impact—to change anything in the world aside from my own sense of accomplishment—I would need to do much of the promotional work myself.

I'd never worked as a publicist, but at *City Limits* I'd learned to do something I called "outreach." Our circulation was small, and I'd realized that if I wanted public officials to change policies based on my work, I needed to ensure that the right people read it. When I published stories, I mailed copies of the magazine to grassroots organizations, advocates, and public officials I thought might find it relevant—and included a note that summarized why I thought it would be interesting to them. I began to do the same thing for my book, but I also needed to draft related essays and op-eds, as well as plan public events. Now in my thirties and a journalist in New York for a decade, I had friends at newspapers and websites—people I genuinely enjoyed, and who could also decide to cover the book or assign me work.

I'd exhausted the zero-percent-interest balance transfers by then. My savings had dropped to about $1,500. And two big expenses loomed: My computer and cell phone, which had become necessary for my work, were both so old and glitchy they were beyond repair. If they failed outright, I'd be unable to do any work on the book at all. I had no confidence that the book would succeed; it was such a long shot. And yet, I wanted to try.

I did some calculations and decided to ask my parents for $10,000. They would not even miss it.

★ ★ ★ ★ ★

Grimly, I knew that if my father offered me the money, he and my step-mother would expect me to let them treat me however they wished. The last time I'd stayed with them, over Christmas in 2008, the visit had ended with both of them chasing me into the basement to scream at me: I was *"a little bitch,"* a *"spoiled brat,"* I caused *"so many problems for everyone."*

My father was my ride to the airport that day—my only way, in those pre-rideshare days, of my getting out of their home and safely back to my own. I saw no choice but to climb into the cab of my father's pickup while he screamed insults at me. I curled in the fetal position in the passenger seat. I could not stop crying and began to repeat *"please stop"* over and over as if it might help. It did not. As I remember it, he yelled at me for the entire ninety-minute drive.

At the airport, I climbed out of the truck and stood motionless, sobbing, on the sidewalk. My father dropped my suitcase at my feet and shoved a wad of bills into my pocket—my Christmas gift. *"We just want you to respect us,"* he said. I did not respond. I could not stop crying until I was home, safe again, in Brooklyn. When I got home, I shoved the money into a card and mailed it back to them. The last thing I wanted was to invite more of that.

And yet, as I prepared to ask them for this loan, I told myself that maybe my father and stepmother had grown. Maybe they would respond to me with kindness. I knew this was unlikely, but I pretended I did not; it was the only way I could get myself to make the request. I was beginning to understand that their behavior had nothing to do with me. They would treat me this way whether I was kind or cruel, whether I borrowed money from them or never asked for any at all.

I made the call from a friend's living room in Oakland, where I was staying after reporting a freelance story. I looked out the window, eyeing the 980 overpass as Dad and Bonnie reminded me I'd been my high school salutatorian and gone to NYU with a scholarship. They pointed out that I was now on food stamps. They asked if I understood I was unmarried, in my thirties, and did not have kids. They told me they were bailing me out of my bad decisions. They asked me why I didn't get a job. I did not have an answer for them. I just remember feeling ashamed of my need, and foolish for having told myself they might have changed. I thrust my tongue out of my mouth and bit down, gently, to keep myself from talking at all.

In the end, though, they said they could loan me the money, interest free, and give me eighteen months before I needed to start paying it back. I sighed with relief and thanked them. After I hung up the phone, I wondered what else they believed I owed them—aside from money—for their generosity.

And I did owe them—or, more accurately, I owed Grandpa Mac. I could not have completed that book and continued my writing career without that loan. Dad and Bonnie would not have had that money to give so freely without the inheritance from Grandpa Mac, who would not have had that money to leave them if he had not been a banker and homeowner in mid-century Ann Arbor, which was only possible because he was white.

And behind all of that, of course, I owed my government. That was what had built the system that made being white so valuable in the first place.

★ ★ ★ ★ ★

My book came out on February 21, 2012, under the title *The American Way of Eating: Undercover at Walmart, Applebee's, Farm Fields and the Dinner Table*. The first review was so negative that a friend called to check on me. The second review was middling. They both felt, to me, like they had read a different book than the one I had written. But if I am honest, the negative reviews were mostly unsettling because I felt they echoed, faintly, the kinds of things my father and Bonnie often told me: I thought I was better than everyone. I didn't give back. I cared only about myself. I was a fraud. I curled up in the corner of my Brooklyn couch-turned-bed and stared at the bookshelves partitioning it from the living room, and let myself wallow for a couple of hours.

I cared deeply about the people and problems I wrote about. I thought it could help people in power understand that people who were poor didn't make bad choices so much as they were given bad options. I thought it might help get affordable supermarkets in neighborhoods that needed them. But I was also sophisticated enough to understand the book's value to me. If the book did well, I thought I might be able to make a living as a journalist covering social inequality. If the book failed, I knew I'd leave journalism, because I could not earn a stable living in it. I knew, especially from my reporting, what a luxury it was to have work that had meaning. I could build a life with a job that just had pay and benefits if I had to. It would be more than most people, in my country and on the planet, get. I could be grateful for that, and find meaning—like most people do—in life outside my work.

And, besides, there wasn't much I could do. I changed the bio on my website and Amazon page to reflect, better than the book did, who I was: the daughter of a lawn-mower salesman and an English major. Someone who grew up with a sick mom and a stressed dad. Someone who had some advantages, but not a surplus of them. Someone who tried to use what she had to make the world a better place. I didn't mention the abuse, which still embarrassed me then. I just wanted to feel like I'd explained myself.

The day my book came out, the *New York Times* ran a generous review of it. "This is a voice the food world needs," wrote the reviewer, who admired my anger at inequity. I was, he wrote, "hardworking" and "blue-collar" and I "traffic[ked] in dark humor." The terms the *Times* reviewer used to describe me felt slightly off-key—I was not, as a journalist riding a bike around Brooklyn, most people's image of "blue-collar." But it was a relief for a reviewer to understand both the anger and empathy in my work—and not only find it justified, but *like* it.

The *New York Times's* stamp of approval, combined with the outreach my publisher and I had done, was enough to create real "buzz." The launch event I organized in Manhattan was standing room only and broadcast on C-SPAN. The first week of publication, it snuck onto the *New York Times* bestseller list.

In April, a prestigious fellowship I'd applied to, the Knight-Wallace Journalism Fellowships at the University of Michigan, offered me one of nineteen slots in the program. As a fellow, I'd earn $70,000 over eight months and have excellent health insurance. And I'd have the extraordinary gift of time to think—and a solid shove into a formal journalism career.

★ ★ ★ ★ ★

I returned to Brooklyn full-time in 2013, after the fellowship. My year in Michigan had yielded more benefits than I'd expected. I had become so accustomed to living frugally that my income felt excessive; I spent only half of what I earned, and was able to replenish my savings.

Affordable access to good health care was an ever bigger boon. At first, I'd stalled on visiting a neurologist in Ann Arbor. I was embarrassed to tell a doctor that my life had been so chaotic, and my income so low, that I'd been lax about taking my medication while I worked on the book. After my first full neurological workup in years, doctors at the university hospital gave me incredible news: it was highly unlikely I actually had multiple sclerosis. I would need to monitor myself closely, but I could consider stopping medication completely.

Something else had shifted, too. Reporting and writing the first book had required me to really think about why my experience in each job—as a farmworker, as a grocery stocker and produce clerk, in the kitchen of an Applebee's—had gone the way it did. And in every one, I'd found that both my gender and my race deeply shaped how people saw me and treated me. Sometimes that had been to my benefit, like when a foreman gave me a ride across a 104-degree peach orchard in an air-conditioned truck. Sometimes it had not, like when a coworker drugged my drink. But for the first time in my life, I had time to study how my race shaped my life. This was a gift that came from writing a book: a shift in my understanding of my life on the scale of tectonic plates instead of a forked road. I wondered what else I might want to understand.

Back in New York, I reconnected with friends and cleaned my apartment. I had a clean bill of health and savings, and a career that was taking off. I just needed to consider the choices before me, all of which were good, and decide what to do next.

* * * * *

Even with the first book's success, I continued to live contract to contract—though contracts came more frequently, and paid more, than they had in the early years of my career. I'd saved half of the money I was paid while on fellowship in Michigan—around $35,000—thinking I'd need it to pay bills. But in the year since I'd finished the program, I hadn't needed to touch it at all. I wondered if there might be a way to use the money to create stability, to create wealth. It was so easy, I thought, to fall into poverty here. If I invested the savings I had well, maybe I could weave my own.

My friend Martina, a journalist in Detroit, began nudging me to buy real estate in 2014. *"You don't have a husband. You're a freelance writer, and that will never pay. It's a lot. You gotta start investing,"* she said to me on her porch in Southwest Detroit, surveying the vacant lot across the street. She knew what she was talking about; the daughter of impoverished Mexican immigrants, she had hauled herself to the edge of the middle class in part by buying property.

Still, I argued with her: I couldn't possibly afford an apartment in New

York. A developer had bought one of the boarded-up warehouses on my block and turned it into condos; I remember price tags around $250,000 for one-bedrooms. Even that was well below Brooklyn's average cost of a home around then: $612,000. Both prices were unfathomable to me; there was no way I could afford that.

Martina rolled her eyes: *Not in New York. Detroit.*

I listened with a mix of interest and skepticism. Interest, because I was leery of the stock market, which felt like gambling. Interest, because owning a house meant I'd have somewhere to go if rent laws changed and my rent went up. Interest, because I loved Detroit just the way it was, with an expansive web of community leaders working to offset the city's problems, as well as a vibrant, multiracial, and working-class web of musicians, writers, and visual artists. Skeptical, because I'd been drawn to Brooklyn for similar reasons—and the changes that had followed my arrival had mostly served to make most housing unaffordable for my friends, my neighbors, and me. I didn't want to contribute to a repeat of that in Detroit. But it was also true that gentrification was coming, whether I invested or not—and its harm, as I saw it, was the displacement it created. Maybe, in a city with a lot of vacant land, I could invest in property without pushing people out.

In June 2014, I clicked on an auction website that Detroit had launched to sell off its abandoned homes. There, the mortgage foreclosure crisis had been followed by a tax foreclosure crisis, leaving the city responsible for thousands of homes. I clicked with interest on a mid-size Victorian in Southwest Detroit, near where I'd lived while reporting the first book. The house had been empty for at least a year then. The roof leaked, and a stairwell was coated in black mold. The kitchen floor was rotting. Patches of ceiling were missing. The basement flooded. But when I visited an open house there with friends, we agreed: It was a nice house. I decided to bid on it.

That August, I won the house with a bid of $27,100, which required a deposit of $2,710. At the time, this was an extravagant price for a Detroit house in disrepair; the median price of a Detroit home—of any condition—that year was $14,000. Elsewhere in the city, properties similar to mine had gone for as little as $500. To afford renovations to make the house habit-able, I had to bundle a construction loan with the purchase. This left me with the responsibility for an $87,211 mortgage, and a four-bedroom house with a yard and garage. My monthly bill, including tax and insurance, was less than $800.

It would be easy for me to follow the script, embraced by middle-class homeowners, about the difficulties of repairs and renovations. I could tell you how the stress was so great that my body broke into hives and my skin began to swell, incapacitating me temporarily and landing me back on an expensive monthly medication I still take today. I could tell you about the contractor who removed part of the basement floor to address drainage issues, then didn't return for weeks, or about how, when I complained, he told me that he was the boss and placed a lien on my property. I could tell you how it took eight months to find a lender who would give me a mortgage, as I was self-employed. I could reach further back and tell you about how I'd lived like a graduate student—in a shared house with strangers—while on fellowship to save the money in the first place, and how much I had struggled to report the book that got me that fellowship. I could tell you the story, so common in this country as to be a national myth, that I got a house because I endured; because I did not give up.

But the truth of how I could afford that house is much grimmer, and far less flattering to me. I am a college-educated investor with some income and wealth—little of which I'd have if I had not been white. More than that, Detroit was the only place where investing in real estate made sense for someone like me—for two reasons. The first reason was social; I'd made friends in Detroit while I'd reported my first book, which gave me places to stay and expertise on which to draw. The second reason was even more important: real estate there was cheap. And Detroit's housing, in turn, was only cheap because racism had first bled, and then plundered, the city.

★ ★ ★ ★ ★

The foreclosure crisis of 2008 was disastrous for Detroit. Before the crisis and its fallout, Detroit was a city of homeowners. That was true in mid-century, when it was a majority-white city, and it stayed true as Detroit became a majority-Black city. In 2000, 52 percent of Black households there owned their homes, well above the national Black homeownership average of 46 percent.

Detroit's status as a city that was majority Black and majority home-owner put it at the center of a crisis started by bankers on Wall Street, which in turn sent its home prices spiraling downward. This is because lenders targeted Black communities for the riskiest and most expensive loans. More than half of the mortgages held by African Americans were subprime—compared to just 18 percent of the mortgages held by white Americans. The most explicit example is Wells Fargo's subprime marketing program aimed at Black homeowners and promoted through churches—internally, the bank's brokers referred to this financing as "ghetto loans." After the financial crisis, white families averaged a drop in wealth of more than one-quarter—while Black families, on average, lost nearly half of their wealth. Indeed, this pattern of incorporating Black Americans into middle-class financial institutions on predatory terms is so pronounced that scholars have coined a term to describe it: "predatory inclusion."[*]

In 2007, nearly 5 percent of the Detroit area's homes went into fore-closure—a greater share than in any other city at the time. Over the next eight years, roughly 65,000 Detroit mortgages would fail; more than half the properties ended up blighted or abandoned. There is no solid figure tallying the dollar value of that loss of wealth, but even a hypothetical loss of just $20,000 in equity per foreclosure would have generated a loss of $1.3 billion in family wealth across Detroit. Research suggests most of that loss was borne by Detroit's Black families, who made up 82 percent of the city.

The house I bought in Southwest entered foreclosure in 2013, in the

---

[*] While the term "predatory inclusion" was introduced in 2017 by Louise Seamster and Raphaël Charron-Chénier to describe the rise of Black educational debt, Keeanga-Yamahtta Taylor aptly applied it to discussion of the mortgage crisis in her 2019 book, *Race for Profit*.

wake of the subprime crisis. There's no public record of the mortgage rate, and the previous owner declined to discuss it with me. But I can tell you that 68 percent of mortgages in Detroit were subprime in 2005—and that in 2007, the previous owner of my house bought it with an $82,450 mortgage.

In Detroit, unlike other cities, *bank* foreclosures were only the first wave of loss. A massive wave of *tax* foreclosure soon followed, beginning in 2014. The 2008 mortgage crisis had driven down home values, but the city did not adjust property taxes to reflect the lowered values. Particularly for the least valuable houses, the city often calculated taxes as if homes were worth as much as nine times over the market value. (It is worth noting that, by failing to make this adjustment, the city frequently violates a state constitutional mandate to limit property tax assessments to half of market value.) Homeowners facing strict state laws and a weakened safety net struggled to keep up; eventually, the county issued tax foreclosure notices to one-third of the city's properties.*

These back-to-back waves of foreclosures left the city's land bank holding nearly 100,000 parcels of land in 2014. That year, the city launched a website to run property auctions for the homes for which it was now responsible. Bidding started at $1,000. That was the summer I sat on Martina's porch, my bank accounts well into five figures for the first time in my life, and thought about investing.

I do not remember what year it was when I realized my house was worth more than what I owed on it, giving me wealth. I do not remember the year my equity climbed into six figures, but I know that the housing market explosion in 2020 spurred it higher still. I felt such relief each time I saw this wealth climb, because it offered me safety. And I felt such bit-

---

* For a more in-depth analysis of the scale, scope, and impact of the tax foreclosures on the city of Detroit, see the work of Bernadette Atuahene, Joshua Akers, and Eric Seymour, as well as a 2020 investigation by Reveal and the *Detroit News*. Keep in mind that homeowners may face bank and tax foreclosure at the same time. Accordingly, figures for bank and tax foreclosures may overlap.

terness, too, because I know it was only possible in Detroit because the banks and the city's tax officials made decisions as if it did not matter whether residents lost their homes. I doubt that would have happened if most of the people in the city were white.

Detroit's loss has been my gain. As a white person who has gained equity from Detroit's losses, I am supposed to take the spoils without comment. I am supposed to know that if I comment, the spoils might be taken away. That is how my family does things, too.

In 2022, my father began to speak, obliquely, about setting up trusts. He explained that my sisters, stepsister, and I would each get "a quarter," minus about $100,000 to be split among their four grandchildren. My father does not use the phrases I expect of someone bequeathing wealth; there is no mention of "inheritance," no talk of an "estate," not even the word "wealth." That year marked the first time my parents had mentioned anything to me about leaving money to their children.

This is the long tail of the mid-century government policies and private practices that gave so much to white Americans and withheld so much from everyone else. An inheritance from my parents, which itself is passed on from Grandpa Mac, is how I might buffer myself against the unpredictable income of a writer, against unexpected expenses from the property I own, against medical bankruptcy if I sicken, against poverty when I am too old to work. It is how I, and my sisters, and my nieces and nephew, will compensate for our government's evident indifference to its people's needs for health care, for affordable shelter, for education that leads to a stable life, for healthy food—an indifference that, over multiple elections, a majority of white Americans have endorsed. And it is why my parents expect me to stay silent as they lie—to themselves and to me—and say they've earned this; that *we* have earned this.

I did not earn this. Not the money. And not this government that takes my taxes, and gives me—and most Americans without great wealth—so little in return.

There are other things I *have* earned. The firm knowledge, gained in writing this book, of the myriad ways racism I did not create benefits me nonetheless. The knowledge that, for me, these benefits are not worth my silence. And the understanding that nothing in this country will get better—health care and housing will not become affordable, wages will not go up, our air and water won't stay clean, the wildfires will not recede—if I do as my family has taught me, and endure silently in hope of getting out alive.

I have earned, in other words, an answer to the questions that began this book. I know, now, something of what racism has given me. And I have earned the conviction that those benefits aren't worth what they cost. At least, not for me.

What about you?

EPILOGUE

Sometime in the 2000s, I visited my parents' house for a family gathering. Maybe it was July 4, maybe it was Christmas. My sister Shana and I were standing in the dining room, eyeing a portrait of my grandfather, an oil painting two feet wide and three feet high. As an adult, it is unsettling to me that I had grown up with this portrait—my grandfather, dapper in a three-piece suit against a dark background—and still had not understood that my grandfather had money. I might have mentioned this to Shana, joked about the naïveté of children. Then I elbowed her and lowered my voice.

"Doesn't Grandpa Mac kind of look Black?"

I remember that, as a child, I thought that Grandpa Mac looked a lot like Grandpa Huxtable, from *The Cosby Show*: tawny skin, close-cut white hair above a graying mustache and dark brows, a broad, prominent nose. I did not share this thought with anyone. No one else in my family ever shared a similar thought. But the striking similarity between the two men stayed in the back of my mind. I was in my thirties before I thought to wonder about Grandpa Mac's race.

Like most white Americans, I'd grown up absorbing the idea of a "one-drop" rule: Any Black heritage, at all, meant a person was Black. In college, I'd learned about that rule and its chilling history, how it meant that white enslavers' rape of the women they held as property created profit. In 2020, I learned, via the work of journalist Isabel Wilkerson, how historians had documented that the German Nazis had found that the American one-drop rule was "too harsh." I did not "believe" it as a rule of science or nature. But, as a product of the society in which I was raised, I still wondered: *What if Grandpa Mac wasn't "white"?*

This was before information about family and genetic heritage was easy to find. I had not heard of Ancestry.com yet. If 23andMe had launched, I considered it niche and eccentric. (And, anyway, since my father had been adopted, testing myself wouldn't be relevant.) I did what I imagine most people did with similar family curiosities when this kind of research was hard. I set it aside.

When I began to look for my grandfather's heritage, in 2018, it was not hard to find answers. The year before Grandpa Mac's parents married, his mother, Ella, lived with her parents in Ontario, Canada. It was 1901, and a census enumerator came to their house in Penetanguishene, a tiny town on Georgian Bay—a vast expanse of Lake Huron northeast of Toronto. The markings on the census sheets are clear. As far as the census taker was concerned, Ella, her father, William, and her two brothers, Norman and William, were Black. Under "colour," he marked "B." Under "racial or tribal origin," he wrote "African." In the margin next to their names, he wrote "negro origin."

These census records are the only hard evidence I can find that Grandpa Mac was the son of a Black woman, and therefore might not have "really" been white. Ella's immigration records mark her as white, and there was great benefit in that—not least of all safety from racial violence. Every document I have found for Grandpa Mac marks him white, too.

"Passing" for white—if that is what Ella did and raised her children to do—was commonplace in the North, then, more so than in the South. In the North, there was little sense of gradation when it came to race. There, being "Black" was generally understood to require dark brown skin. In the

South, by comparison, "Black" was broadly understood to include people of nearly every skin tone. Indeed, while researchers estimate that roughly one-quarter of Black men in the South spent at least some of their lives passing for white in the early twentieth century, they estimate the rate of passing in the North was twice as high.

Learning that Grandpa Mac had a Black parent, but was considered white, is a powerful reminder that "race" is not real, even though the stakes we attach to it are. This is what scholars of racial theory mean by "race is a social construct." It is a reminder, too, that skin color represents vanishingly little—less than one-hundredth of 1 percent—of our DNA. Whatever share of African heritage there may have been in Grandpa Mac's genes, it has been literally immaterial to me. My grandfather had the only two things that make anyone white, ever: The world saw him as white, and he was treated as such. His DNA didn't matter at all.

POSTSCRIPT

WHAT CAME AFTER

A couple of months after the last conversation I had with my father and stepmother for this book, my father wrote me a letter. It arrived in a plain envelope, handwritten on two lined sheets of yellow paper and undated. He writes in the same block lettering I've watched him use all my life. The year this book is published, he will turn seventy-eight.

My father does not want me to write this book, at least not in the way I wrote it. I told him I wanted to talk about racism in my family's life, which seemed to puzzle him, but which he understood on some level. I told him I wanted to talk about the difficult things in my family, the things that had started with my mother's illness, the things that have yet to be settled today. I told him that I loved him and forgave him, but that there were "hard things" I needed to ask him about. I thought he would understand that the "hard things" included his abuse. In early discussions and in three long recorded interviews with him and my stepmother, we moved chronologically through his life. In every conversation, I asked him if he had any questions for me. Every time, he said he did not.

In May 2023, we had our third conversation, covering my teenage years. When I broached the topic of his violence, I said, "I'm sorry to bring it up, but I need to understand this . . . I know what it was like for me, but I don't know what was going on for you." As the conversation progressed, my stepmother told me I had never been in danger. In response, I began to share my memory of my father's attack. Before I finished, my father ordered me and my partner out of his house. I got his letter six weeks later.

The letter begins with insults, saying that Grandma Kate had called me "a drama queen," that I will do "anything to get attention," that he "can't accept this as rational behavior." It includes one specific denial, which is reflected in the book. Then it quickly moves to the leverage my father believes he has: money. "We are in the process of changing our wills and trust, and you will be excluded from both," he wrote. "If you continue on this track, this is the last you will hear from me. . . . Do not attend any service for me when I'm gone. I don't want any crocodile tears."

I've spent my life knowing an unspoken rule, but pretending I did not: *Endure silently, and you will be paid; speak up, and you will pay.* It is rarely said that directly, but in America we reference it all the time: *Don't rock the boat. Don't bite the hand that feeds you. What doesn't kill you makes you stronger.* For my family, it is our rule when it comes to the problem of abuse. In my country, it is our rule for white people when it comes to talking about white supremacy. In capitalism, it is our rule for anyone inclined to protest the greed and cruelty that our economy encourages. Sometimes, I have benefited from playing by these rules, but that is a side-effect—not their intent. These rules of silence and complicity were made for one reason only: to help people with power profit from its abuse.

My father acts as if these rules are immutable and inescapable, but they are not. My family does not have to be like this. Our country does not have to be like this. Our economy doesn't, either. We just have to be willing— as my father is not, as my family is not, as many white people are not, as many people of all races and places are not—to reckon honestly with what we have done and build from there.

A P P E N D I X

THE CASH VALUE OF RACISM

The pages that follow synthesize and tally the material benefits of racism documented for each of the primary subjects in *The White Bonus*.

Just as the stories I tell are not a comprehensive list of everything that has ever happened to each subject, this appendix is not a comprehensive review of *all* the material benefits they have accumulated because of their race. The more closely I studied a subject, including myself, the more advantages that emerged. Accordingly, tallies presented here are a list, only, of what has already been documented and verified in these pages. They are the *absolute minimum* value of each person's "white bonus." And, as I've noted in earlier passages, money is not everything; any reduction of human life to only dollars and cents is blind, flawed, and likely to cause harm.

Nothing here is intended, or presented, as an authoritative accounting of racism's material benefits to white people. I see this as a means of starting a conversation, and hope readers will do the same.

GLOSSARY:

TALLYING THE WHITE BONUS

This work rests on the premise that racial material advantage is not a one-shot deal. I've separated the tallies of white material advantage into two categories, family bonus and social bonus. At the level at which this book operates—individual stories—racism is both a direct payment and a form of compounding interest. One person gets paid more, or gets to buy a house, or doesn't get locked up, because they are white. This is their social bonus. They use that bonus to build wealth. Then, they pass that wealth on to their children, who experience those resources as a family bonus. As these children enter the world as adults, they accumulate their own social bonuses—which in turn become the family bonus they pass on to *their* children.

It's beyond my capacity to take a full tally of how that interplay between social and family bonuses accumulates across whole families. Instead, I have made the following calculations for individual family members—my book subjects—to see what I might find. Much as no single person is the product of only one's parents, no person's "bonus" is the product of only one kind of bonus. The family and social combine in each generation, producing a new family bonus—which will combine with the next generation's social bonus. On and on it goes.

For clarity, I've explained each bonus in greater detail below. Readers seeking more information can find it on whitebonus.com.

Family Bonus

This a rough tally of the money given directly to, or spent on, a single person by family members after they have turned eighteen or left home, whichever comes first. It also includes direct, private spending on the tools of social mobility before eighteen, such as cars and test prep. I have not tallied casual gifts, or those given regularly for birthdays and holidays, primarily because of the difficulty of either documenting or estimating them.

The family bonus is, in part, a reflection of advantages enjoyed by one's parents. I make no claim that I have proven, with scientific rigor, that any of my subjects' wealth can be traced to their race. Instead, I offer figures to prompt a question: How likely is it that they would have had this money if they were not white?

In service of that, each family bonus is accompanied by a list of policies and practices that my research suggests (a) disproportionately benefit white people, and (b) can be linked to the family in question.

As with all estimates of a "white bonus," these figures should be taken as a suggestion of the bare minimum of the material benefit of racism to each subject. It is by no means comprehensive.

Social Bonus

This is a rough tally of financial advantages each subject in part received, as well as financial costs they may have in part avoided, because they are white. As with the family bonus, each subject's social bonus is accompanied by a list of the racist policies I have been able to link, through research, to each subject.

Again, these numbers represent a bare minimum estimate, not a comprehensive figure.

THE WHITE BONUS INDEX

KATRINA RECTENWALD

LINDSEY BECKER

MARYANN BECKER

JARED BUNDE

BARBARA NATHAN KATZ

TRACIE McMILLAN

All figures presented have been adjusted to January 2023 dollar values.

To see full documentation and calculation for this appendix,
or to estimate your own white bonus,
go to whitebonus.com.

FAMILY BONUS
$159,711.14

Sources
Discrimination in unions

Housing discrimination

2002–2012

FAMILY SUBSIDIZED RENT

$44,121.09

page 50

2016

LOAN FOR HOME IMPROVEMENT

$21,467.06

page 51

2012–2023

FAMILY SUBSIDIZED HOUSING IN LIEU OF MORTGAGE

$94,122.99

page 51

SOCIAL BONUS
$15,579.13

Sources

Employment discrimination

Educational discrimination

2008–2009

NURSING SCHOLARSHIP

$15,579.13

page 45

LINDSEY BECKER

FAMILY BONUS
$22,423.39

Sources
Employment and wage discrimination
Privatization of safety net

1993

MONTESSORI SCHOOL

$8,156.89

page 104

2006–2007

ACT PREP AND COST OF TAKING ACT

$253.10

page 114

2007

HALF OF CAR PURCHASE

$1,478.00

page 114

2007–2012

CAR INSURANCE UNTIL FIRST JOB AFTER COLLEGE

$8,678.36

page 114

2007–2012

CELL PHONE UNTIL FIRST JOB AFTER COLLEGE

$3,857.04

page 114

SOCIAL BONUS
$140,256.86

Sources

Educational discrimination

2008–2012

COLLEGE SCHOLARSHIPS

$140,256.86

page 114

FAMILY BONUS
$49,323.44

Sources
Employment and wage discrimination
Privatization of safety net

2010–2012

ACT PREP AND COST OF TAKING ACT

$505.06

page 111

2013

INTEREST-FREE CAR LOAN

$3,630.02

page 114

2012–2018

**CAR INSURANCE UNTIL FIRST JOB
AFTER COLLEGE**

$7,879.51

page 114

2020

**STUDENT DEBT PAYOFF FOR
MARYANN**

$34,791.12

page 119

2012–2016

**CELL PHONE UNTIL FIRST JOB
AFTER COLLEGE**

$2,517.73

page 114

SOCIAL BONUS
$27,717.42

Sources

Educational discrimination

2012

COLLEGE SCHOLARSHIPS

$27,717.42

page 115

FAMILY BONUS
$143,523.82

Sources

Employment and wage discrimination

Privatization of safety net

1994

LAWYER FEES FROM PARENTS

$7,162.07

page 154

1994–1995

SUBSIDIZED RENT AFTER

HIGH SCHOOL

$10,860.53

page 156

1996–1997

TUITION FROM PARENTS

$14,317.57

page 165

2012

DAD COSIGNING STUDENT LOAN

$86,715.94

page 169

2013–2016

SUBSIDIZED RENT FROM MERRIN'S

MOTHER'S ACQUAINTANCE

$24,467.71

page 170

SOCIAL BONUS
$160,993.28

Sources

Implicit deference: criminal justice
Privatization of safety net
Housing discrimination

1994

NOT REQUIRING BAIL FIRST TIME HE WAS ARRESTED

$1,739.36

page 153

1995–1997

WAGES NOT LOST

$52,735.44

page 163

1995–1997

VISITATION NOT REQUIRED

$12,628.73

page 162

1995–1997

COMMISSARY NOT REQUIRED

$1,996.44

page 162

1995–1997

PHONE CALLS NOT REQUIRED

$4,424.50

page 162

2016

MORTGAGE INTEREST SAVED, BECAUSE CREDIT SCORE NOT LOWERED

$15,690.84

page 163

2016–2023

PROPERTY TAXES SAVED DUE TO PROPOSITION 13

$71,777.97

page 174

FAMILY BONUS
$332,410.67

Sources
Educational discrimination
Employment and wage discrimination
Housing discrimination

1971–1975	**1993**
COLLEGE TUITION	HOUSE FROM MIKE'S DAD
$48,372.57	$146,682.72
page 218	page 223
1976–1981	**2001–2012**
HOUSING WITH PARENTS	TRUST FROM CHARLES
$26,665.26	$100,373.91
page 218	page 226
1981	
INHERITANCE FROM UNCLE	
$10,316.21	
page 218	

SOCIAL BONUS
$38,212.57

Sources

Implicit deference

2013–2015

REDUCED RENT AT DISCRETION OF APARTMENT MANAGER

$38,212.57

page 232

*Deceased in 2015

FAMILY BONUS
$146,353.73

Sources

Discrimination in unions

Employment and wage discrimination

G.I. Bill

Housing discrimination

Implicit deference: family preservation

Privatization of safety net

1994

COLLEGE VISITS TO NYU, NORTHWESTERN

$2,770.24

page 204

1994

AVOIDING FOSTER CARE

$15,771.37

page 209

1994–1997

EDUCATIONAL LOANS FROM GRANDFATHER

$52,784.33

page 211

1995

TUITION FROM PARENTS

$5,971.46

page 211

2004

INHERITANCE FROM GRANDFATHER

$40,384.72

page 270

2006

ADDITIONAL CASH FROM PARENTS

$15,086.74

page 271

2011

INTEREST-FREE LOAN FROM PARENTS

$13,584.87

page 290

SOCIAL BONUS
$225,580.57

Sources
Employment and wage discrimination
Housing discrimination
Credit discrimination
Predatory state/governance

1995–1998

JOB AS TUTOR WITH MAGGIE

$26,858.04

page 255

1996–1997

RENT-STABILIZED APARTMENT 1

$1,319.86

page 259

1997–2008

RENT-STABILIZED APARTMENT 2

$8,037.56

page 261

2010, 2011, 2021

ACCESS TO CREDIT, INTEREST-FREE

$37,488.11

page 286

2015–2023

AFFORDABLE HOME-BUYING IN
DETROIT

$151,877.00

page 295

NOTES

Author's Note

xii **"legitimacy to such beliefs":** John Daniszewski, "Why We Will Lowercase White," Associated Press, July 20, 2020, https://blog.ap.org /announcements/why-we-will-lowercase-white.

Introduction

4   **as their white peers:** A massive 2020 analysis of longitudinal data cover- ing the United States from 1989 to 2015 found that "children born into high- income black families have substantially higher rates of *downward* mobility than whites across generations. . . . Indeed, a black child born to parents in the top quintile is roughly as likely to fall to the *bottom* family income quintile as he or she is to remain in the top quintile; in contrast, white children are nearly five times as likely to remain in the top quintile as they are to fall to the bottom quintile." Of children born to parents in the bottom quintile of household income, 10.6 percent of white children were in top-quintile house- holds as adults, compared to 2.5 percent of Black children. Comparatively, of children born to parents in the top quintile of household income, 41.1 percent of white children stayed in top-quintile households as adults, compared to 18.0 percent of Black children. Raj Chetty, Nathaniel Hendren, Maggie R. Jones, and Sonya R. Porter, "Race and Economic Opportunity in the United

States: An Intergenerational Perspective," *Quarterly Journal of Economics* 135, no. 2 (May 2020): 714, https://doi.org/10.1093/qje/qjz042.

4   **more likely to be arrested on drug charges:** For decades, studies have shown that white people may be *more* likely to sell drugs than Black people. A 1991 analysis by Anne Case and Lawrence Katz found that 33 percent of Black teens in Boston reported using illegal drugs compared to 36 percent of their white peers. The same study found that fewer Black teens reported selling illegal drugs or committing a crime: 12 percent of Black teens reported selling illegal drugs, compared to 18 percent of white teens, and 17 percent of Black teens reported committing a crime—compared to 30 percent of their white peers. A 2002 study by Robert Fairlie found similar results nationwide. Jonathan Rothwell at the Brookings Institution analyzed multiple years of arrest data from the Bureau of Justice Statistics and notes, "The black share of people arrested for drug offenses has ranged from 23 percent (in 1980) to 41 percent (in 1991). Blacks remain far more likely than whites to be arrested for selling drugs (3.6 times more likely) or possessing drugs (2.5 times more likely)." Anne C. Case and Lawrence F. Katz, "The Company You Keep: The Effects of Family and Neighborhood on Disadvantaged Youths" (working paper 3705, NBER, Cambridge, MA, May 1991), https://www.nber.org/papers/w3705; Robert W. Fairlie, "Drug Dealing and Legitimate Self-Employment," *Journal of Labor Economics* 20, no. 3 (July 2002): 545–47, https://doi.org/10.1086/339610; Jonathan Rothwell, "How the War on Drugs Damages Black Social Mobility," Social Mobility Memos, Brookings Institution, September 30, 2014, https://www.brookings.edu/blog/social-mobility-memos/2014/09/30/how-the-war-on-drugs-damages-black-social-mobility/; *Results from the 2017 National Survey on Drug Use and Health: Detailed Tables*, Substance Abuse and Mental Health Services Administration, Center for Behavioral Health Statistics and Quality, Rockville, MD, September 7, 2018, https://www.samhsa.gov/data/sites/default/files/cbhsq-reports/NSDUHDetailedTabs2017/NSDUHDetailedTabs2017.pdf.

4   **more likely to be sent to prison than white people:** This fact is widely acknowledged, though rigorous national data on sentencing disparities is hard to come by, given that each state and the federal government are separately responsible for their own criminal legal systems and have varying levels of transparency. But in a sweeping 2000 literature review of forty studies (thirty-two studies of state courts and eight of federal courts), Cassia Spohn

found that *"certain types* of racial minorities—males, the young, the unemployed, the less educated—are singled out for harsher treatment at sentencing" compared with similarly situated whites. This effect is made worse, she notes, when one or more of the following things are true: they are detained in jail while awaiting trial, they are represented by a public defender, they are convicted of drug offenses, they are convicted of minor offenses, they are convicted at trial (as opposed to taking a plea), they have a criminal record, and/or they have a white victim. Cassia C. Spohn, "Thirty Years of Sentencing Reform: The Quest for a Racially Neutral Sentencing Process," in *Criminal Justice 2000*, vol. 3, *Policies, Processes, and Decisions of the Criminal Justice System*, ed. Winnie Reed and Laura Winterfield (Rockville, MD: National Institute of Justice, 2000), 462–63, https://www.ojp.gov/ncjrs/virtual-library/abstracts/thirty-years-sentencing-reform-quest-racially-neutral-sentencing.

4   **13 percent of the wealth of white ones:** Neil Bhutta, Andrew Chang, Lisa Dettling, and Joanne Hsu, "Disparities in Wealth by Race and Ethnicity in the 2019 Survey of Consumer Finances," FEDS Notes, Division of Research and Statistics, Federal Reserve, September 28, 2020, https://www.federalreserve.gov/econres/notes/feds-notes/disparities-in-wealth-by-race-and-ethnicity-in-the-2019-survey-of-consumer-finances-20200928.html. Figures from 2018 put the median wealth of Black families at $24,111, and the median wealth of white families at $188,200.

5   **Not much has changed:** Matthew Desmond, *Poverty, By America* (New York: Crown, 2023), 24–40. Desmond notes that "to graph the share of Americans living in poverty over the past half century amounts to drawing a line that resembles gently rolling hills. . . . There is no real improvement here, just a long stasis."

6   **"target first and worst":** Heather McGhee, "'Sum of Us' Examines the Hidden Cost of Racism—for Everyone," interview by Dave Davies, *Fresh Air*, NPR, February 17, 2021, https://www.npr.org/2021/02/17/968638759/sum-of-us-examines-the-hidden-cost-of-racism-for-everyone.

7   **how much money they make:** Arline Geronimus, interview by the author, June 15, 2023.

8   **whether their economic stability will last:** Research from the Pew Research Center suggests that as the American middle class has shrunk, the share of white adults who are low-income has grown. From 1971 to 2021, the share of Americans in middle-income households dropped from 61 percent to 50 percent. For all racial groups, that shift represented an increase in the number of upper-income households alone. But white Americans were the

only racial group where low-income households also increased over the same period—by just 3 percentage points. This is a relative and modest loss, not an absolute or big one. White Americans remain the group with the largest share of middle-class members, now 52 percent instead of 63 percent in 1971. Our share of low-income members, at 24 percent in 2021, up from 1971, is significantly lower than the share of Black and Hispanic Americans who are low-income: 41 and 40 percent respectively. Rakesh Kochhar and Stella Sechopoulos, "How the American Middle Class Has Changed in the Past Five Decades," Pew Research Center, April 20, 2022, https://www.pewresearch.org/fact-tank/2022/04/20 /how-the-american-middle-class-has-changed-in-the-past-five-decades/.

9   **call it "caste":** Wilkerson, *Caste*, 19, 68–72. Wilkerson writes, "Caste and race are neither synonymous nor mutually exclusive. . . . Race, in the United States, is the visible agent of the unseen force of caste. Race is what we can see, the physical traits that have been given arbitrary meaning and become shorthand for who a person is. Caste is the powerful infrastructure that holds each group in its place." There is also a compelling comparison between racism and caste beginning on page 68.

Chapter 1: My Grandparents

12   **Maybe the early 1940s:** This account is based on personal papers, including family photo albums and scrapbooks, journals and diaries, news clippings and yearbooks.

13   **fur, fish, and timber:** "Story of Our People: The Sault Ste. Marie Tribe of Chippewa Indians," Sault Ste. Marie Tribe of Chippewa Indians, last modified January 28, 2017, https://www.saulttribe.com/history-a-culture/story-of -our-people. Fowle, *Sault Ste. Marie*, 429.

13   **within the bounds of the United States:** "A Brief History of Michigan," in Legislative Service Bureau, *Michigan Manual*, 3–5.

13   **smaller annual payments:** "1836 Treaty Ceded Territory," Sault Ste. Marie Tribe of Chippewa Indians, last modified February 15, 2008, https://www .saulttribe.com/history-a-culture/1836-treaty-ceded-territory.

13   **Canadian side of the river:** Birth Record for John McMillan, Birth Records for July–December 1907, p. 313, no. 287, Steelton, Ontario, Canada, from Ancestry.com.

13   **since the 1850s:** Fowle, *Sault Ste. Marie*, 429.

14   **boosterish account of the period:** Newton, *Story of Sault Ste. Marie*, 193.

14   **feeding city dwellers:** Newton, *Story of Sault Ste. Marie*, 193.

14 **saltwater ports combined:** Fowle, *Sault Ste. Marie*, 7, 45.

14 **it only reached 10,588:** In 1880, the village of Sault Ste. Marie had 1,947 inhabitants (U.S. Census Bureau, 1880 Census, vol. 1, General Population Tables, table 3, "Population of Civil Divisions Less Than Counties," p. 214, https://www2.census.gov/library/publications/decennial/1880/vol-01 -population/1880_v1-10.pdf). By 1900, the Sault was a city of 10,588 (U.S. Census Bureau, 1900 Census, vol. 1, General Population Tables, table 8, "Population of Incorporated Towns, Villages, and Boroughs in 1900," p. 455, https://www2.census.gov/library/publications/decennial/1900/volume-1 /volume-1-p9.pdf).

14 **"prostrated with grief":** "Two Sooites Were Asphyxiated at Cleveland," *Sault Daily Star*, February 10, 1913.

14 **American innkeeper:** Marriage Record of George Coleman and Ella McMillan, August 6, 1919, Chippewa County Return of Marriages for Quarter Ending September 30, 1919, no. 148, from ancestry.com.

14 **this time a painter:** Death Certificate of George Coleman, September 18, 1921, Division of Vital Statistics, Department of State, Michigan; Marriage Record of Alwin Andree and Ella Coleman, September 11, 1923, Chippewa County Return of Marriages for Quarter Ending September 30, 1923, no. 161, from Ancestry.com

14 **on the American side:** Sault Ste. Marie High School, *The Northern Light* (Sault Ste. Marie, MI: 1925), 38.

14 **branch of a national bank:** War Department Personnel Placement Questionnaire completed by John McMillan, July 6, 1944, in the author's possession. The questionnaire includes his work history.

14 **fourth-largest city in the country:** U.S. Census Bureau, 1930 Census, vol. 1, United States Summary, table 11, "Population of Cities Having, in 1930, 100,000 Inhabitants or More: 1790 to 1930," p. 18, https://www2 .census.gov/library/publications/decennial/1930/population-volume-1 /03815512v1ch02.pdf.

14 **leaping into the unknown:** U.S. Census Bureau, 1930 Census, vol. 1, Number and Distribution of Inhabitants, Population-Michigan, table 4, "Population of Counties by Minor Civil Divisions: 1930, 1920, and 1910," p. 520, https://www2.census.gov/library/publications/decennial/1930/population -volume-1/03815512v1ch06.pdf; Census Bureau, "1930, 100,000 Inhabitants or More," p. 512.

14 **to Detroit in 1920:** Petition for Naturalization for Norman Carter, January 7, 1928, Naturalization Service, U.S. Department of Labor, from Ancestry.com.

14 **home-building boom:** Kenneth Snowden (emeritus professor of economics, University of North Carolina at Greensboro), interview by the author, July 6, 2022.

15 **paying the full price outright:** Rothstein, *Color of Law*, 63.

15 **mortgages were short and expensive:** "Decennial Homeownership Rates, 1900–2000," U.S. Census Bureau, accessed April 5, 2023, https://www2.census.gov/programs-surveys/decennial/tables/time-series/coh-owner/owner-tab.txt.

15 **as at the beginning:** Rothstein, *Color of Law*, 63.

15 **B. E. Taylor, a Detroit developer:** U.S. Census Bureau, Population Schedule for Detroit, MI, April 3, 1930, enumeration district 82–841, sheet 7A, lines 30–33, from Ancestry.com. Norman indicated to a census worker that he owned 14255 Hubbell, giving its value as $8,700; my grandfather, going by "Allen," was listed as a roomer.

15 **amenities like sewers and pavement:** *Baist's Real Estate Atlas*, plan 34; Restrictions for B.E. Taylor's Properties, 1919, no. E&M 74D4 333.3, Burton Historical Collection, Detroit Public Library.

15 **linking the neighborhood with downtown:** Schramm, Henning, and Dworman, *Detroit's Street Railways*, 257–58.

15 **houses on every lot:** Restrictions for B. E. Taylor's Properties. Neighborhoods in Norman's part of the city were distinguished from each other in three ways: (1) required setback from street, which increased the size of front yard, (2) maximum home size, and (3) racial restrictions. Monmoor Subdivisions 1 and 2 required houses to be set back ten or twenty feet from the street, respectively; did not allow a home to occupy multiple lots; and lacked racial restrictions. Nearby Monmoor Subdivisions 3 and 4 and Kenmoor had thirty-foot setbacks, the option to build a house across multiple lots, and racial restrictions. Norman's house was in Monmoor 1.

15 **everyone in the Sault, was white:** U.S. Census Bureau, 1920 Census, vol. 3, Composition and Characteristics of the Population by States, Michigan, table 10, "Composition and Characteristics of the Population, for Cities of 10,000 or more," p. 489, https://www2.census.gov/library/publications/decennial/1920/volume-3/41084484v3ch05.pdf; U.S. Census Bureau, 1930 Census, Population Schedule for Detroit, MI, enumeration districts 82–0841 & 82–0842. The 1920 Census reports that Sault Ste. Marie had 11,986 white residents, 49 Black residents, and 61 residents of other races, making it 99.1 percent white. The 1930 Census shows that Norman's stretch of Hubbell was 100 percent white.

15 **that determined your abilities:** Omi and Winant, *Racial Formation*, 23.

15 **hair and eye color:** Natalie Angier, "Do Races Differ? Not Really, Genes Show," *New York Times*, August 22, 2000.

16 **Harlem in New York City:** Yong Chen notes in *Chinese San Francisco* that "Chinatown became a safe haven for many Chinese" (60) not only because it offered unique economic opportunities, but also because it was the one place in San Francisco that did not discriminate against Chinese people in housing or expose them to being a target of racial violence. Roberta Gold, a scholar of New York City's tenant movements, ties the genesis of Harlem as a center of Black culture, in part, to discrimination. "The people who benefited from racial discrimination in housing were landlords. If you don't let Black people rent anywhere but Harlem, and Harlem is jam-packed . . . tenants have to take what they can get even if it is unsafe." (Roberta Gold, interview by the author, January 5, 2022.)

16 **restricting neighborhoods by race:** For more, see Rothstein, *Color of Law*, and Matthew D. Lassiter and Susan Cianci Salvatore, *Civil Rights in America: Racial Discrimination in Housing* (Washington, D.C.: National Park Service, March 2021).

16 **buildings on the block:** McMechen told a reporter, "In the latter part of July four other colored families moved into the same block. Within a few weeks they had spent at least $25 apiece for replacing broken window panes. Just a week ago the house on the corner below me had a front window broken in broad daylight." "Baltimore Tries Drastic Plan of Race Segregation," *New York Times*, December 25, 1910.

16 **up to a year in jail:** "Drastic Plan," *New York Times*.

17 **enforced by the city:** "The moving in of negroes depreciates property," Dashiell told the *New York Times*; "it also tends to the disturbance and destruction of the peace to a marked degree." "Drastic Plan," *New York Times*.

17 **bordered the region:** Allison Shertzer, Tate Twinam, and Randall P. Walsh, "Zoning and Segregation in Urban Economic History" (working paper, NBER, Cambridge, MA, January 2021), 7, http://www.nber.org/papers/w28351.

17 **intervene in a private contract:** Buchanan v. Warley, 245 U.S. 81 (1917).

17 **introduce the assembly line:** Mark Theobald, "O.J. Beaudette Co.," Coachbuilt, updated 2014, http://www.coachbuilt.com/bui/b/beaudette/beaudette.htm; "Ford's Assembly Line Starts Rolling," This Day in History, History.com, updated November 30, 2020, https://www.history.com/this-day-in-history/fords-assembly-line-starts-rolling.

18 **were killed after 1900:** "Lynchings in Missouri," Community Remembrance Project of Missouri, accessed April 24, 2023, https://crp-mo.org/lynchings%3A-1877-1950; Frazier, *Lynchings in Missouri*, 189–202. The Community Remembrance Project has documented sixty "known racial terror lynchings" in Missouri from 1877 to 1950. Frazier's *Lynchings in Missouri* documents lynchings throughout the nineteenth and twentieth centuries in that state. Her work documents the lynching of thirty-three Black men in Missouri from 1900 to 1942.

18 **section without sewers:** Robert K. Nelson et al., "Mapping Inequality," *American Panorama*, ed. Robert K. Nelson and Edward L. Ayers, accessed April 3, 2023, https://dsl.richmond.edu/panorama/redlining/ #loc=12/42.642/-83.369&city=pontiac-mi. HOLC area descriptions for Pontiac and other cities are also available from Mapping Inequality: https://dsl.richmond.edu/panorama/redlining/#loc=5/39.1/-94.58&text=downloads. This description is drawn from the "area descriptions" for sections B2 and C1.

19 **unsafe and income unpredictable:** Dan Clark (professor of history, Oakland University), interview by the author, June 1, 2020.

20 **we do not talk about:** Thierry Devos and Mahzarin R. Banaji, "American = White?" *Journal of Personality and Social Psychology* 88, no. 3 (2005): 463. In this paper, which summarizes six studies, researchers observe: "The conclusion that can be drawn on the basis of the six studies presented here is unambiguous. To be American is to be White." This was based on their finding that white and Asian American test subjects routinely expressed an implicit assumption that Asian American, Hispanic, and African American people were "not as American as White Americans."

20 **arriving in northern cities:** Christy Clark-Pujara and Anna-Lisa Cox, "How the Myth of a Liberal North Erases a Long History of White Violence," *Smithsonian Magazine*, August 27, 2020, https://www.smithsonianmag.com/smithsonian-institution/how-myth-liberal-north-erases-long-history-white-violence-180975661/.

20 **two thousand and eight thousand people each:** Jackson, *Klan in the City*, 129–30. In the 1920s, Detroit-area Klan gatherings—some with cross-burnings, most with thousands of attendees—were documented in Royal Oak, which lies near the Wayne County line, at a vacant lot downtown, at a farm near the intersection of Snyder and Seven Mile Roads, and at the Detroit Riding and Hunt Club.

20 **joined its ranks:** Elaine Fishbaugh (Katheryn Weddle's niece), interview by the author, March 21, 2023.

20 **auto-plant security forces:** Peter H. Amann, "Vigilante Fascism: The
    Black Legion as an American Hybrid," *Comparative Studies in Society and
    History* 25, no. 3 (July 1983): 490–524; Richard Bak, "The Dark Days of the
    Black Legion," *Hour Detroit*, February 23, 2009, https://www.hourdetroit
    .com/community/the-dark-days-of-the-black-legion/; Elmer Graham, "Black
    Legion Shadow over Rubber Workers," *Champ* (Pontiac, MI: Yellow Cab
    Local 594), June 20, 1947.

21 **did not reopen the case:** Report of Black Legion Activities in Oakland
    County, Circuit Court, Oakland County, Michigan, August 31, 1936, 28, Peter
    Amann Papers, box 6, folder 22, Walter P. Reuther Library, Wayne State Uni-
    versity, Detroit, MI; Stanton, *Terror in the City of Champions*, 132–34, 211–12;
    "Dean Reveals Shooting as a Cultist Prank," *Detroit Free Press*, July 26, 1936;
    "Farm Home Held Red Headquarters," *Detroit Free Press*, August 24, 1934;
    Stamp Out the Black Legion, Walter P. Reuther Library, Wayne State Univer-
    sity, Detroit, MI, https://projects.lib.wayne.edu/dropbox/12thstreetdetroit
    /Case_LP001061_3_9_BlackLegion.pdf; Andrew G. Palella, "The Black
    Legion: J. Edgar Hoover and Fascism in the Depression Era," *Journal for
    the Study of Radicalism* 12, no. 2 (Fall 2018): 84, https://muse.jhu.edu/article
    /703882.

21 **became a media sensation:** Bak, "Dark Days"; Report of Black Legion
    Activities, Amann Papers, 6–7; Palella, "The Black Legion," 82.

22 **after the zoning ruling:** Rothstein, *Color of Law*, 76; Ronald Dale Karr,
    "The Evolution of the Elite Suburb: Community Structure and Control
    in Brookline, Massachusetts, 1770–1900" (PhD diss., Boston University,
    1981), 264–66. In 1843, the Linden Place subdivision in the Boston suburb of
    Brookline introduced covenants to its deeds, mandating—as was the case
    in Grandpa Mac's uncle's home in Detroit—setbacks from the street and
    residential use. Before the end of the century, the covenants were amended
    to forbid sales "to any negro or native of Ireland."

22 **Seattle, and Washington, D.C.:** For Charlottesville, see: "1897–
    1948: Charlottesville's First Racially Restrictive Covenants," Mapping
    Cville, January 28, 2019, https://mappingcville.com/2019/01/28/1903-1948
    -charlottesvilles-first-racially-restrictive-covenants/; for Chicago, Minneap-
    olis, and Philadelphia, see: Larry Santucci, "Documenting Racially Restric-
    tive Covenants in 20th Century Philadelphia," *Cityscape* 22, no. 3 (2020):
    242; for Phoenix, see: Carol Rose, "Panel Discussion of *Saving the Neighbor-
    hood*: Author's Introduction," *Arizona Law Review Syllabus* 56, no. 3 (2014):
    13; for San Antonio, see: April Molina, "Couple Shocked by Historical Racist

Deed Restrictions," News 4 San Antonio, September 11, 2016, https://
news4sanantonio.com/news/local/couple-shocked-by-historical-racist
-deed-restrictions. This is hardly a comprehensive list. For the other cities
and for more about covenants in general, see generally Rothstein, *Color of
Law.*

22 **legal and enforceable by law:** Vose, *Caucasians Only,* 52, 55.

22 **"entirely of the Caucasian race":** Brendan Riley, "Brendan Riley's
Solano Chronicles: Racial Redefining in Vallejo," *Times-Herald,* March 25,
2022. Riley's story leads with an image of a 1932 newspaper ad for a whites-
only subdivision for "parents who want to bring up their children in the best
possible environment" particularly as a result of "protective building and
racial restrictions."

22 **from doing the same:** Shelley v. Kraemer, 334 U.S. 1–23 (1948); Jessie
Degollado, "New State Law Will Now Allow Property Owners to Remove
Racial Deed Restrictions Through the Courts," KSAT.com, August 30, 2021,
https://www.ksat.com/news/local/2021/08/30/new-state-law-will-now
-allow-property-owners-to-remove-racial-deed-restrictions-through-the
-courts/.

22 **"property values in that neighborhood":** "Code of Ethics," National
Association of Real Estate Boards, June 6, 1924, National Association
of Realtors, https://www.nar.realtor/about-nar/history/1924-code-of-
ethics.

22 **property values went down:** Slater, *Freedom to Discriminate,* 97.

22 **and circulated it to its members:** Santucci, "Documenting Racially
Restrictive Covenants," 249–50.

23 **"foundation of American citizenship":** Boyle, *Arc of Justice,* 241–42.

23 **"move into white neighborhoods":** Kevin Boyle, interview by the
author, March 14, 2023.

23 **through no fault of their own:** Snowden, interview; Jill Watts, "As
Coronavirus Magnifies America's Housing Crisis, FDR's New Deal Could
Offer a Roadmap Forward," *Time,* April 24, 2020, https://time.com/5826392
/coronavirus-housing-history/.

24 **gain equity as they paid:** *Final Report to the Congress of the United States
Relating to the Home Owners' Loan Corporation: 1933–1951,* Housing and Home
Finance Agency, Home Loan Bank Board, Washington, D.C., March 1, 1952,
FRASER, Federal Reserve Bank of St. Louis, https://fraser.stlouisfed.org
/files/docs/publications/holc/hlc_final_report_1952.pdf.

24 **minority of Black homeowners:** Price V. Fishback, Jonathan Rose,

Kenneth Snowden, and Thomas Storrs, "New Evidence on Redlining by Federal Housing Programs in the 1930s" (working paper, NBER, Cambridge, MA, September 2021), 5, 17; Bruce Mitchell and Juan Franco, *HOLC "Redlining" Maps: The Persistent Structure of Segregation and Economic Inequality*, National Community Reinvestment Coalition, March 20, 2018, https://ncrc.org/holc/.

24 **shaded yellow and red:** Amy E. Hillier, "Redlining and the Homeowners' Loan Corporation," *Journal of Urban History* 29, no. 4 (2003): 397–98; Fishback et al., "New Evidence on Redlining," 15.

24 **affordable to the middle class:** Fishback et al., "New Evidence on Redlining," 6; Rothstein, *Color of Law*, 65.

24 **underwriting whole suburban developments:** Fishback et al., "New Evidence on Redlining," 21; Rothstein, *Color of Law*, 70.

24 **485,933 that year alone:** Grebler, "New Housebuilding," 17, 68.

24 **HOLC did not:** Fishback et al., "New Evidence on Redlining," 23.

25 **danger to property values:** Fishback et al., "New Evidence on Redlining," 27; "Drastic Plan," *New York Times*. In the *New York Times* article, attorney Milton Dashiell argued that, "the destruction in property values is a sufficiently good one to support the ordinance in question. When one considers how whole blocks by the half dozen have had their values cut in two by the advent of half a dozen negro families, it seems conclusive that the city, under its police power, has a right—indeed, not only has the right, but should hold it as its bounden duty—to step in and, by the prohibition of further influx of negro population into the white districts, prevent further destruction in value."

25 **for much of the 1950s:** Rothstein, *Color of Law*, 65–66.

25 **where it held mortgages:** Hillier, "Redlining," 394; Rothstein, *Color of Law*, 64.

25 **in the 1980s:** Hillier, "Redlining," 395.

25 **already possessed through foreclosure:** Fishback et al., "New Evidence on Redlining," 8.

26 **homes that contained old ones:** Fishback et al., "New Evidence on Redlining," 16; Rothstein, *Color of Law*, 87–88.

26 **the basis of race until 1961:** Rothstein, *Color of Law*, 108.

26 **"values in a neighborhood":** U.S. Commission on Civil Rights, "Housing," *1961 Commission on Civil Rights Report*, book 4 (Washington, D.C.: Government Printing Office, 1961), 49. The report quotes a letter received by the commission from FDIC chair Earle Cocke.

27 **into the Great Depression:** Frank Masten, Margaret's father and my great-grandfather, first appears in the 1880 census enumeration for Ann

Arbor, when he was eight years old; his father was a carpenter born in New York, and his mother was born in Michigan to Irish immigrants. Ann Arbor City Directories indicate the family members' professions, including when Margaret started working at a bank in 1928, and show the family moving at least four times between 1920 and 1930. The census enumerations in 1920 and 1930 confirm their status as renters. These documents are all available through Ancestry.com (census enumerations) or Google Books (Ann Arbor Directories). Margaret's study of stenography appears in her high school graduation program, in possession of author.

27 **banks they each worked at merged:** "Ann Arbor Downtown Branch," National Information Center, Federal Financial Institutions Examination Council, accessed May 9, 2023, https://www.ffiec.gov/npw/Institution /Profile/638243?dt=20091107. On February 16, 1936, Farmers and Mechanics Bank, where Grandpa Mac worked, failed. Ann Arbor Savings Bank, where Grandmar worked, failed the same day. These banks, along with another failed bank, First National Savings Bank and Company, merged into Ann Arbor Savings and Commercial Bank.

27 **a hundred miles away:** Marriage Registration of Margaret Masten and J. Alan McMillan, in *Indiana, Marriages, 1810–2001* (Salt Lake City, UT: Fam-ilySearch), 509, from Ancestry.com.

27 **"meant for one another":** Letter from Ella Carter to John A. and Mar-garet M. McMillan, September 19, 1936, copy in possession of author.

27 **in a new subdivision nearby:** Deed for lot 47 of Westwood Hills, Ann Arbor, MI, March 15, 1939, liber 330, p. 533, Washtenaw County Register of Deeds, Ann Arbor, MI.

27 **chose this path:** Snowden, interview.

28 **things had begun to improve:** "Great Depression Facts," Franklin D. Roosevelt Presidential Library and Museum, accessed April 8, 2023, https:// www.fdrlibrary.org/great-depression-facts; CES, *Social Security in America*, 60.

28 **Black men were unemployed:** *Final Report on Total and Partial Unemploy-ment for Michigan; Census of Partial Employment, Unemployment, and Occupations: 1937* (Washington, D.C.: U.S. Government Printing Office, 1938).

28 **a year as a couple:** U.S. Census Bureau, Population Schedule for Ann Arbor, MI, April 5, 1940, enumeration district 81–9, sheet 3A, lines 35–36, from Ancestry.com; U.S. Census Bureau, 1940 Census of Population and Housing: Families, ch. 7, Family Wage or Salary Income in 1939, table 1, Families by Family Wage or Salary Income and Receipt of Other Income in 1939, for the United States, by Regions, Urban and Rural (with Color for the

South), pp. 7–8, https://www2.census.gov/library/publications/decennial/1940/population-families/41272167ch7.pdf. On the 1940 census, John A. McMillan reported earning $2,100 a year, while Margaret M. McMillan reported earning $1,100. My grandfather's salary put him in the 92nd percentile of white men, while my grandmother's put her in the 83rd percentile of white women. Their individual earning exceeded those of 99 and 98 percent of nonwhite workers of the same sex, respectively.

28 **middle and upper-middle class:** This and all subsequent statements about the class of the central figures in this book borrows from the work of Pew Research Center. Rakesh Kochhar at Pew made possible consistent distinctions among five class statuses, as described in the introduction, by generously sharing some of Pew's data with me (hereafter cited as Pew Income Data). Kochhar also helped me retrofit the Pew model to data from censuses before 1970, which reported inconsistently, if at all, on national household income. Where it seems relevant, I will provide a detailed breakdown of a family's class status in an endnote. Here is the one for my grandparents in 1940: In that year, the median annual income for a household of two was $1,680 (see the Family Wage report cited in the previous note). The Pew Center considers the upper-middle class to begin at 200 percent of median annual income, or $3,360. My paternal grandparents' combined income was $3,200, or right on the cusp of upper-middle class.

29 **"persons of African descent":** Deed for lot 47 of Westwood Hills, Ann Arbor, MI, March 15, 1939, liber 330, p. 533, Washtenaw County Register of Deeds, Ann Arbor, MI; Santucci, "Documenting Racially Restrictive Covenants," 250; Deed for lot 47 Westwood Hills, Ann Arbor, MI, September 16, 1927, liber 276, p. 17, Washtenaw County Register of Deeds, Ann Arbor, MI. This last document includes the restrictions.

29 **latter clause snagged Grandpa Mac:** Frank N. Schubert, *Mobilization in World War II*, U.S. Army Center of Military History (Washington, D.C.: Government Printing Office, 1994), https://history.army.mil/brochures/Mobilization/mobpam.htm.

29 **about a quarter of soldiers:** "National Day of the Deployed: Honoring America's Deployed Servicemembers," National WWII Museum, October 26, 2022, https://www.nationalww2museum.org/war/articles/national-day-deployed-honoring-americas-deployed-servicemembers. Of the 16.5 million men and women who served in the US Armed Forces during World War II, 73 percent served overseas.

29 **codified in law:** Kristy N. Kamarck, *Diversity, Inclusion, and Equal*

Opportunity in the Armed Services: Background and Issues for Congress, Congressional Research Service, report R44321, June 5, 2019, 13; MacGregor, *Integration of the Armed Forces*, 36. During World War II, the War Department held separate drafts for Black and white servicemembers. Its trainings were segregated, as were its unit assignments. The army limited its recruitment of Black soldiers to 10 percent of recruits, and all armed forces segregated their blood banks. Top administrators on each base typically followed local custom when it came to racial hierarchies, resulting in segregated theaters, service clubs, and buses.

29 **that hosted segregated events:** Undated photos of Margaret Masten and John A. McMillan, ca. 1944, copies in possession of author. The photos show Grandmar and Grandpa Mac enjoying the beaches and going to the Cricket, where, a note in Grandmar's neat cursive on the reverse of the photo claims, "they serve delicious meals."

29 **college students in the draft:** Albert A. Blum, "The Army and Student Deferments During the Second World War," *Journal of Higher Education* 31, no. 1 (January 1960): 45.

29 **didn't make it past eighth grade:** Thomas D. Snyder, ed., *120 Years of American Education: A Statistical Portrait*, National Center for Education Statistics, Office of Educational Research and Improvement, U.S. Department of Education, January 1993, 7, 19–20. In 1940, 15.1 percent of white American men had four years of schooling or less, 19.0 percent had between five and seven years, and 28.8 percent had eight years, for a combined total of 62.9 percent of white men with an eighth-grade education or less. The same year, 11.2 percent of white men had one year or more of college.

30 **education at all:** Snyder, "American Education," 19. In 1940, Black males completed a median of 5.4 years of school, while 1.7 percent of Black males completed between one and three years of college. Another 1.4 percent completed four or more years of college.

30 **educated recruits, Black or white, did:** Lee, *Negro Troops*, 243, 270. I do not have a copy of Grandpa Don's score on the AGCT, but it required a score of 115 or higher in order for entry into the Army Specialized Training Program, which sent recruits to university courses. At the program's peak in December 1943—during which my grandfather was in the program—105,265 students were being trained under ASTP. Of those, 789 were Black.

30 **engineering classes in 1943:** Separation qualification record for Donald

Weddle, November 14, 1945, obtained from National Archives and Records Administration National Personnel Records Center (NPRC), St. Louis, MO, copy in possession of author.

30 **same reprieve were white:** Lee, *Negro Troops*, 270.

31 **moved back in with his parents:** Honorable discharge for Donald Weddle, November 14, 1945, NPRC, copy in possession of author.

31 **its residents were white:** U.S. Census Bureau, 1950 Census, vol. 1, Number of Inhabitants, Michigan, table 6, "Population of Counties by Minor Civil Divisions: 1930 to 1950," p. 20, https://www2.census.gov/library /publications/decennial/1950/population-volume-1/vol-01-25.pdf. From 1930 to 1950, the year nearest to when Grandpa Don's parents moved there, Waterford Township's population increased from 8,239 to 24,316. While the Michigan census did not publish racial population data for Waterford in 1950, the 1940 and 1960 censuses strongly suggest that the township was almost entirely white. In 1940, Waterford had 27 Black residents. In 1960— after the overall population nearly quadrupled, to 47,107—the number of Black residents was 24.

31 **settling in its neighborhoods:** From 1930 to 1950, the number of Black residents in Pontiac went from 2,553 to 6,870, and their share of residents overall from 3.9 percent to 7.4 percent. See, respectively: U.S. Census Bureau, 1930 Census, vol. 3, Population Reports by States, Part 1: Alabama–Missouri, table 21, "Population by Sex, Color, Age, etc., for Counties by Minor Civil Divisions," p. 1177, https://www2.census.gov/library /publications/decennial/1930/population-volume-3/10612963v3p1ch09.pdf (hereafter cited as 1930 Census Michigan Population Reports, with table and page number); U.S Census Bureau, 1940 Census, vol. 2, Characteristics of the Population, Part 3: Kansas–Michigan, table 28, "Race and Age, by Sex, with Rural-Farm Population, for Minor Civil Divisions, by Counties," p. 856, https://www2.census.gov/library/publications/decennial/1940/population -volume-2/33973538v2p3ch7.pdf; U.S. Census Bureau, 1950 Census, vol. 2, Characteristics of the Population, Part 22: Michigan, General Characteristics, table 33, "Age by Color and Sex, for Standard Metropolitan Areas, Urbanized Areas, and Urban Places of 10,000 or More," p. 73, https://www2 .census.gov/library/publications/decennial/1950/population-volume-2 /37779850v2p22ch3.pdf (hereafter cited as 1950 Census Michigan Population Reports, with table and page number).

31 **intentional, fueled by developers:** Restrictions on Oakwood Manor,

Waterford, MI, August 31, 1940, liber 66, pp. 48–51, Oakland County Register of Deeds, Pontiac, MI.

31 **"owner or tenant," they read:** Deed for lot 77 of Oakwood Manor, Waterford, MI, July 12, 1940, liber 65, p. 458, Oakland County Register of Deeds, Pontiac, MI.

31 **member of the Black Legion:** "Harmon Fired by Commission," *Detroit Free Press*, April 14, 1934; "Identities of 86 Cult Members Bared by Jury," *Detroit Free Press*, September 2, 1936. Ransom was among the "cultists" unmasked; his name was printed in capital letters in the newspaper, along with those of all other government employees found to have been in the Black Legion.

31 **college graduates nationwide:** Katznelson, *Affirmative Action*, 114; "75 Years of the GI Bill: How Transformative It's Been," U.S. Department of Defense, January 9, 2019, https://www.defense.gov/News/Feature-Stories /story/Article/1727086/75-years-of-the-gi-bill-how-transformative-its-been/.

32 **approval of local, white officials:** Katznelson, *Affirmative Action*, 123– 26. Katznelson documents how John Rankin of Mississippi, a famously racist member of the House of Representatives, chaired the committee that crafted the G.I. Bill and put a great deal of effort into making sure that its benefits would not upset the system of white supremacy. "Your bill," Katznelson quotes from a letter to Rankin from a southern college director, "is particularly desirable to the Southern states" (125).

32 **to a college education:** Sarah Turner and John Bound, "Closing the Gap or Widening the Divide: The Effects of the G.I. Bill and World War II on the Educational Outcomes of Black Americans," *Journal of Economic History* 63, no. 1 (March 2003): 149; Katznelson, *Affirmative Action*, 132–33. Among veterans born between 1923 and 1928, 28 percent of white veterans enrolled in college-level training, compared to just 12 percent of Black veterans. This divide reflects not only prejudice on the part of administrators, but a systematic underinvestment in education for Black Americans. Higher education was segregated in the South as a matter of law, and in the North as a matter of practice, leaving fewer seats in classrooms than there were Black veterans interested in sitting in them.

32 **but of racial disparity, too:** "On balance, despite the assistance that black soldiers received, there was no greater instrument for widening an already huge racial gap in postwar America than the GI Bill." Katznelson, *Affirmative Action*, 121.

33 **house on Pontiac's east side:** In 1948, Donald E. and Katheryn C. Wed-

dle are listed in *Polk's Pontiac City Directory* as living at 42 N. Marshall Street in Pontiac. He is listed as working at Reliable Welding. There is no property deed for the Marshall Street property in the Weddle name, so the house must have been a rental.

34 **"second grade," referenced as "B":** HOLC area descriptions for Pontiac and other cities are available from Mapping Inequality: https://dsl.richmond .edu/panorama/redlining/#loc=5/39.1/-94.58&text=downloads. This description draws from the "area descriptions" for sectors B4, where my grandparents lived; D3, which lay to the east; and D6, which lay to the west. According to the census tally of their district, there is only one family whose race is not clearly marked as "W." U.S. Census Bureau, Population Schedule for Pontiac, MI, enumeration district 63–96, April 15, 1940, sheet 13A, lines 19–23.

Chapter 2: Katrina Rectenwald: Work

35 **catch up over wings and cocktails:** This account—and all of the narrative of Katrina and Jasmine in this chapter—is drawn from the many phone and in-person interviews I had with them, especially with Katrina, over the course of eighteen months, from 2021 to 2023. I have indicated where I used information from sources other than the interviews with Jasmine and Katrina.

38 **"racism" in all its work:** Service Employees International Union (SEIU) Resolution 106A, copy in possession of author. The relevant language of Resolution 106A, which was adopted by SEIU in 2016, can be found in any number of sources, perhaps most easily in a Supreme Court brief by SEIU. See: Brief of the National Educational Association and Service Employees International Union as Amici Curiae in Support of Respondents, Students for Fair Admissions v. Harvard, No. 20–1199 (U.S. August 8, 2022).

38 **Simms's job was to find one:** Tinselyn Simms (former assistant director of communications, SEIU), interview by the author, March 15, 2023.

39 **"by not addressing it?":** Ian Haney López, interview by the author, May 31, 2023.

39 **"extent of racial opposition":** Heather McGhee, interview by the author, June 12, 2023.

39 **"implicitly all the time":** Anat Shenker-Osorio, interview by the author, June 12, 2023.

40 **"themselves in," says McGhee:** McGhee, interview.

41 **meant simply not seeing race:** For a comprehensive description and analysis of this phenomenon, see Bonilla-Silva, *Racism Without Racists,*

particularly chapter 1, which sets out the basic framework, and chapter 2, which describes several typologies of the practice.

41 **"at the color of their skin":** Becky Rectenwald, interview by the author, November 10, 2021.

41 **race was biological:** Omi and Winant, *Racial Formation*, 23.

41 **extend the lives of the unfit:** Entman and Rojecki, *Black Image*, 249–52.

41 **were less intelligent than us:** Mildred Schwartz, *Trends in White Attitudes Toward Negroes* (Chicago: National Opinion Research Center, University of Chicago, 1967), 19.

42 **growing up was the "melting pot":** Omi and Winant, *Racial Formation*, 163.

42 **personal conduct and cultural norms:** Michael Omi (associate professor of ethnic studies, University of California, Berkeley), interview by the author, March 15, 2023.

42 **and race-as-culture held:** Omi, interview.

42 **"have to use that defense yet":** Matthew Lassiter (professor of history, University of Michigan), interview by the author, October 18, 2022.

42 **"I like to be colorblind":** *Equal Educational Opportunity: Hearings Before the Select Comm. on Equal Educational Opportunity, Second Session, Part 19B—Equal Educational Opportunity in Michigan*, 92nd Cong. 9869 (1971) (statement of Irene McCabe, chairman, National Action Group, Pontiac, MI).

43 **"cure discrimination with discrimination":** William Bradford Reynolds, "The Focus of Equal Employment Opportunity Programs Under the Reagan Administration" (paper, 4th Annual Conference on Equal Employment Opportunity: Recent Developments in Federal Regulations and Case Law, Civil Rights Division, Department of Justice, Washington, D.C., October 20, 1981), 3; Michael S. Sherrill, "Uncivil Times at Justless: Color-Blind or Blind to the Legacy of Color?" *Time*, May 13, 1985, https://content.time.com/time/subscriber/article/0,33009,968250,00.html.

43 **"the basis of race," wrote Roberts:** Parents Involved v. Seattle School Dist., 551 U.S. 701, 748 (2007).

44 **in a fair-share fee:** Gabe Kramer (former chief of staff, SEIU Healthcare Pennsylvania), email message to the author, December 14, 2022.

44 **found the chapter in 2000:** Zach Zobrist (chief of staff, SEIU Healthcare Pennsylvania), email message to the author, March 12, 2023.

44 **encouraging her to participate:** Cathy Stoddart, interviews by the author, March 11, 2022, March 14, 2023, and June 8, 2023.

44 **all white to 70 percent Black:** Stoddart, interviews.

44 **by the time she attended:** Casey Smith (communications director, PA Department of Education), email to Clarissa Léon (research assistant for the author), November 2022.

44 **battle with medical debt:** Stoddart, interviews; Matt Saxton, "Mingo Junction Steel Mill's Idle Days Could Be Numbered," *Intelligencer* (Wheeling, WV), November 21, 2018.

44 **family of five on fifty dollars a month:** Becky Rectenwald, interview.

45 **in fees and fines:** Becky Rectenwald, interview; Katrina Rectenwald, interview; Criminal Docket for Joseph Rectenwald, no. CP-25-CR-0001197–2003, Court of Common Pleas, Erie County, PA.

45 **while also working full time:** Stoddart, interviews.

45 **degree in 2010:** Transcript for Katrina Rectenwald, Allegheny Community College, copy in possession of author.

46 **also more than 80 percent white:** Molly Kinder, "Essential but Undervalued: Millions of Health Care Workers Aren't Getting the Pay or Respect They Deserve in the COVID-19 Pandemic," Brookings Institution, May 28, 2020, https://www.brookings.edu/research/essential-but-undervalued -millions-of-health-care-workers-arent-getting-the-pay-or-respect-they -deserve-in-the-covid-19-pandemic/.

47 **holding bias and acting on it:** Anthony Greenwald, T. Andrew Poehlman, Eric Luis Uhlmann, and Mahzarin Banaji, "Understanding and Using the Implicit Association Test: III. Meta-analysis of Predictive Validity," *Journal of Personality and Social Psychology* 97, no. 1 (2009): 32, https://psycnet.apa .org/doi/10.1037/a0015575. This paper reports that when people had higher scores of anti-Black bias, they were more likely to be unfriendly to Black interviewers, to vote for John McCain instead of Barack Obama, to laugh at anti-Black humor, and to rate it as funny. Indeed, the test is twice as likely to accurately predict racist behavior as traditional methods of measuring bias, like surveys.

47 **"more with Black Americans":** Tessa Charlesworth (postdoctoral student in psychology, Harvard University), email to Madysen Luebke (author's research assistant), May 2, 2023.

47 **and experience into account:** Jean Moore and Tracey Continelli, "Racial/Ethnic Pay Disparities Among Registered Nurses (RNs) in U.S. Hospitals: An Econometric Regression Decomposition," *Health Services Research* 51, no. 2 (April 2016): 522, https://doi.org/10.1111%2F1475-6773.12337.

47 **unionized nurses is "negligible":** Barry Hisch, David Macpherson, and William Even, "Union Membership and Coverage Database from the CPS,"

section 1, Historical Tables: Union Membership, Density and Employment, By Occupation: 1983–2022 (data for 2021, accessed April 17, 2023), http:// unionstats.com/occ/xls/occ_2021.xlsx; Richard Carey McGregory Jr., "An Analysis of Black-White Wage Differences in Nursing: Wage Gap or Wage Premium?" *Review of Black Political Economy* 40, no. 1 (2013): 35, https://doi .org/10.1007/s12114-011-9097-z.

48 **earned about the same:** Zobrist, email message.

48 **union events, staff took note:** Zobrist, interviews by the author, February 18, 2022, March 9, 2023, and June 15, 2023.

48 **an advocacy group:** Greenhouse, *Beaten Down, Worked Up*, 233–34

48 **unions at *their* jobs:** Daniel Massey (press contact, SEIU), interview by the author, May 30, 2023.

49 **technicians keeping people alive:** Pittsburgh City Council, *Report of the Wage Review Committee on the Impact of Raising Wages for Service Workers at Pittsburgh's Anchor Institutions,* December 8, 2015, https://apps.pittsburghpa .gov/district9/FINAL.Report_of_the_Wage_Review_Committee_12082015 _(1)_(1)_(1).pdf; "AGH's Service, Technical Workers Vote to Join Union," *Pittsburgh Post-Gazette,* June 3, 2015, https://www.post-gazette.com/business /healthcare-business/2015/06/04/Allegheny-General-Hospital-service -technical-workers-vote-to-join-SEIU-Healthcare-Pennsylvania-4/stories /201506040178.

49 **maybe eleven dollars an hour:** Pittsburgh City Council, *Report of Wage Review Committee.*

49 **"when people talk about it":** Zobrist, interviews.

50 **strengthening their own contract:** Zobrist, interviews.

50 **laser-focused on the nurses' wages:** Zobrist, interviews; Kristy Myers (organizer, SEIU Healthcare Pennsylvania), interview by the author, January 13, 2022.

50 **standards of care:** Stoddart, interviews.

50 **Zach invited Katrina to join:** Zobrist, interviews.

50 **had both grown up in:** Deed for [lot redacted] of ward 20, Pittsburgh, PA, May 12, 1981, Deed Book 6368, [page redacted], Allegheny County Division of Real Estate, Pittsburgh, PA.

51 **had passed to Ryan's dad:** Deed for [address redacted], Pittsburgh, PA, May 11, 1962, Deed Book 3991, [page redacted], Allegheny County Division of Real Estate, Pittsburgh, PA. Deed for lot [redacted] of West Liberty Plan, Pittsburgh, PA, May 4, 1981, Deed Book 7112, [page redacted], Allegheny County Division of Real Estate, Pittsburgh, PA.

51 **take over the family house?:** Kim and Jeff Allard (in-laws of Katrina Rectenwald-Allard), interview by the author, March 7, 2023.

51 **parents to pay her brother:** Becky Rectenwald, interview.

51 **once the mortgage is paid off:** Kim and Jeff Allard, interview.

52 **at the turn of the century:** "'New' Lawrenceville Is Coping with Its Own Success," *Pittsburgh Post-Gazette*, September 24, 2016.

52 **had students there, too:** Zach Zobrist, email message to the author, March 15, 2023; Garbie Dukes (labor class participant), interview by the author, March 7, 2023; Harold Grant (labor class participant), interview with the author, March 13, 2023.

52 **1920 mining strike in West Virginia:** Zobrist, interviews.

53 **"and them that don't":** "Union Speech," *Matewan*, directed by John Sayles (1987; New York: Criterion Collection, 2019), Blu-ray Disc.

53 **in the city nearly doubled:** U.S. Census Bureau, 1910 Census, Census Bulletin no. 92, Population by Sex, Nativity, and Color, by Groups of States and Territories, group 9, Pennsylvania, Rhode Island, South Carolina, and South Dakota, table 5, "Native and Foreign Born and White and Colored Population, Classified by Sex, for Places Having 2,500 Inhabitants or More," p. 7, https://www2.census.gov/library/publications/decennial/1900/bulletins/demographic/92-population-sex-nativity-color-pa-ri-sc-sd.pdf; Trotter and Day, *Race and Renaissance*, 203.

53 **Black men as strikebreakers:** Foner, *Organized Labor*, 144.

53 **compared to Pittsburgh:** Trotter and Day, *Race and Renaissance*, 9; Kelley, *Hammer and Hoe*, 1.

54 **"yourself and your buddies":** Nelson Lichtenstein, interview with author, October 18, 2022.

54 **as if it were private property:** *Status of Negroes in Craft Unions . . . Pittsburgh Labor Market: A Special Report of Mayor's Commission on Human Relations*, p. 2, box 15, folder 21, Subseries 18: Mayor's Commission on Human Relations, 1964–1966, Series IV: Reports on Pittsburgh (city), 1910–1985, Pittsburgh Public Administration Reports and Studies, University of Pittsburgh.

54 **the historian Joe Trotter:** Trotter and Day, *Race and Renaissance*, 51.

54 **Black workers in construction unions:** "Job Protest Spurs Pittsburgh Clash," *New York Times*, August 27, 1969; "City's Protesters Taking a Break Over Labor Day," *Pittsburgh Post-Gazette*, August 30, 1969; *What Does Trouble Mean?: Nate Smith's Revolution*, directed by Jim Seguin (Pittsburgh: Center for Documentary Production and Film Study, Robert Morris University, 2009), DVD.

54 **were 100 percent white:** Dubinsky, *Trade Union Discrimination*, 24.

54 **and 20 percent Black:** U.S. Census Bureau, 1970 Census, vol. 1, General Population Characteristics, part 40, Pennsylvania, section 1, table 24, "Age by Race and Sex, for Areas and Places," p. 129, https://www2.census.gov/library /publications/decennial/1970/population-volume-1/00496492v1p40s1ch3 .pdf.

54 **any Black apprentices at all:** Dubinsky, *Trade Union Discrimination*, 24.

55 **"'these people,'" says Lichtenstein:** Lichtenstein, interview.

55 **were 100 percent white:** "Bethlehem Steel Faces Rights Test," *New York Times*, February 10, 1973; Foner, *Organized Labor*, 430–31.

55 **blast furnace, the coke oven:** *Struggles in Steel*, directed by Ray Henderson and Tony Buba (San Francisco: California Newsreel, 1996), Vimeo, 9:17, https:// vimeo.com/ondemand/strugglesinsteel; Foner, *Organized Labor*, 430.

55 **fired when layoffs arrived:** Foner, *Organized Labor*, 430; Needleman, *Black Freedom Fighters*, 211–12.

55 **"actually it's structured":** Lichtenstein, interview.

55 **the benefits of union membership:** Joe Rectenwald, interview by the author, November 16, 2021.

55 **protesting *against* integration:** Becky Rectenwald, interview.

56 **family size—functionally poor:** *Occupational Outlook Handbook* (Washington, D.C.: Bureau of Labor Statistics, May 1992), 418; Pew Income Data. In 1990, the year closest to when Joe got his journeyman's book for which there is data, the median income for an excavation machine operator was $430 a week, or $17,200 for a 40-week year (most heavy construction workers do not have work the whole year). Becky would cut hair at home a couple times a month, charging $5 a cut. She'd pick up work with a friend's catering business maybe once a month, earning, she remembers, $50 for a twelve-hour shift. A rough estimate would put their combined income at $18,640. Census data analyzed by the Pew Research Center puts the national median income for a family of six that year at $47,744, putting the Rectenwalds' income at well below half of the median—a rough proxy for poverty.

56 **"don't feel bad in any way":** Becky Rectenwald, interview by the author, March 7, 2023..

56 **even in hospitals:** Susan Kocin, "Basic Provisions of the 1966 FLSA Amendments," *Monthly Labor Review* 90, no. 3 (March 1967): 1; Fair Labor Standards Act of 1938, Pub. L. No. 718, §13(a), 52 Stat. 1060, 1067 (1938).

56 **right to organize unions, too:** Fox, *Three Worlds of Relief*, 262; Juan F. Perea, "The Echoes of Slavery: Recognizing the Racist Origins of the Agri-

cultural and Domestic Worker Exclusion from the National Labor Relations Act," *Ohio State Law Journal* 72, no. 1 (2011): 96n2.

56 **or service jobs:** U.S. Census Bureau, 1940 Census, vol. 2, Characteristics of the Population, part 1, United States Summary, table 22, Population by Race with Individual Minor Races, by Divisions and States, p. 52, https://www2.census.gov/library/publications/decennial/1940/population -volume-2/33973538v2p1ch2.pdf; U.S. Census Bureau, 1940 Census, vol. 3, The Labor Force, part 1, United States Summary, table 4, Employment Status of the Population, by Race and Sex, for the United States by Regions, p. 18, https://www2.census.gov/library/publications/decennial/1940/population -volume-3/33973538v3p1ch2.pdf. In 1940, Black workers accounted for 35.7 percent of all workers in the South—but they were clustered in service work and agriculture. That year, Black workers accounted for 32.9 percent of all service workers other than domestic and protective (i.e. firefighters and police) service, 39.4 percent of general laborers, 48.3 percent of all farmers and farm managers, 69.4 percent of domestic workers, and 72.0 percent of farm laborers. With the exception of general laborers, all of these industries were excluded from the labor protections of the New Deal.

56 **during debate on the bill:** 82 Cong. Rec. 1404 (1937).

57 **"to apply to domestic help":** Transcript of Press Conference #447, April 1, 1938, Series 1: Press Conference Transcripts, Press Conferences of President Franklin D. Roosevelt, 1933–1945, Franklin D. Roosevelt Presidential Library and Museum, Poughkeepsie, NY, http://www.fdrlibrary.marist.edu /_resources/images/pc/pc0064.pdf.

57 **"I just can't take that risk":** William F. Pinar, "The N.A.A.C.P. and the Struggle for Antilynching Legislation, 1897–1917," *Counterpoints* 163 (2001): 727, https://www.jstor.org/stable/42977760; White, *Man Called White*, 168–70.

57 **46 percent of Black workers overall:** Marc Linder, "Farm Workers and the Fair Labor Standards Act: Racial Discrimination in the New Deal," *Texas Law Review* 65 (1987): 1366. Linder's authoritative study of farmworkers and labor protections over time documents that, by 1940, only 53 percent of Black workers were covered by Social Security. Drawing on an unpublished dissertation from 1939, Linder also documents that in 1930, 54 percent of Black male workers and 87 percent of Black female workers were excluded by the Social Security Act.

57 **old-age protection:** Fox, *Three Worlds of Relief*, 270.

57 **the right to minimum wages:** Winant, *Next Shift*, 157; Fair Labor Standards Amendments of 1974, Pub. Law No. 93–259, §7, 88 Stat. 55, 62, (1974).

57 **lower, to a "tipped" wage:** Kocin, "1966 FLSA Amendments," 1; Kai Filion and Sylvia Allegretto, *Waiting for Change: The $2.13 Federal Subminimum Wage* (Washington, D.C.: Economic Policy Institute, February 23, 2011), https://www.epi.org/publication/waiting_for_change_the_213_federal _subminimum_wage/.

58 **to the house for dinner:** Joe Rectenwald, interview.

58 **best friend, who is Black:** Becky Rectenwald, interview.

58 **workers starting in 1970:** Trotter and Day, *Race and Renaissance*, 112.

58 **writes historian Gabriel Winant:** Winant, *Next Shift*, 183.

58 **Pittsburgh lost 133,000 jobs:** Bill Toland, "In Desperate 1983, There Was Nowhere for Pittsburgh's Economy to Go but Up," *Pittsburgh Post-Gazette*, December 23, 2012, https://www.post-gazette.com/business /businessnews/2012/12/23/In-desperate-1983-there-was-nowhere-for -Pittsburgh-s-economy-to-go-but-up/stories/201212230258.

58 **before Katrina was born:** Toland, "In Desperate 1983."

58 **had taken the place of industry:** Fuchs, *Service Economy*, xxiii. In 1968, U.S. health economist Victor Fuchs coined the term "service economy" to describe the economy that had emerged in the United States after World War II.

59 **women had provided at home:** Winant, *Next Shift*, 160, 180–81, 206–07, 214.

59 **mental illness all spiked:** Winant, *Next Shift*, 187–88, 200. Economists documented a 10-to-15 percent increase in the mortality rate in the Pittsburgh region following the collapse of steel, while other researchers documented an increase in alcohol-related offenses and domestic violence in the same era.

59 **185,000 jobs in health care:** Winant, *Next Shift*, 7.

59 **near the bottom of the income ladder:** Kinder, "Essential but Undervalued."

59 **and $24,755, respectively:** Bianca K. Frogner and Malaika Schwartz, "Examining Wage Disparities by Race and Ethnicity of Health Care Workers," *Medical Care* 59, no. 10, S5 (October 2021): table 2, https://doi.org/10 .1097%2FMLR.0000000000001613. In 2018, white nursing aides earned an average of $24,809 and $24,755. According to the Bureau of Labor Statistics, that is the equivalent of $29,944 and $29,879 in January 2023. While the study of health care wages cited here was made considerably later than Katrina's early years in health care—when her earnings, in 2023, were equal to roughly $31,000—I believe it provides a useful point of comparison.

60 **that assumed low wages:** Winant, *Next Shift*, 138, 243–44.

63 **Squirrel Hill and Point Breeze:** "The Pittsburgh Neighborhood

Disadvantage Map," Pittsburgh Neighborhood Project, June 9, 2020, https://pittsburghneighborhoodproject.blog/2020/06/09/the-pittsburgh-neighborhood-disadvantage-map/.

63   **grow up in poor families:** Sharkey, *Stuck in Place*, 113.

64   **for help as they age:** Joe Rectenwald, interview.

Chapter 3: My Parents' Childhoods

66   **likely describes them, too:** U.S. Census Bureau, Current Population Reports, Consumer Income, series P-60, no. 9, March 25, 1952, Income of Families and Persons in the United States: 1950, table 4, Distribution of Families and Unrelated Individuals by Total Money Income and Major Source of Earnings, by Size of Family, for the Unites States: 1950, p. 24, https://www.census.gov/library/publications/1952/demo/p60-009.html; *Occupational Outlook Handbook* (Washington, D.C.: Bureau of Labor Statistics, May 1951), 214; Pew Income Data. The Weddle family had five members in 1952. In 1949, the closest year for which data is available, the national median income for a family of five was $3,687.00 and the national median income for a Class A welder in a city was $3,421.60. That is just over 92 percent of the median income, likely placing the Weddles in the lowest tier of the middle class, but out of poverty.

66   **"Caucasian race" from living there:** Declaration of Use and Building Restrictions for Seminole Hills Subdivision, Pontiac, MI, October 4, 1945, liber 1825, pp. 224–29, Oakland County Register of Deeds, Pontiac, MI.

66   **fifteen years earlier:** Robert K. Nelson et al., "Mapping Inequality," https://dsl.richmond.edu/panorama/redlining/#loc=13/42.643/-83.334&city=pontiac-mi&area=A3.

67   **since filing its first case in 1909:** Vose, *Caucasians Only*, ix.

67   **the tools you needed:** Katznelson, *Affirmative Action*, 124, 140.

67   **debate over the bill:** 90 Cong. Rec. 4339, 4342 (Statements of Rep. Rankin).

68   **homes from 1946 to 1951:** McGhee, *Sum of Us*, 81; Katznelson, *Affirmative Action*, 115–16, 208n11; Grebler, *Federal Credit Aids*, 68.

68   **to assess homes, would approve:** Rothstein, *Color of Law*, 70.

68   **without government help:** Brown, *Whiteness of Wealth*, 66.

68   **went to Black homebuyers:** Community Relations Program, American Friends Service Committee, *Equal Opportunity in Housing*, March 1955, p. 7, Loren Miller Papers, box 26, folder, 15, Huntington Library, San Marino, CA.

68 **38 percent of Black Americans:** F. John Devaney, *Tracking the American Dream: 50 Years of Housing History from the Census Bureau: 1940 to 1990*, Current Housing Reports, Series H121/94–1 (Washington, D.C.: Government Printing Office, 1994), 29.

69 **limit nonwhite student admissions:** Sarah Turner and John Bound, "Closing the Gap or Widening the Divide: The Effects of the G.I. Bill and World War II on the Educational Outcomes of Black Americans," *Journal of Economic History* 63, no. 1 (March 2003): 147n5; Katznelson, *Affirmative Action*, 129–30.

69 **8 percent of Black men:** Olson, *G.I. Bill*, 74; Charles G. Bolte and Louis Harris, *Our Negro Veterans,* Public Affairs Pamphlet, No. 128. 1947, cited in Turner and Bound, "Closing the Gap," 152–53; Thomas Snyder, ed., "120 Years of American Education: A Statistical Portrait," National Center for Education Statistics, Office of Educational Research and Improvement, U.S. Department of Education, January 1993, 18–19.

69 **"almost exclusively for whites":** Katznelson, *Affirmative Action*, 114.

69 **Oneida with its help:** "75 Years of the GI Bill: How Transformative It's Been," U.S. Department of Defense, January 9, 2019, https: //www.defense .gov/News/Feature-Stories/story/Article/1727086/75-years-of-the-gi-bill -how-transformative-its-been/. The site notes that about eight million veterans took advantage of the bill in the first seven years after its passage.

69 **nearly half of all new homes:** Grebler, *Federal Credit Aids*, 17.

69 **significantly after the war:** Bruce Annett (vice president, marketing and public affairs, Lawrence Tech.), email message to the author, August 16, 2019.

70 **"Fractured spine, ruptured liver, shock":** Death certificate for Harley Nichols, September 13, 1952, copy in possession of author.

70 **news story in the local paper:** "City Man Dies from Injuries," *Pontiac Daily Press*, September 11, 1952.

70 **my great-grandfather's funeral:** "Pontiac City Workers Connected with Black Legion, Ex-Police-Chief Says," *Detroit Free Press*, May 25, 1936; "Dismissed Cultist Upheld in Sermon," *Detroit Free Press*, December 7, 1936; "Sermon Stirs Pontiac Anew," *Detroit Free Press*, December 8, 1936; "Pontiac Ousts Cultist Leader," *Detroit Free Press*, September 12, 1936.

70 **up to $7,500 for its members:** United Automobile, Aerospace, and Agricultural Implement Workers of America, *Thirty-Three Years of Progress* (Pontiac, MI: UAW Local 594, 1972), Bentley Historical Library, Ann Arbor, MI. In 1950, UAW Local 594 added life and accidental death insurance coverage to its

members' benefits. The same contract also introduced pensions for workers and added coverage for hospitalization.

71 **facilities were "inherently unequal":** Brown v. Board of Education, 347 U.S. 496 (1954). The following year, after seeing that *Brown* was largely ignored, the court was even more explicit in *Brown II*, stating, "Racial discrimination in public education is unconstitutional" (348 U.S. 298). Unfortunately, the justices also urged the integration of schools "with all deliberate speed" (348 U.S. 301), a notoriously vague phrase that allowed most southern school districts to "deliberate" and delay for at least a decade, until the Civil Rights Act of 1964 allowed the federal government to force schools to comply.

71 **for their own children:** According to a Gallup poll, "nearly two out of three Northern white persons approved of the Supreme Court decision [to end school segregation], they were split on the issue of wanting their children to attend a school where a majority of the pupils were Negro." "Integration Gets Firm Backing of Public Today," *Detroit Free Press*, August 29, 1958.

71 **and 16.7 percent Black:** 1930 Census Michigan Population Reports, table 21, p. 1177; 1950 Census Michigan Population Reports, table 33, p. 73; U.S. Census Bureau, 1960 Census, vol. 1, Characteristics of the Population, part 24, Michigan, table 21, "Characteristics of the Population, for Standard Metropolitan Statistical Areas, Urbanized Areas, and Urban Places of 10,000 or More," p. 82, https://www2.census.gov/library/publications/decennial /1960/population-volume-1/37722966v1p24ch3.pdf. In 1930, Pontiac had 61,529 white residents, 2,553 Black residents, and 846 residents categorized as other. In 1950, Pontiac had 85,585 white residents, 6,870 Black residents, and 118 residents categorized as other. In 1960, Pontiac had 68,256 white residents, 13,744 Black residents, and 203 residents categorized as other.

71 **prepare for integrated schools:** "It's a Problem in Facing Fact," *Detroit Free Press*, August 29, 1958.

72 **Central High School for nine months:** "1958 School Blast United a Divided Tennessee Town," *Los Angeles Times*, October 16, 1988; "Ike Orders Troops to Leave Little Rock May 29," *Detroit Free Press*, May 9, 1958.

72 **part of the city:** U.S. Census Bureau, 1960 Censuses of Population and Housing, vol. 3, Census Tracts for Detroit, MI, table P-1, p. 70, tract OA-0088, https://www2.census.gov/library/publications/decennial/1960/population -and-housing-phc-1/41953654v3ch06.pdf.

72 **yielded $3,100 in profit:** Deed for lot 92 of Seminole Hills, Pontiac, MI, June 16, 1960, liber 4085, p. 849, Oakland County Register of Deeds, Pontiac, MI.

72 **fifteen miles west:** Mortgage for Pine Lot Estates lot 14, August 14, 1961, liber 4216, p. 110, Oakland County Register of Deeds, Pontiac, MI.

72 **homebuyers in mortgage lending:** "15 Guilty in Sit-In," *Detroit Free Press*, December 13, 1963.

72 **"who require the 'right' address":** Brochure for Pine Lake Estates, copy in possession of author.

73 **99.3 percent, were white:** Bloomfield Hills High School, *Hillcrest*, 1963.

73 **cowboys and Indians the next:** These descriptions of my father's childhood are drawn from photos and other ephemera in my possession.

73 **become a branch manager:** Letter from Bill [last name unknown] to John A. McMillan, November 1, 1954, copy in possession of author.

73 **white men until 1972:** R. E. Reichert, "Ann Arbor Bank Announces Major Changes at Three Bank Offices," undated press release, copy in possession of author; Kelly Bouchard, "Maine Civil Rights Figure Recalls Prom Protest," *Portland Press Herald*, August 26, 2013; Moose Lodge No. 107 v. Irvis, 407 U.S. 163 (1972). Even after *Moose Lodge v. Irvis*, many "lodge" organizations ignored the Supreme Court's order to desegregate; in 2001, the *Times* reported on an Elks group in Norwich, NY, that rejected Black applicants: "No Room at the Lodge," *New York Times*, January 7, 2001.

73 **into the upper-middle class:** Pew Income Data; *Occupational Outlook Handbook: 1961 Edition* (Washington, D.C.: Bureau of Labor Statistics, 1961), 601. The Department of Labor indicated that junior executives at large city banks would start their executive career around $10,000 a year, eventually reaching "more than twice that figure." Given that my grandfather was serving as a junior executive in the post of junior cashier, and had been in banking for more than thirty years at that point, I feel $15,000 is a fair ballpark estimate. The same year, the national median income for a family of three was $5,793.00, putting my father's childhood family at 259 percent of median income and well into the upper-middle class.

74 **"didn't make sense to me":** John McMillan, interview by the author, Bonnie McMillan and Matthew Van Meter present; February 19, 2022 (hereafter cited as JM interview, February 2022).

75 **he had won a football scholarship:** JM interview, February 2022; Transcript for John McMillan, John Carroll University, 1966, copy in possession of author.

76 **instituting a random lottery:** JM interview, February 2022; Transcript for John McMillan; Haney López, *Dog Whistle Politics*, 24; Congressional

Budget Office, "The All-Volunteer Military: Issues and Performance," CBO, July 1, 2007, p. 5, https://www.cbo.gov/sites/default/files/110th-congress -2007-2008/reports/07-19-militaryvol_0.pdf.

76 **under sketches of the constellations:** JM interview, February 2022.

76 **early 1973, he came home:** Honorable discharge for John McMillan, February 3, 1973, copy in possession of author.

76 **count on his parents for emergencies:** JM interview, February 2022.

76 **more wealth to share with him:** Comm. on Veterans Affairs, S. Rep. No. 93–18, at 105 (1973); Amitabh Chandra, "Labor-Market Dropouts and the Racial Wage Gap: 1940–1990," *American Economic Review* 90, no. 2 (May 2000): 336; Francine D. Blau and John W. Graham, "Black-White Differences in Wealth and Asset Composition," *Quarterly Journal of Economics* 105, no. 2 (May 1990): 323, 327, 336.

77 **their next meeting, and went:** JM interview, February 2022.

77 **she dropped out:** This and subsequent descriptions of my mother's young adulthood are drawn from photos, journals, yearbooks, transcripts, and other ephemera in my possession.

77 **who died in 1971:** Death notice for Bert Weddle, *Daily Journal*, January 13, 1971.

77 **the rest of her life:** Bonnie McMillan (née Huston), co-interview with John McMillan, conducted by the author with Matthew Van Meter present, March 2, 2023 (hereafter cited as JM and BM interview, March 2023).

77 **about $510 a year:** Undergraduate Catalog 1971–1972, *Eastern Michigan University Bulletin* 61, no. 1 (May 1971): 14, https://commons.emich.edu/cgi /viewcontent.cgi?article=1148&context=catalog.

78 **An antisorority sorority, Barb said:** Barb Stevens, interview by the author, August 11, 2019.

78 **called themselves the Beavers:** Kappa Beaver Sigma Pledge Book, February 1973, copy in possession of author; Barb Stevens, interview by the author, August 12, 2019. The "official song" of the Beavers goes: "I'm a Kappa Beaver Sigma, / A kappa Beaver all the way, / A real live shooter from the crotch on down, / We're always good for a lay. / Brown and yellow are our colors, / The dandelion's our flower true (our flower true) / Soooooo sock it to me / One more time— / Don't you wish you were a Beaver, too!"

79 **it had more than tripled:** NCES, Digest of Education Statistics 2007, table 320, "Average Undergraduate Tuition and Fees and Room and Board Rates Charged for Full-Time Students in Degree-Granting Institutions, by

Type and Control of Institution: 1964–65 Through 2006–07," https://nces.ed
.gov/programs/digest/d07/tables/dt07_320.asp; Jennifer Ma, Matea Pender,
and CJ Libassi, "Trends in College Pricing and Student Aid 2020," College
Board, October 2020, p. 10, https://research.collegeboard.org/media/pdf
/trends-college-pricing-student-aid-2020.pdf. In 1970–71, when both my parents were working on their degrees, the average "sticker price" for a year of
public university tuition was $478—the equivalent in January 2023 of $3,593.
By the time I headed to college in 1994, it had risen to $5,859 after adjusting
for inflation. In 2020, one year of public, four-year college tuition averaged
$12,077 after adjusting for inflation.

79 **"fees from students and families":** Claudio Sanchez, "How the Cost of
College Went from Affordable to Sky-High," NPR, March 18, 2014, https://
www.npr.org/2014/03/18/290868013/how-the-cost-of-college-went-from
-affordable-to-sky-high.

79 **two-thirds to one-third:** Sanchez, "Cost of College"; President's Commission on Higher Education, Higher Education for American Democracy, vol.
1 (Washington, D.C.: Government Printing Office, 1947), 25, 47.

79 **the cost of school:** Sanchez, "Cost of College"; President's Commission on
Higher Education, 25, 47; Brian Haynes, "Black Undergraduates in Higher
Education: An Historical Perspective," *Metropolitan Universities* 17, no. 2
(2006): 13; NCES, Digest 2013, "Fall Enrollment, 1947 through 2023." NCES
does not report race for 1950, but it records a total of 2,281,298 students at
degree-granting postsecondary institutions in 1950, and Haynes writes that,
in that year, there were 76,600 Black college students, or 3.36 percent of the
total.

79 **One-quarter of students needed loans:** NCES, Digest of Education Statistics 1994, table 33, "Estimated Total Expenditures of Educational Institutions, by Level, Control of Institution, and Source of Funds: 1975–76 to
1991–92," 37; NCES, Digest of Education Statistics 2020, table 306.10, "Total
Fall Enrollment in Degree-Granting Postsecondary Institutions, by Level
of Enrollment, Sex, Attendance Status, and Race/Ethnicity or Nonresident
Alien Status of Student: Selected Years, 1976 through 2018," https://nces
.ed.gov/programs/digest/d19/tables/dt19_306.10.asp.

79 **Half of students needed loans:** CBO, "The Volume and Repayment of Federal Student Loans: 1995 to 2017," November 2020, https://www.cbo.gov
/publication/56754; NCES, Digest of Education Statistics 2013, table 303.10,
"Total Fall Enrollment in Degree-Granting Postsecondary Institutions,
by Attendance Status, Sex of Student, and Control of Institution: Selected

Years, 1947 through 2023," https://nces.ed.gov/programs/digest/d13/tables /dt13_303.10.asp.

79 **80 percent of nonwhite students:** Mark Huelsman, "The Debt Divide: The Racial and Class Bias Behind the 'New Normal' of Student Borrowing," Demos, May 19, 2015, https://www.demos.org/research/debt-divide-racial -and-class-bias-behind-new-normal-student-borrowing.

79 **political power became clear:** Haney López, *Dog Whistle Politics*, 48.

80 **Haney López calls "strategic racism":** "George Wallace, Segregation Symbol, Dies at 79," *New York Times*, September 14, 1998; Haney López, *Dog Whistle Politics*, 48.

80 **deserved help were receiving it:** Haney López, *Dog Whistle Politics*, 30.

80 **everyone was on their own:** American National Election Studies (ANES), Top Tables, "Government Guaranteed Job and Standard of Living, yes/no 1956–2002," accessed June 3, 2022, https://electionstudies.org /resources/anes-guide/second-tables/?id=144m; ANES, Second Tables, "Government Guaranteed Job and Standard of Living, yes/no by Mode," accessed June 3, 2022, https://electionstudies.org/resources/anes-guide/top -tables/?id=33. Hat tip to Heather McGhee for her discussion of this. N.b.: ANES recently removed the above tables from its website, but spreadsheet-savvy readers may find the data at https://electionstudies.org/data-center /anes-time-series-cumulative-data-file/.

81 **and the Allman Brothers Band:** "Billboard Hot 100 for Week of October 27, 1973," Billboard, accessed April 9, 2023, https://www.billboard.com /charts/hot-100/1973-10-27/.

81 **was there when they met:** Derek Spinei, "Plenty of Elbow Room," *Ypsilanti Gleanings* (Fall 2010): 21.

81 **no plan beyond that:** JM interview, February 2022. The scenes of the early years of my parents' relationship are drawn from dozens of photos and personal papers in my possession in addition to the cited interviews.

82 **Burger King on the way home:** JM interview, February 2022.

82 **appeared in the local paper:** JM interview, February 2022.

82 **approved of the match more easily:** Barb Stevens, interview, August 11, 2019.

83 **a mishap of scheduling:** Barb Stevens, interview, August 11, 2019.

83 **loved—and married—him anyway:** Barb Stevens, personal communication with the author, July 13, 2013. I did not record this informal meeting, but I have contemporaneous notes written shortly thereafter.

84 **buy the booze for the reception:** JM interview, February 2022.

84 **pay for the wedding:** JM interview, February 2022.

85 **help from my father's parents:** JM interview, February 2022; James Durston, "Best of Boeing: 10 Revolutionary Aircraft," CNN, June 4, 2012. Durston quotes aviation journalist Tom Ballantyne, who points out that long-haul international travel was not made affordable until the Boeing 747 first flew in 1970.

85 **hard work and careful spending:** JM interview, February 2022.

85 **their father's house in Waterford:** Land contract for lot 56 of Oakwood Manor, Waterford, MI, June 12, 1974, liber 6324, p. 796, Oakland County Register of Deeds, Pontiac, MI.

85 **and illegal for eight:** Rothstein, *Color of Law*, 85; "History of Fair Housing," U.S. Department of Housing and Urban Development, accessed April 9, 2023, https://www.hud.gov/program_offices/fair_housing_equal_opp /aboutfheo/history.

85 **remained all-white:** U.S. Census Bureau, 1970 Census of Population and Housing, part 6, Census Tracts for Detroit, MI, General Characteristics of the Population, table p-1, tract 1106.01, p. 22, https://www2.census.gov/library /publications/decennial/1970/phc-1/39204513p6ch09.pdf. (Hereafter cited as 1970 Census Tracts for Detroit SMSA, with tract number and page.)

85 **same home would in a mixed-race neighborhood:** Junia Howell and Elizabeth Korver-Glenn, "The Increasing Effect of Neighborhood Racial Composition on Housing Values, 1980–2015," *Social Problems* 68, no. 4 (2021): 1052.

85 **equivalent of $256,798 in 2023:** Land contract for Oakwood Manor lot 56, Waterford, MI, June 12, 1974, liber 6324, pp. 796–97, Oakland County Register of Deeds, Pontiac, MI.

85 **split the proceeds down the middle:** Order Allowing Final Account and for Distribution of Residuary Assets, In re The Estate of Bert Weddle, deceased, December 27, 1974, Oakland County Probate Court, no. 104,798, liber 6414, pp. 707–08, Oakland County Register of Deeds, Pontiac, MI.

85 **paying off their mortgage:** *Occupational Outlook Handbook: 1972–1973 Edition* (Washington, D.C.: Bureau of Labor Statistics, 1973), 499; Pew Income Data.

86 **wouldn't've even entered my mind:** John McMillan, JM and BM interview, March 2023.

Chapter 4: Lindsey and Maryann Becker: School

88 **Rosie and Lewis, Lindsey's father, noticed, too:** This passage and subsequent accounts of the Becker family's experiences, unless otherwise cited, are

drawn from multiple interviews with members of the family: Lindsey, Mary-ann, Lewis, and Rosie (all pseudonyms, as noted in the chapter), and also on private documents and papers I reviewed, such as photos and college transcripts.

88 **after all, was majority Black:** This and all subsequent accounts of school demographics in Hattiesburg and the state of Mississippi were calculated from a database created by the author (hereafter cited as Author's Education Database). The data was drawn from a number of public and private sources, as follows: For individual schools in Hattiesburg, 1970–1987, data was drawn from a 1987 report filed with the U.S. District Court for the Southern District of Mississippi as part of ongoing proceedings in *United States v. State of Mississippi* (Civil Action No. 4706) and available at the National Archives in Atlanta. Data for individual facilities in Magee Schools was drawn from the *Directory of Public Elementary and Secondary Day Schools, 1968–69*, available from the National Center for Educational Statistics. For districtwide and statewide data on public schools, data was drawn from four sources: (1) Most years before 1970 were drawn from various editions of the *Mississippi Biennial Report of the State Superintendent of Education*, available in hard copy and microfilm at the Mississippi Department of Archives and History in Jackson (MDAH). (2) For many years from 1960–1970, data was drawn from the Mississippi State Department of Education's *Ten Year Trend Study on Local School Districts 1960–61 Through 1969–70*, which is available in hard copy at MDAH. (3) Some gaps were filled with data from the Urban Institute's Education Data Explorer, at educationdata.urban.org/data-explorer. (4) Some hard-to-find data about 1969 in Hattiesburg and 1969–1970 statewide was drawn from the archival research notes of Charles Bolton for his book, *The Hardest Deal of All*, which were generously shared with me by Bolton. For more information, visit whitebonus.com.

88 **city residents were Black:** Author's Education Database; U.S. Census Bureau, 1990 Census, CP-1, General Population Characteristics, part 26, Mississippi, table 6, "Race and Hispanic Origin," p. 25, https://www2.census.gov/library/publications/decennial/1990/cp-1/cp-1-26.pdf.

89 **they were in the 1960s:** Sean F. Reardon and Ann Owens, "60 Years After *Brown*: Trends and Consequences of School Segregation," *Annual Review of Sociology* 40 (July 2014): 215, https://doi.org/10.1146/annurev-soc-071913-043152. This study found that while segregation in schools had decreased from the mid-1960s through the early 1970s, "school racial segregation has changed little" between the 1970s and the date of the study.

90   **Hattiesburg did nothing to integrate:** "Stupid Decision," *Hattiesburg American*, May 17, 1954.

91   **to preserve racial segregation:** Bolton, *Hardest Deal*, 68–69.

91   **to provide "equal" ones:** Bolton, *Hardest Deal*, 33.

91   **than per Black student:** Author's Education Database; Stephanie Rolph (associate professor of history, focused on the American South, at Millsaps College) interview by the author, March 21, 2023. The spending in Hatties-burg Schools reflects the fact that public education in Mississippi has long been deeply underfunded for all students, of all races. "When *Brown v. Board of Education* is decided, no Mississippians are getting a quality education—not really. The system itself is underfunded across the board, but Black schools are even more horrifically underfunded," Rolph, a historian whose work focuses on mid-century Mississippi, told me. Indeed, some of the leading opponents of school integration in Mississippi were hostile to public education for Black and white residents alike, as a "way to keep them satisfied with the low wages and with the status quo is to not let them get too well educated."

91   **first, if modest, decline:** Author's Education Database.

91   **Hattiesburg adopted it in 1965:** "'Freedom of Choice' Decisions Today," *Hattiesburg American*, September 1, 1965.

92   **enrolling twenty students that year:** "Dedication Ceremony Sched-uled Sunday at Beeson Academy," *Hattiesburg American*, April 11, 1969.

92   **"manifestation of massive resistance":** Bolton, *Hardest Deal*, 140n41.

92   **ended the practice by 1970:** Bolton, *Hardest Deal*, 126n17.

92   **a few of its schools:** Alexander v. Holmes County Board of Education, 396 U.S. 19, 20 (1969) (per curiam: "no person is to be effectively excluded from any school because of race or color"). In a case with the same name decided earlier in 1969, Justice Black wrote, "There is no longer the slightest excuse, reason, or justification for further postponement of the time when every public school system in the United States will be a unitary one, receiv-ing and teaching students without discrimination on the basis of their race or color," 396 U.S. 1218, 1221 (1969).

92   **more than 80 percent white:** Author's Education Database.

92   **the district, put it to me:** Tracy Williams, interview by the author, December 11, 2022.

92   **two high schools in 1971:** Author's Education Database; U.S. v. Miss., 622 F.Supp. at 623. In 1970, prior to the start of integration in Hattiesburg's public schools, Davis, Eaton, and Walthall elementaries were 55.6 percent, 48.1 percent, and 49.1 percent white, and Hawkins Jr. High was 49.9 white.

Four of the remaining elementaries were more than 90 percent Black (Love, Jones, Eureka, Bethune), and the other four were more than 80 percent white (Camp, Grace Christian, Thames, Woodley). Burney Jr. High was 98.5 percent Black, while Thames Jr. High was 93.4 percent white; Rowan High School was 97.6 percent Black, and Blair High School was 80.6 percent white.

93 **handful of schools reflected that mix:** Author's Education Database.

93 **putting down just $1,500:** Deed for Becker home, Hattiesburg, MS, September 16, 1992, Lamar County Chancery Clerk, Purvis, MS. A down payment of $1,500 is drawn from the recollections of Rose Becker, who also remembers using an FHA loan that required a 3 percent down payment for that purchase. Provided Becker has correctly remembered the percentage, the amount is likely in the ballpark of the actual down payment. The mortgage for the property in question was $50,083. If that amount is 97 percent of the purchase price, the house price would have been $51,632—a difference of $1,548.96.

93 **bought a larger home:** Deed for Becker home, Hattiesburg, MS, October 15, 1992, Lamar County Chancery Clerk, Purvis, MS.

93 **"for white flight reasons":** Rose Becker, interview by the author, September 7, 2022.

93 **dropped, too:** Bolton, *Hardest Deal*, 190.

94 **fund that county's schools:** "Clyde Smith Case Wins Top Story," *Hattiesburg American*, December 29, 1994; "Hub Schools Want to Annex Kids, Tax Base," *Hattiesburg American*, April 19, 1989. The description of the consequences of development in Lamar County is generally true, but I have simplified in the interest of brevity. Any city's school and tax politics are esoteric and complex. Hattiesburg's are even more so, as it has the unusual distinction of being part of two counties simultaneously—Forrest County, which holds most of Hattiesburg, and of which Hattiesburg is the county seat, and Lamar County, of which the city's west side is a part.

94 **district and its revenues sat:** M. E. Williams, "City Sees Potential Fortune Slip Away," *Hattiesburg American*, April 15, 1987; "Hub Schools," *Hattiesburg American*; "Hub Loses Bid to Annex Lamar Land," *Hattiesburg American*, December 5, 1991. Although there is no published history of the annexation discussion between Hattiesburg and the surrounding counties, contemporaneous news accounts suggest that annexing students as well as adjacent county land was a particularly difficult fight in Mississippi. In 1977, state representative Billy Andrews introduced a successful bill that banned cities from annexing school districts when they expanded boundaries over county lines—which was precisely what Hattiesburg Public Schools proposed to

do in Lamar County, where it hoped to annex twenty-three square miles. Then, in 1986, legislators approved a law that banned city school districts from expanding with city limits. The 1989 suit from the Hattiesburg Public Schools challenged both laws, arguing to federal officials that they were unconstitutional. Opposition to annexation in Lamar County was immediate and intense, led in part by Andrews, who was then serving as the Lamar County school board's attorney—and who, after all, had penned the 1977 legislation Hattiesburg now sought to overturn.

94 **"students who had moved":** Gordon Walker, interview by the author, December 12, 2022.

94 **facing the same problem:** "Hub Loses Bid," *Hattiesburg American*.

95 **of a single race:** Bolton, *Hardest Deal*, 189–90; Timothy Leake, "Case: *United States of America v. State of Mississippi*," case summary, Civil Rights Litigation Clearinghouse, University of Michigan Law School, March 1, 2019, https://clearinghouse.net/case/13782/.

95 **each grade into fewer buildings:** Author's Education Database. When classes began in the fall of 1987, administrators had closed six of its eleven elementaries. It restructured the remaining five, turning three into schools for students in kindergarten through fourth grade, and two into schools for fifth- and sixth-grade students. Out of three junior highs, one became a magnet school for kids in second through sixth grade; and one closed. One of the district's two high schools became a junior high. This left the district with five elementaries, two junior highs, and one high school.

96 **Hopkins told me:** Jimmy Hopkins (former associate superintendent of Hattiesburg Public Schools), interview by the author, December 21, 2022.

96 **in the first year:** Tim Doherty, "Schools' 'White Flight' More Than Forecast," *Hattiesburg American*, December 15, 1987.

96 **of 16.6 percent:** Author's Education Database. In 1987, the Hattiesburg school district reported enrollment of 2,243 white students. In 1988, the first year of integration, it reported 1,871 white students, a drop of 372—or 16.6 percent.

96 **in the district's history:** Author's Education Database. From 1954 to 1988, the steepest two-year decline in white enrollment in Hattiesburg's public schools came between 1986 and 1988, when white enrollment dropped by 25 percent, from 2,487 to 1,871. Prior to that, the largest two-year drop in white enrollment had come between 1970, when the Supreme Court's decision in *Alexander v. Holmes* mandated immediate integration, and 1972.

Over those two years, white enrollment in Hattiesburg's public schools had dropped by 20 percent, from 4,200 to 3,371.

96 **Petal's grew by 626:** Author's Education Database. From 1987 to 1997, overall enrollment in Hattiesburg's public schools dropped by 764, from 6,026 to 5,262. Over the same period, Oak Grove's enrollment grew from 1,706 to 3,372, and Petal's grew from 2,995 to 3,621, respectively.

97 **Beeson Academy two years later:** Stuart Levin, "Beeson Academy/ Hattiesburg Prep: A History in Context," *Journal of Mississippi History* 82, no. 3/4 (Fall/Winter 2020): 126–34, 140. Beeson Academy was among eleven Mississippi schools that lost tax-exempt status in 1970 for practicing racial discrimination. The decision increased the cost of tuition, and the student body changed "from the predominantly blue-collar background of the founding families to a more affluent demographic." In 1969, Beeson merged with Hattiesburg Academy. In 1978 the school rebranded itself as Hattiesburg Prep. After it closed in 1986 the school sold its furniture and books to Presbyterian Christian School. For a fascinating discussion of the intersection of Christian ideology and white supremacy at PCS by one of its former students, see: Rachel Winstead, "Basements Below the Sanctuary: A Story of the Church School" (honors thesis, University of Mississippi, 2020).

97 **tax-exempt status:** Suitts, *Overturning Brown*, 17.

97 **admit only whites:** David Nevin and Robert E. Bills, *The Schools That Fear Built: Segregationist Academies in the South* (Acropolis Books: 1976), 3.

98 **schools in 1970:** Annual Report of the State Superintendent of Public Education (Jackson, MS: State Department of Education, 1970–71), 120; Nonpublic Schools, 1970-71 (Jackson, MS: State Department of Education), 16. Information about white enrollment in Mississippi public in 1970 is from Charles Bolton's research notes, copy in possession of the author. In 1970, there were 63,242 students enrolled in nonpublic schools in Mississippi, and 534,411 enrolled in public schools. Of the latter, 259,304 were white.

98 **opposition to integration:** Rolph, interview.

99 **speech he titled "Black Monday":** McMillen, *Citizens' Council*, 17–19.

99 **resistance to school integration:** Thomas P. Brady, *A Review of Black Monday* (Winona, MS: Association of Citizens' Councils of Mississippi, 1954), 5, https://archive.org/details/1954Brady; McMillen, *Citizens' Council*, 19.

99 **springing up across the country:** Rolph, *Resisting Equality*, 58; McMillen, *Citizens' Council*, 120–21, 143–44, 150–53, 154n60. Historians have documented the Citizens' Council's presence in fifteen states: Alabama, Arkansas, California—where there were chapters in five counties—Colorado, Florida,

Louisiana, Maryland, Mississippi, Missouri, South Carolina, Texas, Georgia, North Carolina, Virginia, and Tennessee. In 1994, Neil McMillen, in a revised edition of his 1974 history of the councils, cautioned against taking the Council's own estimates of membership at face value. "No reliable figures are available," he wrote. "And until Council records are open to the researcher (and it does not appear that they will ever be), there can be no precise means of gauging the organization's maximum strength." His best guess for the Council's membership at its peak was 250,000 people.

100 **dropped by nearly two-thirds:** Sturkey, *Hattiesburg*, 271.

100 **from inception to dissolution:** Rolph, interview.

101 **"who fail[ed] to cooperate":** Rolph, 40.

101 **"Save Our Public Schools":** "How to Keep Schools Open," ca. 1958, box 1, folder 11, Citizens' Council Collection, Special Collections Department, Mississippi State University Libraries, Mississippi State University, MS; "How to Save Our Public Schools," ca. 1959, box 1, folder 11, Citizens' Council Collection.

101 **"think it could happen, either":** "The Little Rock School Board's Plans for Your Child," ca. 1958, box 2, folder 15, Citizens' Council Collection.

101 **Emmett Till was murdered:** William Sturkey, interview by the author, November 17, 2022. Sturkey, author of the history *Hattiesburg: An American City in Black and White*, says, "When politicians drill down on hate speech, it helps mobilize and embolden people who will actually go and do these horrendous acts. And the Emmett Till case is very much about *Brown v. Board of Education*, with every single politician in the state falling over each other to issue the most damning statement about *Brown v. Board of Education*, centering the rape of white girls by black boys." He continued, "It's just absolute hysteria over school desegregation."

101 **this idea of desegregation:** Rolph, interview.

101 **90 percent or more Black:** Erica Frankenberg, Jongteon Ee, Jennifer Ayscue, and Gary Orfield, *Harming Our Common Future: America's Segregated Schools 65 Years After* Brown (Los Angeles: Center for Education and Civil Rights, Civil Rights Project, University of California, Los Angeles, May 10, 2019), https://www.civilrightsproject.ucla.edu/research/k -12-education/integration-and-diversity/harming-our-common-future -americas-segregated-schools-65-years-after-brown/Brown-65-050919v4 -final.pdf.

101 **that of the district:** Monica P. Carter, "Biracial Panel Monitors Transition," *Hattiesburg American*, February 3, 1999.

101 *classrooms* **met that standard:** Author's Education Database. In 1997, Thames Elementary was 13.69 percent white, while the district overall was 14.6 percent white. The city of Hattiesburg, meanwhile, was 58.2 percent white in 1990 and 49.9 percent in 2000.

101 **released it from oversight:** Nikki Davis Maute and Monica Carter, "Hattiesburg Schools Not Race-Based," *Hattiesburg American*, October 25, 1997.

102 **school closest to their home:** Carter, "Biracial Panel."

102 **to relieve overcrowding:** Delmont, *Why Busing Failed*, 39–40.

102 **"of the same coin":** Matthew Delmont, interview by the author, May 31, 2023.

103 **173 students, attended Thames:** Author's Education Database; Maute and Carter, "Not Race-Based." In 1997, the year that Hattiesburg was declared unitary, the local paper reported the following share of white students at each elementary school: At Grace Christian Elementary, 15 percent of students were white; at Hawkins Elementary, 84 percent were; at Lillie Burney, 19 percent; at Thames, 16 percent; at Jones, 9 percent; at Woodley, 17 percent. In 1999, of 306 white students enrolled in Hattiesburg's six operating elementaries, 1 attended Lillie Burney, 17 attended Hawkins, 19 attended Jones, 30 attended Grace Christian, 66 attended Woodley, and 173 attended Thames.

103 **one-third white, after all:** Author's Education Database.

103 **outside of their neighborhood:** Felicia Johnson (former assistant principal, Thames Elementary), interview by the author, December 13, 2022; Tracy Williams (former principal, Thames Elementary), interview by the author, November 10, 2022.

103 **the "special visa," too:** Alan Oubre (director of student support services, Hattiesburg Public Schools), interview by the author, November 9, 2022.

104 **or by that name:** James Davis (former superintendent, Hattiesburg Public Schools), interview by the author, December 14, 2022; Hopkins, interview.

105 **one's own thought processes:** *Suggested Outcomes for Intellectually Gifted Education Programs Grades 2–8 in Mississippi* (Jackson, MS: Office of Gifted Education Programs, Mississippi State Department of Education, 1994), 5–6.

105 **did not exceed 4 percent:** This and other data on gifted and talented programs was calculated based on a database created by the author (hereafter cited as Gifted and Talented Database). The original data was drawn from a number of sources: (1) The Mississippi Department of Education's District and School Data site, available at https://newreports.mdek12.org/. (2) The Urban Institute's Education Data Explorer, available at https://educationdata.urban.org/data

-explorer. (3) The U.S. Department of Education's Civil Rights Data Collection site, available at https://ocrdata.ed.gov/flex/Reports.aspx.

105 **documented similar trends:** Jason A. Grissom and Christopher Redding, "Discretion and Disproportionality: Explaining the Underrepresentation of High-Achieving Students of Color in Gifted Programs," *AERA Open* 2, no. 1 (January–March 2016): 8, https://doi.org/10.1177/2332858415622175. There is little evidence that gifted and talented programs provide a significant boost to the academic achievement or social mobility of the students enrolled in them. Even so, the assignment of students to gifted and talented programs is a clear decision about which students deserve to have resources targeted toward them. An extensive body of scholarship documents how, in American schools, white and Asian students are more likely to be found deserving of this help than Black and Hispanic students. The 2016 study, by educational scholars Jason Grissom and Christopher Redding, is an authoritative one; a look through its bibliography offers a solid guide to this body of literature. Lay readers seeking a broader introduction should see: Jill L. Adelson, D. Betsy McCoach, and M. Katherine Gavin, "Examining the Effects of Gifted Programming in Mathematics and Reading Using the ECLS-K," *Gifted Child Quarterly* 56, no. 1 (January 2012): 25–39, https://doi.org/10.1177/0016986211431487; Sa A. Bui, Steven G. Craig, and Scott A. Imberman, "Is Gifted Education a Bright Idea? Assessing the Impact of Gifted and Talented Programs on Achievement" (working paper 17089, NBER, Cambridge, MA, May 2011), https://doi.org/10.3386/w17089; Christopher Redding and Jason A. Grissom, "Do Students in Gifted Programs Perform Better? Linking Gifted Program Participation to Achievement and Nonachievement Outcomes," *Educational Evaluation and Policy Analysis* 43, no. 3 (September 2021): 520–44, https://doi.org/10.3102/01623737211008919; Danielle Dreilinger, "Why Decades of Trying to End Racial Segregation in Gifted Education Haven't Worked," Hechinger Report, October 14, 2020, https://hechingerreport.org/gifted-educations-race-problem/.

105 **district's white elementary students:** Gifted and Talented Database. In the 2002–2003 school year, Thames Elementary's gifted and talented program enrolled the most gifted and talented students of the district's six elementaries in both raw number and percentage of students. That year, Thames enrolled 132 out of its 567 students in gifted and talented programs—compared to 47 students out of 528 at Lillie Burney; 62 students out of 540 at Grace Christian; 83 out of 510 at Woodley, 50 out of 373 at Hawkins; and 40 out of 337 at Jones. It was also by far the whitest school. Of the 253 white students enrolled across Hattiesburg's public elementaries in 2002–2003, 165 attended Thames.

105 **intensified in the upper grades:** Author's Education Database. The

district did not provide complete demographic data for gifted and talented programming across the district's elementary schools over time, citing privacy concerns that required the redaction of any enrollment data referencing fewer than ten students. In 2002–2003, the earliest year for which the district provided full enrollment demographics for Thames, the program served 68 white students (out of 165 total white students at the school); 58 Black students (out of 378 total); and 8 students of other races (out of twenty-four total). This put 41 percent of Thames's white students into gifted and talented programming, and 15 percent of Black students.

105 **4 percent of Black students:** Gifted and Talented Database; Author's Education Database. In 2009, 25 white students took AP classes at Hattiesburg High, compared to 45 Black students. The same year, the school enrolled 59 white students, and 1,135 Black students. That means 42.37 percent of white students were in AP, compared to 3.96 percent of Black students. That is the year Maryann began classes at the high school in tenth grade, graduating in 2012.

106 **years of court-ordered integration:** Walker, interview, November 2022.

107 **the days of debutante balls**: "Debs End Year with Gala New Year's Eve Ball," *Hattiesburg American*, January 1, 1952; "Now You're Talking!: Exclusive Clubs," *Hattiesburg American*, June 8, 1990. The 1990 letter (or, rather, phone message) to the editor is a complaint that Hattiesburg High students won't allow Oak Grove students to join the Debs, even if they are residents of Hattiesburg. The righteously indignant teen wrote that, if the Hattiesburg Debs wanted to keep discriminating against their suburban classmates, "their sorority needs to be sponsored by the school and also include blacks."

107 **the high school integrated:** Williams, interview, November 2022.

108 **Black youth with crime and violence:** There is an extensive body of scholarship documenting white Americans' steady presumption that Black people, of all ages and genders, are prone to criminality and violence. This is rooted in racist stereotypes dating back to enslavement, and carries through to the present day. Kristin Henning's *The Rage of Innocence* provides a thoughtful contemporary window into the problem; Michelle Alexander's *The New Jim Crow* does an excellent job of deconstructing the mechanisms by which these stereotypes work.

108 **that of the state and nation:** "State and National Violent Crime Rates: 1990 to 2021," and "Summary Crime Reported by the Hattiesburg Police Department," Crime Data Explorer, Federal Bureau of Investigation, accessed June 12, 2023, https://cde.ucr.cjis.gov/LATEST/webapp/#/pages/explorer/crime/crime-trend. From 2000 to 2010, Hattiesburg's violent crime rate was beneath that of both Mississippi and the United States. From 2000 to 2010,

Hattiesburg's violent crime rate dropped from 351 crimes per 100,000, to 251 per 100,000. The violent crime rate in Mississippi and the United States dropped from 361 and 507 per 100,000 to 250 and 405 per 100,000, respectively.

108 **of Oak Grove's enrollment:** Author's Education Database.

108 **"had every opportunity":** Johnson, interview.

109 **share of the population:** Author's Education Database.

109 **3.5 percent of the school:** Author's Education Database.

109 **enrolled in her grade:** The Urban Institute's Data Explorer lists only two female white students in Maryann's graduating class.

111 **90th percentile nationwide:** *ACT Profile Report-National: Graduating Class 2012*, ACT, accessed April 24, 2023, https://www.act.org/content/dam /act/unsecured/documents/Natl-Scores-2012-National2012.pdf.

112 **the economic padding:** Information about the share of students receiving free or reduced lunch is from the Urban Institute's Data Explorer, available at https://educationdata.urban.org/data-explorer/explorer.

113 **"just a waste of time":** Ashley McGhee, interview by the author, December 16, 2022.

115 **higher than Maryann's score:** Luc Hatlestad (director of media relations and internal communications, Gustavus Adolphus College), email to Madysen Luebke, March 31, 2023.

116 **the 2020 pandemic paused rankings:** Alan Burrow (executive director for district and school performance), Mississippi Department of Education, emails with Chris Rickert (fact-checker for author), June 6, 11, 2023; "Historical Data," Mississippi Department of Education, accessed June 15, 2023, https:// newreports.mdek12.org/Dataset/State.

116 **came from low-income homes:** Author's Education Database.

116 **poverty rate of 32.0 percent:** "QuickFacts: Hattiesburg City, Mississippi," accessed May 19, 2023, U.S. Census Bureau, https://www.census.gov /quickfacts/fact/table/hattiesburgcitymississippi/RHI225221.

116 **90 percent or more Black:** John Logan, Deirdre Oakley, and Jacob Stowell, "Resegregation in U.S. Public Schools or White Decline? A Closer Look at Trends in the 1990s," *Children, Youth and Environments* 16, no. 1 (2006): 49–68.

116 **that is 68 percent low-income:** Gary Orfield, Jongyeon Ee, Erica Frankenberg, and Genevieve Siegel-Hawley, Brown *at 62: School Segregation by Race, Poverty and State* (Los Angeles: Civil Rights Project, University of California, Los Angeles, May 16, 2016), 7, https://www.civilrightsproject.ucla .edu/research/k-12-education/integration-and-diversity/brown-at-62-school -segregation-by-race-poverty-and-state/Brown-at-62-final-corrected-2.pdf.

116 **achievement of Black students:** Sean F. Reardon et al., "Is Separate Still Unequal? New Evidence on School Segregation and Racial Academic Achievement Gaps" (working paper 19–06, CEPA, Stanford Center for Education Policy Analysis, 2019).

117 **guaranteed by a college degree:** Rakesh Kochhar and Stella Sechopoulos, "How the American Middle Class Has Changed in the Past Five Decades," Pew Research Center, April 20, 2022, https://www.pewresearch .org/short-reads/2022/04/20/how-the-american-middle-class-has-changed -in-the-past-five-decades/. As described by the Pew Research Center, from 1971 to 2021, the share of American high school graduates who were lower income more than doubled, while the share in the middle and upper class dropped by one-quarter. Over that period, the share of adults with only a high school diploma who were low-income nearly doubled, while the share of adults with a bachelor's degree who were upper income increased.

117 **middle-class rules and norms:** Orfield et al., Brown *at* 62, 6.

120 **long drop looming below:** Sheldon Danziger (president, Russell Sage Foundation), email to author, June 12, 2023. Note that this is a summary of an exchange, not a direct quote.

121 **if they were hired:** Marianne Bertrand and Sendhil Mullainathan, "Are Emily and Greg More Employable than Lakisha and Jamal? A Field Experiment on Labor Market Discrimination," (working paper 9873, NBER, Cambridge, MA, July 2003), http://www.nber.org/papers/w9873; Valerie Wilson, Ethan Miller, and Melat Kassa, "Racial Representation in Professional Occupations," Economic Policy Institute, June 8, 2021, https://www .epi.org/publication/racial-representation-prof-occ/. A 2003 working paper analyzing employer response to 5,000 sets of nearly identical resumes sent out with identifiably Black or white names ("Lakisha Washington" and "Emily Walsh") found that white names were 50 percent more likely to get a call back from potential employers, leading the researchers to conclude that "racial discrimination is still a prominent feature of the labor market." A 2021 audit of 83,000 fake job applications found that applications with "Black" names were still less likely to get calls back than were applications with "white" names.

122 **the end of their lives:** Deed for Becker land, Simpson County, MS, February 1, 2022, Simpson County Chancery Clerk, Mendenhall, MS.

122 **Mississippi by the 1810s:** This sentence is drawn from information in a self-published book by a descendant of the early Beckers, name withheld to preserve the family's anonymity, as he shares a last name with the Beckers.

122 **came to nearly $23,725:** U.S. Census Bureau, 1860 Census enumeration tables, schedule 1, Free Inhabitants, Jones County, MS, July 23, 1860, p. 8, lines 2–34, from Ancestry.com. The several Becker families enumerated together in Jones County, all listed as "farmers," had personal estates totaling $27,225. The bulk of that sum ($21,000, or around $750,000 today) came from the household of James Becker, who owned nineteen of the family's twenty-four enslaved people, who were presumably the source of his wealth.

123 **nearly $875,000 today:** Danielle Cabot (public affairs, Federal Reserve Bank of Minneapolis), email to Madysen Luebke, June 13, 2023. Cabot estimated that "$25,375 in 1860 would be the equivalent in 2023 of $874,497.69."

123 **88 percent of Americans:** Fabian T. Pfeffer and Asher Dvir-Djerassi, "The U.S. Wealth Distribution: Off the Charts," *Socius* 8 (December 2022), https://journals.sagepub.com/doi/full/10.1177/23780231221143957. The median wealth of Americans in 2019 was $121,800. Using the Pew Research Center's benchmarks delineating class, wealth of $365,000 or above would rank a household as upper class.

123 **their parents or grandparents:** Several psychological studies have shown that white Americans often respond to "meritocratic threat," the possibility that they have unearned advantages, by downplaying or denying the existence of racial advantage. For more on this, see the work of Negin Ghavami, Angélica Gutiérrez, Eric Knowles, Brian Lowery, and Miguel Unzueta.

124 **a quarter of Americans can say:** Deed of release for Becker home, Hattiesburg, MS, February 22, 2013, Lamar County Chancery Clerk, Purvis, MS; "Housing Taxation in OECD Countries," OECD, last updated July 21, 2022, https://stat.link/kfq1ve. In this study of renting, mortgages, and outright ownership of homes across twenty-eight countries, researchers found that the United States had one of the lowest rates of outright ownership in the world: 22.8 percent. Another 42 percent of Americans held mortgages for homes, and 35.2 percent of Americans were renters.

Chapter 5: My Parents as Parents

125 **in the lower-middle class:** *Occupational Outlook Handbook: 1972–1973* (Washington, D.C.: Bureau of Labor Statistics, 1973), 323–24. In 1970, the average wage for a beginning secretary at a small firm was $522 a month, or $6,264 for twelve months. The same year, "young people starting in routine jobs" in sales earned minimum wage ($1.60 an hour), with wages going up to $3.00 an hour for experienced salespeople. I've estimated wages for my

father, who would have been inexperienced, at minimum wage, for fifty weeks a year, forty hours a week: $3,200. Combined, this puts my parents' income at $9,464—just over the threshold into the middle class.

125 **they bought their first home:** JM interview, February 2022; Intake Information and Patient Assessment for Charyl McMillan, March 21, 1985, Clinical Resources, Inc., copy in possession of author. The intake form discusses my mother's work.

125 **money for one, interest free:** JM interview, February 2022.

126 **across Detroit's northern border:** Deed for lot 54 of Beautiful Irvington, Oak Park, MI, October 17, 1975, liber 6564, p. 683, Oakland County Register of Deeds, Pontiac, MI.

126 **it was considered diverse:** JM and BM interview, March 2023.

126 **many of them Christian Iraqis:** "Oak Park, Mich.: Focus of Modern U.S. Diversity," *New York Times*, December 20, 1983.

126 **Oak Park was 99 percent white:** U.S. Census Bureau, 1970 Census, vol. 1, Characteristics of the Population, part 24, Michigan, table 29, "Household Relationship and Type of Family by Race, for Places of 10,000 to 50,000," p. 141, https://www2.census.gov/prod2/decennial/documents /1970a_mi-01.pdf.

126 **and immigrant families stayed:** U.S. Census Bureau, 1980 Census, vol. 1, Characteristics of the Population, chapter C, General Social and Economic Characteristics, part 24, Michigan, table 162, Social Characteristics by Race and Spanish Origin for Places of 10,000 to 50,000, p. 24–61, https://www2 .census.gov/library/publications/decennial/1980/volume-1/michigan/1980a _mic-01.pdf. From 1970 to 1980, the population and racial/ethnic makeup of the city of Oak Park changed dramatically. Overall population decreased from 36,762 to 31,537. Nearly 9,000 whites had left—most of them native-born rather than immigrant—and their population dropped from 36,525 to 27,120. Black residents increased from 72 to 3,794. Residents classified as "other" increased from 165 to 215.

126 **all there was to it:** JM interview, February 2022.

126 **especially in the North:** Douglas S. Massey and Jonathan Tannen, "Suburbanization and Segregation in the United States: 1970–2010," *Ethnic and Racial Studies* 41, no. 9 (2018): 1594–595.

127 **a much higher price tag:** Richard Rothstein, "A 'Forgotten History' of How the U.S. Government Segregated America," interview by Terry Gross, *Fresh Air*, NPR, May 3, 2017, https://www.npr.org/2017/05/03/526655831/a -forgotten-history-of-how-the-u-s-government-segregated-america.

127 **and 12 percent Black:** U.S. Census Bureau, 1980 Census, vol. 1, Characteristics of the Population, part 24, Michigan, chapter B, General Population Characteristics, table 14, "Summary of General Characteristics," p. 11, https://www2.census.gov/prod2/decennial/documents/1980/1980censusofpopu80124uns_bw.pdf. (Hereafter cited as 1980 Census Michigan Population Characteristics, with table and page number.)

127 **25 percent Black:** 1970 Census Tracts for Detroit SMSA, tract 1101, p. 15; 1980 Census Tracts for Detroit SMSA, tract 1101, p. 29.

127 **Park, and gained Black residents:** Massey and Tannen, "Suburbanization and Segregation," 1594–1611; Daniel T. Lichter, Brian C. Thiede, and Matthew M. Brooks, "Racial Diversity and Segregation: Comparing Principal Cities, Inner-Ring Suburbs, Outlying Suburbs, and the Suburban Fringe," *RSF: The Russell Sage Foundation Journal of the Social Sciences* 9, no. 1 (February 2023): 27, https://doi.org/10.7758/RSF.2023.9.1.02. The share of all Americans who live in suburbs has climbed steadily since 1970, when 45.2 percent of us lived in suburbs, to 55.4 percent in 2010, according to a study published in 2018. The most recent study of the racial composition of suburbs, which used slightly different metrics, put the share of residents in suburbs even higher in 2020, at 64.5 percent. The degree of that change has differed markedly by racial group. From 1970 to 2010, the share of white residents in suburbs increased by more than one-quarter, going from 49.1 percent to 63.1 percent. Meanwhile, the share of Black residents in suburbs more than doubled, going from 18.2 percent to 39.9 by 2010. The share of both groups in suburbs continued to grow from 2010 to 2020, with white residents in suburbs increasing by about 1 percent, and the share of Black residents increasing by about 9 percent. Note that, due to the lack of a comprehensive data set charting suburbanization from 1970 to 2020, the statistics cited here rely on slightly different metrics for measuring suburbanization and so are not directly comparable. I rely on Massey and Tannen from 1970 to 2010, and Lichter, Thiede, and Brooks for data from 2010 to 2020.

127 **the Black neighbors arrived:** Clarence J. Wurdock, "Neighborhood Racial Transition: A Study of the Role of White Flight," *Urban Affairs Quarterly* 17, no. 1 (September 1981): 75–89; Orser, *Blockbusting in Baltimore*, 184.

127 **Black family for a high price:** "Blockbusting," *Georgetown Law Journal* 59, no. 1 (October 1970): 170–71; Aba Heiman, "Nonsolicitation and Cease and Desist Orders Against Real Estate Brokers in New York," *Fordham Urban Law Journal* 15, no. 3 (1987): 607.

128 **paid more than double:** "Blockbusting: A Novel Statutory Approach to

an Increasingly Serious Problem," *Columbia Journal of Law and Social Problems* 7, no. 3 (Summer 1971): 543.

128 **researchers documented in Brooklyn:** "Blockbusting: Novel Statutory Approach," 539n9, 542.

128 **"minority buyers," wrote the authors:** "Blockbusting: Novel Statutory Approach," 544–45.

128 **holding that they violated free speech:** Linmark Associates v. Township of Willingboro, 431 U.S. 85 (1977).

128 **concerns about "sign pollution":** Cathy Trost, "Oak Park Sign Ban Challenged," *Detroit Free Press*, August 26, 1977.

128 **"They can't make their own rules":** *CBS Evening News*, August 16, 1977 (abstract), Vanderbilt Television News Archive, https://tvnews.vanderbilt .edu/broadcasts/253670; Trost, "Sign Ban Challenged."

128 **struck down Oak Park's rule:** "U.S. Judge Suspends Oak Park Sign Ban," *Detroit Free Press*, September 28, 1977.

128 **36 percent white:** "QuickFacts: Oak Park City, Michigan," accessed August 25, 2023, U.S. Census Bureau, https://www.census.gov/quickfacts/fact /table/oakparkcitymichigan/PST045222.

129 **starting families after World War II:** Keith McClellan (local historian), interview by the author, December 9, 2019.

130 **showing me off to their friends:** This description is taken from my mother's notes in a monthly calendar, and the narrative in this passage is generally derived from photographs, calendars, and other personal documents in my possession unless otherwise indicated.

130 **any family other than themselves:** Sung S. Park, Emily E. Wiemers, and Judith A. Seltzer, "The Family Safety Net of Black and White Multigenerational Families," *Population and Development Review* 45, no. 2 (June 2019): 371; Colleen M. Heflin and Mary Pattillo, "Poverty in the Family: Race, Siblings, and Socioeconomic Heterogeneity," *Social Science Research* 35, no. 4 (2006): 818; Elizabeth Higginbotham and Lynn Weber, "Moving Up with Kin and Community: Upward Mobility for Black and White Women," *Gender and Society* 6, no. 3 (September, 1992): 430. Black Americans are 10 to 20 percentage points more likely to have a poor family member than whites, putting pressure on those with financial stability to help out. Researchers have shown clearly that this divide is largely a function of disparities in income and wealth, and recedes when comparing Black and white Americans of the same economic means. Other research suggests that white families are also less likely to feel obligated to help their poorer kin. Higginbotham and Weber

found that working- and middle-class Black women were significantly more likely than white women of the same classes to feel obligated to help family members. When researchers asked white women, "Generally, do you feel you owe a lot for the help given to you by your family and relatives?," they noted that many white women "were perplexed and asked what the question meant."

131 **were not yet commonplace:** Stuart Campbell, "A Short History of Sonography in Obstetrics and Gynecology," *Facts, Views and Vision: Issues in Obstetrics, Gynecology and Reproductive Health* 5, no. 3 (2013): 222.

132 **instead of retail's late nights:** JM interview, February 2022.

132 **"So, we ended up moving":** JM and BM interview, March 2023.

133 **an affluent suburb nearby:** Deed for Fox Run Green Subdivision No. 7 lot 239, November 16, 1978, liber 7375, p. 589, Oakland County Register of Deeds, Pontiac, MI.

133 **community was 97.5 percent white:** 1980 Census Michigan Population Characteristics, table 14a, p. 23.

133 **in Boston by four years:** John Kifner, "Violence Mars Busing in Boston," *New York Times*, September 13, 1974.

134 **hell to heaven:** Davis v. School District of City of Pontiac, 309 F. Supp. 734 (E.D. Mich. 1970); Davis v. School District of City of Pontiac, 95 F. Supp. 2d 688 (E.D. Mich. 2000); *Equal Educational Opportunity: Hearings Before the Select Comm. on Equal Educational Opportunity, Second Session, Part 19B—Equal Educational Opportunity in Michigan*, 92nd Cong. 9881–9887, 9889–9892 (1971) (statements of Jo Ann Walker, reading teacher, Pontiac City School System, and Patricia Johnson, teacher, Pontiac City School System), https://www.google.com/books/edition/Equal_Educational_Opportunity /8FGQAAAAMAAJ.

134 **no obligation to fix that:** *Davis*, 309 F. Supp. at 736.

134 **to delay integration there:** William K. Stevens, "5 Years of Busing in Pontiac, Mich.: Gains and Losses," *New York Times*, December 3, 1975.

134 **temporarily closing two GM plants:** Fred Sparks, "Pontiac Schools Half Empty," *Detroit Free Press*, September 8, 1971; Agis Salpukas, "Wider Plot Laid to Pontiac Klan," *New York Times*, September 11, 1971; Jerry M. Flint, "Antibusing Pickets Close 2 Car Plants," *New York Times*, September 15, 1971.

134 **celebrity for protesting "forced busing":** *Equal Educational Opportunity: Hearings, Part 19B*, 9869–9870 (statement of Irene McCabe, chairman, National Action Group, Pontiac, MI).

134 **"busing" the cause of the protests:** A representative photo caption

from the *Free Press* referred to "all the emotion and anguish that busing has brought to many American cities in this and past Septembers." Sparks, "Half Empty." A glance through news accounts of desegregation plans in the North and West shows that "busing" clearly refers not to the transportation of students, but to the racial integration of schools.

134 **"That is my personal feeling":** *Equal Educational Opportunity: Hearings, Part 19B,* 9840 (statement of William Lacy, school administration, Pontiac Public Schools).

134 **"They were called n—lovers":** *Equal Educational Opportunity: Hearings, Part 19B,* 9875 (statement of Carole Sweeney, mother, Pontiac, MI).

135 **looked down and said, *"Black people":*** I did not record the conversation I had with Debbie Hudson in the summer of 2019, so I have indicated in the text that these quotations are drawn from memory, rather than from the transcript of a formal interview.

135 **neighborhood, which was white:** Elaine Fishbaugh, interviews with the author, March 22, March 23, and June 9, 2023. These interviews form the basis of the next six paragraphs unless otherwise noted.

135 **got blown up in Pontiac:** Stevens, "5 Years of Busing."

136 **but they did not know this:** Report of Black Legion Activities in Oakland County, Circuit Court, Oakland County, Michigan, August 31, 1936, 28, Peter Amann Papers, box 6, folder 22, Walter P. Reuther Library, Wayne State University, Detroit, MI, 27; "Farm Held Red Headquarters," *Detroit Free Press,* August 22, 1934. Interview with John and Bonnie McMillan, May 25, 2023.

137 **middle-class people to buy them:** Dorothy Weddell, "Housing Takes a Bigger Bite," *Detroit Free Press,* February 6, 1982.

137 **for $26,500 six years earlier:** Deed for lot 54 of Beautiful Irvington, Oak Park, MI, October 17, 1975, liber 6564, 683, Oakland County Register of Deeds, Pontiac, MI; Deed for lot 54 of Beautiful Irvington, Oak Park, MI, June 11, 1981, liber 8029, 204, Oakland County Register of Deeds, Pontiac, MI. The first deed records the sale to my parents, the second their sale of it.

137 **mortgage for their new house:** JM interview, February 2022; Deed for lot 4 of Cambridge Knolls, June 11, 1981, liber 8026, 764, Oakland County Register of Deeds, Pontiac, MI.

137 **based on word of mouth:** JM interview, February 2022.

137 **in Michigan and elsewhere:** William Harold Gerritz, "Family Preferences for K–12 Education: An Explanatory Model" (PhD diss., University of California, Berkeley, 1987), 57, 59. Gerritz found that about half of

middle-class parents searched for good schools for their children, while 40 percent of lower-class parents and 81 percent of upper-class parents did.

137 **the top quintile of schools statewide:** *Michigan K–12 Public School Districts Ranked by Selected Financial Data: 1980–1981* (Lansing: Michigan State Board of Education), 28–29. In the 1980–1981 school year, Ferndale schools spent $2,566 per student in total general funds, ranking it sixty-third out of the state's 529 districts. Oak Park schools, by comparison, spent $3,763 that year, ranking it second in the state.

137 **rank around the state average:** "1981–82 MEAP Test Scores," *Detroit Free Press*, January 6, 1982; Chris Christoff, "School Test Scores Don't Always Reflect the Payout," *Detroit Free Press*, April 14, 1983. During the 1981–1982 school year, 76.2 percent of Ferndale fourth graders passed the Michigan Educational Assessment Program (MEAP) test for math, compared to 78 percent of all fourth graders in the state. The same year, 71.1 percent of Ferndale's fourth graders passed the MEAP test for reading, compared to 76 percent of all Michigan fourth graders.

138 **districts in the state:** *Michigan School Districts Ranked*, 28–29.

138 **"just be out of reach":** "Holly High School Retains Accreditation," *Herald Advertiser* (Holly, MI), April 26, 1984.

138 **"teachers in other districts":** Steven Gaynor (former principal, Davisburg Elementary School), interview by the author, December 4, 2019.

138 **"less of a priority in the city":** JM and BM interview, March 2023.

138 **desegregate its elementary schools:** William Grant, "Retrial Ordered on Ferndale Integration," *Detroit Free Press*, May 18, 1978; William Grant, "Schools Add 1,200 to Plan for Integration," *Detroit Free Press*, September 10, 1975. In 1969, the United States Department of Health Education and Welfare charged the Ferndale School District with running a segregated school, Grant Elementary. This marked the first desegregation case brought against a school system by the federal government outside the South.

138 **he never heard about that, either:** JM and BM interview, March 2023.

138 **the district was colorblind:** Burton Shifman to Ira Polley, February 11, 1969, (state superintendent of education), Michigan Office of Hispanic Education Records, RG 87-21, series 1, Archives of Michigan, Lansing, MI.

138 **3,500 elementary students overall:** Jo Thomas, "Milliken Defends Ferndale School Funds," *Detroit Free Press*, January 31, 1975.

139 **The district lost its appeal:** Grant, "Schools Add 1,200." The Ferndale School Board's case lost every appeal it filed up to the Supreme Court, which remanded the case to the U.S. Sixth Court of Appeals—where the school

district of Ferndale lost, finally, in 1972. Once the legal concerns had been cleared, the Department of Health, Education, and Welfare withheld the district's funds as penalty for failing to provide Black students an equal education to that offered to white students.

139 **The district chose the latter:** Roger Mills, *Justice Delayed and Denied: HEW and Northern School Desegregation* (Washington, D.C.: Center for National Policy Review, Catholic University School of Law, 1974), 48. Mills notes that, as of the writing of his 1974 report, Ferndale was the only northern or western school district to actually have its funds terminated (57).

139 **send their children to Grant Elementary:** "Ferndale Plan Rejected," *Lansing State Journal*, February 26, 1975; William Grant, "Ferndale Pulls Whites to Black School," *Detroit Free Press*, September 4, 1975. In 1975, the Justice Department rejected four proposals from Ferndale Public Schools that relied on voluntary enrollment to achieve integration. "We do not reject 'freedom-of-choice' or voluntary plans as inadequate on their face," wrote Thomas Keeling, head of the education section. He continued, "Our experience in circumstances similar to Ferndale has been that such plans do not work."

139 **sued Ferndale under the new law:** Grant, "Schools Add 1,200."

139 **"clearly does not do that":** Grant, "Ferndale Pulls Whites."

139 **Sixth Circuit Court of Appeals:** Grant, "Retrial Ordered"; William Grant, "Justice Dept. Appeals Ferndale School Case," *Detroit Free Press*, September 10, 1975.

139 **taught in shifts:** Gregory Skwira and Patricia Montemurri, "Ferndale Schools Must Desegregate, Appeals Court Says," *Detroit Free Press*, January 31, 1978.

140 **"logic at all" in her ruling:** Katherine Green, "Busing Gets an A," *Detroit Free Press*, June 12, 1981; Skwira and Montemurri, "Ferndale Schools Must Desegregate."

140 **take classes at Grant:** "Ferndale Draws Up New Busing Plan," *Detroit Free Press*, July 29, 1980.

140 **"white students," wrote Gilmore:** Marianne Rzepka, "Ferndale Busing Will Begin Jan. 5 for 350 Students," *Detroit Free Press*, October 9, 1980.

140 **integrated its elementary schools:** Rzepka, "Ferndale Busing"; Donna Britt, "Ferndale Pupils Move," *Detroit Free Press*, January 6, 1981.

140 **"Success in Ferndale":** Green, "Busing Gets an A." Green reported that the district had forgone $250,000 a year in federal funds, for eight years, for failing to desegregate its schools."

141 **monthly payments of $70:** Land Contract for lot 3 of Cambridge Knolls, June 11, 1981, liber 8042, p. 170, Oakland County Register of Deeds, Pontiac, MI; Deed for lot 3 of Cambridge Knolls, August 23, 1989, liber 11104, p. 697, Oakland County Register of Deeds, Pontiac, MI; JM and BM interview, March 2023; John A. McMillan to lot owner, May 6, 1989, copy in possession of author.

141 **once far-flung rural towns:** Dan Lichter (Ferris family professor emeritus of sociology and public policy, Cornell University), interview by the author, July 11, 2022.

141 **and work in a suburb:** Michael Bader (associate professor of sociology, Johns Hopkins), interview by the author, March 17, 2020.

142 **"sprawl" and "exurbs" are others:** Lichter, Thiede, and Brooks, "Racial Diversity and Segregation," 27.

142 **counties that, technically, were suburban:** Daniel T. Lichter, David L. Brown, and Domenico Parisi, "The Rural-Urban Interface: Rural and Small Town Growth at the Metropolitan Fringe," *Population, Space and Place* 27, no. 3 (2020): 5, e2415, https://doi.org/10.1002/psp.2415.

142 **far more than cities or even suburbs:** Alan Berube, Audrey Singer, Jill Wilson, and William Frey, "Finding Exurbia: America's Fast-Growing Communities at the Metropolitan Fringe," *Brookings Institution Living Census Series* (October 2006): 23, https://www.brookings.edu/wp-content/uploads/2016/06/20061017_exurbia.pdf. This 2006 study found that, on average in 2004, 47 percent of city residents were white, as were 55 percent of inner suburbs, 74 percent of outer suburbs, and 83 percent of fringe communities.

142 **diversifying metro areas for outlying areas:** Lichter, Thiede, and Brooks, "Racial Diversity and Segregation," 31, 35. The Simpson's Diversity Index (SDI) measures the likelihood that any two residents within a given geographic area will be from different ethnoracial groups. The higher the score, the more integrated the place. Principal city residents had an SDI score of 62.8, inner-ring suburbanites a score of 52.7, outer-ring suburbanites a score of 50.9, and exurbanites a score of 34.1.

142 **Jewish families on the north:** Cecil Angel and Georgea Kovanis, "Oak Park Faces Test of Tolerance," *Detroit Free Press*, March 23, 1991.

142 **function of whole cities or suburbs:** Daniel T. Lichter, Domenico Parisi, and Michael C. Taquino, "Toward a New Macro-Segregation? Decomposing Segregation Within and Between Metropolitan Cities and Suburbs," *American Sociological Review* 80, no. 4 (August 2014): 844.

142 **had become majority Black:** "QuickFacts: Oak Park City, Population,

Census, 2010 Census," U.S. Census Bureau, accessed April 15, 2023, https://www.census.gov/quickfacts/fact/table/oakparkcitymichigan/POP010210. In 1970, five years before my parents moved to Oak Park, the city was 99.4 percent white and 0.2 percent Black. In 1980, a year before we moved, the balance had shifted to 85.7 percent white and 12.1 percent Black. By 2020, the most recent year for which census data is available, it was 55.6 percent white and 36.8 percent Black.

142 **landed in exurban places like Holly:** 1980 Census Michigan Population Characteristics, table 15a, "Persons by Race for Towns/Townships," p. 36. In 1980, Holly had 8,204 white residents and 209 Black residents, making it 96.7 percent white.

142 **"following the racial script":** Dan Lichter, interview by the author.

142 **"and others living side by side":** Shirley Uridge, "Don't Ruin Rose Community!" letter to the editor, *Herald Advertiser* (Holly, MI), May 21, 1987.

143 **racial mix remained 98 percent white:** 1980 Census Michigan Population Characteristics, table 15a, "Persons by Race for Towns/Townships," pp. 35–41. In 1980, the five townships feeding into Holly Area Schools (Groveland, Holly, Rose, Springfield, and White Lake) had 47,230 residents, of whom 46,300 residents, or 98.0 percent, were white.

143 **that fact being widely understood:** Nancy Strole, interview by the author, August 29, 2019; Ina Golden, interview by the author, September 10, 2019.

143 **longstanding presence of a Black community in Holly:** U.S. Census Bureau, 1930 Census, vol. 3, Population Reports by State, Michigan, table 21, "Population by Sex, Color, Age, etc., for Counties by Minor Civil Divisions," p. 75. As early as 1930, the first year that Holly had grown large enough to be reported in census publications, the town had ten Black residents. That is the highest proportion among the townships that would later form the Holly School District: Groveland Township counted two Black residents, and Rose, Springfield, and White Lake Townships had no Black residents at all.

143 **who stayed there after dark:** "Fenton," History and Social Justice, accessed April 15, 2023, https://justice.tougaloo.edu/sundowntown/fenton-mi/. The historian and sociolologist James Loewen documented the breadth of "sundown towns" across the U.S., counting thousands of places that could be considered as such. Fenton is listed as a "probable" sundown town in an ongoing list maintained by historians online.

143 **my mother's brother did in 1981:** JM and BM interview, March 2023;

undated photograph of the author's uncle, ca. 1981, copy in possession of author.

143 **bottom of the middle class:** *Occupational Outlook Handbook: 1982–1983* (Washington, D.C.: Bureau of Labor Statistics, 1983), Pew Income Data. In 1980, the median earnings for a wholesale sales worker ranged from $23,000 in hardware, plumbing, and heating materials to $30,800 in lumber and building materials. As a ballpark number, I believe the midpoint between the two—$26,900—is a fair proxy for my father's annual income in 1980. That year, the national median income for a household of five was $26,988, placing us in the lower end of the middle class: between two-thirds and 100 percent of median income.

144 **as they walked to the car:** JM and BM interview, March 2023.

145 **degenerative neurological disease:** Medical records for Charyl McMillan, December 26, 1981–January 1, 1982, St. Joseph Mercy Hospital, Pontiac, MI, copy in possession of author.

146 **were in car seats:** Johanna McMillan, interview by the author, March 6, 2022.

146 **The roads were dry:** "The Weather," *Detroit Free Press*, February 14, 1984; Def. Albert Tipolt's Answers to Interrog. 7, McMillan v. Tipolt, No. 84–277752-NI (Oakland County Cir. Ct., 1984), copy in possession of author.

146 **He stuck to local roads after that:** Def. Albert Tipolt's Answers to Interrog. 6, McMillan v. Tipolt, No. 84–277752-NI (Oakland County Cir. Ct., 1984), copy in possession of author.

147 **they cried and called for her:** Service records for Charyl McMillan, February 14, 1984, Holly Volunteer Ambulance Company, copy in possession of author.

147 **cuts across her face:** Bill for medical services for Charyl McMillan, March 3, 1984, Associated Radiologists of Oakland County, copy in possession of author; Emergency Department records for Charyl McMillan, February 13, 1984, St. Joseph Mercy Hospital, Pontiac, MI.

147 **to the hospital in Pontiac:** Records for Charyl McMillan, Holly Ambulance; Pl.'s Answers to Def. Charles H. Wilson, Inc.'s Interrog., McMillan v. Tipolt, No. 84–277752-NI (Oakland County Cir. Ct., 1984), copy in possession of author.

148 **could cause serious injury:** The mainstream medical establishment did not consider brain injury, including concussion, as a significant problem until the 1990s. In the early 1990s, only twelve states even required brain injuries to be reported as part of maintaining health statistics on their residents, and

federal financing agencies had no reimbursement protocol for health care related to brain injury. Congress finally took the issue up in 1992, when the Department of Health and Human Services recommended "to establish traumatic brain injury (TBI)" as a category of injury in reporting systems. *Rehabilitation Facilities for People with Head Injuries, Hearing Before the Human Resources and Intragovernmental Relations Committee of the Committee on Government Operations*, 102nd Congress (1992), 228, https://hdl.handle.net/2027 /pst.000020337179.

Chapter 6: Jared Bunde: Crime

151 **"the acid guy," said Jared:** Jared's narrative in this chapter, unless otherwise cited, is drawn from numerous in-person and phone interviews with Jared and from a number of nonpublic personal papers, such as school transcripts, which I have cited only if they feel crucial to establishing the provenance of a fact in the text.

153 **parents of Black children to make:** Keisha April, Lindsey M. Cole, and Naomi E. S. Goldstein. "Let's 'Talk' About the Police: The Role of Race and Police Legitimacy Attitudes in the Legal Socialization of Youth," *Current Psychology* 42, no. 18 (2022): 1–16.

153 **Rick assumed he deserved it:** Rick Bunde, interview by the author, March 4, 2023.

154 **from 1987 to 2011:** Michael Lawlor, interview by the author, April 28, 2022.

154 **"do the time," says Lawlor:** Lawlor, interview.

154 **"you know, start that way:** Rick Bunde, interview.

154 **to "accelerated pretrial rehabilitation":** Mark Oullette to Jared Bunde, May 19, 1995, copy in possession of author. This letter from Jared's attorney outlines the state's offer and Jared's options.

154 **than they'd risk at trial:** Ram Subramanian, et al., *In the Shadows: A Review of the Research on Plea Bargaining* (Brooklyn, NY: Vera Institute of Justice, September 2020), 2, https://www.vera.org/downloads/publications/in -the-shadows-plea-bargaining.pdf.

155 **three years to less than two:** Margaret Werner Cahalan and Lee Anne Parsons, *Historical Corrections Statistics in the United States, 1850–1984*, Bureau of Justice Statistics, U.S. Department of Justice (Rockville, MD: Westat, December 1986), table 6–17, "Average Time Served and Percent of Sentence Served for First Release from Federal Facilities by Offense: Selected Years 1955–1983," p. 163, https://bjs.ojp.gov/content/pub/pdf /hcsus5084.pdf.

155 **doubled within a decade:** William J. Sabol and John McGready, *Time Served in Prison by Federal Offenders, 1986–97*, Bureau of Justice Statistics, U.S. Department of Justice (Rockville, MD: Westat, June 1999), table 4, "Average Time to Be Served by Offenders Released from Federal Prison, by Offense of Conviction, 1986–97," p. 7, https://bjs.ojp.gov/content/pub/pdf/tspfo97.pdf.

155 **commonly used by white adults:** United States Sentencing Commission, *1994 Guidelines Manual* (USSC), §2D1.1(c)(7) (November 1, 1994), https://www.ussc.gov/guidelines/2015-guidelines-manual/archive/1994-partd; USSC (1994), table 01A, "Sentencing Table," https://www.ussc.gov/guidelines/2015-guidelines-manual/archive/1994-table01a.

155 **"need to bring them to heel":** "Hillary Clinton Campaign Speech," aired January 25, 1996, C-SPAN, 23:45, https://www.c-span.org/video/?69606-1/hillary-clinton-campaign-speech.

155 **harsher system of punishment:** Michelle S. Phelps, "Rehabilitiation in the Punitive Era: The Gap Between Rhetoric and Reality in U.S. Prison Programs," *Law and Society Review* 45, no. 1 (March 2011): 35, https://doi.org/10.1111/j.1540-5893.2011.00427.x.

155 **a *Harper's* writer in 1994:** Dan Baum, "Legalize It All: How to Win the War on Drugs," *Harper's Magazine*, April 2016, https://harpers.org/archive/2016/04/legalize-it-all/.

155 **drugs other than marijuana:** Michael Lawlor, "Reforming Mandatory Minimum Sentences in Connecticut," *Federal Sentencing Reporter* 15, no. 1 (October 2002): 10–13, https://doi.org/10.1525/fsr.2002.15.1.10.

155 **childcare centers, or public housing:** Lawlor, "Sentences in Connecticut," 11. The introduction of greater penalties within a set distance from a school subjected large swaths of densely populated areas—like cities, where a disproportionate number of Black people lived, compared to less-densely populated areas like suburbs and rural areas—to increased penalties. After Connecticut legislators expanded school-zone laws to include 1,500-foot zones around schools, housing projects, and daycare centers, for example, the only places in New Haven *without* heightened drug sentences were a golf course, a marsh, and a landfill.

155 **if he was convicted:** Jennifer Dukes (U.S. Sentencing Commission), email message to Graham Hacia (fact-checker), June 6, 2023; "1994 Table 01A," USSC, "Sentencing Table."

156 **Jared would be going to prison:** Oulette to Bunde, May 19, 1995.

157 **the bill's sponsor, Mark Souder:** Eric D. Blumenson and Eva S. Nilsen, "How to Construct an Underclass, or How the War on Drugs Became a War

on Education," *Journal of Gender, Race and Justice* 6, no. 61 (2002): 69; Bradley D. Custer, "The History of Denying Federal Financial Aid to System-Impacted Students," *Journal of Student Financial Aid* 50, no. 1 (2021), article 2, https://doi.org/10.55504/0884-9153.1710. In 1998, three years after Jared's charges, Congress passed a law *automatically* banning anyone convicted of a felony from getting federal loans, grants, or work study assistance. It stayed law until 2005, when Congress narrowed the provision to only prevent students who committed crimes while receiving aid from continuing to do so.

158 **convicted of the same charges:** Eileen Poe-Yamagata and Michael A. Jones, *And Justice for Some* (Davis, CA: National Council on Crime and Delinquency, April 2000), 20, https://files.eric.ed.gov/fulltext/ED442882.pdf.

158 **hours of community service:** Mark Oulette to Jared Bunde, June 16, 1995, copy in possession of author. This letter from Jared's attorney outlines Jared's sentence.

158 **entire thing would disappear:** There is no data (good or otherwise) on racial disparities in criminal records that are sealed by a judge, as Jared's was—they are, after all, sealed. But research into other ways of sealing records, such as "expungement" or "clean slate" laws, shows troubling differences in race. For more, see the scholarship of Alyssa Mooney, Alissa Skog, and Amy Lerman.

158 **for Jared in this way:** Rick Bunde, interview.

158 **well into the middle class:** *Occupational Outlook Handbook: 1992–1993* (Washington, D.C.: Bureau of Labor Statistics, 1993), 66, 260; Pew Income Data. In 1990, the average salary for midlevel engineers of all kinds was $49,165 for Level IV, and $59,162 for Level V (out of eight levels). The midpoint of those two incomes is $54,179. The same year, the average salary for a postal worker who'd put a few years in with the agency would have been around $26,500. In 1994, when Jared was arrested on drug charges, both of his parents—who each had custody of one child—would have been considered two-person households. That put his father, an engineer, just shy of the upper-middle class. Jared's mother, meanwhile, would have been in the lower-middle class.

158 **finished the degree in 1987:** Rick Bunde, interview.

159 **pushed for changes:** R. D. G. Wadhwani, "Kodak, FIGHT, and the Definition of Civil Rights in Rochester, New York: 1966–1967," *Historian* 60, no. 1 (Fall 1997): 59.

159 **most dangerous jobs:** Third Amended Complaint at 17–19, 24, Employees

Committed for Justice v. Eastman Kodak, No. 6:04-cv-06098-CJS (W.D. N.Y., March 1, 2006).

159 **important to Jared's sentencing:** Rick Bunde, interview.

160 **"lives," he says:** Rick Bunde, interview.

160 **"beg to say no":** Rick Bunde, interview.

160 **could not manage their child:** Tracie McMillan, "What Do We Think Poverty Looks Like?" *New York Times*, July 8, 2017, https://www.nytimes .com/2017/07/08/opinion/sunday/poverty-snap-food-stamps-.html.

160 **in the courtroom for every hearing:** Allen Dupree and Wendell Primus, *Declining Share of Children Lived with Single Mothers in the Late 1990s* (Washington, D.C.: Center on Budget and Policy Priorities, June 15, 2001), 13; *Poverty in the United States: 1991* (Washington, D.C.: U.S. Census Bureau, August 1991), 15, 100. In 1995, 47.1 percent of Black children lived with a single mother, 2.9 percent lived with a cohabiting mother, and another 3.8 percent lived with a cohabiting or single father. In 1990, the nearest year for which I found reliable data, 58 percent of Black single mothers worked. The same year, 56.1 percent of Black families with a single mother were poor.

160 **study after study after study:** Nazgol Ghandnoosh and Christopher Lewis, *Race and Punishment: Racial Perceptions of Crime and Support for Punitive Policies* (Washington, D.C.: The Sentencing Project, 2018), 14–17, https:// www.sentencingproject.org/app/uploads/2022/08/Race-and-Punishment .pdf; Lincoln Quillian and Devah Pager, "Black Neighbors, Higher Crime? The Role of Racial Stereotypes in Evaluations of Neighborhood Crime," *American Journal of Sociology* 107, no. 3 (November 2001): 718–19, https://doi .org/10.1086/338938; Kelly Welch, "Black Criminal Stereotypes and Racial Profiling," *Journal of Contemporary Criminal Justice* 23, no. 3 (August 2007): 276–77; Gabbidon, Taylor Greene, and Young, *African American Classics*, 135– 58. This is not, of course, a comprehensive list.

161 **and incarceration: "collateral consequences":** *Collateral Consequences: The Crossroads of Punishment, Redemption, and the Effects on Communities, Briefing Before the United States Commission on Civil Rights* (Washington, D.C.: U.S. Commission on Civil Rights, June 2019), 11–12.

161 **"legal financial obligations," or LFOs:** The work of sociologist Alexes Harris, particularly in her book *A Pound of Flesh*, provides an excellent and thorough analysis of the rise of legal financial obligations, their disproportionate effect on the poor, and the ways that these policies further entrench racial inequalities. For the denial of federal benefits, see: Custer, "Denying

Federal Financial Aid"; 24 C.F.R. § 982.553 (2001) ("Denial of admission and termination of assistance for criminals and alcohol abusers").

162 **more likely to be incarcerated:** Besiki L. Kutateladze, Nancy Andiloro, Brian Johnson, and Cassia Spohn et al., "Cumulative Disadvantage: Examining Racial and Ethnic Disparity in Prosecution and Sentencing," *Criminology* 52, no. 3 (August 25, 2014): 534–36, https://doi.org/10.1111/1745–9125 .12047.

162 **forty-two states, including Connecticut:** Conn. Gen. Stat. § 51–298 (2018) ("The commission shall have a claim against any person represented by a public defender . . . for the reasonable value of services rendered to him"); *At What Cost? Findings from an Examination into the Imposition of Public Defense System Fees* (Washington, D.C.: National Legal Aid and Defender Association, July 2022), 5, https://www.nlada.org/sites/default/files/NLADA_At _What_Cost.pdf. NLADA found that eighteen states have statutory upfront application/appointment fees, forty-two states and D.C. have statutory recoupment fees, and seventeen states have statutes authorizing both fees. Only seven states "have no statutory public defense system fees."

162 **they often must pay bail:** Alexes Harris, Tyler Smith, and Emmi Obara, "Justice 'Cost Points': Examination of Privatization Within Public Systems of Justice," *Criminology and Public Policy* 18 (2019), 345.

162 **the cost of electronic monitoring:** Kiren Jahangeer, "Fees and Fines: The Criminalization of Poverty," American Bar Association, October 13, 2021.

162 **for their room and board:** "State-by-State Court Fees," NPR, May 19, 2014, https://www.npr.org/2014/05/19/312455680/state-by-state-court-fees.

162 **each time he called home:** Keith Phaneuf, "MCI Said Improperly Halting Collect Prisoners' Calls," *Journal Inquirer* (Manchester, CT), January 12, 2001, https://www.journalinquirer.com/archives/mci-said -improperly-halting-collect-prisoners-calls/article_0e6ea733–059a-5c58 -adf3–025f2b59b510.html; Jennifer Brady and Amanda Gordon, *Inmate Work Activities* (Hartford, CT: Office of Legislative Research, May 6, 2011), https:// www.cga.ct.gov/2011/rpt/2011-R-0191.htm; "Inmate Assignment and Pay Plan," Administrative Directive 10.1 § 6(B), Connecticut Department of Correction, October 22, 2015, https://portal.ct.gov/-/media/DOC/Pdf/Ad /ad1001pdf. In 2001, in-state phone calls from Connecticut prisons were billed at a rate of $0.09–$0.23 per minute, plus a flat $1.75 surcharge. Author calculations; for full documentation see whitebonus.com.

162 **in the late 2010s:** Stephen Raher, "The Company Store: A Deeper

Look at Prison Commissaries," Prison Policy Initiative, May 2018, https://www.prisonpolicy.org/reports/commissary.html.

162 **is about a hundred miles:** Nancy G. La Vigne, "The Cost of Keeping Prisoners Hundreds of Miles from Home," Urban Institute, February 3, 2014, https://www.urban.org/urban-wire/cost-keeping-prisoners-hundreds-miles-home.

162 **if they do not:** Michael McLaughlin et al., "The Economic Burden of Incarceration in the U.S." (working paper, Concordance Institute for Advancing Social Justice, George Warren Brown School of Social Work, Washington University in St. Louis, July 2016).

162 **left in prison, alone:** *The Effects of Prison Visitation on Offender Recidivism* (St. Paul, MN: Minnesota Department of Corrections, November 2011), 27, https://mn.gov/doc/assets/11-11MNPrisonVisitationStudy_tcm1089-272781.pdf.

163 **probation and supervision:** "Court Fees," NPR.

163 **per family, at $13,600:** Beatrix Lockwood and Nicole Lewis, "The Hidden Cost of Incarceration," Marshall Project, December 17, 2019, https://www.themarshallproject.org/2019/12/17/the-hidden-cost-of-incarceration.

163 **$19,050 in 2023:** This estimate reflects costs Jared's family would have incurred in terms of visitation, which would have required time, gas, and wear and tear on their cars; commissary; and phone calls. Readers can find a fuller accounting of costs in the appendix, the White Bonus Index at the end of the book, or online at whitebonus.com.

163 **$53,000 in 2023:** Adjusted for inflation to 2023 dollars, three years of full-time work at minimum wage from mid-1995 through mid-1998 would have yielded $52,735.

163 **thirty-two points per year:** Grey Gordon, John Bailey Jones, Urvi Neelakantan, and Kartik Athreya, "Incarceration, Earnings, and Race" (working paper 20–11, Federal Reserve Bank of Richmond, Richmond, VA, July 2, 2021), 2, https://www.richmondfed.org/publications/research/working_papers/2021/wp_21–11. Adjusted for inflation to 2022 dollars, three years of full-time work at minimum wage from mid-1995 through mid-1998 would have yielded $51,389.34.

164 *without* **a criminal record:** Devah Pager, Bruce Western, and Bart Bonikowski, "Discrimination in a Low-Wage Labor Market: A Field Experiment," *American Sociological Review* 74 (October 2009): 786. This study of employment discrimination in New York City's low-wage labor market found that, for whites, "the stigma of a felony conviction appears to be no greater than

that of minority status." The study found that white men with a criminal record applying for jobs received callbacks or job offers 17.2 percent of the time, compared to 13.0 percent of Black applicants who had no criminal record at all—a difference of 32.3 percent.

164 **of preincarceration income:** Christopher J. Lyons and Becky Petit, "Compounded Disadvantage: Race, Incarceration, and Wage Growth," *Social Problems* 58, no. 2 (May 2011): 259–60, https://doi.org/10.1525/sp.2011 .58.2.257. There is a rich body of evidence showing a correlation between prior incarceration and low wages. Notably, Lyons and Petit found that it was the fact of incarceration alone—more than arrest, conviction, or time spent in jail—that correlated with a drop in income.

164 **to gain work experience:** Robert Apel and Gary Sweeten, "The Impact of Incarceration on Employment During the Transition to Adulthood," *Social Problems* 57, no. 3 (August 2010): 468, 472, https://doi.org/10.1525/sp .2010.57.3.448.

164 **63 percent of Black released prisoners:** Leonardo Antenangeli and Matthew R. Durose, *Recidivism of Prisoners Released in 24 States in 2008: A 10-Year Follow-Up Period (2008–2018)* (Washington, D.C.: Bureau of Justice Statistics, U.S. Department of Justice, September 2021), 1–4, https://bjs.ojp.gov/BJS_PUB /rpr24s0810yfup0818/Web%20content/508%20compliant%20PDFs.

164 **overlap with each other:** For more on the connection between recidivism and heightened surveillance, refer to the scholarship of Alexes Harris, Cecelia M. Klingele, Patrick Sharkey, and Jacob William Faber.

165 **white person somewhere before:** Peggy McIntosh, "White Privilege: Unpacking the Invisible Knapsack," *Peace and Freedom* (July/August 1989), 10–12. Jared's experience of it being unusual to be the only white person in a public space tracks closely with McIntosh's essay. On a list of twenty-six examples of white privilege, the first reads: "I can if I wish arrange to be in the company of people of my race most of the time. "

168 **to be breaking the law:** Al Baker, "New York Minorities Frisked 9 Times as Often, Data Find," *New York Times*, May 12, 2010, https://www.nytimes .com/2010/05/13/nyregion/13frisk.html; Ashley Southall and Michael Gold, "Why 'Stop-and-Frisk' Inflamed Black and Hispanic Neighborhoods," *New York Times*, November 17, 2019, https://www.nytimes.com/2019/11/17 /nyregion/bloomberg-stop-and-frisk-new-york.html.

169 **public health school in the country:** "Best Public Health Schools," *U.S. News and World Report*, accessed April 21, 2023, https://www.usnews.com /best-graduate-schools/top-health-schools/public-health-rankings.

169 **$33,000 a year:** Tammy Berwanger (assistant dean of marketing and communications, Johns Hopkins School of Nursing), email message to Madysen Luebke, April 19, 2023.

169 **and pale, freckled skin:** This passage and all of the following sections about Merrin are drawn from my numerous interviews with Merrin Clough.

170 **at the time was around $2,000:** *2015–2023 Housing Element* (El Cerrito, CA: Community Development Department, El Cerrito City Council, April 2015), 42, https://el-cerrito.org/900/Housing-Element-2015–2023.

170 **more than $130,000 a year:** "Results for Jared Bunde," Transparent California, https://transparentcalifornia.com/salaries/search/?q=jared +bunde.

170 **safely in the middle class:** According to the Department of Housing and Urban Development's Family Median Income Documentation System (available at https://www.huduser.gov/portal/datasets/il/il2020/select_Geography .odn), the 2020 median household income in the Oakland-Fremont metropolitan area (roughly speaking, the East Bay) was $119,200. That puts the annual income range of the middle class (for all sizes of households) from $79,864 at the low end to $238,400 at the high end.

171 **twelve years later, in 2008:** John Eligon, "Does Race Matter in America's Most Diverse ZIP Codes?" *New York Times*, November 24, 2017, https:// www.nytimes.com/2017/11/24/us/does-race-matter-in-americas-most -diverse-zip-codes.html.

172 **would require less paperwork:** Korver-Glenn, *Race Brokers*, 108.

173 **in common with the seller:** Joann S. Lublin, "Can I Buy Your House, Pretty Please?" *Wall Street Journal*, January 10, 2013, https://www.wsj.com /articles/SB10001424127887323482504578227703128967098.

173 **"to fair housing violations":** "Love Letters or Liability Letters?" National Association of Realtors, October 23, 2020, https://www.nar.realtor /fair-housing-corner/love-letters-or-liability-letters.

173 **she realized the couple was Black:** Memorandum & Order, Clinton-Brown v. Hardick, No. 1:21-cv-00176 (D. Mass., April 15, 2021). The case was transferred to Rhode Island and settled for an undisclosed amount in October 2021.

173 **insisted on them anyway:** If my world is any indication, the practice has been slow to recede. In June 2021 I wrote a "love letter" at the suggestion of a Realtor. In July 2021, a white friend of mine, unaware of NAR's directive and encouraged by another Realtor, wrote a successful one, too.

173 **down payment and closing costs:** Deed for [block and lot redacted], Vallejo, CA, November 23, 2016, document no. 201600108977, Solano County Assessor/Recorder, Fairfield, CA; Estimated Buyer's Settlement Statement for Jared Bunde and Merrin Clough, Old Republic Title Company, November 30, 2016; copy in possession of author.

174 **home's value grows:** Toni Vranjes, "Proposition 13 Under Increased Scrutiny as California Faces Economic Crisis," KCET (Los Angeles), October 13, 2020, https://www.kcet.org/shows/the-first-angry-man/proposition-13-under -increased-scrutiny-as-california-faces-economic-crisis.

174 **outside of the family:** "[Proposition] 58: Taxation. Family Transfers," in March Fong Eu and John Vickerman, *California Ballot Pamphlet, General Election* (Sacramento, CA: California Secretary of State, 1986), 24–27; "Proposition 193: Property Taxation: Purchase or Change in Ownership: Parent-Child Transfer Exclusion," California Legislative Analyst's Office, March 1996, https://lao.ca.gov/ballot/1996/prop193_3_1996.html; "Proposition 19: Changes Certain Property Tax Rules. Legislative Constitutional Amendment," California Legislative Analyst's Office, November 3, 2020, https://lao.ca.gov/ballot/2020/Prop19-110320.pdf.

174 **destined to shrink government:** Conor Dougherty, "California Tax Revolt Faces a Retreat, 40 Years Later," *New York Times*, October 27, 2020, https://www.nytimes.com/2020/10/27/business/economy/california -property-tax-proposition-15.html; Adam Clymer, "Reagan Urges Party to Support Tax Cuts," *New York Times*, June 25, 1978.

174 **taxes double in just a few years:** Doerr, *California's Tax Machine*, 131.

174 **lobbyist named Howard Jarvis:** "Generals of a Rebellion by California Taxpayers," *New York Times*, June 8, 1978.

174 **"life, liberty, and illegal aliens":** *The First Angry Man*, directed by Jason Cohn and Camille Servan-Schreiber (Berkeley, CA: Bread and Butter Films, 2019), PBS (streaming), 28:29.

174 **use of "forced busing":** *First Angry Man*, 37:49, 38:13. For a clear discussion of the link between the California "tax revolt," spearheaded by Harold Jarvis, and opponents of school integration, the filmmakers' interviews with "anti-busing" activist Bobbi Fiedler are instructive, as is the archival footage used in the film.

175 **"their piece of the system":** *First Angry Man*, 39:20.

175 **arrived on the other side:** Slater, *Freedom to Discriminate*, 64.

175 **low- and moderate-cost housing:** *Proposition 13: Its Impact on California and Implications* (Sacramento, CA: California Budget Project, April

1997), 10, https://calbudgetcenter.org/app/uploads/2018/09/Issue-Brief
_Proposition-13-Its-Impact-on-California-and-Implications_04.1997.pdf.

175 **were no longer a good bet:** *Proposition 13*, 10.

176 **saved $12 million:** *First Angry Man*, 40:44.

176 **savings of $462 a month:** These figures are based on an original cal-
culator developed by Madysen Luebke in support of this book, referred to
hereafter as Author's Proposition 13 Calculator. Many thanks to Patrick J.
Murphy, director of resource equity and public finance at the Opportunity
Institute for guidance on methodology. Calculations and methodology are
available on whitebonus.com.

176 **and threatened public programs:** O'Sullivan, Sexton, and Sheffrin, *Property Taxes*, 32–33.

176 **value climbed by 65 percent:** This is according to a Redfin search for
Jared and Merrin's address in April 2023.

176 **went up by 9 percent:** Jared and Merrin purchased their house in 2016
for $445,000. By early summer 2022, the property website Redfin estimated
its value at $774,814. That is an increase of $329,814, or 74 percent. The tax-
able value, increasing by 2 percent a year as per state law, began at $445,000
in 2017 and in 2022 sat at $486,668, an increase of $41,668—or just 9.36 percent. That is the equivalent of gaining $288,146 in untaxed wealth.

177 **more than $68,000:** Author's Proposition 13 Calculator, www.whitebonus
.com.

178 **students are white:** "District Performance Review: Vallejo City Unified," California School Dashboard, accessed April 21, 2023, https://
www.caschooldashboard.org/reports/48705810000000/2022; "QuickFacts:
Vallejo, California," accessed August 27, 2023, U.S. Census Bureau, https://
www.census.gov/quickfacts/fact/table/vallejocitycalifornia/POP010220.

178 **being socioeconomically disadvantaged:** "Vallejo City Unified," Cal.
School Dashboard.

179 **"very low" in academic performance:** Sean F. Reardon, "School Segregation and Racial Academic Achievement Gaps," *RSF: The Russell Sage Foundation Journal of the Social Sciences* 2, no. 5 (September 2016): 49–51, https://doi
.org/10.7758/RSF.2016.2.5.03.

179 **$20,942 a year for secondary?:** Melanie Hanson, "Average Cost of Pri-
vate School," Education Data Initiative, last updated March 25, 2023, https:
//educationdata.org/average-cost-of-private-school.

180 **either low or very low quality:** "Vallejo City Unified," Cal. School
Dashboard.

Chapter 7: My Childhood

181 **she was having suicidal thoughts:** Summary of neuropsychological examination for Charyl McMillan, December 13, 1985, Midwestern Educational Resources Center, copy in possession of author; Test. of Steven Newman 119–20, McMillan v. Auto Club Ins. Ass'n., No. 86–318–187-CK (Wayne County Cir. Ct., 1989), copy in possession of author. Hereafter, filings and records from this case will be cited by giving the full document name and pincite, followed by: *McMillan v. Auto Club.* Full citations are given to the case's various appeals.

181 **showed "moderate degenerative changes":** X-ray report for Charyl McMillan, November 3, 1984, William Beaumont Hospital, Royal Oak, MI, copy in possession of author.

182 **advice about how to pay for it:** Exhibit prepared for arguments in *McMillan v. Auto Club.*

182 **he still collects from today:** Stephen Hopkins (plaintiffs attorney in *McMillan v. Auto Club*), interview by the author, January 24, 2020; JM and BM interview, March 2023.

182 **modifying our home or hiring help:** Wayne Miller (family attorney in no-fault case), interview by the author, June 16, 2023.

182 **increasingly clear she needed:** Miller, interview.

182 **covering my mother's care:** Stephen Hopkins to Sandra Beck, December 6, 1984, copy in possession of author.

182 *Why should the insurer have to pay:* Test. of Sandra Beck 73–76, *McMillan v. Auto Club.*

183 *"I don't understand what happened":* Progress notes for Charyl McMillan, November 19, 1984, Pathways Clinic, copy in possession of author; Test. of John McMillan 160, *McMillan v. Auto Club*; Test. of Igor Grant 45, *McMillan v. Auto Club*; Neurophysical exam report for Charyl McMillan, September 29, 1986, copy in possession of author.

183 **having "severe to profound impairment":** Progress notes for Charyl McMillan, November 19, 1984.

183 **"taken on [the children's] behalf":** Summary of neuropsychological evaluation for Charyl McMillan, December 13, 1985.

184 **was not an option:** Shira Turrentine, interview by the author, March 23, 2023; Turrentine v. General Motors, 499 N.W.2d 411 (Mich. Ct. App. 1993).

184 **volunteering to help:** Turrentine, interview.

184 **and "cannot be managed":** Erica L. Green, "Why Are Black Students Punished So Often? Minnesota Confronts a National Quandary," *New York*

Times, March 18, 2018, https://www.nytimes.com/2018/03/18/us/politics
/school-discipline-disparities-white-black-students.html.

185 **than their white counterparts:** James F. Gregory, "The Crime of
Punishment: Racial and Gender Disparities in the Use of Corporal Punish-
ment in U.S. Public Schools," *Journal of Negro Education* 64, no. 4 (Autumn
1995): 458; Daniel Losen et al., *Are We Closing the School Discipline Gap?* (Los
Angeles: Center for Civil Rights Remedies, University of California, Los
Angeles, 2015), 6; Richard Welsh and Shafiqua Little, "The School Disci-
pline Dilemma: A Comprehensive Review of Disparities and Alternative
Approaches," *Review of Educational Research* 88, no. 5 (October 2018): 757;
Richard O. Welsh (assistant professor of educational leadership and policy
studies, new york university), email to Madysen Luebke, July 28, 2022.

185 **Total Therapy Management:** Test. of John McMillan 254–55, *McMillan
v. Auto Club.*

185 **there were 266:** "Our History," Brain Injury Association of America,
accessed April 16, 2023, https://www.biausa.org/about/history.

186 **attracted investment capital:** Susan Connors (president, Brain Injury
Association of America), interview by the author, July 12, 2021; Lester M. Sal-
amon, "The Resilient Sector: The State of Nonprofit America," in *The State
of Nonprofit America*, ed. Salamon (Washington, D.C.: Brookings Institution
Press, 2012), 15; *Rehabilitation Facilities for People with Head Injuries, Hearing
Before the Human Resources and Intragovernmental Relations Committee of the
Committee on Government Operations*, 102nd Congress (1992), 301, https://hdl
.handle.net/2027/pst.000020337179.

186 **with "enormous growth potential":** Milt Freudenheim, "Rehabilitation in Head Injuries," *New York Times*, December 29, 1987.

186 **worked, and which did not:** *Head Injuries Hearing*, 102nd Congress,
191–92.

186 **$400 a day for residential care:** Freudenheim, "Rehabilitation in Head
Injuries."

186 **operated in the United States:** Freudenheim, "Rehabilitation in Head
Injuries"; Peter Kerr, "Treating of Severe Brain Injuries Is Profitable, but Not
for Patients," *New York Times*, March 16, 1992.

186 **accreditation ensuring standards of care:** *Head Injuries Hearing*, 102nd
Congress, 191–92.

186 **held a hearing to parse them:** *Head Injuries Hearing*, 102nd Congress, 2.

186 **investigation into the industry:** Kerr, "Treating of Severe Brain Injuries."

187 **do not remember being told at all:** Johanna McMillan, interview; Shana McMillan, interview by the author, March 5, 2023.

188 **"take care of herself," he says:** JM and BM interview, March 2023.

188 **"that she previously enjoyed":** Progress note for Charyl McMillan, March 23, 1988, Total Therapy, copy in possession of author.

188 **we had bills totaling $45,265:** Bill for treatment for Charyl McMillan, April 31, 1988, Total Therapy, copy in possession of author.

189 **find another way to care for her:** Kay Farnell to John McMillan, December 17, 1987, copy in possession of author.

189 **one-third of what remained:** Wayne Miller, interview by the author, June 19, 2023.

189 **providing adult foster care:** Pamela Lamb to John McMillan, January 6, 1988, copy in possession of author. The letter encloses the admission policy and indicates that Total Therapy has a license for adult foster care.

189 **maintaining a quality of life:** Rebecca Gepner to John McMillan, April 22, 1988, copy in possession of author; Progress note for Charyl McMillan, May 5, 1988, Total Therapy, copy in possession of author.

189 **would cost $77,000 a year:** Brant E. Fries et al., "A Screening System for Michigan's Home-and Community-Based Long-Term Care Programs," *Gerontologist* 42, no. 4 (August 2002): 463–64; Wayne Miller, interview by the author, June 15, 2023; Martha Shipley (case manager) to Wayne Miller, May 4, 1987. The medical insurance my family had at the time covered modest health costs like occupational therapy. It did not cover the ongoing costs of care for a person disabled by a car accident, let alone the cost of providing that care at home. As for public health care options available in the late 1980s and early 1990s, Michigan did not begin providing Medicaid coverage for adults who were elderly or disabled until 1992.

190 **scope of services had *decreased*:** Cost breakdown for Charyl McMillan, undated (ca. 1988), Total Therapy, copy in possession of author. In May 1988, Total Therapy billed my family $9,013 for my mother's care, which comprised $7,500 for room and board, $1,163 for therapeutic treatments, and $350 for day programs. By November, the total cost was $13,440, which comprised $10,500 for room and board, which had increased by $50 a day; the therapeutic program had been discontinued; and $2,965 for day programs, the unit cost of which had increased by 70 percent without explanation.

190 **we had been billed $145,784:** I arrived at this number by tallying the bills my family received from Total Therapy for the year of 1988.

191 **Burger King and Sbarro:** Full-page advertisement for Summit Place Mall, *Detroit Free Press*, March 9, 1989.

192 **denial of claims "standard procedure":** Voir Dire 37, *McMillan v. Auto Club*.

192 **"hard enough to knock her out":** Def.'s Closing Arg. 102–03, *McMillan v. Auto Club*.

192 **had made her MS worse:** Pl.'s Opening Statement 64, *McMillan v. Auto Club*.

193 **was for Total Therapy:** Pl.'s Closing Argument 149–50, 153–55, *McMillan v. Auto Club*.

193 **covered by no-fault insurance:** Miller, interview, June 15, 2023.

193 **work within three months?:** Rebecca W. Rimel, et al., "Disability Caused by Minor Head Injury," abstract, *Neurosurgery* 9, no. 3 (September 1981): 221–28.

193 **billed for her care:** Statement of Juror 7 (foreperson) 173–74, *McMillan v. Auto Club*.

194 **car accident or no:** Post-Trial Hr'g 19, *McMillan v. Auto Club*.

194 **the case's exhibits:** Miller, interview, June 15, 2023.

194 **would be covered by the insurer:** McMillan v. Auto Club Ins. Ass'n., 502 N.W.2d 48 (Mich. Ct. App. 1993).

194 **for ongoing care:** McMillan v. Auto Club Ins. Ass'n., 491 N.W.2d 593 (Mich. Ct. App. 1992).

194 **consider them for future cases:** Julie Camden to Wayne Miller, February 16, 1990, copy in possession of author.

194 **send her somewhere else:** JM and BM interview, March 2023; Bill for treatment of Charyl McMillan, December 31, 1989, copy in possession of author.

195 **"we went along with that":** JM and BM interview, March 2023.

195 **"importance of marriage":** Wayne Miller, interview by the author, June 19, 2023.

195 **"in charge of their own mother":** Test. of John McMillan 99–100, *McMillan v. Auto Club*.

195 **steps be taken on our behalf:** Summary of neuropsychological evaluation for Charyl McMillan, December 13, 1985.

195 **we all endured without complaint:** JM and BM interview, March 2023.

195 **he was dating:** Elaine Fishbaugh, interview by the author, March 22, 2023.

196 **someone she could help:** JM and BM interview, March 2023.

196 **in February 1990:** Default J. of Divorce, McMillan v. McMillan, No. 90–384510-DM (Oakland County Cir. Ct., 1990).

196 **"Time will tell":** Katheryn Weddle, journal entry, February 16, 1990, copy in possession of author. This journal, along with medical records, aided in the timeline of the passages covering my mother's death.

196 **couple weeks before:** Default J. of Divorce, McMillan v. McMillan.

199 **first labor laws in the 1930s:** "History of Federal Minimum Wage Rates Under the Fair Labor Standards Act, 1938–2009," U.S. Department of Labor, accessed April 16, 2023, https://www.dol.gov/agencies/whd/minimum -wage/history/chart.

199 **to pay Black workers fairly:** Juan F. Perea, "The Echoes of Slavery: Recognizing the Racist Origins of the Agricultural and Domestic Worker Exclusion from the National Labor Relations Act," *Ohio State Law Journal* 72, no. 1 (2011): 129–32.

200 **She regrets this:** Shana McMillan, interview.

201 **entitled to no-fault benefits:** McMillan v. Auto Club Ins. Ass'n., 502 N.W.2d 48 (Mich. Ct. App. 1993). This subsequent appeal was on remand from the Michigan Supreme Court.

202 **250 studies used that language:** Anne Elixhauser, Bryan Luce, William Taylor, and Joseph Reblando, "Health Care CBA/CEA: An Update on the Growth and Composition of the Literature," *Medical Care* 31, no. 7 (July 1993): JS7.

202 **they can be fed to create it:** For a compelling and thorough discussion of these practices, see Caitlin Rosenthal's *Accounting for Slavery: Masters and Management.*

202 **"paid to do so," they write:** Kevin Lander and Jonathan Pritchett, "When to Care: The Economic Rationale of Slavery Health Care Provision," *Social Science History* 33, no. 2 (Summer 2009): 155–82.

209 **as similar Black families:** U.S. Department of Health and Human Services, Children's Bureau, *National Study of Protective, Preventive, and Reunification Services Delivered to Children and Their Families* (Washington, D.C.: Government Printing Office, 1997), 7–18. This report documents that among families with child welfare cases who were not enrolled in cash welfare, 23 percent of white children were placed in foster care, as were 30 percent of Hispanic children and 62 percent of African American children. This means that 77 percent of white families were left intact, compared to 38 percent of Black families.

209 **children into foster care:** 130 Cong. Rec. S21779 (1984); Hatcher, *Poverty Industry,* 146n6; U.S. Census Bureau, *Money Income and Poverty Status of Families and Persons in the United States: 1984,* Current Population Reports,

P-60, no. 149, table 1, "Selected Characteristics of Families—Number of Families and Median Income in 1984 and 1983 of All Families and Families with Householders Working Year Round Full Time, by Race and Spanish Origin of Householder," pp. 11–12; Daniel L. Hatcher, "Collateral Children: Consequence and Illegality at the Intersection of Foster Care and Child Support," *Brooklyn Law Review* 74, no. 4 (2009): 1344.

209 **any state interested in doing so:** Hatcher, "Collateral Children," 1346–47.

209 **Michigan was interested:** Bob Wheaton (public information officer, Michigan Department of Health and Human Services), email message to Madysen Luebke, September 6, 2022.

209 **have faced a new monthly bill:** Maria Cancian, Steven Cook, Mai Seki, and Lynn Wimer, "Making Parents Pay: The Unintended Consequences of Charging Parents for Foster Care," *Children and Youth Services Review* 72 (2017): 109, http://dx.doi.org/10.1016/j.childyouth.2016.10.018.

210 **cost my family nearly $8,000:** Friend of the Court Bureau, *Michigan Child Support Guideline Manual* (Lansing, MI: Friend of the Court Advisory Committee, State Court Administrative Office, January, 1991), 44. This is the manual that was effective at the time, and it includes tables for calculating costs for foster care based on parent income. For full documentation and calculations, see whitebonus.com.

Chapter 8: Barbara Nathan Katz: Poverty

212 **International House of Pancakes:** Irma Perez, interviews by the author, March 24, 2022, and January 23, 2023.

212 **Mike, who'd go first:** The accounts of Barb's life and family, unless otherwise cited, are drawn from my interviews with her sisters: Anita Beckenstein, Debbie Nathan, and Miriam Lerner between February 2022 and June 2023.

214 **in the late 1990s:** John Nova Lomax, "Is Texas Southern, Western, or Truly a Lone Star?," *Texas Monthly*, March 3, 2015, https://www.texasmonthly.com/the-daily-post/is-texas-southern-western-or-truly-a-lone-star/.

214 **two mentioned southern heritage:** Light Cummins, "History, Memory, and Rebranding Texas as Western for the 1936 Centennial," in McCaslin, Chipman, and Torget, *This Corner of Canaan*, 47n37, 48n38, 49–50.

214 **limit Jewish enrollment:** Susan H. Greenberg, "Intellectuals at the Gate," Inside Higher Ed, September 21, 2022.

215 **instead, graduating in 1948:** Melissa Kean, "William Max Nathan, Class of 1916," Rice History Corner, Rice University, December 3, 2010,

https://ricehistorycorner.com/2010/12/03/william-max-nathan-class-of
-1916/.

215 **murdering a teenage girl, in 1915:** "Leo M. Frank Dies; Georgia Lynch-
ers Tie Him to Tree," *University Missourian* (Columbia, MO), August 17, 1915.
The Library of Congress has a page dedicated to coverage of Leo Frank:
https://guides.loc.gov/chronicling-america-leo-frank/selected-articles.

215 **minds in the postwar years:** "SS and Foreign Policy," Holocaust Ency-
clopedia, United States Holocaust Memorial Museum, accessed June 20, 2023,
https://encyclopedia.ushmm.org/content/en/article/ss-and-nazi-policy.

215 **happened with startling frequency:** Clive Webb, "Counterblast: How
the Atlanta Temple Bombing Strengthened the Civil Rights Cause," *Southern Spaces*, June 22, 2009, https://southernspaces.org/2009/counterblast-how
-atlanta-temple-bombing-strengthened-civil-rights-cause/.

215 **between 1957 and 1958:** Faygie Holt, "How a Spate of Synagogue Bombings in the 1950s Is Impacting Us Today," Aish, May 17, 2022, https://aish
.com/how-a-spate-of-synagogue-bombings-in-the-1950s-is-impacting-us
-today/.

215 **brought his bride back to Houston:** Marriage License for Charles
Nathan and Sylvia Laufe, May 25, 1948, from Ancestry.com.

216 **to 29 percent white:** U.S. Census Bureau, 1950 Census, vol. 3, Census
Tract Statistics, ch. 24, Houston, TX, table 1, "Characteristics of the Population, by Census Tracts," tract 39, p. 19, https://www2.census.gov/library
/publications/decennial/1950/population-volume-3/41557421v3p2ch05.pdf.

216 **99.5 percent white, in 1949:** U.S. Census Bureau, 1950 Census, vol. 2, Characteristics of the Population, part 43, Texas, table 34, "General Characteristics of the Population for Standard Metropolitan Areas, Urbanized Areas, and
Urban Places of 10,000 or More," p. 100, https://www2.census.gov/library
/publications/decennial/1950/population-volume-2/11027772v2p43ch3.pdf;
U.S. Census Bureau, 1960 Census, vol. 1, Characteristics of the Population, part
45, Texas, table 21, "Characteristics of the Population for Standard Metropolitan
Areas, Urbanized Areas, and Urban Places of 10,000 or More," p. 117, https://
www2.census.gov/library/publications/decennial/1960/population-volume-1
/33255142v1p45ch04.pdf; Deed for lot 8 of Teas Garden, Harris County, TX,
August 30, 1949, vol. 1988, p. 459, Harris County Clerk, Houston, TX.

216 **workplace of white women's homes:** A significant body of scholarship
documents and explores the ways that domestic work in the twentieth century mimicked the master-slave relationship of the nineteenth. See: Judith
Rollins, *Between Women*, and Premilla Nadasen, *Household Workers Unite*.

216 **and labor law protections:** Hugh Schutte, "Household Help Is Scarce, Expensive in South, Too," *Kilgore* (TX) *News Herald*, May 18, 1958. This Associated Press article about domestic work in the Deep South reported that daily maid service typically ran eight hours a day and paid $4.00 to $5.00 for the day. Meanwhile, minimum wage for jobs covered by the Fair Labor Standards Act was at $1.00 an hour. The rates in 1959, reported the AP, were considered "expensive" by southern women; before World War II, maids could be hired at $2.00 per day, at a time when the minimum wage was $0.30 an hour ($2.40 per day).

216 **"of the Caucasian race":** Restrictions for Teas Gardens, Harris County, TX, February 1, 1949, vol. 1949, p. 586–90, Harris County Clerk, Houston, TX; Restrictions for Post Oak Plaza, Harris County, TX, June 24, 1948, vol. 1948, pp. 348–51, Harris County Clerk, Houston, TX.

216 **the end of the century:** U.S. Census Bureau, Census 2000, PHC-1-45, Summary Population and Housing Characteristics for Texas, table 4, "Race and Hispanic or Latino," p. 206, https://www2.census.gov/library/publications/2002/dec/phc-1-45.pdf.

217 **they were concerned:** Anita Beckenstein (Barb's sister), interview by the author, January 11, 2023.

217 **loved one to an asylum:** Frank and Glied, *Better but Not Well*, 72; David A. Rochefort, "Origins of the 'Third Psychiatric Revolution': The Community Mental Health Centers Act of 1963," *Journal of Health Politics, Policy and Law* 9, no. 1, (Spring 1984): 12–13, https://doi.org/10.1215/03616878-9-1-1.

218 **feel close to anyone at all:** Jennifer S. Williams, Shelley A. Riggs, and Patricia L. Kaminski, "A Typology of Childhood Sibling Subsystems That May Emerge in Abusive Family Systems," *Family Journal* 24, no. 4 (October 2016): 3–5, https://doi.org/10.1177/1066480716663182.

218 **position at the university:** "New Tech Director," *Albuquerque Journal*, June 16, 1977.

219 **relatively complacent workforce:** Friedan, *Global Capitalism*, 242.

219 **passed from 1933 to 1939:** Historians distinguish between the First and Second New Deals. The first began when Roosevelt took office in 1933 and passed nine acts in the first hundred days of his administration, all of them aimed at jump-starting the economy. It took until 1935 for policies aimed at addressing the hardships of the underpaid and unemployed, called the Second New Deal, to begin being passed. See: Katznelson, *Fear Itself*.

219 **on behalf of workers:** Social Security Act of 1935, Pub. L. No. 74–271, §§

201, 301, 501, 49 Stat. 620, 622, 626, 629 (1935); National Labor Relations Act of 1935, Pub. L. No. 74–198, §§ 7–9, 49 Stat. 449, 452–453 (1935).

219 **overtime pay for covered workers:** Fair Labor Standards Act of 1938, Pub. L. No. 75–718, §§ 6–7, 52 Stat. 1062–1063 (1938).

219 **was absent from the list:** Starr, *Social Transformation*, 269.

220 **with organized white supremacy:** Katznelson, *Fear Itself*, 128.

220 **ignore you all night:** Katznelson, *Fear Itself*, 260.

221 **call it American exceptionalism:** For more on this topic, see Seymour Lipset's *American Exceptionalism*, which explores the differences between the United States and Europe at great length.

221 **social benefits of any kind:** Béland et al., *Welfare State*, 78–81. Nineteen European countries established pensions prior to 1926, and sixteen introduced unemployment insurance prior to 1928, compared to the United States' introduction of similar policies in 1936 with the Social Security Act. Fifteen European countries introduced family allowances, which the United States has not introduced, between 1930 and 1947.

221 **more than half their children:** Sheila B. Kamerman, "A Global History of Early Childhood Education and Care" (paper commissioned for Education for All Global Monitoring Report 2007, *Strong Foundations: Early Childhood Care and Education*), 2006, 71. This paper documented that Germany, France, Italy, the Netherlands, Belgium, Luxembourg, Ireland, Denmark, Greece, and Spain provided 50–95 percent of their nations' children with free childcare from age three until school attendance began. Portugal reported providing care for thirty-five percent of its children, and the United Kingdom reported providing care for 35–40 percent of its children.

221 **insurance or national health care:** *Health Care Systems in the EU: A Comparative Study* (working paper, Directorate General for Research, European Parliament, Luxembourg, May 1998), 17–18, 126–27.

221 **on safety net programs:** Lindert, *Making Social Spending Work*, 105.

222 **half to political institutions:** Alesina and Glaeser, *Fighting Poverty*, 75, 181, 217.

222 **declined an average of $138:** Alesina and Glaeser, *Fighting Poverty*, 148, 165.

222 **Jill Quadagno and Cybelle Fox:** Quadagno, *Color of Welfare*, 194; Fox, *Three Worlds of Relief*, 26–27.

223 **on Dallas's northwest border:** Deed for unit 409 of Forest West Condominiums Phases I & II, Dallas, TX, February 9, 1983, vol. 83028, p. 2115, Dallas County Clerk, Dallas, TX.

223 **cannot say for sure:** Debbie Nathan, text messages with the author, June 9, 2023.

223 **a Cadillac each year:** Irma Perez, interview.

223 **defaulted on the condo's mortgage:** Substitute Trustee's Deed for unit 409 of Forest West Condominiums Phases I & II, Dallas, TX, June 13, 1994, vol. 93199, p. 3525, Dallas County Clerk, Dallas, TX.

223 **Mike had inherited from his father:** Deed for lot 27 of Sixth Installment of Crest Meadow Estates, Dallas, TX, February 13, 1996, vol. 96030, p. 5730, Dallas County Clerk, Dallas, TX.

223 **a new, upscale subdivision:** Deed for lot 27 of [Sixth] Installment of Crest Meadow Estates, Dallas, TX, February 26, 1971, vol. 71040, p. 1999, Dallas County Clerk, Dallas, TX.

224 **in the years since:** Jennifer Martel and Laura Kelter, "The Job Market Remains Strong in 1999," February 2000, Monthly Labor Review, Bureau of Labor Statistics, https://www.bls.gov/mlr/2000/02/art1full.pdf; "Industries at a Glance: Food and Drinking Places," accessed August 27, 2023, Bureau of Labor Statistics, https://www.bls.gov/iag/tgs/iag722.htm. According to these reports, there were 7,946,000 workers in food and drinking places in 1999, which jumped 54 percent, to 12,235,800 in 2023.

224 **tipped workers like servers:** "Tip Credit and Tip Pooling Provisions of the Fair Labor Standards Act," Congressional Research Service, June 27, 2018, https://crsreports.congress.gov/product/pdf/IF/IF10917/2.

224 **make up the rest with tips:** The 1966 amendments took more than a decade to bring the newly covered workers up to minimum wage. In 1966, the jobs originally covered by the FLSA had a minimum wage of $1.40. Non-farm jobs added in 1966 were at $1.00 an hour, and did not reach parity with other jobs until 1978. See: "History of Federal Minimum Wage Rates Under the Fair Labor Standards Act, 1938–2009," Wage and Hour Division, U.S. Department of Labor, accessed April 23, 2023, https://www.dol.gov/agencies/whd/minimum-wage/history/chart.

225 **to minimum wage at all:** Kai Filion and Sylvia Allegretto, *Waiting for Change: The $2.13 Federal Subminimum Wage* (Washington, D.C.: Economic Policy Institute, February 23, 2011), https://www.epi.org/publication/waiting_for_change_the_213_federal_subminimum_wage/.

225 **$2.13 an hour:** "Minimum Wages for Tipped Employees," Wage and Hour Division, U.S. Department of Labor, January 1, 2023, https://www.dol.gov/agencies/whd/state/minimum-wage/tipped.

225 **around $26,000 a year:** "Waiters and Waitresses—Occupational Out-

look Handbook," U.S. Bureau of Labor Statistics, U.S. Department of Labor, last updated September 8, 2022, https://www.bls.gov/ooh/food-preparation -and-serving/waiters-and-waitresses.htm.

225 **without ever dirtying their ties:** Perez, interviews.

225 **Social Security in those days:** Bryant, interview.

226 **rarely got above $25,000:** I've drawn this estimate from what Mike and Barb's acquaintances and coworkers remember about their incomes. The manager of the Corinthians, Bill Bryant, remembered that Mike was getting $800 a month from social security, or about $9,600 a year. Combined with the $15,000 that Irma Perez estimated she made each year (and suggested Barb would have likely earned as well) their household income would have been around $24,600.

226 **nation's lowest-income households:** Pew Income Data.

226 **to cover basic expenses:** Amy Glasmeier, "Living Wage Calculation for Denton County, Texas," Living Wage Calculator, Massachusetts Institute of Technology, accessed June 16, 2023, https://livingwage.mit.edu /counties/48121. The required annual income, before taxes, to support two adults in Denton County in 2022 was $58,664. While there is no similar calculation available for the year 2015, adjusting for inflation suggests that a ballpark required annual income for two adults that year would have been $48,765.

226 **Use as they liked:** Miriam Lerner, interview, June 8, 2023.

228 **much contact with the working poor:** Lerner, interview.

228 **they were disabled or a parent:** "A Guide to the Supreme Court's Decision on the ACA's Medicaid Expansion," Kaiser Family Foundation, August 1, 2012, https://www.kff.org/health-reform/issue-brief/a-guide-to-the-supreme -courts-decision/.

229 **had owned enslaved people:** U.S. Census Bureau, 1860 Census enumeration tables, schedule 2, Slave Inhabitants, Scott County, MS, district 3, June 18, 1860, p. 5, right column, line 39, and p. 6, left column, line 1. Census records show that Barb's great-great-grandparents, David and Babette Carb, enslaved two people in Hillsboro, MS: a thirteen-year-old girl and a twenty-three-year-old woman (the census did not name enslaved people). Readers can search the U.S. Census Slave Schedules on Ancestry.com, on familysearch .org, or on microfilm at their local federal depository.

229 **Black students until 1962:** Katharine Shilcutt, "'The Legal Battle over Desegregating Rice' Gives Context to Historic Decision," Office of Public Affairs, Rice University, November 9, 2020, https://news.rice.edu/news/2020 /legal-battle-over-desegregating-rice-gives-context-historic-decision.

229 **to stand in for wages:** Hopkins, *Stable Condition*, 24.

229 **a central political concern:** Starr, *Social Transformation*, 251, 367–68, 370. Starr provides an excellent overview of the political and business interests that gave rise to Medicaid and Medicare.

230 **"will stop this," he said:** Zelizer, *Taxing America*, 21, 151–53; Jonathan Zelizer, interview by the author, June 8, 2023. The historic record does not show legislators, including Mills, speaking openly about race when discussing cash aid or health care programs, Zelizer told me. "It wasn't always explicitly discussed—but everyone knew who you were talking about," he said. "[Mills] has no doubt about who he's talking about when he talks about the poor and welfare. So I wouldn't imagine that wasn't true also for Medicaid," he said.

230 **Black women in New York City:** Douglas S. Reed, "Court-Ordered School Finance Equalization: Judicial Activism and Democratic Opposition," *Developments in School Finance, 1996* (Washington, D.C.: National Center for Education Statistics, U.S. Department of Education, July 1997), 93, http://nces.ed.gov/pubs97/97535g.pdf; Mark Toney, "Revisiting the National Welfare Rights Organization," *Colorlines*, November 29, 2000, https://colorlines.com/article/revisiting-national-welfare-rights-organization/.

231 **fueled Ronald Reagan's rise:** "'Welfare Queen' Becomes Issue in Reagan Campaign," *New York Times*, February 15, 1976.

231 **Black subjects as dysfunctional:** Martin Gilens, "Race and Poverty in America: Public Misperceptions and the American News Media," *Public Opinion Quarterly* 60, no. 4 (Winter 1996): 521.

231 **the largest share of the poor:** John Creamer et al., *Poverty in the United States: 2021* (Washington, D.C.: U.S. Census Bureau, September 2022), 5, https://www.census.gov/content/dam/Census/library/publications/2022/demo/p60-277.pdf. In 2021, the most recent year for which data was available, the largest racial group among the poor were white, non-Hispanic Americans, who made up 40 percent of the poor. The next largest group was Hispanic Americans, at 28 percent, then Black Americans, at 22 percent. Asian Americans that year comprised 5 percent of America's poor, while both American Indians and mixed-race Americans each made up 3 percent of the poor.

232 **$1,700 a month:** Bryant, interview. Bryant told me that most units at Corinthians cost $1,700–1,900 a month. As he often did with residents he felt compassionate toward, he said, he charged Barb and Mike less than the sticker price; he remembers they paid $800. After Barb died, says Bill, Mike sat in his office and cried about struggling to make rent. Bryant told me he dropped

it to $600. "I didn't go through the company, nothing like that. I didn't want them to be on the street," he said.

232 **say advocates, is seven:** Angela Browne, "Fear and the Perception of Alternatives: Asking 'Why Battered Women Don't Leave' Is the Wrong Question," in *The Criminal Justice System and Women*: Offenders, Victims, and Workers, ed. Barbara Raffel Price and Natalie J. Sokoloff (Boston: McGraw-Hill, 1995): 228–45.

233 **10 percent by 2020:** Carter C. Price and Christine Eibner, "For States that Opt Out of Medicaid Expansion: 3.6 Million Fewer Insured and $8.4 Billion Less in Federal Payments," *Health Affairs* 32, no. 6 (2013): 1031, https://doi .org/10.1377/hlthaff.2012.1019; 42 U.S.C. § 1396d(y)(1) (2022). This portion of the Social Security Act, as amended by the ACA, sets the schedule for diminishing payments.

233 **before the expansion:** 42 U.S.C. § 18051(d). This portion of the ACA sets out the rules for payments to the states to defray the cost of Medicaid expansion.

233 **stop the ACA:** National Federation of Independent Business v. Sebelius, 567 U.S. 519 (2012).

233 **rights of their citizens:** Amended Complaint at 4, Florida v. U.S. Department of Health and Human Services, No. 3:10-cv-91-RV/EMT (N.D. Fla. May 14, 2010). After appeal, Fla. v. Dep't of Health and Human Serv., 648 F.3d 1235 (11th Cir., 2011), was combined with Nat'l Fed. of Ind. Bus. v. Sebelius, 567 U.S. 519 (2012) when it went to the Supreme Court.

234 **sneakers or cupcakes:** Paul Gottlieb, "Peninsula Residents Disappointed, Elated by Health Law Ruling," *Peninsula Daily News* (Port Angeles, WA), June 29, 2012, https://www.peninsuladailynews.com/news/peninsula-residents -disappointed-elated-by-health-law-ruling/.

234 **Black or Hispanic:** Samantha Artiga, "The Impact of the Coverage Gap for Adults in States not Expanding Medicaid by Race and Ethnicity,"KFF, October 26, 2015, https://www.kff.org/racial-equity-and-health-policy /issue-brief/the-impact-of-the-coverage-gap-in-states-not-expanding-medic aid-by-race-and-ethnicity/. In 2015, 3.1 million Americans were in the "coverage gap." Of those, 56 percent—1.7 million—were people of color.

234 **they broadly supported it:** Mark Schlesinger and Tae-ku Lee, "Is Health Care Different? Popular Support of Federal Health and Social Policies," *Journal of Health Politics, Policy and Law* 18, no. 3 (Fall 1993): 613.

234 **feature of the Republican party:** Michael Henderson and D. Sunshine Hillygus, "The Dynamics of Health Care Opinion, 2008–2010: Partisanship,

Self-Interest, and Racial Resentment," *Journal of Health Politics, Policy and Law* 36, no. 6 (December 2011): 951–53.

234 **than supporters of Democrats:** For a thorough overview of scholarship linking party identification with racial attitudes, particularly with regard to its relationship to the Affordable Care Act, the work of political scientist Dan Hopkins in *Stable Condition* is instructive.

234 **Medicaid expansion under the ACA:** Daniel Lanford and Jill Quadagno, "Implementing ObamaCare: The Politics of Medicaid Expansion Under the Affordable Care Act of 2010," *Sociological Perspectives* 59, no. 3 (September 2016): 638, http://dx.doi.org/10.1177/0731121415587605.

234 **"open racism in America":** Howard F. Stein and Seth Allcorn, "A Fateful Convergence: Animosity Toward Obamacare, Hatred of Obama, the Rise of Donald Trump, and Overt Racism in America," *Journal of Psychohistory* 45, no. 4 (Spring 2018): 237–39.

235 **"bigotry of low expectations":** "Remarks by Administrator Seema Verma at the National Association of Medicaid Directors (NAMD) 2017 Fall Conference," U.S. Centers for Medicare and Medicaid Services, November 7, 2017, https://www.cms.gov/newsroom/fact-sheets/speech-remarks -administrator-seema-verma-national-association-medicaid-directors-namd -2017-fall.

235 **Medicaid work requirements:** Tracie McMillan, "How One Company is Making Millions Off Trump's War on the Poor," *Mother Jones*, January/ February 2019, https://www.motherjones.com/politics/2018/12/how-one -company-is-making-millions-off-trumps-war-on-the-poor/. Maximus has taken down its 2017 calls, but I reported on the call as part of my story for *Mother Jones*. You can hear a partial recording of the earnings call in question in "Profits and Perverse Incentives," episode 5 of *The Uncertain Hour*, Krissy Clark's 2023 investigative podcast from Marketplace.

235 **the point was moot:** "Section 1115 Waiver Tracker Work Requirements," Kaiser Family Foundation, April 20, 2023, https://www.kff.org /report-section/section-1115-waiver-tracker-work-requirements/.

235 **"do anything about it":** Anne Dunkelberg (advocate with Every Texan), interview by the author, January 24, 2023.

235 **more than any other state:** Anne Dunkelberg, "2021 Census Data Provides Insight into the Uninsured Population of Texas," Every Texan, October 28, 2022, https://everytexan.org/2022/10/28/2021-census-data-provides -insight-into-the-uninsured-population-of-texas/.

235 **paperwork simply forgo insurance:** Dunkelberg, interview.

235 **still had not expanded Medicaid:** "Status of State Medicaid Expansion Decisions: Interactive Map," Kaiser Family Foundation, May 24, 2023, https://www.kff.org/medicaid/issue-brief/status-of-state-medicaid-expansion-decisions-interactive-map/. As of May 2023, ten states had not adopted Medicaid expansion: Alabama, Florida, Georgia, Kansas, Mississippi, South Carolina, Tennessee, Texas, Wisconsin, and Wyoming.

235 **expanded in every state:** Sarah Miller, Norman Johnson, and Laura R. Wherry, "Medicaid and Mortality: New Evidence from Linked Survey and Administrative Data" (working paper 26081, NBER, Cambridge, MA, July 2019), 23, https://www.nber.org/papers/w26081.

236 **per two-week pay period:** Perez, interview.

236 **$2,300 a year:** The premium was calculated by entering Barb's information into Kaiser Family Foundation's 2015 Health Insurance Marketplace Calculator, available at https://www.kff.org/interactive/subsidy-calculator-2015/.

237 **behavioral economics: tunneling:** In their book *Scarcity*, the behavioral economists Eldar Shafir and Sendhil Mullainathan explore the concept of tunneling at length, framing it as an expression of scarcity. This is particularly important, they argue, in understanding the behavior of the poor—who, they are careful to note, have the "same psychological quirks as everyone else" (268), but fewer material resources to compensate for them.

238 **for being a good friend:** Perez, interview.

238 **joined Barb at the table:** Elena Errofeva, interviews by the author, March 22, 2022, and January 21, 2023. This passage and the rest of the account of Barb's death, unless otherwise cited, is drawn from these interviews with Elena.

238 **a sweet, almost rotten, smell:** Pranita Ghimire and Amit S. Dhamoon, "Ketoacidosis," StatPearls, last updated August 8, 2022, https://www.ncbi.nlm.nih.gov/books/NBK534848/; Yu Kuei Lin, interview by the author, January 23, 2022. This and the subsequent descriptions of the physical process of ketoacidosis are drawn from my interview with Dr. Lin or from the Ghimire and Dhamoon article.

240 **freezing the tipped minimum:** Maddie Oatman, "The Racist, Twisted History of Tipping," *Mother Jones*, May/June 2016, https://www.motherjones.com/food/2016/04/restaurants-tipping-racist-origins-saru-jayaraman-forked/; Sylvia Allegretto and David Cooper, *Twenty-Three Years and Still Waiting for Change: Why It's Time to Give Tipped Workers the Regular Minimum Wage* (Washington, D.C.: Economic Policy Institute, July 10, 2014), https://www.epi.org/publication/waiting-for-change-tipped-minimum-wage/.Led

by Herman Cain, the National Restaurant Association became a "lobbying powerhouse" in the 1990s. In 1996, Cain and the NRA successfully
lobbied the Clinton administration to decouple the tipped wage—used
predominantly in restaurants—from the minimum wage. Prior to this
change, the tipped minimum wage was set at 50 to 60 percent of the
minimum wage.

241 **spending had increased their profits:** "The Profitability of Health Insurance Companies," Council of Economic Advisors, Office of the President,
March 2018, https://trumpwhitehouse.archives.gov/wp-content/uploads
/2018/03/The-Profitability-of-Health-Insurance-Companies.pdf; Reed Abel-
son, "Major U.S. Health Insurers Report Big Profits, Benefiting from the
Pandemic," *New York Times*, August 5, 2020, https://www.nytimes.com/2020
/08/05/health/covid-insurance-profits.html. Between implementation of the
Affordable Care Act in 2014 and early 2018, health insurance stocks outperformed the S&P 500 by 106 percent, according to the Council of Economic
Advisers. When the pandemic hit in 2020, insurers reported net earnings
roughly doubled: Anthem went from $1.1 billion in the second quarter of
2019 to $2.3 billion for the same quarter in 2020; UnitedHealth went from
$3.4 billion to $6.7 billion; and Humana reported net income rising from
$940 million to $1.8 million over the same period.

241 **standards of the ACA:** "Cost-Sharing for Plans Offered in the Federal
Marketplace for 2015," Kaiser Family Foundation, accessed June 20, 2023,
https://www.kff.org/slideshow/cost-sharing-for-plans-offered-in-the-federal
-marketplace. As noted earlier, Barb's household income is likely to have been
as low as $24,600 a year. If Barb's plan from her employer had been based
on the ACA's affordability standard for such plans (9.5 percent of household
income), she would have been responsible for paying an estimated $2,337 a
year in premiums. Because this was an employer-provided plan, she would
not have been eligible for government subsidy through the marketplace to
offset its cost.

241 **no longer had to pay:** "Cost sharing," KFF; Matthew Rae, Krutika Amin, and
Cynthia Cox, "ACA's maximum out-of-pocket limit is growing faster than
wages," KFF, July 22, 2022, https://www.healthsystemtracker.org/brief
/aca-maximum-out-of-pocket-limit-is-growing-faster-than-wages. According to KFF, the average deductible for bronze plans nationwide in 2015 was
$5,331. The cap for out-of-pocket maximums, which is usually equal to the
bronze plan maximum, were capped at $6,600 that year.

242 **modest and predictable:** "What Does Medicare Cost?," Centers for

Medicare and Medicaid Services, accessed June 20, 2023, https://www .medicare.gov/basics/get-started-with-medicare/medicare-basics/what-does -medicare-cost. Generally speaking, any individual on Medicare with less than $97,000 of income in 2023 would pay about $165 a month for an insurance premium, and be subject to a $226 deductible.

242 **5 percent of household income:** Medicaid Program; Medicaid and Children's Health Insurance Program (CHIP) Managed Care Access, Finance, and Quality, 88 Fed. Reg. 28092 (May 3, 2023) (proposed rule).

242 **insured through private plans:** Charlie M. Wray, Meena Khare, and Salomeh Keyhani, "Access to Care, Cost of Care, and Satisfaction with Care Among Adults with Private and Public Health Insurance in the US," *JAMA Network Open* 4, no. 6 (2021): e2110275, https://doi.org/10.1001 /jamanetworkopen.2021.10275. This survey of 149,290 Americans found that people with employer-sponsored insurance were less likely than people with Medicaid and Medicare to report instability in insurance coverage, difficulty seeing a physician or taking medication because of costs, and having medical debt. People insured through Medicare—the universal program designed with white, middle-class workers in mind—were more satisfied with their insurance than those with employer-sponsored coverage or Medicaid.

242 **called it caste:** Wilkerson, *Caste*, 22–32.

243 **and expensive system:** Based on lobbying records analyzed by Open Secrets.org, one of the loudest opponents of the Affordable Care Act before its passage, Ohio congressman John Boehner, raised $79 million in campaign donations during his last decade in Congress. The insurance industry ranked among the top five donors to Boehner in those six cycles. In presidential years, the insurance industry's largest donations have gone to national candidates including John McCain, Barack Obama, Hillary Clinton, Mitt Romney, and Donald Trump.

Chapter 9: My Young Adulthood

244 **educational grant at the end:** *Hearing on the Accounting and Management Practices of the Corporation for National Service, Before the Subcomm. on Education and the Workforce, First Session*, 105th Cong. 71 (1997) (testimony of Harris Wofford, chief executive officer of the Corporation for National Service). My income from AmeriCorps is a rough estimate, based on memory, personal records, and the few public reports detailing payment for part-time workers in AmeriCorps. Both my memory and a checking account ledger I maintained in college suggest AmeriCorps paid me around $50 a week; program documents

indicate that part-time workers enrolled in college worked 300 hours each year—roughly 10 hours a week. At the time, minimum wage was $4.25 an hour. As for the tuition grant, Wofford said that a full-time AmeriCorps member received an educational voucher for $4,725 "to help pay for college or pay off college loans." I was part-time, so I received roughly half of that.

245 **what that's like:** Jennifer Engle, "Postsecondary Access and Success for First-Generation College Students," *American Academic* 3, no. 1 (2007): 33.

248 **did not file a report:** John McMillan, co-interview with Bonnie McMillan, conducted by author with Matthew Van Meter present, May 25, 2023; hereafter cited as JM and BM Interview, May 2023. Shana McMillan, interview by the author, March 5, 2022; Johanna McMillan, interview interview by the author, March 6, 2022. My parents tell me they do not remember the incident in September, but they do remember that my father threw my sister and the police were called. My sisters do not want to discuss these events with me. During our conversations, it became clear to me that sometimes "I don't remember" was an honest statement, and sometimes it meant "I don't want to talk about it."

249 **treated like that:** JM and BM interview, May 2023.

255 **around $140 every two weeks:** *National Service Programs: AmeriCorps*USA—Early Program Resource and Benefit Information*, U.S. General Accounting Office, Health, Education, and Human Services Division (Washington, D.C., August 29, 1995), 40.

255 **squarely within functional poverty:** *Housing New York City 1996* (New York: NYC Department of Housing, September 1999), 149; Pew Income Data. During the years that I worked for AmeriCorps and Maggie during the school year, then waited tables and picked up odd jobs in the summer, I earned around $18,900 a year. That was enough, in 1995, to push me above the two-thirds-of-median-income standard that marks the beginning of the middle class for a single adult. Once I paid tuition, which I remember being around $9,000 a year out of pocket, the income off of which I lived totaled about $9,900. That income was equivalent to about 39 percent of Brooklyn's median income for a single person, placing me well below the 50-percent-of-median ceiling for functional poverty.

256 **a "detective for the people":** Wayne Barrett, "Time for Something New," *Village Voice*, January 4, 2011, https://www.villagevoice.com/2011/01/04/wayne-barrett-time-for-something-new/.

256 **investigating sweatshops in Chinatown:** Wayne Barrett, "Cheap Lives: How Rudy Stonewalled the Families of Nine Dead Black Students,"

Village Voice, April 21, 1998; Wayne Barrett and Tracie McMillan, "Geraldine Ferraro: Sweatshop Landlord," *Village Voice*, March 10, 1998.

259 **10 percent just three times:** New York City Rent Guidelines Board, "Rent Guidelines Board Apartment Orders #1 through #54," uploaded June 2022, https://rentguidelinesboard.cityofnewyork.us/wp-content/uploads /2022/06/2022-Apartment-Chart.pdf.

259 **twice that:** Registration Apartment Information for Apt. 2B, 5313 6th Ave., Brooklyn, NY, 11220, New York State Division of Housing and Community Renewal, February 9, 2022, copy in possession of author; James Devitt (managing director of Public Affairs, New York University), email message to Madysen Luebke, October 28, 2021.

259 **set "rent controls" in 1942:** Timothy L. Collins, *An Introduction to the New York City Rent Guidelines Board and the Rent Stabilization System*, rev. ed. (New York: New York City Rent Guidelines Board, January 2020), 22, https://rentguidelinesboard.cityofnewyork.us/wp-content/uploads/2020/01 /intro2020.pdf.

259 **rather than supporting city housing:** Jackson, *Crabgrass Frontier*, 213, 230, 241; Rothstein, *Color of Law*, 70–72.

259 **inclusion instead of exclusion:** Gold, *When Tenants Claimed*, 21–27, 32.

260 **and when it could increase:** Collins, *Rent Guidelines Board*, 24–25.

260 **in the country: rent stabilization:** Collins, *Rent Guidelines Board*, 26; Brittany Lyte, "The Three Best Cities for Rent Control," *Christian Science Monitor*, May 6, 2016, https://www.csmonitor.com/Business/Saving-Money /2016/0506/The-three-best-cities-for-rent-control.

261 **my third and current one:** *Housing New York City 1996*, report summary, New York City Department of Housing Preservation and Development (New York, September 1999), 10, https://rentguidelinesboard.cityofnewyork .us/wp-content/uploads/2019/08/96summary.pdf; Registration Apartment Information for Apt. 4R, 77 Lefferts Pl., Brooklyn, NY, 11238, New York State Division of Housing and Community Renewal, February 9, 2022, copy in possession of author.

261 **service of the common good:** McGhee, *Sum of Us*, xxii.

261 **income, benefit from that:** Barika Williams, "The 2017 AMI Cheat Sheet," Association for Neighborhood and Housing Development, August 17, 2017, https://anhd.org/report/ami-cheat-sheet-2017; C. R. Waickman, J. B. R. Jerome, and R. Place, *Sociodemographics of Rent Stabilized Tenants*, New York City Department of Housing and Preservation (New York, 2018), 1, 5, https://www.nyc.gov/assets/hpd/downloads/pdfs/services/rent-regulation

-memo-1.pdf. In 2017, the last year for which data is available, there were 946,514 rent-stabilized units in New York City with a median annual household income of $44,560, compared to $66,000 for households in unregulated private rentals. The median annual income in New York City overall for that year was $85,900.

261 **bear for them ever since:** Registration for 77 Lefferts Pl., Brooklyn; Registration for 53136 6th Ave., Brooklyn.

263 **to submit than to fight:** Van der Kolk, *Body Keeps the Score*, 82–85, 87, 148; Laura Starecheski, "Take the ACE Quiz—and Learn What It Does and Doesn't Mean," NPR, March 2, 2015, https://www.npr.org/sections/health -shots/2015/03/02/387007941/take-the-ace-quiz-and-learn-what-it-does-and -doesnt-mean. In an unofficial tally of my Adverse Childhood Experiences (ACEs) from the source cited above, I answered *yes* to seven out of ten questions, which indicates increased risk of a long list of mental and physical ailments ranging from depression to kidney disease to diabetes. The threshold for an increased risk of sexual assault is four *yes* answers. See: "Adverse Childhood Experiences (ACEs)," CDC, last modified August 23, 2021, https:// www.cdc.gov/vitalsigns/aces/index.html.

266 **know her attacker:** Cassia Spohn, Clair White, and Katharine Tellis, "Unfounding Sexual Assault: Examining the Decision to Unfound and Identifying False Reports," *Law and Society Review* 48, no. 1 (March 2014): 161–92.

266 **who investigated sexual violence:** Barbara Bradley Hagerty, "An Epidemic of Disbelief," *Atlantic*, July 22, 2019, https://www.theatlantic.com /magazine/archive/2019/08/an-epidemic-of-disbelief/592807/.

267 **Black men raping white women:** Powdermaker, *After Freedom*, 389. In Hortense Powdermaker's 1939 survey of 256 white Southerners about their attitudes towards Black people, 64 percent of whites surveyed said that lynching for rape was justifiable. Divided by gender, 66 percent of white women agreed that lynching for rape was justifiable, compared to 61 of white men.

267 **no evidence:** Ida B. Wells-Barnett, "History of Some Cases of Rape," in *The Red Record* (Chicago, 1895; Project Gutenberg, 2005), chap. 6, https://www .gutenberg.org/files/14977/14977-h/14977-h.htm.

267 **let alone convicted of it:** Paula Giddings, *When and Where I Enter: The Impact of Black Women on Race and Sex in America* (New York: William Morrow, 1984), 28. As Giddings recounts, journalist Ida B. Wells researched the specifics of 728 lynchings from 1884 to 1892. Wells found that only one-third

of Black men murdered in those lynchings "were even accused of rape, much less guilty of it."

267 **"claiming devotion to woman":** Ida B. Wells-Barnett, "Lynching, Our National Crime," Address at the National Negro Conference, New York, NY, June 1, 1909, Archives of Women's Political Communication, Carrie Chapman Catt Center for Women and Politics, Iowa State University, Ames, IA, https://awpc.cattcenter.iastate.edu/2017/03/09/mob-murder-in-a-christian-nation-june-1-1909/.

267 **terrorizing Black people was:** The rape of *Black women* by *white men* was widely accepted by white society, sufficiently so that early civil rights efforts incorporated the protection of Black womanhood into activists' demands. Danielle McGuire's *At the Dark End of the Street* provides an introduction to and analysis of this history.

267 **feminist goals "carceral feminism":** Gruber, *Feminist War on Crime*, 7, 148.

267 **protect any person from harm:** Town of Castle Rock v. Gonzales, 545 U.S. 748 (2005). Justice Antonin Scalia wrote in *Castle Rock* that the issue of the duty of police to protect citizens had in fact been settled seventeen years earlier, in *DeShaney v. Winnebago County Dept. of Social Servs.*, 489 U.S. 189 (1989). Chief Justice William Rehnquist wrote definitively in *DeShaney* that "nothing in the language of the Due Process Clause itself requires the State to protect the life, liberty, and property of its citizens against invasion by private actors" (195).

268 **are ever convicted:** "The Criminal Justice System: Statistics," RAINN, accessed June 20, 2023, https://www.rainn.org/statistics/criminal-justice-system.

268 **longer than eighteen years:** Lawrence A. Greenfield, *Prison Sentences and Time Served for Violence*, Bureau of Justice Statistics, U.S. Department of Justice (Washington, D.C., April 1995), 1, https://bjs.ojp.gov/library/publications/prison-sentences-and-time-served-violence; Danielle Kaeble, *Time Served in State Prison, 2018*, Bureau of Justice Statistics, U.S. Department of Justice (Washington, D.C., March 2021), 2, https://bjs.ojp.gov/content/pub/pdf/tssp18.pdf.

268 **38 percent of arrests for rape:** Michael Planty et al., *Female Victims of Sexual Violence, 1994–2010* (Washington, D.C.: Bureau of Justice Statistics, March 2013), 5; *Crime in the United States: 1998* (Washington, D.C.: Federal Bureau of Investigation, October 17, 1999), 228. Researchers estimate that from 1994 to 1998, white men committed 70 percent of all sexual assaults, and Black men committed 18 percent of all sexual assaults. In 1998, the FBI

reported that 60.2 percent of all rape charges were against white individuals, while 37.5 percent were against Black individuals.

270 **Congress sped up the reduction:** Peter R. Orszag and William G. Gale, "Bush Administration Tax Policy: Introduction and Background," Brookings Institution, September 13, 2004, https://www.brookings.edu/articles/bush -administration-tax-policy-introduction-and-background/.

270 **$1.5 million tax-free:** "The Federal Estate Tax," Center on Budget and Policy Priorities, last updated November 7, 2018, https://www.cbpp.org/sites /default/files/atoms/files/policybasics-estatetax.pdf.

270 **his house, four years early:** Mortgage for lot 74 of Cambridge Knolls, Holly, MI, June 29, 1993, liber 13762, p. 147, Oakland County Register of Deeds, Pontiac, MI; Mortgage Release, Satisfaction, and Discharge for lot 74 of Cambridge Knolls, Holly, MI, June 22, 2004, liber 33566, p. 149, Oakland County Register of Deeds, Pontiac, MI.

271 **wealth in the country:** Pfeffer and Dvir-Djerassi, "U.S. Wealth Distribution." According to the Bureau of Labor Statistics, $1,500,000 in 2023 was the equivalent of $1,262,052 in 2019, the year for which Pfeffer and Dvir-Djerassi analyzed wealth brackets. This puts my parents between the 89th percentile ($1,082,047) and the 90th percentile ($1,343,276) in 2019.

271 **"We're comfortable":** John and Bonnie McMillan, interview with author, May 25, 2023.

273 **or brown, were human:** "The CEO Poverty Measure" (working paper, New York City Center for Economic Opportunity, New York, NY, August 2008), 62. This report documented that 19.4% of New York City's poor are white, while 27.1% of the city's poor are Black, 11.8% are Asian, and 40% are Hispanic. For comparison, the city's overall population was 34.7% white, 23.5% Black, 11.8% Asian, 27.8% Hispanic, and 2.2% "other."

273 **"men's eyes and white perspective":** *Kerner Commission Report on the Causes, Events, and Aftermaths of the Civil Disorders of 1967* (Rockville, MD: National Advisory Commission on Civil Disorders, National Institute of Justice, 1967), 213.

273 **"She's Not a Bad Parent":** Tracie McMillan, "Market Babies," *City Limits*, January 2003.

273 **the aesthetics of legumes:** Tracie McMillan, "The Action Diet," *City Limits*, July/August 2004.

274 **"Will You Adopt Me?":** Cover, *City Limits*, June 2004, https://www.scribd .com/document/80173195/City-Limits-Magazine-June-2004-Issue.

274 **and the *Washington Post*:** Lisa Ann Batitto, "Harry Chapin Media Award

Winners Announced" (press release), World Hunger Year, ca. 2005, copy in possession of author.

277 **"will ruin their appetites":** Pollan, *Omnivore's Dilemma*, 12.

278 **a realistic goal:** Matthew Flamm, "Publishers Rewrite Book," *Crain's New York Business*, May 24, 2009, https://www.crainsnewyork.com/article /20090524/FREE/305249979/publishers-rewrite-book.

278 **by major publishing houses:** The spreadsheet generated by #Publishing PaidMe, hosted by the Transparency Project, includes by my count 270 entries that are some form of nonfiction comparable to my work (non-fiction, memoir, reportage, narrative nonfiction, and journalism). Of those, the median reported deal for an *agented* proposal ran from $60,000 across all sizes of publishers to $92,500 bought by the "Big Five." Unagented propos-als reported to the data set, by comparison, have a median value of $3,000. Author analysis of #PublishingPaidMe data set: https://docs.google.com /spreadsheets/d/1Xsx6rKJtafa8f_prlYYD3zRxaXYVDaPXbasvt_iA2vA/edit #gid=1798364047.

278 **survive on that contract alone:** "Authors Guild Survey Shows Drastic 42 Percent Decline in Authors Earnings in Last Decade," Authors Guild, January 5, 2019, https://authorsguild.org/news/authors-guild-survey-shows -drastic-42-percent-decline-in-authors-earnings-in-last-decade/.

278 **write fiction were white:** Richard Jean So and Gus Wezerek, "Just How White Is the Book Industry?" *New York Times*, December 11, 2020, https:// www.nytimes.com/interactive/2020/12/11/opinion/culture/diversity -publishing-industry.html.

278 **about 82 percent:** *#PUBLISHINGPAIDME* [Google Sheets spreadsheet], accessed April 18, 2023, https://docs.google.com/spreadsheets/d/1Xsx6rKJtafa8f _prlYYD3zRxaXYVDaPXbasvt_iA2vA.

Chapter 10: My Adulthood

281 **"poor" by most researchers:** Low-income housing credit regulatory agreement between Quincy Street Owners, LLC and New York State Divi-sion of Housing and Community Renewal, July 28, 2009, document ID 2009074100334001, Office of the City Register, New York City Department of Finance, New York, NY. This use of "poor" does not reflect the federal pov-erty standard, which is based on an estimate of expenses rather than median incomes. As elsewhere in the book, I am drawing on the Pew Research Cen-ter's income class boundaries, which sets poor at 50 percent or less of the median income.

281 **a starting rent of $599:** LIHC agreement, Quincy Street Owners.

283 **the Toren:** "Toren, 150 Myrtle Avenue," City Realty, accessed July 1, 2023, https://www.cityrealty.com/nyc/downtown-brooklyn/toren150-myrtle -avenue/review/40806; "Toren Condominium Program," New York City Department of Housing Preservation and Development, accessed July 1, 2023, https://www.nyc.gov/site/hpd/services-and-information/toren -condominium-program.page. The city's housing department indicates that the income limit for "affordable" units at the Toren in 2019 equaled 195 percent of the area median income. As per the Pew Research Center class designations, that would put these households just shy of New York City's upper-middle class (200 to 300 percent of the median income).

283 **anywhere in the city:** "Still Subsidizing Luxury Development," Pratt Center for Community Development, December 6, 2006, https://prattcenter .net/uploads/1221/1639011796138432/PrattCenter-421a-Stillsubsidizingluxury development.pdf; Samuel Stein, Debipriya Chatterjee, "Rising Cost, Diminishing Returns" (Community Service Society, New York, February 2022); Hayley Raetz and Matthew Murphy, "The Role of 421-a During a Decade of Market Rate and Affordable Housing Development" (Furman Center, New York University, February 2022). The program in question, referred to as 421(a), was introduced in 1971 by Mayor John Lindsay. It was expanded in 1987 under Mayor Ed Koch. In 2007, after the documents providing for my building were signed, the Bloomberg administration and City Council tightened the requirements for 421(a). That fall, the city began to require that developers build affordable units if they received a tax break for projects in expensive and gentrifying parts of Manhattan, Queens and Brooklyn. There was no mandate to build affordable units in the same building as market-rate units until 2017. Combined, the three reports cited here offer an excellent overview of the program's history, as well as a discussion of inclusionary zoning.

283 **two miles from the rich:** Lower Income Housing Plan Application Pursuant to the Inclusionary Housing Program for [lot and block redacted], Brooklyn, NY, Quincy Street Owners LLC. May 23, 2006. New York City Department of Housing Preservation and Development. Developer Donald Capoccia submitted a Lower Income Housing Plan Application for Inclusionary Zoning for my building on May 23, 2006. The plan indicates that the "compensated development," is at 160 Myrtle/245 Flatbush—the same address as the Toren.

284 **wealthy residents are white:** "The Racial Dimension of New York's

Income Inequality," Fiscal Policy Institute, March 2017, http://fiscalpolicy.org /wp-content/uploads/2017/03/Racial-Dimension-of-Income-Inequality.pdf.

284 **are *not* white:** New York City Center for Economic Opportunity, "The CEO Poverty Measure" (working paper, CEO, August 2008), 62.

284 **by more than half:** "Population FactFinder," New York City Department of Planning, accessed June 21, 2023, https://popfactfinder.planning.nyc.gov/; Casey Berkovitz (press secretary, New York City Department of City Planning), email message to Madysen Luebke, April 14, 2023. From 2000 to 2020, the share of white residents in Clinton Hill increased from 19 percent to 45 percent of the population, while the share of Black residents dropped from 58 percent to just 26 percent. Data from 2020 is from the city's website; data from 2000 was provided by the Department of City Planning.

285 **$3,700 a month:** Corcoran Report on Brooklyn Rental Market, February 2023, 3, https://www.ecorcoran.com/uploaded_doc/Corcoran_February _2023_Brooklyn_Rental_Market_Report_FINAL.pdf

286 **two hundred dollars a month:** At the time I applied for food stamps, I had earned about $4,200 in the final quarter of 2010 by copyediting and successfully applying for a small grant to support the book. At the time, the state of Michigan only used income, and did not include assets, when determining eligibility for aid. In November 2011, the administration of then new governor Rick Snyder introduced asset tests restricting food aid to households that had no more than $5,000 in their accounts. I no longer have bank records for that time period, but my memory is that I had spent most of my savings and would likely have qualified for much of 2011 under the stricter guidelines.

287 **jobs left in newsrooms:** Penny Abernathy, "The State of Local News," Local News Initiative, Medill School of Journalism, Northwestern University, June 29, 2022, https://localnewsinitiative.northwestern.edu/research/state -of-local-news/report/. This report documented that in 2006 there had been 365,460 jobs in newspapers across the United States, of which 75,000 jobs were in newsrooms. By 2021, the overall number of jobs at newspapers had fallen to 106,580, with 31,400 of those jobs remaining in newsrooms.

288 **(of any income) or poor:** Raphaël Charron-Chénier and Louise Seamster, "Racialized Debts: Racial Exclusion from Credit Tools and Information Networks," *Critical Sociology* 47, no. 6 (September 2021): 977–92, https://doi .org/10.1177/0896920519894635. Scholars of the racial wealth gap note that access to affordable, stably priced debt is a key component of social mobility and economic stability in the United States. Black households have much

less access to credit cards and bank accounts than do white households, are less likely to be approved for credit, and are more likely be sold predatory loan products like payday loans. This is a critical gap in a place like the U.S., where the social safety net is so thin, and the terms of employment so punishing. Here, debt is what allows many Americans to weather unexpected and immediate expenses like car and home repairs—it is, functionally, a safety net that comes at a price. The above study observed that "racial differences in financial literacy also have essentially no effect on racial disparities in financial access net of income and asset differences. These differences are differences in access, not [personal] choices" (989).

288 **"already have some wealth":** Charron-Chénier and Seamster, "Racialized Debts," 979.

289 **a pebble dropped into a lake:** Burcu Yucesoy, Xindi Wang, Junming Huang, and Albert-László Barabási, "Success in Books: A Big Data Approach to Bestsellers," *EPJ Data Science* 7 (2018), article 7, https://epjdatascience .springeropen.com/articles/10.1140/epjds/s13688-018-0135-y. This study of *New York Times* bestseller list titles found that while more than 100,000 books debut each year, only about 500 ever make it onto the bestseller list—an approximate, if not perfect, measure of impact on public debate.

290 **to about $1,500:** "Request for a Hearing," prepared for Michigan Department of Human Services, February 2, 2011; in possession of author.

293 **in dark humor:** Dwight Garner, "Before the Food Arrives on Your Plate, So Much Goes on Behind the Scenes," *New York Times*, February 21, 2012.

294 **104-degree peach orchard:** Historical weather data from National Weather Service's San Joaquin Valley Forecast Office, available at https://www .weather.gov/wrh/climate?wfo=hnx. On July 17, 2009, temperatures in Visalia peaked at 104 degrees, part of a six-day stretch of temperatures over 100 degrees.

295 **then: $612,000:** C. J. Hughes, "Nets Players May Find Brooklyn a Tempting Place to Live," *New York Times*, September 4, 2012, https://www.nytimes .com/2012/09/04/sports/basketball/brooklyn-offers-tempting-real-estate -choices-for-nets.html.

296 **as little as $500:** Drew Philp, "Why I Bought a House in Detroit for $500," *BuzzFeed*, January 9, 2014, https://www.buzzfeed.com/drewphilp /why-i-bought-a-house-in-detroit-for-500; Robin Runyan, "Detroit Home Sale Prices Up, Downtown Much Pricier Than Neighborhoods," *Curbed Detroit*, January 22, 2019, https://detroit.curbed.com/2019/1/22/18192222/detroit

-home-sale-prices-up-downtown-much-pricier-sales-than-neighborhoods. Runyan's piece features a screenshot of data from Realcomp that includes median home prices for Southeast Michigan from 2014 to 2018.

297 **became a majority-Black city:** "How Diverse is Your City?," Priceonomics, accessed July 1, 2023, https: //priceonomics.com/how-diverse -is-your-city.

297 **average of 46 percent:** *Growing Detroit's African-American Middle Class* (Detroit, MI: Detroit Future City, February 2019), 55; U.S. Census Bureau, 2000 Census, Historical Census of Housing Tables: Homeownership by Race and Hispanic Origin (dataset), https://www.census.gov/data/tables/2000 /dec/coh-ownershipbyrace.html.

297 **held by white Americans:** Richard Rothstein, "Subprime Loan Debacle Intensified Segregation," Economic Policy Institute, April 3, 2012, https:// www.epi.org/publication/subprime-loan-debacle-intensified-segregation/.

297 **nearly half of their wealth:** Signe-Mary Mckernan, Caroline Ratcliffe, Eugene Steuerle, and Sisi Zhang, "Disparities in Wealth Accumulation and Loss from the Great Recession and Beyond," *American Economic Review* 104, no. 5 (May 2014): 244; Fabian T. Pfeffer, Sheldon Danziger, and Robert F. Schoeni, "Wealth Disparities Before and After the Great Recession," *Annals of the American Academy of Political and Social Science* 650 (November 2013): 108.

297 **any other city at the time:** Ben Rooney, "Rust and Sun Belt Cities Lead '07 Foreclosures," *CNN Money*, February 13, 2008, https://money.cnn.com /2008/02/12/real_estate/realtytrac/.

297 **ended up blighted or abandoned:** Christine MacDonald and Mark Betancourt, "Effort to Stave Off Detroit Foreclosures Leaves Many Deeper in Debt," *Detroit News*, December 4, 2019, https://www.detroitnews.com/story/news /local/detroit-housing-crisis/2019/12/05/detroit-foreclosures-effort-wayne -county-treasurer-puts-many-residents-into-deeper-debt/1770381001/; Christine MacDonald and Joel Kurth, "Foreclosures Fuel Detroit Blight, Cost City $500 Million," *Detroit News*, June 3, 2015, https://www.detroitnews .com/story/news/special-reports/2015/06/03/detroit-foreclosures-risky -mortgages-cost-taxpayers/27236605/.

297 **82 percent of the city:** Mike Wilkinson, "Whites Get Half of Mortgages in Detroit, Nation's Largest Majority Black City," *Bridge Michigan*, June 13, 2019, https://www.bridgemi.com/urban-affairs/whites-get-half-mortgages -detroit-nations-largest-majority-black-city.

298 **wake of the subprime crisis:** Sheriff's Deed on Mortgage Sale for portion of [redacted], Detroit, MI, July 11, 2013, [liber and page redacted], Wayne County Register of Deeds, Detroit, MI.

298 **subprime in 2005:** McDonald and Kurth, "Foreclosures Fuel Detroit Blight"; Mike Wilkinson, "Whites Get Half of Mortgages in Detroit, Nation's Largest Majority Black City," Bridge Michigan, June 13, 2019, https://www.bridgemi.com/urban-affairs/whites-get-half-mortgages-detroit-nations-largest-majority-black-city.

298 **an $82,450 mortgage:** Wilkinson, "Whites Get Half of Mortgages in Detroit, Nation's Largest Majority Black City"; Mortgage for portion of lot [redacted], Detroit, MI, September 12, 2007, [liber and page redacted], Wayne County Register of Deeds, Detroit, MI; MacDonald and Kurth, "Detroit Blight." MacDonald and Kurth note that the average mortgage on a foreclosed home in Detroit at the time was $83,000.

298 **over the market value:** Notably, overassessments were most egregious with lower-valued properties. In 2009, writes scholar Bernadette Atuahene, Detroit's Assessment Division assessed low-value properties at eighteen times the state-mandated limit; middle-value properties at double the limit; and high-value properties below the limit. See Bernadette Atuahene, "Predatory Cities," *California Law Review* 108 (February 2020): 113, https://doi.org/10.15779/Z38NS0KZ30.

298 **half of market value:** Atuahene, "Predatory Cities," 110.

298 **struggled to keep up:** Michele Oberholtzer (housing advocate), email messages to the author, May 10–11, 2023.

298 **one-third of the city's properties:** Atuahene, "Predatory Cities," 112; MacDonald and Betancourt, "Detroit Foreclosures." The city does have an appeals process, but it has been poorly advertised and requires rapid and diligent response.

298 **parcels of land in 2014:** In late 2014, Data Driven Detroit listed 16,504 properties as "City Transfer to DLBA [Detroit Land Bank Authority]," 48,907 as "City Ownership, Post-DLBA Transfer," 7,784 as "DLBA Inventory Pre-City Transfer," and 23,593 "DLBA Inventory, Post-City Transfer," yielding 96,788 properties in DLBA. Data Driven Detroit, Technical Documentation for dataset LikelyPublicOwnership_2014_Final.mdb, updated November 25, 2014. See also: Christine Ferretti, "Detroit Land Bank Funds at Limit as Inventory Grows," *Detroit News*, April 11, 2016, https://www.detroitnews.com/story/news/local/detroit-city/2016/04/11/detroit-land-bank-funds-limit-inventory-grows/82880806/.

Epilogue: What Came Before

302 **one-drop rule was "too harsh":** Wilkerson, *Caste*, 80–88. Wilkerson provides a compelling overview of Yale historian James Q. Whitman's book *Hitler's American Model: The United States and the Making of Nazi Race Law.*

302 **he wrote "negro origin":** 1901 Census of Canada, Schedule 1, Population, enumeration table for Ontario, district 113 East Simcoe, subdistrict A, subdivision 5 in Tiny Township, p. 10, lines 13–17, from Ancestry.com.

303 **passing in the North was twice as high:** Emily Nix and Nancy Qian, "The Fluidity of Race: 'Passing' in the United States, 1880–1940" (working paper 20828, NBER, Cambridge, MA, January 2015), 1, 8, 33, 37–38, 51. https://www.nber.org/papers/w20828. Nix and Quan estimate that, nationwide, between 19 and 32 percent of Black males "passed" for white at some point during their lifetime between 1880 and 1940. They put the rate of passing in the South at 23 percent, and the rate of passing in the North at 48 percent.

303 **"race is a social construct":** Omi and Winant, *Racial Formation*, 12.

303 **of our DNA:** Natalie Angier, "Do Races Differ? Not Really, Genes Show," *New York Times*, August 22, 2000.

BIBLIOGRAPHY

Alesina, Alberto, and Edward L. Glaeser. *Fighting Poverty in the US and Europe: A World of Difference*. Oxford: Oxford University Press, 2004.

Baist's Real Estate Atlas of Surveys of Detroit, Michigan. Vol. 2. Philadelphia: G. Wm. Blaist's Sons, 1929.

Banaji, Mahzarin R., and Anthony G. Greenwald. *Blindspot: Hidden Biases of Good People*. New York: Penguin, 2014.

Béland, Daniel, Kimberly J. Morgan, Herbert Obinger, and Christopher Pierson, eds. *The Oxford Handbook of the Welfare State*. 2nd ed. Oxford: Oxford University Press, 2021.

Bolton, Charles C. *The Hardest Deal of All: The Battle over School Integration in Mississippi, 1870–1980*. Jackson: University Press of Mississippi, 2005.

Bonilla-Silva, Eduardo. *Racism Without Racists: Color-Blind Racism and the Persistence of Racial Equality in the United States*. Lanham, MD: Rowman & Littlefield, 2003.

Boyle, Kevin. *Arc of Justice: A Saga of Race, Civil Rights, and Murder in the Jazz Age*. New York: Henry Holt, 2004.

Brokaw, Tom. *The Greatest Generation*. New York: Random House, 1998.

Brown, Dorothy A. *The Whiteness of Wealth: How the Tax System Impoverishes Black Americans—and How We Can Fix It*. New York: Crown, 2021.

Brown, Karida L. *Gone Home: Race and Roots Through Appalachia*. Chapel Hill: University of North Carolina Press, 2018.

Chen, Yong. *Chinese San Francisco, 1850–1943: A Trans-Pacific Community*. Stanford, CA: Stanford University Press, 2002.

Cherry, Robert and William M. Rodgers III, eds. *Prosperity for All? The Economic Boom and African Americans*. New York: Russell Sage Foundation, 2000.

Committee on Economic Security. *Social Security in America*. Washington, D.C.: Social Security Board, 1937. https://www.ssa.gov/history/reports/ces/cesbook.html.

Cramer, Katherine J. *The Politics of Resentment: Rural Consciousness in Wisconsin and the Rise of Scott Walker*. Chicago: University of Chicago Press, 2016.

Delmont, Matthew F. *Why Busing Failed: Race, Media, and the National Resistance to School Integration*. Berkeley: University of California Press, 2016.

Doerr, David R. *California's Tax Machine: A History of Taxing and Spending in the Golden State*. 2nd ed. Sacramento: California Taxpayers Association, 2008.

Dubinsky, Irwin. *Reform in Trade Union Discrimination in the Construction Industry: Operation Dig and Its Legacy*. New York: Praeger, 1973.

Entman, Robert M., and Andrew Rojecki. *The Black Image in the White Mind: Media and Race in America*. Chicago: University of Chicago Press, 2001.

Foner, Philip S. *Organized Labor and the Black Worker, 1619–1973*. New York: Praeger, 1974.

Fowle, Otto. *Sault Ste. Marie and Its Great Waterway*. New York: G. P. Putnam's Sons, 1925.

Fox, Cybelle. *Three Worlds of Relief: Race, Immigration, and the American Welfare State, from the Progressive Era to the New Deal*. Princeton, NJ: Princeton University Press, 2012.

Frank, Richard G., and Sherry A. Glied. *Better but Not Well: Mental Health Policy in the United States Since 1950*. Baltimore: Johns Hopkins University Press, 2006.

Frazier, Harriet C. *Lynchings in Missouri, 1803–1981*. Jefferson, NC: McFarland, 2009.

Friedan, Jeffry. *Global Capitalism: Its Rise and Fall in the Twentieth Century*. New York: Norton, 2006.

Fuchs, Victor R. *The Service Economy*. Cambridge, MA: National Bureau of Economic Research, 1968. https://www.nber.org/books-and-chapters/service-economy.

Gabbidon, Shaun L., Helen Taylor Greene, and Vernetta D. Young. *African American Classics in Criminology and Criminal Justice*. Thousand Oaks, CA: Sage, 2002.

Gaines, Doris Townsend, and Carolyn Hall Abrams, eds. *The Class of 1968: A Thread Through Time.* Conneaut Lake, PA: Page, 2020.

Gold, Roberta. *When Tenants Claimed the City: The Struggle for Citizenship in New York City Housing.* Urbana: University of Illinois Press, 2014.

Grebler, Leo. "New Housebuilding Under FHA and VA Programs." In *The Role of Federal Credit Aids in Residential Construction.* Cambridge, MA: NBER, 1953.

———. *The Role of Federal Credit Aids in Residential Construction.* Cambridge, MA: NBER, 1953.

Greenhouse, Steven. *Beaten Down, Worked Up: The Past, Present, and Future of American Labor.* New York: Alfred A. Knopf, 2019.

Gruber, Aya. *The Feminist War on Crime: The Unexpected Role of Women's Liberation in Mass Incarceration.* Berkeley: University of California Press, 2021.

Haney López, Ian. *Dog Whistle Politics: How Coded Racial Appeals Have Reinvented Racism and Wrecked the Middle Class.* Oxford: Oxford University Press, 2014.

Harris, Alexes. *A Pound of Flesh: Monetary Sanctions as Punishment for the Poor.* New York: Russell Sage Foundation, 2016.

Hatcher, Daniel L. *The Poverty Industry: The Exploitation of America's Most Vulnerable Citizens.* New York: New York University Press, 2016.

Hopkins, Daniel J. *Stable Condition: Elites' Limited Influence on Health Care Attitudes.* New York: Russell Sage Foundation, 2023.

Hudson, Hosea, and Nell Irvin Painter. *The Narrative of Hosea Hudson: His Life as a Negro Communist in the South.* Cambridge, MA: Harvard University Press, 1979.

Ignatiev, Noel. *How the Irish Became White.* New York: Routledge, 1995.

Jackson, Kenneth T. *Crabgrass Frontier: The Suburbanization of the United States.* New York: Oxford University Press, 1987.

———. *The Ku Klux Klan in the City, 1915–1930.* New York: Oxford University Press, 1967.

Katznelson, Ira. *Fear Itself: The New Deal and the Origins of Our Time.* New York, Liveright, 2013.

———. *When Affirmative Action Was White: An Untold History of Racial Inequality in Twentieth-Century America.* New York: W. W. Norton, 2006.

Kelley, Blair LM. *Black Folk: The Roots of the Black Working Class.* New York: Liveright, 2023.

Kelley, Robin D. G. *Hammer and Hoe: Alabama Communists During the Great Depression.* Chapel Hill: University of North Carolina Press, 1990.

Kinder, Donald R., and Lynn M. Sanders. *Divided by Color: Racial Politics and Democratic Ideals.* Chicago: University of Chicago Press, 1996.

Korver-Glenn, Elizabeth. *Race Brokers: Housing Markets and Segregation in 21st Century Urban America*. New York: Oxford University Press, 2021.

Legislative Service Bureau. *Michigan Manual, 2001–2002*. Lansing: Legislative Service Bureau, Michigan Legislative Council, 2001.

Lee, Ulysses. *The Employment of Negro Troops*. Washington, D.C.: U.S. Army Center of Military History, 1963.

Lichtenstein, Nelson. *State of the Union: A Century of American Labor*. Princeton, NJ: Princeton University Press, 2003.

Lindert, Peter H. *Making Social Spending Work*. Cambridge: Cambridge University Press, 2021.

Lipset, Seymour Martin. *American Exceptionalism: A Double-Edged Sword*. New York: W. W. Norton, 1996.

MacGregor, Morris J., Jr. *Integration of the Armed Forces, 1940–1965*. Washington, D.C.: U.S. Army Center of Military History, 1981.

McCaslin, Richard B., Donald E. Chipman, and Andrew J. Torget, eds. *This Corner of Canaan: Essays on Texas in Honor of Randolph B. Campbell*. Denton: University of North Texas Press, 2013.

McGhee, Heather. *The Sum of Us: What Racism Costs Everyone and How We Can Prosper Together*. New York: One World, 2021.

McGuire, Danielle L. *At the Dark End of the Street: Black Women, Rape, and Resistance—a New History of the Civil Rights Movement from Rosa Parks to the Rise of Black Power*. New York: Vintage, 2011.

McMillen, Neil R. *The Citizens' Council: Organized Resistance to the Second Reconstruction, 1954–64*. Urbana: University of Illinois Press, 1971.

Merritt, Keri Leigh. *Masterless Men: Poor Whites and Slavery in the Antebellum South*. Cambridge: Cambridge University Press, 2017.

Nadasen, Premilla. *Household Workers Unite: The Untold Story of African American Women Who Built a Movement*. Boston: Beacon Press, 2015.

Needleman, Ruth. *Black Freedom Fighters in Steel: The Struggle for Democratic Unionism*. Ithaca, NY: ILR Press, 2003.

Nevin, David, and Robert E. Bills. *The Schools that Fear Built: Segregationist Academies in the South*. Acropolis Books, 1976.

Newton, Stanley. *The Story of Sault Ste. Marie and Chippewa County*. Sault Ste. Marie, MI: Sault News, 1923.

Olson, Keith W. *The G.I. Bill, the Veterans, and the Colleges*. Lexington: University Press of Kentucky, 1974.

Omi, Michael, and Howard Winant. *Racial Formation in the United States*. 3rd ed. New York: Routledge, 2014.

Orser, W. Edward. *Blockbusting in Baltimore: The Edmondson Village Story*. Lexington: University Press of Kentucky, 1994.

O'Sullivan, Arthur, Terri A. Sexton, and Steven M. Sheffrin. *Property Taxes and Tax Revolts: The Legacy of Proposition 13*. Cambridge: Cambridge University Press, 1995.

Painter, Nell Irvin. *The History of White People*. New York: Norton, 2010.

Pollan, Michael. *The Omnivore's Dilemma: A Natural History of Four Meals*. New York: Penguin, 2006.

Powdermaker, Hortense. *After Freedom: A Cultural Study in the Deep South*. New York: Viking, 1939.

Quadagno, Jill. *The Color of Welfare: How Racism Undermined the War on Poverty*. New York: Oxford University Press, 1996.

Roberts, Dorothy. *Torn Apart: How the Child Welfare System Destroys Black Families—and How Abolition Can Build a Safer World*. New York: Basic Books, 2022.

Roediger, David R. *The Wages of Whiteness: Race and the Making of the American Working Class*. New York: Verso, 1991.

Rollins, Judith. *Between Women: Domestics and Their Employers*. Philadelphia: Temple University Press, 1985.

Rolph, Stephanie R. *Resisting Equality: The Citizens' Council, 1954–1989*. Baton Rouge: Louisiana State University Press, 2018.

Rosenthal, Caitlin. *Accounting for Slavery: Masters and Management*. Cambridge, MA: Harvard University Press, 2018.

Rothstein, Richard. *The Color of Law: A Forgotten History of How Our Government Segregated America*. New York: Liveright, 2017.

Schottenstein, Allison E. *Changing Perspectives: Black-Jewish Relations in Houston During the Civil Rights Era*. Denton: University of North Texas Press, 2021.

Schramm, Jack E., William H. Henning, and Thomas J. Dworman. *Detroit's Street Railways*. Vol. 2, *City Lines, 1922–1956*. Chicago: Central Electric Railfans' Association, 1980.

Sharkey, Patrick. *Stuck in Place: Urban Neighborhoods and the End of Progress Toward Racial Equality*. Chicago: University of Chicago Press, 2013.

Slater, Gene. *Freedom to Discriminate: How Realtors Conspired to Segregate Housing and Divide America*. Berkeley, CA: Heyday Books, 2021.

Stanton, Tom. *Terror in the City of Champions: Murder, Baseball, and the Secret Society That Shocked Depression-Era Detroit*. Guilford, CT: Lyons Press, 2016.

Starr, Paul. *The Social Transformation of American Medicine: The Rise of a Sovereign Profession and the Making of a Vast Industry*. New York: Basic Books, 1982.

Sturkey, William. *Hattiesburg: An American City in Black and White.* Cambridge,
    MA: Belknap Press, 2019.

Suitts, Steve. *Overturning Brown: The Segregationist Legacy of the Modern School
    Choice Movement.* Montgomery, AL: NewSouth Books, 2020.

Taylor, Keeanga-Yamahtta. *Race for Profit: How Banks and the Real Estate Industry
    Undermined Black Homeownership.* Chapel Hill: University of North Carolina
    Press, 2019.

Trotter, Joe W., and Jared N. Day. *Race and Renaissance: African Americans in Pitts-
    burgh Since World War II.* Pittsburgh: University of Pittsburgh Press, 2010.

Van der Kolk, Bessel. *The Body Keeps the Score: Brain, Mind, and Body in the Healing
    of Trauma.* New York: Penguin, 2014.

Vose, Clement E. *Caucasians Only: The Supreme Court, the NAACP, and the Restric-
    tive Covenant Cases.* Berkeley: University of California Press, 1959.

White, Walter. *A Man Called White: The Autobiography of Walter White.* Athens: Uni-
    versity of Georgia Press, 1995. First published 1948 by Viking (New York).

Wilkerson, Isabel. *Caste: The Origins of Our Discontents.* New York: Random
    House, 2020.

Winant, Gabriel. *The Next Shift: The Fall of Industry and the Rise of Health Care in
    Rust Belt America.* Cambridge, MA: Harvard University Press, 2021.

Zelizer, Julian E. *Taxing America: Wilbur D. Mills, Congress, and the State, 1945–1975.*
    New York: Cambridge University Press, 1998.

ACKNOWLEDGMENTS

I am indebted to more people than I have space to thank. Folks named here generally were behind the scenes and this will be the one moment I get to name them for the way they've helped my work. As with all my work, anything good in it was only possible because of the generosity others showed me. All its flaws and mistakes, however, are mine alone.

I offer extraordinary thanks to the families who shared their time and stories with me in writing this book. These are not easy conversations to have. I am so grateful that you've trusted me with your stories in hopes that more of us can have them. In Pittsburgh, those are the Rectenwalds and Toneys. In Mississippi, the "Beckers." In Connecticut and California, the Bundes and Cloughs. In Texas and points beyond, the Nathans. In Michigan, it is the broad world of Nicholses, Weddles, and McMillans. Thank you for trusting me to tell your stories accurately and fairly.

I could not have proposed this work, at this scale, without the counsel and advocacy of my agent, David Black, and his staff, including Ayla Zuraw-Friedland, Bin-Bin Jiang, Ellen Scott, Emma Peters, Gary Morris, and Matt Belford. I would not have done this work, at this scale, without the support of Henry Holt, most notably my editor, Serena Jones, and her assistants, Zoë Affron and Anita Sheih. It has also required the vast patience, support, and firm hand of the team at Holt, including production editor Molly Bloom, copyeditor Shelly Perron, art director Christopher Sergio, designer Omar Chapa, and legal counsel Laury Frieber. And I doubt I would have even thought of any of it in the first place without the unsolicited—but entirely welcome—counsel of James Oseland, who in 2016 told me I really should write a second book. Without his insistence that I stop worrying about what kind of book I might be able to *sell*, and to think instead about what book I *wanted* to write, I wouldn't have even tried.

* * * * *

My primary research assistant, Madysen Luebke, is not only a stellar, dogged reporter of infinite curiosity and patience, she's a delight to work with. I also benefited from the skilled research of Clarissa Léon, Eileen Markey, Nushrat Rahman, Shaun Raviv, and Sydney Sinclair. Writing counsel, research, and endnote assistance from Matthew Van Meter was integral to this work, as was fact-checking done by Chris Rickert, Geraldine Holden, Graham Hacia, Hilary McClellen, Julie Schwietert-Collazo, Karen Rose Stave, and Nandini Rathi. Kerch McConologue keeps me online, and Kavya Beheraj makes my data look good.

* * * * *

Because this was in part a national story, I drew on many experts who spend their work lives looking at America, writ large. Rakesh Kochhar at the Pew Research Center, Patrick J. Murphy and Austin Zheng at Opportunity Insights, and Fabian Pfeffer at the Stone Center for Inequality Dynamics went far beyond standard reporter questions to help me ensure that my work was on sound footing. I'm also indebted to scholars George Yancy, Jacquelyn Dowd-Hall, Louis Hyman, Nathan Connolly, Robin D. G. Kelley, William A. Darity, and the late William Spriggs for their early generosity with their extraordinary expertise. Dan Hopkins and Gwyneth McClendon helped me parse the body of social science on the safety net. Shannon Felton Spence, formerly of Opportunity Insights, was patient with endless follow up questions. Angela Hanks, of Demos; Danyelle Solomon at the Center for American Progress; and Jen Wagner of the Center on Budget and Policy Priorities, helped me work through policy questions. Cynthia Cox and Chris Lee at KFF helped me work through federal Medicaid policy. Jaime Ventura at the American National Election Survey helped reconstruct a newly offline data set so that I could complete my work. Kenneth Snowden showed infinite patience in explaining early homeownership and mortgages. Gina Neff was patient and generous as I explored—and then dropped—research on the tech industry. Jacob Rugh helped orient me on contemporary homeownership and race, while Mark Klee at the U.S. Census helped me parse arcane data. Beth Howard, Carla Wallace, Celina Culver, Pam McMichael and others from Showing Up for Racial Justice shared valuable insights on whiteness and class.

Librarians are a gift and I am grateful to have had help from the following in that profession: Adam Oster at the Library of Michigan; Janet Bunde at New York University's Bobst Library; Jennifer Dietz, an archivist in the Tampa City Clerk's archives; Laney Chavez, archivist for Harris County; Matthew Peek in North Carolina's Department of Cultural Resources; Meredith Sommers at the Bayliss Public Library in Sault Sainte Marie; Nora Dolliver in the New York Public Library's special collections; and Sara Brewer at the National Archives in Atlanta. William Thompson, at the Mississippi Department of Archives and History, went above and beyond to help me track down data hidden in hard-copy reports that are eighty and ninety years old.

* * * * *

Because these stories lived and died in the places they occurred, local expertise also proved invaluable—and harder to come by. In order by state, I need to thank the following people who gave me their time so I could do my work.

In Florida, Peyton Jones and Charles "Fred" Hearns helped me document the lived experience of Jim Crow in wartime Tampa.

In Michigan, the battalion of friends, acquaintances, and experts who helped reconstruct personal and local history I never knew includes Barb Stevens, Chris Samida, Debbie Hudson, Ina Golden, Katie Golden, Mary Ann Dame, Mike Mishler, Nancy Strole, Stephen Hopkins, Steven Gaynor, Susan Schreiber, and Tom Michalski. Dan Clark and Graham Cassano helped unearth Pontiac history. Jackie Doig of the Center for Civil Justice put in herculean unpaid work to help me estimate my family's likely qualification for Medicaid more than thirty years ago. Marie Sheehan at Coalition for Tax Justice and Michele Oberholtzer explained Detroit home foreclosures in meticulous detail. Brigitte Maxey, Laura Berman, and Keith and Marian McClellan did their best to help me understand Oak Park at the time my parents lived there.

In Mississippi, RL Nave was generous and thoughtful with me as I began my search for a subject, as were Alan Huffman, Ellen Ann Fentress, Marcie Cohen Ferris, and Stuart Rockoff. The work of Ko Bragg compelled me to dig deeper into local history, for which I'm very grateful, and Kate Medley and Laura Sorey opened doors I needed to get through. Historians Charles C. Bolton, Stephanie Rolph, and William Sturkey, all of whose work I cite in the text, deserve a special thank you for their extraordinary generosity in explaining their work and related scholarship to me. In Hattiesburg, I also learned a lot from educators Scott Waldrop and Michael Marks.

In Missouri, Carole Goggin and Mark Hodges were generous with their knowledge of Southeast Missouri and lead mines, respectively. Colin Gordon's work on racial covenants in St. Louis was key to my early research, and I'm grateful he took the time to discuss it with me.

In New York, Sam Stein was invaluable in reconstructing Bloomberg-era housing policy aims.

In Ontario, Guylaine Pétrin, Janie Cooper-Wilson, and Karolyn Smardz Frost helped me learn about Afro-Canadian history and its possible ties to my family.

In Pennsylvania, I am indebted to Gabe and Erin Kramer, whose knowledge of Pittsburgh and its labor movement was invaluable. So were their introductions to Jeffrey Shook, Kate Giammarise, Lisa Frank, Ray Engel, and Sara Goodkind, who were incredibly generous with me. I also benefited from conversations and time with Celine Roberts, Chris Briem, Hal Klein, Kacy McGill, Michael Glass, Natalia Rudiak, Nick Cotter, and Tony Norman.

In Texas, Anita Hassan, Anne Dunkelberg, Chris Tomlinson, Christian Wallace, David McSwane, Jason Ford, Karisa King, Michelle García, Robert Laurence, Sofia Sepulveda, and Stacey Pogue helped me consider the state more fully, as well as understand its history around Medicaid. I also drew on the phenomenal oral history of civil rights in that state overseen by Max Krochmal and Todd Moye, who were generous with their expertise.

★ ★ ★ ★ ★

I had the extreme good fortune of support from several institutions in completing this work. The Russell Sage Foundation, MacDowell, and the Wildacres Residency all offered needed, and generous, support that I doubt I can ever fully repay—but I plan to pay it forward.

These places also offered the extraordinary luxury of colleagueship—a particular rarity for independent folks like myself. At Russell Sage, I had the huge fortune to have meaningful exchanges with Aixa Cintrón-Vélez, Amada Armenta, Arline Geronimus, Dan Hopkins, David Haproff, Diana Hernández, Gwyneth McClendon, Ira Katznelson, James Wilson, John Bound, Kirsten Swinth, Maria Abascal, Monica Bell, Pilar Gonalons-Pons, Samuel Myers, Sareeta Amrute, Sheldon Danziger, Steven Roberts, and Suzanne Nichols. At MacDowell, Sharon Bandy, Wo Chan, Benji Hart, and Kay Ulanday Barrett helped me think more critically, and more creatively, about my work—and were generous in sharing theirs.

In both places, organizational staff from building maintenance to head chefs made it possible for me to work without worrying about facilities or feeding myself. These are the unsung heroes of every professional workplace. At MacDowell I'm grateful to Babette Haley, Ann Hayashi, Colette Lucas, Courtney Bethel, Dan Millbauer, David Macy, Deb Marsh, Ellen Gordon, Jamie Sargent, Jeannine Wegmueller, Jeromy Brett, John

Sieswerda, Jonathan Gourlay, Karen Keenan, Robin Cherof, and Scott Tyle. At Russell Sage, I benefited from the hard work of Andre, Bethzaida Rivera, Briceida Cirilo, David Haproff, Hyacinth Johnson, Ivan Ramos, Jackie Cholmondeley, Junior Oliveira (Junior), Jimmy Beglan, Jorge Ortiz, Mitch Dorfman, Rosa Fermin, Sage Overskei North, and Tina Arboleda. Their work makes mine possible. The least I can do is say thank you.

* * * * *

It takes a village to do anything worthwhile—including, for me, writing books. In pulling together this one, I've directly benefited from the work, kindness, and counsel of the following colleagues and friends in those journalism and publishing: Abbie Fentress Swanson, Adriana Gallardo, Alexis Gargagliano, Alyssa Katz, Annia Ciezadlo, Allie Gross, Amanda Hickman, Anna Clark, Ava Chin, Barry Estabrook, Barry Lynn, Bernice Yeung, Bill McGraw, Cassi Feldman, Charles William Wilson, Charles Yao, Christopher Leonard, Clara Jeffery, Dan Charles, Danny Feingold, Debbie Nathan, Eileen Markey, Esther Kaplan, Fergus McIntosh, Garrett Therolf, Georgia Freedman-Wand, Gustavo Arellano, Indrani Sen, Jaeah Lee, Janice Hui, Jennifer Block, Jennifer Gonnerman, John T. Edge, John Gravois, John Hoeffel, Kai Wright, Karen Shimizu, Kate Giammarise, Katie O'Donnell, Kelsey Ronan, Kevin Young, Kiese Laymon, Kit Rachlis, Krissy Clark, Lynette Clemetson and Wallace House, Maggie Bowman, Maha Ahmed, Maria Godoy, Martina Guzmán, Mayukh Sen, Melissa Segura, Michelle García, Mohamad Bazzi, Mosi Secret, Natalia Fidelholtz, Pableaux Johnson and the red beans table, Peter Hong, Poh Si Teng, Rachel Dry, Rakia Clarke, Rebecca Friedman, Ricardo Sandoval-Palos, Robin McDowell, Roz Bentley, Sam Fromartz, Sara Bonisteel, Sarah Blustain, Seth Wessler, Suzette Hackney, Suzy Khimm, Terry Parris, Vanessa Mobley, Von Diaz, Wayne Barrett (RIP), and Zahir Janmohamed.

* * * * *

At various times I was in need of housing or workspace as I worked on drafts, went on reporting trips, or, a couple times, took a break. In

Alabama, thank you to the Shimizu-Michels Birmingham stopovers. In California, Jessica Warner and Jason and Taiyo Sanders made it easy to be in the Bay Area. Temescal Works made it affordable for me to report there for long stretches. Jess Basta and Ben, Aeris and Leo make LA a delight. I'm grateful for Anne and Paul Chesnut's way station in Santa Barbara, and for the garrulous hosting of Gustavo Arellano and Delilah Snell in Santa Ana. In Kentucky, Lora Smith and Rachel Laudan eased the journey with their guest rooms. In Maine, Belfast Coworking made it possible for me to still see family while on deadline. In Michigan, Detroit's 27th Letter Books, Room Project writing space, and Source Booksellers have all provided not only wonderful spaces but true community. In Mississippi and New Orleans, Theo Hummer, Lucy Faust and Trey Parker (not the one you're thinking of), Julie Corts Burks, and Bethany Fayard made it easy for me to spend long stretches there. In New Mexico, Stephen and Lloyd Goding, as well as Susan and Richard Lindeborg, have made visiting a beautiful place possible. In New York, Mike and Elana Gold provided a welcome respite in Brooklyn when "redevelopment" on my block proved too noisy. In Pennsylvania, Pittsburghers Beth Kracklauer, Sherrie Flick, Eric Lipsky, and Megan Rooney were incredible hosts; Carla and Kenny Hoover gave me a place to stopover in rural PA on the way home. In Texas, outside of San Marcos, Tawni Bates and Lebeth Lammers provided a welcome respite from motels and generous shelter during an ice storm. In Washington, D.C., thank you to the Thomases and the Zezima-Shaws. Maybe most of all, in New Jersey, Maine, and Massachusetts, Larry and Peggy Van Meter have made space for me in every sense of the word. I am so lucky.

As a human, I could not have managed this work without the support of friends and institutions who have nothing to do with my career and don't much care whether it succeeds or fails: Alyson, Geoff, Miriam, Lou, and Ginger; Andrea, Paul, Emmett, and Mavis; Amanda and EJ; Ava and Walter; Christina Guzman and family; Chris Kim; Colleen, Munaf, and Farrah; Denisse, Seth, and Camino; Elissa, Oscar, Asa, and Isaac; Faye and Gary; Gabriel Guerrero; Heidi and Phil; Hilary, Rico, and Mirah; Isabel and Fabien; Jen, Carlos, and Anna; Jillian and Dylan; Julie, Lou,

Nettie, and Max; Keene, Bethany, Rachel, and Sara; Larry Owens; Milton Saunders and Gobi of Lefferts Place, RIP; Mimi Owens; Pit and Taliah; Poh, Mayank, and Navin; Shakirah and Ahn; Sue, Mike, and Kate; Toya Williford; Yasmin, Bill, and Ora Luz. And thank you to the Iyengar Yoga Detroit Cooperative and the Park Slope Food Coop for keeping things that are good for me within my budget.

Thank you to my mother and grandparents, who've all passed, for every good thing you did for me. Thank you to my father and stepmother for the same, and for speaking with me as long as you were able. Thank you to my sisters and their families. They are my heart.

And thank you, in every possible way, to Matty. Thank you for holding me and giving me roots. Thank you for being on my team. I ain't going nowhere.

INDEX

ABOUT THE AUTHOR

Tracie McMillan has written for publications including the *New York Times*, the *Washington Post*, the *Los Angeles Times, Mother Jones, Harper's Magazine, Slate*, and *National Geographic*. She trained under Wayne Barrett at the *Village Voice* before serving as the managing editor of the award-winning magazine *City Limits* from 2001 to 2005. McMillan is also the author of the bestselling *The American Way of Eating: Undercover at Walmart, Applebee's, Farm Fields and the Dinner Table*. Her work has been recognized by the Hillman Book Prize, the James Beard Foundation Journalism Awards, and Investigative Reporters and Editors. In 2013 she completed a Knight-Wallace Journalism Fellowship at the University of Michigan; in 2020 she was a MacDowell fellow; and in 2022 she was a Visiting Journalist at the Russell Sage Foundation. She is based in Brooklyn, New York, and keeps an office in Detroit, Michigan.